Third Edition

American Politics

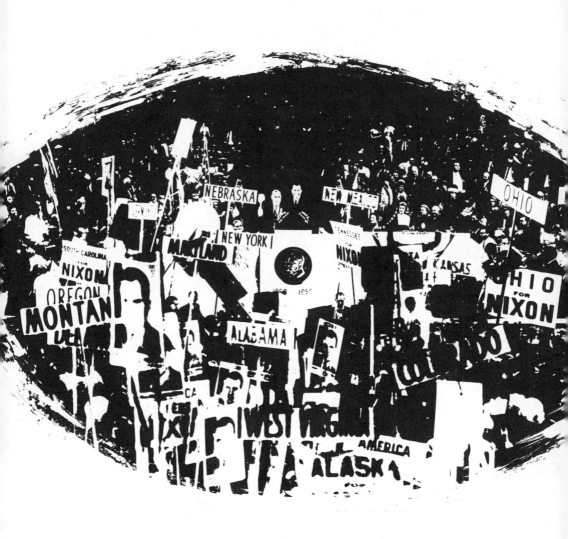

Third Edition **American Politics**

Stephen V. Monsma
Professor of Political Science
Member, Michigan House of
Representatives

The Dryden Press
Hinsdale, Illinois

For my father Martin Monsma (1893–1968), who showed me the Way.

Preface

The bicentennial celebration of the United States has seen an apparently endless outpouring of descriptions and praises of the American political heritage. It would appear that by July 4, 1976, all would surely have been said—all facets of the American political experience explored and even the more unlikely episodes in American political history lauded.

Yet much has been left unexplored and unsaid. To gain a true understanding of American politics we must move beyond mere descriptions and uncritical acclaim. We must engage in hard analysis and a search for facts, whether we find those facts and analyses comforting and supportive of past ideas or disturbing and contrary to them. This book presents the facts of American politics and analyzes them in an attempt to provide the student with a true understanding of the American way of politics.

In presenting these analyses and facts I have incorporated three basic qualities into this book—qualities that distinguish it from other American politics textbooks and, I hope, help it convey an accurate understanding of the American way of politics. The first is organizational: the disparate elements of American politics are organized and analyzed in a general framework that draws together concepts from systems analysis, structural-functional analysis, and public policy analysis. This framework, I believe, serves as a useful means of presenting to students without a strong background the often bewildering elements of American politics in an organized, integrated— and therefore understandable—way.

In this third edition I have given a stronger emphasis to policy analysis than I did in the first two editions, finding many elements of policy analysis helpful to students in their efforts to integrate the many facets of American politics. Two new chapters have been added, categorizing and analyzing several types of public policy-making processes. They should be especially useful in drawing together the disparate elements of American politics discussed throughout the first ten chapters of the book.

A second quality of this book is its eclecticism. I have not relied on any one particular methodological or theoretical movement in political science, but have used insights and information gathered by a wide range of scholars. The book is not wedded to any one particular approach.

A third quality I have incorporated here—as I sought to do in the first two editions—is conciseness and readability. Given the wealth of excellent supplementary material that is available, I wanted this book to be concise enough to use with that material. Yet I also have tried to make it comprehensive enough—covering the basic facts of American politics—to stand by itself as an explanation and analysis of American politics. Constantly striving for readability, I hope that the book will be clear and understandable to all students. If so, class time can be spent in elaborating ideas presented in the book or in discussing supplementary material, instead of elucidating areas the book has not made clear.

It is important to note that I present a description-analysis of the American political system, not an evaluation of it. I have eschewed evaluation, not because I believe it unimportant or because I believe there are no normative bases on which to rest evaluations, but because of the very practical need to keep this book limited in scope and because of my conviction that understanding and knowledge must precede evaluation. I have included, however, a set of evaluative questions at the end of each chapter in order to stimulate students to think through some crucial normative questions.

In writing such a book as this one acquires many debts. I cannot begin to mention them all, but I must particularly thank Mary Ellen Stocker of The Dryden Press for her editorial help. A different, and even deeper debt is owed to my family for the hours together of which this edition has robbed them. Finally I make the traditional, nonetheless sincere, affirmation that the responsibility for all errors of fact and judgment is mine alone.

S.V.M.
Grand Rapids, Michigan
September 1975

Contents

Third Edition   # American
Politics

The Context
of Politics

The Political
Environment

Part One

Introduction
to Part One

American government is big. Some three million civilians and another
three million armed forces personnel are employed by the federal
government. American government is complex. Its millions of
employees are scattered throughout eleven major departments, more
than forty independent regulatory agencies and commissions, sixteen
offices and councils in the White House, the court system, and
numerous congressional offices and agencies.

Within the vastness and complexity that is the federal government
major policy decisions affecting all Americans—and many
non-Americans around the globe—are made on a daily basis. Whether
it is a major question of war and peace in reaction to renewed warfare
between Israel and the Arabs or whether it is a highly detailed
question dealing with the size of the lettering required in a warning on
electrical toys, the federal government is making decisions every day.
Out of this daily stream of specific decisions public policies are made
and implemented—public policies that can send some of us half way
around the globe to fight and die or that can result in unemployment
and poverty for some and steady employment and affluence for others.

The importance of public policies cannot be denied. The evidence is
all around us. Matters become difficult, however, when we try to work
back from the public policies themselves and locate the processes by
which they were made. And that is what this book is really all about.
It seeks to answer two very basic questions: How are public policies
made? Why are the public policies made in the way they are? To state
the questions is easy; to answer them at all adequately will take all the
that come after.

There are two reasons why these questions are difficult to answer.
First is the sheer size and complexity of the federal government,
combined with the fact that policy making goes on in all aspects and
on all levels of government. Policy making is not limited to Congress,
or to the presidency, or to any other one institution or structure.

Rather, a wide variety of persons, agencies, and institutions all contribute—some in major ways, others in minor ways—to the formulation of any given policy. A second reason why it is difficult to describe and analyze public policy making is that no single policy-making process exists for all policies. One process exists for one type of policy, another process for another policy. There is no one public policy-making process. There are many. They vary with the type of policy—whether it deals with domestic or foreign affairs, whether its effects are broad in scope or narrow, whether it deals with one subject field or another.

To understand how public policies are made and why they are made as they are, we first need perspective on the whirling, confusing array of persons, events, processes, ideas, institutions, and—sometimes —crimes that make up the American way of politics. The three chapters in Part One attempt to give the necessary perspective by placing American politics in its theoretical, human, and constitutional contexts.

Chapter 1　**The Political System**　　The Theoretical Context

One of the tools that we would find it difficult to get along without is the map. Maps guide families on their weekend camping trips, enable both ocean-going ships and weekend sailors to reach their ports safely, and—more recently—guide astronauts in their explorations of the moon. But as is often the case with familiar objects taken for granted, many of us would be hard pressed to give an accurate definition of exactly what a map is. We are likely to define it in terms of purpose ("Something to show me how to get where I want to go"), rather than in terms of what it really is.

A little thought, however, would reveal three basic characteristics of a map. First, it is a symbolic representation of physical, geographic features. The red line on a road map is a symbol that represents a freeway, the little circle on the red line represents an interchange, and the blue spot represents a lake. Second, a map is a simplification of reality. The road map does not show every tree, house, and curve in a road; rather, it selects those aspects of reality that are judged essential and symbolically represents them. Third, a map represents those physical features that are important for the purposes for which the map was made. A road map, for example, represents a lake simply by a distinctive blue color and shows in detail the roads leading to it, whereas a navigational map shows the different currents, depths, and sand bars of the same lake in great detail and simply indicates the land area around the lake by a single green or brown color. The two maps symbolize wholly different physical features because their purposes are wholly different. The boatman on the lake would be as lost with the road map as the automobile driver would be with the navigational map. And both would be equally confused if left without any map at all.

The student of the American way of politics—and of the public policy-making processes encompassed by American politics—is often as lost and bewildered as would be a boatman or driver without a map. In many respects his need is the same as that of the boatman or driver: it is for a map that symbolically represents the unknown terrain of American politics, simplifying reality by highlighting those features of American politics

4

that are most important for his purposes and then relating them to each other. Armed with a map such as this, he can then sort out the important from the less important and recognize how one fact or description relates to the whole and to other facts and descriptions. The rest of this chapter presents such a map or conceptual framework, the framework around which this book is organized.[1]

Systems and Functions

The Concept of System

The title of this chapter refers to the political system. But exactly what is meant by the term *system?* We use the word every day, speaking of the circulatory system, the economic system, or a school system. But normally, we would not look at a stone and call it a system. Why not? Because most people view a stone as a single, united whole, whereas a system is made up of a variety of units. Within the circulatory system are units, such as blood vessels and a heart; within an economic system are goods, producers, and consumers; and within a school system are separate schools. Thus, the first necessary characteristic of a system is that it contain separate, distinguishable units.

Normally, several persons waiting for a bus on a street corner or a row of cars lined up on a used-car lot would not be considered a system either. We have a number of distinct units, but they are not united in the sense of working together to achieve any goals—they do not interact with each other, and therefore do not form a functioning "team." A car could be removed from the used-car lot and the other cars would not be affected; one of the persons on the street corner could decide to walk home and the others would not be affected. Neither the cars nor the people were interacting with each other and as a result they were not affecting each other. But if the heart or any other part of the circulatory system were to be taken away, the entire system could no longer function. If one took away a school from a school system, the other schools would clearly be affected.

In summary, a system possess two distinguishing characteristics: It is composed of separate, distinguishable units that interact in order to perform certain functions; hence, the removal of any unit directly affects the

1. This theoretical framework is based upon concepts and theories presented in the following works: Gabriel A. Almond and G. Bingham Powell, Jr., *Comparative Politics: A Developmental Approach* (Boston: Little, Brown, 1966); David Easton, *The Political System* (New York: Knopf, 1953); David Easton, *A Framework for Political Analysis* (Englewood Cliffs, N.J.: Prentice-Hall, 1965); William C. Mitchell, *The American Polity* (New York: Free Press, 1962); and Talcott Parsons and Edward A. Shils, eds., *Toward a General Theory of Action* (New York: Harper & Row, 1962) [first published in 1951].

others. In the terms most frequently used by scholars, a system is marked by *differentiation* (the existence of distinct units) and *integration* (the interaction of the units in order to perform the functions of the system).

The Concept of Function

A *function,* as the term is used in the preceding paragraph, is the result or consequence of system activities. Thus, to determine the function(s) of a system, we must first determine what its activities are and then determine the result of those activities. The activities of the circulatory system include the pumping and carrying of blood throughout a living body; the result of this activity (that is, the circulatory-system function) is that it provides essential, life-sustaining materials to the body's cells and carries away waste material. In the same way, the activities of a school system include recruiting teachers, ordering educational materials, holding class sessions, and dispensing grades; the end result or function of these activities is, presumably, the education of children. To a limited degree, one might say that a *systems function* is the goal or purpose of its activities, but this is not always true. In the example of the school system, the activities of a particularly inept school system may not result in educating children but in frustrating and thwarting their desire to learn. Then the goal or purpose of the school system would be to educate children; its function (that is, the actual result or consequence of its activities) would be to frustrate and thwart the children's desire to learn.

In determining which units are part of a system and which units are not —that is, in determining the boundaries of a system—we must determine what the function of the system is and include only those units that are directly involved in the performance of that function. Because the function of the circulatory system is the bringing of essential, life-sustaining materials to the body's cells and the carrying away of waste materials, we can conclude that capillaries, for example, play an integral part in performing this function and therefore are part of the circulatory system; on the other hand, the stomach does not participate in this function and therefore is not part of the circulatory system.

The Political System and its Function

In order to conceive of the political system as a system in the sense described above, it is first of all necessary to determine the function of the political system. Only then can one begin to include and exclude units as parts of that system.

Many political scientists have suggested that the chief function of the political system is making authoritative policies for an entire society.[2] There are three crucial aspects of this function that set it off as a function belonging uniquely to the political system. One is that policy making lies at the heart of the political system's function. A *policy,* as the term is being used here, is a course of action chosen in response to an existing set of circumstances and alternative ways of reacting to those circumstances. Typically a policy is arrived at by a number of more specific decisions, all of which are related by their being addressed to a single set of circumstances, to an interrelated area of concern. Thus the American government has a Middle Eastern policy, a health care policy, and an energy conservation policy. Each of these examples constitutes a policy area because each is reacting to a single set of circumstances found within an interrelated area of concern.

Many organizations other than the political system make policies, however. A local garden club may make a policy in regard to membership requirements; a church may have a policy in regard to the celebration of certain holy days. Thus the political system's basic function has two additional aspects we need to examine—aspects that distinguish political, or public, policy making from the policy making of private organizations. Public policy making is authoritative. This means public policies are not suggestive or advisory in nature; force or the threat of force is behind them, plus certain feelings that they ought to be obeyed. If we fail to obey the decision of the state legislature to establish a statewide speed limit of fifty-five miles an hour, we find that political decisions are, in fact, authoritative. And if on occasion—or even frequently—we disobey this decision, we probably still feel that we *should* obey it. The fact that we feel the need to find excuses to justify exceeding the speed limit (we were in a hurry or the traffic was very light) in itself shows that we normally accept an obligation to obey it. These feelings are what political scientists call *legitimacy,* the acceptance or recognition by the public that it ought to obey the decisions of the political system.

Finally, public policies are made for an entire society, not merely for some subgroup or subsection within a society. A labor union or a church may be able to make authoritative policies, but their policies apply only to their own membership. Their authority stops with their membership. But the authority of the political system encompasses the entire society. Every person, institution, and group is subject to the policies enacted by the political system.

Thus, the basic function of the political system (that is, the result or consequences of all its activities) is the making of authoritative policies for an entire society. Therefore, in order to determine the boundaries of the

2. See especially Easton, *The Political System,* chap. 5, and Mitchell, *The American Polity,* chap. 1.

political system—to determine which units are part of it and which are not —we must ask which units are directly involved in making authoritative policies for an entire society and which units are not.

The Units of the Political System

The Concept of Units   Integration is one mark of the political system; differentiation is another. The political system consists of a number of distinct, differentiated units. To understand the nature and significance of these units, we must take a closer look at the concept of differentiated units that make up a system.

In the previous example of the circulatory system, it is obvious that one unit in the circulatory system is the heart: It is marked by *differentiation* (it is distinguishable from the rest of the system) and also by *integration* (it takes part in fulfilling the systems function). But a single cell of the many that go to make up the heart is also marked by differentiation (it, too, is distinguishable) and integration (it, too, aids in fulfilling the system's function). Thus, when we refer to the units within the circulatory system, are we referring to individual cells, to major units such as the heart or arteries, or to parts of major units? The answer: all of these. On the one hand are the basic units, units that cannot be further subdivided. For the layman at least, these would be the cells. Between the cells and the total system are other units with varying degrees of complexity. Biologists speak of cells making up tissues; tissues, organs; and organs, the total system. The units at each level of complexity are made up of a combination of units from the next lower level. And the units at each level are marked by differentiation and integration.

Although the situation is, unfortunately, not as neat and simple, the units of a political system can be viewed in the same manner. We can start out with certain basic units and then conceive of other units of varying degrees of complexity.

The Basic Unit   The *basic unit* of the political system is the individual person who takes a direct part in making authoritative policies for an entire society (the political system's function). Individual judges, congressmen, lobbyists, bureaucrats: as long as they have a direct hand in making public policy they are all basic units of the political system.

Subsystems   Just as there are units of varying complexity between individual cells and the total circulatory system, there are units of varying complexity between individuals and the total political system. These units are called *subsystems,* for they are systems in the sense that they are composed of differentiated units (individuals) that are integrated in performing certain functions. They are *sub*systems in the sense that each one is only a part of the total political system. In fact, there is a hierarchy of subsystems, with the lowest subsystems made up of individuals and the higher composed of lower subsystems, or of lower subsystems and a number of individuals. The judicial subsystem is one of the subsystems of the American political system. The Supreme Court is, in turn, one of the subsystems within the judicial subsystem, and the Supreme Court subsystem is made up of the individual Supreme Court justices and their clerks.

The Dynamics of the Political System

The political system is not a static entity, carved in granite and unchanging forevermore. Instead, it is a living, pulsating entity, affecting and being affected by the society of which it is a part and even by forces outside its society. Just as the circulatory system could not exist and would be meaningless without the general organism of which it is a part, the political system could not exist and would be meaningless without the society of which it is a part. There is a constant interchange between the political system and its environment. In the process, neither the environment nor the political system remains the same. To understand more clearly the nature and effects of the interrelations between the political system and the world in which it exists, it is helpful to conceive of inputs that flow into the political system from the environment. These inputs, by means of several conversion functions, are changed into authoritative outputs; and these outputs, by means of a feedback process, condition the inputs flowing into the political system. (See Figure 1.1 for a simplified diagram of this process.) This section of the chapter considers this all-important, never-ending input-conversion-output-feedback cycle.

Inputs

Two types of inputs flow into the political system from its environment. The first input is *support.* No political system could last long without the support of the society of which it is a part. Without a minimal level of support a political system would be extremely unstable, likely to fall prey to a coup d'etat or to disintegrate into several separate political systems. Support can take many forms. Simply accepting the decisions of the political system as being legitimate and obeying them is the most common way of showing support.[3] The ordinary citizen sending in his income tax return on April 15 is showing support for the political system. But support can also take more active forms: Voting, speaking or writing in support of the "American way of life" or the Constitution, and showing respect for such symbols of the country as the flag or the national anthem are examples.

3. To repeat, legitimacy refers to the feeling or recognition by the public that the decisions of the political system should or ought to be obeyed.

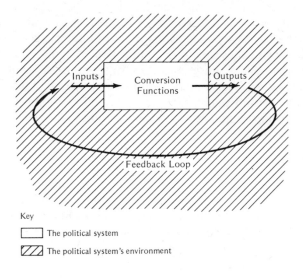

Key

☐ The political system

▨ The political system's environment

Figure 1.1   The political system and its environment: Simplified diagram

The second type of input is *demands* that certain policy decisions be made by the political system. Such demands are expressed in every society. The sources of these demands range from the general public to small, elite cliques; in form, they vary from virtual commands to rather timid requests; and their means of expression range from voting to rioting. In short, demands vary greatly in their sources, forms, and means of expression, but they are all indications of desires that certain decisions be made by the political decision makers.

Up to this point, inputs have been pictured as though they arise only from within the society of which the political system is a part. However, they may also arise from outside the society. When a foreign government threatens retaliation if American troops are landed in a neighboring country, demands are being made; when another foreign government pledges support to the American government in a crisis situation, support is being given. Most inputs, however, and normally the most important inputs, arise from within the society of which a political system is a part.

Conversion Functions

There is a very wide gap between the many competing, often particularistic, and sometimes barely articulated demands and the almost semiconscious support given the political system on the one hand and the authoritative outputs of the political system on the other hand. This gap is filled by the four *conversion functions:* the means by which inputs—

demands and supports—are converted into authoritative policies. Thus, the basic, over-all function of the political system—making authoritative policies for an entire society—can be broken down into its component parts, because the over-all function is accomplished by the performance of these four subsidiary functions or subfunctions.

Interest Representation   The first of the conversion functions is interest representation. Demands in and by themselves are merely expressions of certain desires that are present "out there," somewhere in society. Often they are very narrow in nature, concerned with very specific issues that affect only a limited number of persons. Sometimes they are expressed with force and vigor; at other times they are barely articulated, consisting more of vague feelings that things are not going well and that changes are needed. Support, by its very nature, tends to be diffuse and is often given more out of habit than conscious choice. Yet the depth and nature of the support that is present for the government as a whole, its current leaders, and current policies will condition what the political system can do and how it can go about doing it. Therefore, for demands and supports to become part of the authoritative policy-making processes, they must somehow be fed into the political system and be brought to bear at crucial points in the policy-making processes.

To do so they must be channeled into the political system so that they can mold and shape both the policy alternatives being considered and the conditions under which policy decisions are made. This is what *interest representation* does: it is the channeling of demands and supports into the political system, thereby determining the policy alternatives to be considered and the conditions under which policy decisions are made. Exactly which demands and supports will be channeled into the political system is an open question. They can be those of the general public or of some elite group within the public. But whatever their source, as long as demands and supports are being brought into the political system in an effective manner, interest representation is going on.

When, for example, there is a general feeling of dissatisfaction with the rate of inflation and a general feeling of confidence that governmental action can be effective, a highly respected Harvard economist, the Senate Finance Committee, and the national AFL-CIO may each urge on the political system a particular course of action each believes would be effective. This is a form of interest representation.

Rule Initiation   The second conversion function is *rule initiation,* that is, making authoritative decisions that initiate or establish new rules or make basic changes in old ones. Continuing with the example from the preceding paragraph: When Congress passes legislation raising taxes as an anti-inflationary move, rule initiation has occurred. A new rule has been established. What must be stressed is that an initiated rule is general, not specific, in nature. It establishes certain categories and says that all persons (or situations) falling into those categories must do such and such. The new anti-inflation rule might say, for example, that all persons in the $15,000 to $20,000 a year income bracket must pay a five percent income tax surcharge—it would not say that Mr. Thomas Jefferson of Charlottesville, Virginia, must pay a five percent income tax surcharge. As a result, the establishment or initiation of a new rule is not the end of the matter: The generalized rule must be brought to bear in specific situations. Initiated rules do not carry themselves out automatically. Thus the two remaining conversion functions—rule application and rule interpretation—are needed.

Rule Application   *Rule application* is making authoritative decisions that apply generalized rules in specific situations. The general rule that all persons with incomes of $15,000 to $20,000 a year must pay a five percent income tax surcharge is brought to bear on Mr. Jefferson, who must pay an added five percent on top of the $2,462 tax he is already paying on his $17,500 income.

Rule Interpretation   *Rule interpretation* is making authoritative decisions that determine the intent of rules in order to settle conflicts that have arisen over their meaning.[4] Sometimes disputes arise over the correct application of a rule. Then the meaning of the rule must be authoritatively determined. Thomas Jefferson may claim that $3,000 of the money he received was not "income" in the sense that income is defined in the law (perhaps it is money he won through illegal gambling), thus his taxable income is in the "under $15,000" income bracket, and he does not need to pay the surcharge. Clearly, in such a case the meaning of the rule and its correct application must be determined.

Summary   Making authoritative policies for an entire society is the result of four different activities: interests are represented; out of this representation, rules are initiated; these rules are then applied to specific situations; and finally, disputes arising out of the application of the rules are settled. Figure 1.2 shows the relationship of these conversion functions schematically. Interest representation is involved in all three of the other conversion functions in the sense that the representation of interests affects and conditions all of them. Thus, in Figure 1.2, arrows are drawn between interest

---

4. It should be noted that interpretation, as the word is normally used, is involved in the application of a general rule. As it is applied to specific cases, a particular interpretation is consciously or unconsciously being given it. But the term *rule interpretation* is used in a more narrow sense in this book to refer only to the process of establishing the meaning of a general rule whenever a conflict arises over its proper application.

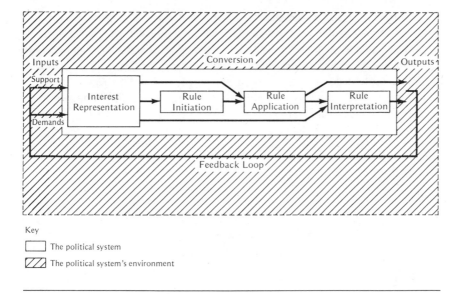

Key

☐ The political system

▨ The political system's environment

Figure 1.2   The political system and its environment

representation and the other three conversion functions. Once rules are initiated, they must be carried out—this means application. Normally, this is the end of the process by which authoritative policies are made. But sometimes desputes arise; then a third conversion function must be performed—rule interpretation.

In some political systems, all four of these conversion functions are performed by the same institution or person, but in the American political system there is a strong tendency toward specialization of function, with different units in the political system performing the different conversion functions. As is discussed in detail in Part Three, Congress is primarily involved in rule initiation, the bureaucratic structures are primarily involved in rule application, the judiciary is primarily involved in rule interpretation, and the presidency is involved in all three. Interest representation goes on throughout the major political structures and institutions and by means of semiofficial and unofficial channels of communication. These forms of interest representation will be discussed at various points in Parts Two and Three.

Outputs

The *outputs* of the political system consist of *authoritative decisions*—authoritative decisions that are either applications or interpretations of rules. This follows logically from our previous discussion of the conversion functions of the political system. What flows from the political system into its environment are not abstract, generalized rules, but specific applications of general rules and interpretations of general rules that are made whenever disputes arise over their meaning. Both the application and interpretations are, of course, authoritative decisions. They have force and the threat of force behind them and are invested with the element of legitimacy. Taken together, the authoritative application and interpretation of rules in a single area of concern constitutes a public policy.

Feedback

When the outputs of a political system flow into the political system's environment, the matter is not ended, for the outputs of a political system in turn affect the inputs flowing into it. There is a *feedback* effect. When a political system initiates a particular rule and that rule is applied and interpreted, the support and demands flowing into the political system are all affected. If, for example, a political system decides, as part of its health care policy, to establish a program of governmental health insurance for all citizens, then clearly the general society would be affected by this policy decision, as, ultimately, would be the support and demands flowing into the political system. Citizens who feel that the political system has responded to their demands and adopted a program that assures them of better medical care and fewer worries over crippling medical bills may give greater *support* to the political system. But the new programs may tax the existing number of doctors and medical facilities to their limit, leading to *demands* that the political system aid in the construction of new hospitals or help in the establishment of additional medical schools!

Feedback can be either positive or negative; it can either add to the support being given the system and lead to demands that existing policies be kept and expanded or reduce the support being given the system and lead to demands that existing policies be dropped or radically changed.

Policy Making

Policy making in a particular area of concern is the process whereby inputs flow into the political system, are converted into authoritative outputs, and in turn affect the inputs flowing into the political system. The crucial point is that policy making in any given area is not like a straight line, moving from inputs to conversion to outputs, and then starting fresh in another area with inputs to conversion to outputs again. Instead, policy making—as Figure 1.2 pictures it—is a continuous, never-ending process. No matter where one breaks into this circle, whether at the input, conversion, output, or feedback stage, that part of the process is being affected and conditioned by the preceding parts of the circle and is affecting and conditioning what comes after. It is a dynamic, ever-flowing situation. As long as the political system exists, there is no end—or beginning.

System-maintenance Functions

Thus far we have considered two types of functions: the basic, over-all function of the political system and the conversion functions, that is, the specialized subfunctions of which the over-all function consists. There is a third and final type of function. Not only must the political system perform conversion functions whereby inputs are converted into authoritative decisions, but it must also perform certain functions that help assure its continuance as a stable, viable system. These are the *system-maintenance functions*—and without them a political system would soon cease to exist. Just as the most basic instinct of all animals is the instinct for self-preservation, so also every political system must have an instinct for self-preservation.[5] Political systems help preserve themselves by performing three basic system-maintenance functions.

Conflict Resolution

The first system-maintenance function is *conflict resolution.* A political system and its subsystems are constantly subjected to conflicting demands. Sweeping advantages and disadvantages are being allocated—the stakes are high and conflict is the norm. Thus, there is a constant danger that a political system will disintegrate, gradually sinking into civil war or anarchy or splitting up into a number of smaller political systems. To prevent these developments, ways and means must be found to resolve the conflicts—not necessarily to everyone's or every group's satisfaction, but at least to the extent that persons and groups feel they can "live with" the results. They must be willing to accept the results instead of attempting to withdraw from or destroy the system. When, for example, the decision-making processes of a political system provide for and encourage negotiation and compromise among conflicting points of view, they are aiding the successful resolution of conflicts.

Generating Support

Another system-maintenance function is the *generating of support.* As we have already seen, a political system cannot long exist without support. A large part of the support gained (or lost) by a political system is the result of its own actions. By its decisions and by *how* it makes it decisions, it can generate support for itself—a function that must be performed successfully if the system is to survive for any length of time. When, for example, a

---

5. It should be noted that what the system-maintenance functions maintain is the political system, not necessarily existing policies, existing patterns of decision making, or an existing hierarchy of privilege among societal groups. In fact, one of the most effective ways for a political system to maintain itself is to be flexible and adaptable as it relates to a changing environment and changing demands.

political system responds to certain demands being put upon it and makes policy changes in keeping with those demands, support will be generated, since those making the demands will view favorably a political system that satisfies their desires. Or when a political system allows a wide variety of viewpoints to be heard before it makes a certain decision, support can be generated even among those who lose in the final decision, for they will at least feel they have been given a fair hearing and have been allowed to express their positions.

Creating Legitimacy

A third system-maintenance function is that of *creating legitimacy.* Legitimacy—the people's conviction that the political system is legitimate and that they ought to obey its decisions—is also essential for a stable, viable system. No political system can be sustained solely by coercion. As is true of generating support, a political system itself can do much to create legitimacy by accentuating and using traditions, ideologies, and symbols; by the decisions it makes; and by the *way* in which it makes decisions. If it cannot do so, it is bound to decline and eventually disappear. Somehow, a political system must be able to invest its decisions and activities with the aura of legitimacy. When, for example, a political system develops certain rituals and ceremonies, such as an elaborate, colorful swearing-in ceremony for a new head of state, it is helping to create legitimacy. Exactly how the American political system performs these three essential system maintenance functions is considered at various points throughout the remaining chapters.

Inputs and Outputs Within the Political System

Only one more elaboration is needed to complete our framework of American politics. With only a few modifications, what was stated concerning the political system as a whole and its environment can be applied to the units that make up the political system. The subsystems and individuals in the political system have inputs flowing into them and outputs flowing out from them.

Inputs   The *inputs* consist of supports and demands: the Supreme Court makes a decision and the President *supports* it by calling for compliance with it; the Speaker of the House *requests* a House committee to report out a certain bill. In short, the units of the political system have the same two types of inputs flowing into them that the total political system has.

Outputs   The *outputs* flowing from the units of the political system are decisions—as are the outputs of the total political system—but they are not necessarily *authoritative* decisions. In our examples, the President's call for compliance meant a decision on his part, and clearly the Speaker of the House had to decide to make his request. The first example could also be considered an authoritative decision. Anyone disobeying the President by violating the Supreme Court decision might find sanctions being taken against him. In the example of the Speaker, however, the decision to request a committee to report out a bill cannot be considered authoritative. The committee may feel little obligation to grant the Speaker's request, and if it fails to do so, there probably is little the Speaker can do. Thus, the output of the subsystems and of individuals in the political system consists of decisions, but these decisions may or may not be authoritative in nature.

It should be noted that within the political system, a single interaction can be either an input or an output, depending on how we view it. The request of the Speaker to the committee is an output for the Speaker and an input for the committee. The environment of the units within the political system consists of the rest of the political system, the society as a whole, and even forces outside the society.

The Political System and the Political Elite

The Issue   The conceptual framework or "map" of the political terrain presented in this chapter says nothing about what proportion of a population is included in a political system. Conceivably a political system could consist of all persons in a society. This would be the case if all persons were directly involved in governing (that is, in making authoritative policies for an entire society). Such is the ideal of *direct* or *participatory democracy:* the people directly ruling themselves. Then all persons make certain demands on the political system and give it their support, and all are involved in all four of the conversion functions whereby these demands and supports are translated into public policies. Government is by the people.

The Realities   The basic fact, however, is that, with the possible exception of a few isolated cases, societies are divided into the few who govern and the many who are governed.[6] Direct or participatory democracy is a myth. Political systems consist of relatively small numbers of persons who represent interests and who make, apply, and interpret rules; the vast majority are excluded from direct participation. As Harold Lasswell has

6. Many writers have stressed the elite nature of government, although they have differed on the nature of that elite rule. See, for example, Gaetano Mosca, *The Ruling Class* (New York: McGraw-Hill, 1939); Floyd Hunter, *Community Power Structure* (Chapel Hill, N.C.: University of North Carolina Press, 1953), Robert Dahl, *Who Governs?* (New Haven, Conn.: Yale University Press, 1961); and Peter Bachrach, *The Theory of Democratic Elitism* (Boston: Little, Brown, 1967).

Table 1.1   Roles of the major political institutions and structures in the performance of the political system's functions

Functions	Institutions		
Conversion:	*Political Parties*	*Interest Groups*	*The Presidency*
Interest Representation	Highly significant especially by nominating candidates	Highly significant plead particularistic interests; give information	Significant articulate perceived societal demands
Rule Initiation	Virtually none	Virtually none unless possess overwhelming power	Significant especially in leadership role in Congress
Rule Application	Virtually none	Virtually none unless possess overwhelming power	Significant especially in leadership role in bureaucracies
Rule Interpretation	Virtually none	Virtually none unless possess overwhelming power	Significant especially in leadership role in judiciary
System Maintenance:			
Conflict Resolution	Significant aggregate particularistic interests	Minor large, inclusive groups may moderate conflicting demands	Significant President drawn into all major conflicts
Generating Support	Significant represent many interests and overtly praise the system	Significant give access to the system	Significant President highly visible
Creating Legitimacy	Virtually none	Minor by-product of giving access to the system	Significant traditions of Presidency

Table 1.1

	and Structures	
Congress	*The Bureaucracies*	*The Judiciary*
Significant many interests directly represented	Minor sometimes become spokesmen for certain interests	Virtually none
Highly significant enacts basic rules of political system	Significant makes recommendations to President and Congress; have been delegated rule-making powers	Minor some major, landmark decisions can be considered as initiated rules
Significant overse bureaucracies	Highly significant applies rules to specific situations	Virtually none
Minor reacts to judicial decisions; Senate approves judicial appointments	Minor some regulatory agencies do so to a degree	Highly significant interprets Constitution and laws
Highly significant many interests represented and seeks agreement among them	Significant settle conflicts over proper rule applications	Significant Courts only involved when conflict present
Significant by giving many interests a say in rule making	Highly significant citizens have direct contact with bureaucracies	Minor prestige and rituals of Courts can help support
Significant its right to make basic rules is accepted	Minor perceived fairness can aid legitimacy	Highly significant places stamp of legitimacy on decisions of other institutions

written: "Government is always government by the few."[7] Government by the people is not attainable—not in the Soviet Union and China, or in the United States and Britain.

This concentration of political decision making in the hands of the few is true for two reasons. First, except in the smallest of political units (such as a village of 300 or so persons), it is physically impossible for all or even a large proportion of the people to be directly involved in running the government. Chaos could be the only result. Second, most persons do not have the interest and motivation necessary to be able to govern themselves directly. To govern requires time taken away from other pursuits (such as recreation or earning money), and the person who is willing to spend so valuable a resource on political pursuits is rare. Governing therefore goes by default to those with the interest and motivation to spend large amounts of time on politics.

Elite Political Systems and Democracy Thus all political systems are composed of and run by *political elites*—not the general public. But this does not mean that all political systems are undemocratic. Harold Lasswell has stated the case succinctly: "To confuse the percentage of leaders at any given moment with the test of democracy is to make an elementary mistake, since a society may be democratic and express itself through a small leadership. The key question turns on accountability."[8]

The crucial question asks whether the political elite is a closed circle, accountable only to itself and influenced by no forces outside itself, or whether the elite is open to anyone having the requisite interest and skill and is held accountable to the general public for its decisions and thereby is significantly influenced by that public. In either case an elite—not the people—rules, but the nature of that elite and the conditions of its rule differ widely. The former is an autocratic elite; the latter a democratic elite.

In summary, we can safely assume that the American political system is composed of a relatively small number of elite decision makers, who perform the conversion and system maintenance functions. But the nature of that elite and the conditions of its rule are questions to be explored in the remaining chapters of the book.

The Political System, Politics, and Policy Making

The American way of politics is complex. If nothing else is clear, that much should be by now. To understand the making of public policies, therefore,

7. Harold D. Lasswell, Daniel Lerner, and C. Easton Rothwell, *The Comparative Study of Elites* (Stanford, Calif.: Stanford University Press, 1952), p. 7.

8. Lasswell et al., *The Comparative Study of Elites,* p. 7.

some way of organizing or putting together the chaotic world of American politics must be found. This chapter has suggested a way of organizing the key facets. It offers a map—a simplified, symbolic representation—of the difficult American political terrain. It thereby offers a means by which we can gain a clearer, more accurate understanding of how public policies are made in the United States and why they are made as they are. The rest of the book is organized around this framework.

The remaining two chapters of Part One analyze the environment of the American political system, which constantly affects American politics. Parts Two and Three zero in on the basic structures or subsystems found in the political system, such as the political parties, the Congress, and the presidency. The nature of each one's involvement in public policy making is analyzed by considering what role each plays in the performance of the four basic conversion functions that make up the policy-making processes. The role of each in performing the three system-maintenance functions is also noted. This will help us see both how each subsystem or structure contributes to policy making and how each of the functions crucial to policy making is performed. Table 1.1 summarizes both the role the major institutions and structures play in the performance of the political system's functions (the vertical columns), and the means by which the major functions of the political system are performed (the horizontal rows).

In Part Four much of what is discussed earlier in the book is put together from the point of view of the public policy-making processes. Public policy making processes are divided into several subcategories, and the chief characteristics of policy making in each of the categories are explored.

Some Exploratory Questions

1. Does an explicit theoretical framework like that presented in this chapter force the real political world into an artificial, overly simplified mold, or does it help organize the real political world into a more understandable, learnable whole?

2. Does the framework presented in this chapter, by stressing the regular input-conversion-output-feedback flow and the performance of system-maintenance functions, contain a hidden conservative bias, which values stability over change, continuity over revolution?

Bibliographical Essay

Three studies that consider the nature and use of theoretical frameworks in the study of politics and are sufficiently clear and basic to be of value to most beginning students are Arthur S. Goldberg, "Political Science as Science," in Nelson W. Polsby, Robert A. Dentler, and Paul A. Smith, eds., *Politics and Social Life* (Boston: Houghton Mifflin, 1963), pp. 26–35; David Easton, *The Political System,* 2d ed.

(New York: Knopf, 1971), especially chap. 2; and Karl W. Deutsch, *The Nerves of Government* (New York: Free Press, 1963), especially chap. 1.

Three works that are clear, readable introductions to the systems type of approach to politics are David Easton, *A Framework for Political Analysis* (Englewood Cliffs, N.J.: Prentice-Hall, 1965); Gabriel A. Almond and G. Bingham Powell, Jr., *Comparative Politics: A Developmental Approach* (Boston: Little, Brown, 1966); and William C. Mitchell, *The American Polity* (New York: Free Press, 1962). Additional, more involved explanations can be found in David Easton, *A Systems Analysis of Political Life* (New York: Wiley, 1965), and in the book by Karl Deutsch (*The Nerves of Government*) cited in the preceding paragraph.

For discussions of the nature of politics and the political process, see the short, introductory books by Robert Dahl, *Modern Political Analysis,* 2d ed. (Englewood Cliffs, N.J.: Prentice-Hall, 1970); and Harold Lasswell, *Politics: Who Gets What, When, How* (Cleveland: World Publishing, 1958). On the elite nature of political systems see Gaetano Mosca, *The Ruling Class* (New York: McGraw-Hill, 1939) and C. Wright Mills, *The Power Elite* (New York: Oxford University Press, 1956), both of which stress the autocratic tendencies of elite rule, and Robert Dahl, *Who Governs?* (New Haven, Conn.: Yale University Press, 1961) and Nelson Polsby, *Community Power and Political Theory* (New Haven, Conn.: Yale University Press, 1963), both of which show the possibility of democracy coexisting with elite rule. For a balanced, readable analysis of the American political system from an elitist perspective see Kenneth Prewitt and Alan Stone, *The Ruling Elites* (New York: Harper & Row, 1973).

On the policy-making approach to the study of politics see Charles Lindblom, *The Policy-Making Process* (Englewood Cliffs, N.J.: Prentice-Hall, 1968) and Ira Sharkansky, ed., *Policy Analysis in Political Science* (Chicago: Markham, 1970).

Chapter 2

**The
Political
Culture**

The Human Context

Wall Street lawyers, blacks trapped in urban ghettoes, wealthy oil tycoons, white ethnics from middle America, and rugged Wyoming ranchers seem to be so different as to make generalization impossible. American society appears to be so big and so various that it defies description. Nevertheless, through all this diversity certain basic threads do in fact run. Underlying the many varied elements of American society are patterns of attitude and belief. To study the politics of a nation without studying these patterns of attitude and belief would be as foolish as to study zoologically a species of animal without studying its natural habitat. The people of a nation, with their attitudes, values, hopes, and fears, constitute a crucial part of the political system's environment.

In order to give greater precision and focus to the study of societies and their impact on politics, political scientists have developed the concept of political culture. The *political culture* of a nation refers to its people's politically relevant attitudes, beliefs, and patterns of behavior.[1] The significance of a nation's political culture lies in the fact that no political system exists in a vacuum, cut off and isolated from the society of which it is a part. Instead, it is both influencing and being influenced by its society. As was stressed in Chapter 1, outputs are constantly flowing from the political system into the society and inputs flow from the society into the political system. As a consequence, the nature of that society and its attitudes, beliefs, and behavior patterns that relate to the political system have the profoundest effect on that system.

This chapter explores American political culture in terms of the support given the political system, how the demands made upon the political system are culturally conditioned, and certain broad values and beliefs held by Americans.

1. For a good explanation of the concept of political culture, see Lucian W. Pye, "Political Culture," in David L. Sills, ed., *International Encyclopedia of the Social Sciences,* vol. 12 (New York: Macmillan and Free Press, 1968), pp. 218–224.

American Political Culture and Support

Perhaps the most important set of attitudes that constitute a nation's political culture is the one that determines the nature and level of *support for its political system.* As noted in Chapter 1, no political system can last long without this support. Political regimes with extremely low levels of support are marked by their great instability and usually by their attempts at coercion and repression undertaken to maintain political power. Such regimes frequently fall victim to coups or revolutions and sometimes break up into a number of smaller political units. Although all political systems with a minimal amount of stability must have some support, they differ greatly in its level and nature.

Level of Support

Until the mid-1960s it was possible to speak confidently of the high level of support that Americans gave their political system. In many ways Americans exhibited a very high level of trust, confidence, and pride in their political system. Although there always had been some skepticism toward politicians and big government,[2] this skepticism was counterbalanced by a firm structure of strong support. A 1960 study, for example, found in response to a general question concerning what things about the United States they were most proud of, some 85 percent of a cross section of Americans reported pride in some aspect of their political institutions or processes.[3] And a 1964 study found that 76 percent of the population believed they could trust the government to do what is right either always or most of the time.[4]

But since the mid-1960s Americans' trust and confidence in their government have been dealt one blow after another. There was the Vietnam War, in which the doves saw the government following a brutal, aggressive policy, and the hawks saw the government following an uncertain policy that refused to grasp military victory. Then in the late 1960s came the riots and disturbances in the black urban ghettoes and the massive and sometimes violent antiwar demonstrations—both of which made the government appear unable to maintain peace and order. And just when direct American military involvement in Southeast Asia had been ended and the ghettoes and campuses had returned to at least an outward calm, Water-

2. More on this later in the chapter in the consideration of certain basic common beliefs of Americans.

3. Gabriel A. Almond and Sidney Verba, *The Civic Culture* (Princeton, N.J.: Princeton University Press, 1963), p. 102.

4. Center for Political Studies, University of Michigan, "Election Time Series Analysis of Attitude of Trust in Government," mimeograph report (Fall 1971).

gate burst onto the scene: the highest officials in the land—including the President and the Vice-President—were found lying, obstructing justice, and giving and taking bribes. The mid-1970s saw the added impact of severe economic troubles that the government was unable to control: a recession led to massive unemployment, combined with the highest inflation since the 1940s. The results these hammer blows have had on Americans' sense of trust in their government is revealed in Figures 2.1 and 2.2.

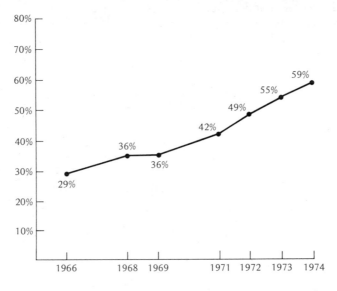

Figure 2.1   Population feeling alienated, 1966–1974[a]

[a] Based on the average percentage of persons giving an alienated or powerless response to the following four items: (1) The rich get richer and the poor get poorer. (2) The people running the country don't really care what happens to you. (3) What you think doesn't count much anymore. (4) You feel left out of things going on around you.

Source: United States Senate, Committee on Government Operations, *Confidence and Concern: Citizens View American Government* (Washington, D.C.: GPO, 1973), p. 30. updated by means of Harris Associates news releases.

Figure 2.1 shows that feelings of alienation as measured by one survey doubled from 1966 to 1974. Figure 2.2 shows that trust in government has declined sharply in recent years among both black and white Americans. (More on the racial differences shortly.) The fact that more than one measure of trust and confidence in government shows the same decline and the fact that the decline is a fairly long-term one, lasting over ten years, seem to indicate that the decline in trust is serious and deep-rooted. This is the conclusion reached by political scientist Arthur Miller, who has intensively studied trust in government. He has written: "A situation of widespread, basic discontent and political alienation exists in the U.S.

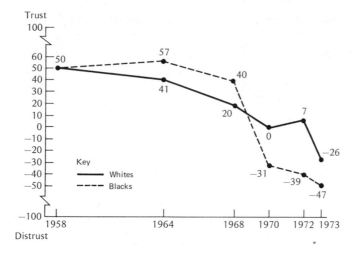

Figure 2.2   Index of trust in government by race, 1958–1973[a]

[a] The index numbers were obtained by subtracting the percentage of persons ranking low in trust from the percentage of those ranking high in trust. Thus a positive number indicates more persons were high in trust than were low in trust, and a negative number indicates more persons were low in trust than were high in trust.

Source: Arthur H. Miller, "Change in Political Trust: Discontent with Authorities and Economic Policies, 1972-1973," paper given at the 1974 Annual Meeting of the American Political Science Association, p. 32.

today."[5] Later he went on: "To summarize, political cynicism is related to feelings of political inefficacy, to the belief that government is unresponsive, and to an apparent desire for structural and institutional reform. The trend toward increased distrust, therefore, reflects a growing dissatisfaction and discontent with the performance of government in the United States. . . . The trend is a serious statement that government in the U.S. is perceived as falling far short of democratic goals."[6]

Does all this mean that the United States today is marked by low support for the political system? Does it mean that the potential for revolution or some other illegal take-over of government associated with low support is now present in the United States? Three factors argue against the position that the United States has moved from a situation of high support to one of dangerously low support, and in favor of the position that the United States has moved from a situation of high support to one of mixed support for the political system.

First is the fact that substantial minorities, as seen in Figures 2.1 and 2.2, still maintain their trust and confidence in government. In Figure 2.1, 41

5. Arthur H. Miller, "Political Issues and Trust in Government: 1964–1970," *American Political Science Review,* 68 (September 1974), 951.

6. Arthur H. Miller, "Rejoinder to 'Comment' by Jack Citrin: Political Discontent or Ritualism?" *American Political Science Review,* 68 (September 1974), 992.

percent were not yet disenchanted with government in 1974, and in Figure 2.2 the negative 1973 measures of trust for both whites and blacks were still far from the −100 which would indicate no trust at all. Distrust is high compared to what it was ten years ago, but it is still only moderately high.

A second factor indicating there is still a significant level of support in the United States is reflected in continued reports of optimism and hope among the American public. A recent study by Louis Harris Associates reports: "In the forest of the disenchanted, there are actually sturdy trees of faith and traditional trust. Americans who evidence doubt about the quality of both life and political leadership nonetheless believe strongly that government can work and should continue an active, innovative role in society."[7] Only 32 percent of the people agreed that "the best government is the government that governs the least." And 67 percent agreed that "it's about time we had a strong federal government again to get this country moving again."[8] This study also showed that 58 percent of the people still felt they could do something effective about an unjust or corrupt official.[9] The situation appears to be one in which the people's faith in the system of government has been shaken, but an underlying layer of faith in the possibility of improvement by political action remains.

A third factor that has been studied is the extent to which the current decline in trust is tied, first, to very specific current policies and current public officials and, second, to the much more serious long-term, generalized feeling of distrust of the whole system or way of governing. If it is the first, changes in current policies and personnel could result in quick increases in trust; if it is the second, a more serious, genuine loss of basic support is indicated. Although the evidence is mixed there are some indications the especially severe loss of trust and confidence is centered more on current officials and policies than on the political system as such. The authors of a before-and-after-Watergate study of university students concluded: "Trust in officials on the average declined most, trust in government much less, and trust in the system slightly less than that. This is evidence of the somewhat limited—but nonetheless significant—nature of the impact of Watergate. It is certainly understandable that faith in the people who operate the government declined during the year of the Watergate revelations. It is important and noteworthy that confidence in the government as a whole and in the system declined a good deal less."[10]

7. United States Senate, Committee on Government Operations, *Confidence and Concern: Citizens View American Government* (Washington, D.C.: GPO, 1973), p. 64.

8. United States Senate, Committee on Government Operations, *Confidence and Concern,* p. 236.

9. United States Senate, Committee on Government Operations, *Confidence and Concern,* p. 260.

10. Robert Entman, James Prothro, and Edward Sharp, "The Mass Media, Dissonant Events, and Alienation: A Panel Study of the Effects of the Watergate Scandals on Political Attitudes," paper given at the 1974 Annual Meeting of the American Political Science Association, p. 17.

Table 2.1   Political trust and attitudes toward the American form of government, 1972

	Trust in government			
	Low (n=419)	Middle (n=373)	High (n=224)	Total (n=1016)
Pride in Government				
I am proud of many things about our form of gov't.	74.3%	91.8%	97.9%	86.0%
I can't find much about our form of gov't to be proud of	25.8	8.2	2.1	14.0
Total	100.1	100.0	100.0	100.0
Change Our Form of Government?[a]				
Keep our form of gov't as is	43.2	63.3	80.8	58.8
Some change needed	31.7	27.6	14.3	26.4
Big change needed	25.1	9.1	4.9	14.7
Total	100.0%	100.0%	100.0%	99.9%

[a] The exact wording of this question is: "Some people believe that change in our whole form of government is needed to solve the problems facing our country, while others feel no real change is necessary. Do you think . . . ?"

Source: Jack Citrin, "Comment: The Political Relevance of Trust in Government," *American Political Science Review*, 68 (September 1974), 975.

Table 2.1 offers additional evidence in support of this point. Even among those scoring low in trust, majorities still report being proud of the American form of government and reject changing the whole form of government. The Gallup Poll showed that from April to August 1974, during which time the House Judiciary Committee's televised impeachment hearings were held, public approval of Congress climbed from 30 percent to 48 percent,[11] a rise that indicates that public approval or disapproval of government is subject to rather wide fluctuations depending on how the public sees the short-run performance of government.

In summary, it appears that a uniformly high level of support given the political system a decade ago has been replaced by a mixture in which a strong measure of support remains—especially a long-term faith that the basic system can still be made to work—but tempered by a suspicion and skepticism, especially toward current policies and officials. It appears that the American political system is not in imminent danger of disintegration or revolution due to loss of support. Yet the heightened feelings of suspicion and distrust may foreshadow an era in which the political pendulum will swing more widely, with one leader or one party being in favor one year and out of favor the next; in which office holders running for re-election will frequently be defeated; and in which policy preferences will change rapidly. Chapter 4 reports evidence indicating that all these phenomena are becoming more common in American politics. Thus the changing level of support is likely to lead to more frequent and more rapid

11. See *Time* (September 9, 1974), p. 17.

changes in policy and leadership but is unlikely to lead to revolution or political disintegration. At least that is the current picture. Only the future will reveal whether the present situation will continue without much change, whether higher support will reassert itself, or whether a further decline in support, with greater chances of political instability, will occur.

Blacks and Support

That support for the political system may be low among black Americans is suggested by the fact that blacks have suffered centuries of oppression and discrimination in the United States. Figure 2.1, as we have seen, compares trust in government by blacks and whites and offers some support for such a conclusion. It shows that in the mid-1960s—when the federal government's civil rights activities were highly visible—blacks were actually slightly more trustful of the government than were whites. But since 1968 that trend has reversed itself, and now blacks are in fact less trustful of the government than are whites. Table 2.2 shows that whites have more confidence in the effectiveness of elections than blacks do.

Nevertheless, there is persuasive evidence that blacks generally are not as alienated from the American political system as a superficial consideration might indicate. This is a conclusion reached by many studies done at the time of the ghetto riots of the late 1960s.[12] The black attitudes revealed in Figure 2.1 and Table 2.2, although somewhat more negative than those of whites, are not all that different from those of the whites. A

Table 2.2   Confidence in the institution of elections by race, 1972–1973

Confidence in elections[a]	1972			1973		
	Total	Whites	Blacks	Total	Whites	Blacks
A good deal	55.8%	57.0%	43.2%	32.8%	33.2%	28.5%
Some	36.5	35.7	44.7	38.1	39.2	26.8
Not much	7.7	7.3	12.1	29.2	27.6	44.7
Total	100.0%	100.0%	100.0%	100.0%	100.0%	100.0%

[a] The question used to measure confidence in elections was worded as follows: "And how much do you feel that having elections makes the government pay attention to what the people think—a good deal, some, or not much?"

Source: Arthur H. Miller, "Change in Political Trust: Discontent with Authorities and Economic Policies, 1972–1973," paper given at the 1974 Annual Meeting of the American Political Science Association, p. 36.

12. See William Brink and Louis Harris, *Black and White* (New York: Simon and Schuster, 1966); Angus Campbell and Howard Schuman, "Racial Attitudes in Fifteen American Cities," in *Supplemental Studies for the National Advisory Commission on Civil Disorders* (Washington, D.C.: GPO, 1968), pp. 1–67; Edward S. Greenberg, "Children and Government: A Comparison Across Racial Lines," *Midwest Journal of Political Science,* 14 (May 1970), 249–275; and David O. Sears, "Black Attitudes Toward the Political System in the Aftermath of the Watts Insurrection," *Midwest Journal of Political Science,* 13 (November 1969), 515–544.

1966 study found that 87 percent of black Americans reported they would be willing to fight for the United States in a future war.[13]

The total picture that emerges from a consideration of black support for the political system is that, over-all, blacks give somewhat less support to the political system than do whites. The recent falling off in support among whites is also observable among blacks, leading to a situation in which support for government—while still present to a significant degree—has been compromised. Thus, only the incurable optimist or the most undiscerning observer would argue that black disaffection with American society and its political system is of no consequence. Nevertheless, American society still appears to have the opportunity to hold the continuing support of the black minority for the political system. Much depends on the future policies pursued by the political system.

American Political Culture and Demands

The political culture is related in two ways to *the making of demands.* First, the political culture outlines the policy areas within which demands may be made by delineating which social and economic concerns are the proper concern of government—and which are not. A recent study showed, for example, that 89 percent of the American people agree that the federal government should handle such matters as "how to control inflation, avoid depression, and how to achieve peace in the world."[14] Active involvement in creating economic stability and active work for peace in the world are both accepted as legitimate, and even necessary, areas of governmental effort, and thus demands are constantly being made on the government in these policy areas. During an earlier period, the political culture defined the economy and the international political arena as two policy areas that the federal government should for the most part stay out of, and thus there were few demands for specific public policies in those areas. In much the same way today, no demands are made on the government to directly subsidize churches or to nationalize basic industries because the political culture is agreed that it would be improper for the government to do so.

Second, the political culture defines the *way* in which demands may legitimately be made. The American political culture rejects assassination, physical assault, riots, and bribes as suitable means of making demands, although they obviously are not rejected by a few persons. Instead, de-

13. Brink and Harris, *Black and White,* pp. 274–275. The Commission on Civil Disorders found similar, although somewhat less favorable, attitudes among the Detroit and Newark blacks. See the National Advisory Commission on Civil Disorders, *Report,* p. 178.

14. United States Senate, Committee on Government Operations, *Confidence and Concern,* p. 236.

mands are to be made by way of strictly defined procedures: petitions, letters, voting, pressures of interest groups, and so forth. Even when legally permissible, making demands by picketing, marches, and other types of demonstrations are suspect to most Americans. Less than 20 percent would approve of "taking part in protest meetings or marches that *are permitted by the local authorities."*[15] Following clashes between the Chicago police and antiwar demonstrators at the 1968 Democratic convention, the evidence indicates more persons felt the police had used too little force than felt the police had used too much force[16] —this in spite of television coverage admittedly sympathetic to the demonstrators and clear violations by the police of basic rules of proper police conduct.[17] It appears that although Americans will sometimes approve of demonstrations and marches—particularly those supporting dominant values and beliefs—Americans remain inherently suspicious of them and—particularly when they run counter to dominant values and beliefs and surely when they involve violence or illegal acts—will question or reject them as legitimate means of making demands.

American Political Culture and Basic Political Beliefs

In order to understand how American political culture serves as an environment for American politics, a third important aspect of that culture must be grasped. This aspect—in distinction from the more sharply focused aspects of political culture relating to support and to demands—is concerned with a wide range of *general beliefs and values.* Beliefs concerning equalitarianism, big government, political power, and other such topics are heavily involved in the creation of the climate of opinion that has the profoundest effect on the politics of any society. But these beliefs are difficult to analyze and describe with precision. Furthermore, the number of beliefs held by the American people that have been suggested by historians, philosophers, political scientists, sociologists, and general commentators on American society is seemingly infinite. What this section of the chapter does is to focus on three basic beliefs out of the welter of possibilities. They have been selected—and others rejected—both because of the strong evidence in support of their existence and because of their especially great relevance to the political system.[18]

15. See Philip E. Converse, Warren E. Miller, Jerrold G. Rusk, and Arthur C. Wolfe, "Continuity and Change in American Politics: Parties and Issues in the 1968 Election," *American Political Science Review,* 63 (December 1969), 1105.

16. See Lewis Chester, Godfrey Hodgson, and Bruce Page, in *An American Melodrama* (New York: Viking, 1969), pp. 592–595.

17. See Daniel Walker, *Rights in Conflict* (New York: Dutton, 1968).

18. For a very able discussion of the three points raised below as well as additional points, all of which are interpreted as being part of a classical liberal tradition that has had a profound impact in American thought and culture, see Donald J. Devine, *The Political Culture of the United States* (Boston: Little, Brown, 1972) especially chap. 4.

Suspicion of Big, Centralized Government

From the days of the thirteen colonies to the present, Americans have been suspicious of big, centralized government. This suspicion reveals itself in two particularly significant ways: a preference for local or state governmental action over federal government action, and a belief in the desirability of keeping political power divided and splintered. Support for both of these ideas can be seen as early as 1787 in the words of James Madison in defense of the new Constitution before its ratification by the thirteen states: "In the compound republic of America, the power surrendered by the people is first divided between two distinct governments, and then the portion allotted to each subdivided among distinct and separate departments. Hence a double security arises to the rights of the people."[19]

That almost two hundred years later most Americans still believe in the evil of concentrated political power is seen in the almost universal acceptance of the concept of dividing political power between the legislative, judicial, and executive branches of government. No serious suggestions that the United States abandon the separation of powers within the federal government have ever been made. And all the states have followed the federal pattern of having separated legislative, executive, and judicial branches. Only one state—Nebraska—has even taken the fairly modest step of creating a one-house legislature. This belief in the efficacy of the separation of powers was reinforced by the Watergate scandals, when the independent judiciary and legislative branches were credited with bringing into line an executive that was abusing its power.[20]

Table 2.3 reveals current public attitudes in regard to making the three different levels of government stronger.[21] The pervasive American belief

Table 2.3   Beliefs in the desired strength of federal, state, and local governments, 1973[a]

	Federal	State	Local
Should be stronger	32%	59%	61%
Should be weaker	42	11	8
Should be kept as is	17	22	23
Not sure	9	8	8
Total	100%	100%	100%

[a] The exact wording of the question was: "Do you think each of the following levels of government should be made much stronger, somewhat less strong, or should have power taken away from it?"

Source: United States Senate, Committee on Government Operations, *Confidence and Concern: Citizens View American Government* (Washington, D.C.: GPO, 1973), p. 299.

19. James Madison, *The Federalist* (#51).
20. See, for example, the editorial, "Transfer of Power" *The New York Times* (August 9, 1974), p. 32.
21. For additional evidence on this point see Devine, *The Political Culture,* pp. 167–172.

Table 2.4   Attitudes Toward federal, state, and local government

	Respondents agreeing
Each state in the country has different people with different needs, so it is mainly the states that should decide what government programs ought to be started and continued	74%
The federal government has become so big and bureaucratic that it should give more of its tax money to the states and local communities to do what they think it is best to do	73%
Local government is closer to the people, so as many governmental services as possible should be given to local governments to handle	72%
Federal government has deep responsibility for seeing to it that the poor are taken care of, that no one goes hungry, and that every person achieves a minimum standard of living	68%
It's about time we had a strong federal government again to get this country moving again	67%

Source: United States Senate, Committee on Government Operations, *Confidence and Concern: Citizens View American Government* (Washington, D.C.: GPO, 1973), p. 236.

in the inherent greater trustworthiness of state and local government over centralized government is revealed in a willingness of majorities to make both state and local governments stronger and an unwillingness to make the federal government stronger. But Table 2.4 reveals ambiguities in Americans' preference for state and local action over federal governmental action. The first three statements—all of which state a preference for state or local governmental action over federal governmental action—have strong majority support as would be expected. But the last two statements, both of which call for strong federal action, also have strong majority support. The feeling seems to be suspicion and wariness toward big, centralized government more than outright rejection of big, centralized government.

Suspicion of Political Parties and Politicians

Americans have a curious love-hate affair with their political parties and politicians. Their beliefs about parties and politicians harbor many ambiguities and even flat contradictions. A cross section of the population, for example, was asked to evaluate some ninety occupations, indicating whether they thought the "general standing" of each was excellent, good, average, somewhat below average, or poor. The ten most highly respected occupations (in the order in which they were rated) were United States

Supreme Court justice, physician, state governor, cabinet member in the federal government, diplomat in the United States foreign service, mayor of a large city, college professor, scientist, United States representative in Congress, and banker.[22] The significant fact for us here is that six of the ten most highly respected occupations were political offices. Nevertheless, another nationwide survey found a majority of the population (54 percent) were opposed to their sons or daughters entering politics as a career.[23] Most cited the "dirty" nature of politics as the reason for their opposition, and even many of those not opposed to a political career for their children felt that their children should be able to "clean up the mess" or get the best of the "dirty politicians." Americans seem both to oppose political careers for their offspring and to respect those successful in political careers!

The explanation for this contradiction seems to flow from the admiration of political offices and institutions in the abstract—the Supreme Court, Congress, a governorship of a state, and the like—but a deep-seated distrust of persons perceived as politicians and activities perceived as partisan politics.[24] The existence of deep-seated distrust can be seen in the number of negative terms that are applied to politicians and party politics, for example, "bosses" instead of leaders, "party hacks" instead of followers, "smoke-filled rooms" instead of conference rooms, and "deals" instead of agreements.

The sense of distrust of political parties is also revealed by Table 2.5. The public was found to be sharply divided in its attitudes toward political parties, with majorities taking an antiparty position on a number of items —but with majorities taking proparty positions on the last two items. The author of the study from which this table is taken concludes that, in terms of the public's attitude toward political parties, "the general image which emerges is that public feeling is lukewarm and somewhat mixed."[25]

Equalitarianism and Trust in Popular Rule

Although the Declaration of Independence proudly proclaims, "All men are created equal," it is clear that Americans are very unequal in wealth, education, physical strength, and a host of other qualities. Yet there is a

22. Albert J. Reiss Jr., *Occupations and Social Status* (New York: Free Press, 1961), p. 54.

23. American Institute of Public Opinion (Gallup Poll), March 3, 1965. Also see William C. Mitchell, "The Ambivalent Social Status of the American Politician," *Western Political Quarterly,* 22 (1959), 683–698 and Maurice Klain, " 'Politics'—Still a Dirty Word," *Antioch Review,* 15 (Winter 1955), 457–466.

24. For a discussion of possible sources of this distrust see Klain, " 'Politics'—Still a Dirty Word," pp. 461–464.

25. Jack Dennis, "Support for the Party System by the Mass Public," *American Political Science Review,* LX (September 1966), p. 606.

Table 2.5   Public support for the political party system

	Percentage of Respondents[a]				
	Agreeing	Uncertain	Disagreeing	Not Determined	Total
The political parties more often than not create conflicts where none really exist	64	13	15	8	100%
The parties do more to confuse the issues than to provide clear choice on them	54	19	21	6	100%
The conflicts and controversies between the parties hurt our country more than they help it	47	14	35	4	100%
Our system of government would work a lot more efficiently if we could get rid of conflicts between the parties all together	53	8	34	5	100%
It would be better if, in all elections, we put no party labels on the ballot	22	7	67	4	100%
Democracy works best where competition between parties is strong	68	12	12	8	100%

[a] Based on a 1964 survey conducted in Wisconsin only.

Source: Jack Dennis, "Support for the Party System by the Mass Public," *American Political Science Review*, 60 (September 1966), 605–606.

sense in which American society insists that persons are in fact equal. The American view of equality is not, however, a leveling view; it is not a belief in the merit of wiping out or even reducing differences in wealth and material possessions (these are seen as the proper fruit of one's hard work or perhaps of fortuitous circumstances). Rather, the key feature of American equalitarianism is its belief that wealth, education, or acclaim does not make anyone a better person than the next. Thus no one owes such people deference. They may be wealthier or more famous, but not better. They may be admired and envied, but not given deference.

As political scientist E. E. Schattschneider wrote: "Translated into modern terms, 'equal in the eyes of God' does not mean that all men are equally wise or good or strong. Men are equal in the one dimension that counts: each is a human being, infinitely precious because he is human.

All else is irrelevant.''[26] Inequalities such as those in wealth, education, and health are recognized by American society—but are considered irrelevant in assessing a person's true worth.

This sense of equalitarianism quite naturally leads to a strong faith in the ability of the people to rule themselves. Lincoln's famous ''government of the people, by the people, for the people'' seems to be carved as deeply and as lastingly in the hearts and minds of the American people as it is in the granite of the Lincoln Memorial. In response to the question ''In general, how much trust and confidence do you have in the wisdom of the American people when it comes to making political decisions?'' some 76 percent of the people indicated they had a great deal or a good deal of trust and confidence.[27]

In an intensive study of a small group of working-class men, Robert Lane found the men committed to popular rule, even while admitting its weaknesses. He wrote that ''most, indeed, almost all, of the men both understood the frailties of popular government and accept it'' and asks, ''Why do these Americans, representative of working-class Eastport, and of New Haven, Springfield, Baltimore, Akron, Flint, and a large portion of urban America, adopt the ideology of popular government so completely?''[28]

Another indication of the faith Americans have in popular rule is the fact that their typical response to allegations of corruption in government or the political parties is to call for more popular rule. The direct primary and the use of the referendum were adopted in much of the country in the early twentieth century in response to revelations of widespread political corruption. And more recently, following the Watergate scandal, there have been renewed calls for more direct public participation in public and party affairs.

Summary

This brief treatment of three of the basic American political beliefs that heavily influence the politics of the United States suggests that Americans are suspicious of big government, political parties, and politicians, having conflicting ideas about the acceptance and the rejection of them, and that they have an abiding faith in the equal worth of all human beings and of the people's ability to rule their own affairs well. The consequences of these beliefs for the political system and the policy-making processes will

---

26. E. E. Schattschneider, *Two Hundred Million Americans in Search of a Government* (New York: Holt, Rinehart and Winston, 1969), p. 45. Also see James Bryce, *The American Commonwealth* (New York: Macmillan, 1911), pp. 810–821.

27. See Lloyd A. Free and Hadley Cantril, *The Political Beliefs of Americans* (New Brunswick, N.J.: Rutgers University Press, 1968), p. 193.

28. Robert E. Lane, *Political Ideology* (New York: The Free Press, 1962), p. 86.

be noted throughout the remaining chapters of the book. Very briefly, however, they make it difficult to put together in the United States concentrations of political power to deal with national problems. There tends to be a preference for decentralized policy making and certainly for decentralized administration of public policies. In addition, support and legitimacy for public policies have to be obtained by the constant demonstration of the ties between the policies and popular support for them.

Some Exploratory Questions

1. Is the level and nature of the support given the political system so high that needed changes in the system are made difficult to achieve? Or is it now so low that the stability and sense of community necessary for an orderly society is threatened?

2. As American society and the political system are confronted with such fundamental problems as energy shortages, economic instability, and urban crises, are the three basic political beliefs discussed in this chapter likely to form a strong basis on which to develop and carry through the needed public policies, or are they likely to make it more difficult to achieve and carry through the needed public policies?

Bibliographical Essay

Probably the single most helpful analysis of American political culture is found in Donald J. Devine, *The Political Culture of the United States* (Boston: Little, Brown, 1972). Also very helpful, but becoming somewhat dated by now, is Gabriel A. Almond and Sidney Verba, *The Civic Culture* (Princeton, N.J.: Princeton University Press, 1963). This is a comparative study of the political attitudes of the citizens of the United States, Britain, West Germany, Italy, and Mexico. It has been published in an abridged, paperback edition (Boston: Little, Brown, 1965). V. O. Key, *Public Opinion and American Democracy* (New York: Knopf, 1961) also sheds light on American political culture. Especially helpful is Key's discussion of consensus and cleavage in the United States. For a study that sheds much light on the way children learn support for the political system, see David Easton and Jack Dennis, *Children in the Political System* (New York: McGraw-Hill, 1969).

A good source of recent data dealing with American support for the political system can be found in a study the United States Senate commissioned Louis Harris Associates to do: United States Senate, Government Operations Committee, *Confidence and Concern: Citizens View American Government* (Washington, D.C.: GPO, 1973). Also helpful in giving poll data bearing on American political attitudes are William Watts and Lloyd Free, *State of the Nation* (New York: Universe Books, 1973) and Lloyd Free and Hadley Cantril, *The Political Beliefs of Americans* (New Brunswick, N.J.: Rutgers University Press, 1968).

The question of black support for the political system is analyzed by Angus Campbell and Howard Schuman, "Racial Attitudes in Fifteen American Cities," *Supplemental Studies for the National Advisory Commission on Civil Disorders* (Washington, D.C.: GPO, 1968). Also helpful is the National Advisory Commission on Civil Disorders, *Report of the National Advisory Commission on Civil Disorders* (New York: Bantam Books, 1968). William Brink and Louis Harris, *Black and White* (New York: Simon and Schuster, 1966) reports both white and black attitudes toward racial and political questions. On white attitudes toward blacks, see the very helpful work by Angus Campbell, *White Attitudes Toward Black People* (Ann Arbor, Mich.: Institute for Social Research, University of Michigan, 1971).

A host of books seek to analyze more general underlying political values and beliefs of Americans. The Devine and Almond and Verba books cited earlier are good. Also see Seymour M. Lipset, *Political Man* (Garden City, N.Y.: Doubleday, 1960) and Seymour M. Lipset, *The First New Nation* (New York: Basic Books, 1963). For other books that seek to analyze the basic political beliefs of Americans, but rely less on survey data and more on personal insight, see David M. Potter, *People of Plenty* (Chicago: University of Chicago Press, 1954), Dennis W. Brogan, *The American Character* (New York: Knopf, 1944), and Jean-Francois Revel, *Without Marx or Jesus* (Garden City, N.Y.: Doubleday, 1971). Also still full of helpful insights is Alexis de Tocqueville, *Democracy in America,* trans., George Lawrence (Garden City, N.Y.: Doubleday, 1969). Tocqueville was an early nineteenth-century Frenchman who came to America to observe the new American democracy and reported and analyzed what he saw in a very perceptive manner.

Chapter 3   **The Consti-**   The Legal Context
               tution

Is a proper understanding of a political system more dependent on a knowledge of its societal, cultural environment or on a knowledge of its constitutional, legal structure? To debate such a question is about as useful as debating which wing of an airplane is more important! Just as an airplane is useless with only one of its wings, so also our understanding of a political system is equally distorted with knowledge only of its societal environment or only of its constitutional environment. Both are essential.

The previous chapter considered the cultural or human context of politics: the attitudes, aspirations, and beliefs of the American people. This chapter supplies the other crucial aspect of a political system's environment: the constitutional or legal environment. First, the origins and basic nature of the Constitution are considered. Next, civil liberties, which are legally provided by the Constitution and other laws, are discussed. And, finally, the federal structure provided by the Constitution is considered. Knowledge of these facets of the Constitution and other laws will set the legal context within which the political processes and struggles described in succeeding chapters take place, just as the previous chapter set the human context within which the political processes and struggles take place.

A Constitution

Sometimes the most basic term, one which appears to be clear and simple, is discovered upon closer examination to be neither clear nor simple. *A constitution* is such a term. At first thought almost all Americans would feel able to state what *the American Constitution* is. After all, is it not that document written in 1787 that establishes the American government and prescribes its basic institutions and procedures? The answer is both yes and no. The American Constitution is, in fact, that document written in 1787 (with the addition of its subsequent amendments), but it is also more than that. If the chief distinguishing characteristic of any constitution is its establishing of the basic structure of the government and the basic procedures and processes by which that government operates, then laws that created such governmental agencies as the Federal Communications Commission and the National Labor Relations Board or traditions such as the President's forming a Cabinet composed of the heads of the executive departments should be considered as much a part of the American constitution as the formal, written document. For they play as much a role in defining the structure of government and in determining how it is to operate as do the various sections of the formal Constitution.[1]

Thus it is wise to define a *constitution* as all documents, laws, official decisions, and traditions that help establish the basic structure of a government and the procedures and processes by which it operates. The American constitution thereby includes the formal, written Constitution, but it also includes those laws passed by Congress, executive orders of the presidency, basic decisions of the bureaucracy, decisions of the Supreme Court, and customs and traditions that help establish the structure of government and the procedures and processes by which it operates. The American constitution in this broader sense is considered at numerous points throughout the book; this chapter, however, focuses upon the formal Constitution.

Origins of the American Constitution

The American Constitution has proved to be a most remarkable document. It has lasted more than 180 years, surviving the impact of the change from a relatively static, rural, and agrarian society to a mobile, urban, and industrial society. This fact, which makes the United States Constitution the most enduring national constitution in history, testifies to its fundamental strengths and to the ability of the men who chartered it—and to the ability of succeeding political leaders who have made the Constitution work.

Americans often tend to discount the impact that past events have played in shaping the present. And so it is with the Constitution—Americans often talk as if it were divinely inspired and revere the "founding fathers" as if they were national saints, instead of viewing the Constitution as growing naturally out of the historical context in which it was written. The Constitution was in fact particularly influenced by four historical factors: the colonial experience, the struggle for independence, the Articles of Confederation, and contemporary political theories.

1. For purposes of clarity, when the American Constitution in the sense of the formal document written in 1787 is intended, *Constitution* will be capitalized; when constitution is used in the broader sense to refer to all documents, laws, decisions, and traditions that help establish the government and its procedures, *constitution* will not be capitalized.

The Colonial Experience At the time the Constitution was written in 1787, colonies had been in existence on the shores of America for over 150 years. In fact, the writing of the Constitution stands not too far from the midpoint between the founding of the first colonies and the present. Clearly, the experiences of this long period of development—commercial and economic development, and also political development—were bound to have an impact on the writing of the new Constitution. During the colonial period, for example, each of the colonies, all except Pennsylvania, had a bicameral legislature. The members of the lower houses were generally selected by popular vote, and the members of the upper houses were either appointed by the British monarch or needed his approval. During the colonial period, the lower houses insisted that they alone had the power to raise taxes. Hence, the pattern of a bicameral legislature in which the popularly elected branch alone could initiate tax legislation was an established pattern, ready for incorporation into the Constitution in 1787.

Most of the governors of the colonies were either appointed by the British monarch or served only with the Crown's approval. Only Rhode Island and Connecticut—which selected their governors through their colonial legislatures—appointed their own governors independently of the British monarch. Thus, a separation of legislative and executive powers had already evolved during the colonial experience. In all the colonies, judges were appointed directly by the monarch. This was one of the means by which Great Britain could ensure that the laws of the colonies were in conformity with the laws of the mother country. Here we can see the precursor of the American concept of federalism, in which central and regional governments each have areas of autonomy and sovereignty, while at the same time legal conflicts between these governmental units are settled by the central government.

The Independence Struggle In 1760, King George III came to power in Great Britain, and he insisted that the American colonists should bear a larger portion of the costs incurred by the British in protecting the colonies from both the French and the Indians. Under his leadership, the British Parliament passed a number of new taxes, the brunt of which fell upon the American colonists. The colonists argued that the taxes were unjust because the colonists themselves were denied direct representation in the British Parliament. The British Parliament, with notable exceptions such as Edmund Burke, argued that it was only fair that the colonists should pay for their own protection. The colonists also felt that a number of other measures passed by the British Parliament were aimed at enriching Britain at the expense of the colonies.

The rift between the colonists and Britain quickly widened as both the colonists' resistance to the British measures and British attempts to enforce the measures escalated. The end result came on July 4, 1776: the Second

Continental Congress adopted a resolution, drafted primarily by Thomas Jefferson, that became known as the Declaration of Independence. The Declaration of Independence did more than merely attempt to justify the rebellion against British authority—it set forth the ideals for which the new American nation would become known:

We hold these truths to be self-evident, that all Men are created equal, that they are endowed by their Creator with certain unalienable Rights, that among these are Life, Liberty, and the Pursuit of Happiness—That to secure these Rights, Governments are instituted among Men, deriving their just Powers from the Consent of the Governed, that whenever any Form of Government becomes destructive of these Ends, it is the Right of the People to alter or abolish it, and to institute new Government, laying its Foundation on such Principles, and organizing its Powers in such Form, as to them shall seem most likely to effect their Safety and Happiness. . . .

While the Declaration of Independence sought to vindicate a political rebellion against British colonial authority, it was not accompanied by a social revolution of any magnitude. Indeed, many of the "revolutionaries" themselves would refuse to call the American rebellion a revolutionary war. Rather, they saw themselves as taking arms only in a last resort to secure the principles of government already established in the colonial period.

Probably the most important legacy of the struggle for independence was a negative view of government. The colonists' clash with the British monarchy had encouraged the development of a view of government as a distant force constantly threatening to restrict personal freedoms. The struggle for independence implanted a fear of executive authority; it also fostered the fear of centralized governmental authority that we recognize today (noted in Chapter 2).

The Articles of Confederation   After declaring the thirteen colonies' independence from Britain, the Continental Congress set to work to draft a charter to unify the colonies. By 1781, each of the colonies had agreed to the Articles of Confederation. The Articles soon proved unworkable, however, for several reasons. Because of the colonists' fear of centralized, executive authority, the Articles created a very weak centralized government: there was no provision for a chief executive; and the central government had no power to raise revenues or regulate interstate commerce.

Without the power to levy taxes, the central government had to rely on essentially voluntary financial contributions from the states and, as might be expected in such a situation, it was continually threatened with impending bankruptcy. Without the power to regulate interstate commerce, the individual states quickly erected trade barriers to protect their individual commercial interests, thus hindering any significant degree of economic integration. The new government under the Articles faced not only an economic crisis, but also a military crisis. Unable to raise revenues, it could not supply a reliable defense system against potential British, French, Spanish, and Indian enemies, or against piracy on the high seas.

The colonists' experience with the distant British Crown was directly reflected in the Articles of Confederation, but the Articles quickly taught the now independent colonists that their basically weak central government brought new problems.

Contemporary Political Theory In addition to the impact of the colonists' historical experiences on the writing of the Constitution was the impact of the contemporary political theories accepted by most of the authors of the Constitution.[2] Fundamental to their theory of politics was a basic fear and distrust of both the citizenry and the rulers. As James Madison wrote: "But what is government itself, but the greatest of all reflections on human nature? If men were angels, no government would be necessary. . . . In framing a government which is to be administered by men over men, the great difficulty lies in this: you must first enable the government to control the governed; and in the next place oblige it to control itself."[3]

More specifically, the authors feared the development of factions—or groups of citizens—within the population that would pursue purely selfish goals and be able to twist government to their favor and to the detriment of the rest of the populace.[4]

In light of these fears, the authors believed in the "science of politics," which had recently "received great improvement" and led to the discovery of "various principles" that were "now well understood," and by which "the excellencies of representative government may be retained and its imperfections lessened or avoided."[5] The authors had a somewhat mechanistic conception of politics—they believed that by way of certain structural features they could assure effective, equitable government.

Personal Motivations The Constitution was written in a context of impressions, hopes, and fears created by the new Americans' historical experiences and by current political theories. But we ought not to forget that it was written by very real persons, subject to very real pressures, and possessing very real concerns and interests. This elementary—yet some-

2. For an excellent summary of the theoretical perspective of the writers of the Constitution, see Wilson C. McWilliams, "The American Constitution," in Gerald M. Pomper, ed., *The Performance of American Government* (New York: The Free Press, 1972), pp. 13–25.
3. James Madison, *The Federalist* (#51).
4. This fear is particularly well expressed in the famous Federalist Paper #10, written by James Madison.
5. Alexander Hamilton, *The Federalist* (#9).

times forgotten—fact was stressed and developed in 1913 by the historian Charles Beard in his book *An Economic Interpretation of the Constitution.* He examined the background of each of the members of the Constitutional Convention and concluded that almost all the authors of the Constitution were from the landed and commercial classes of their day and that their aim was to protect their own private interests: "The members of the Philadelphia Convention, which drafted the Constitution, were, with few exceptions, immediately, directly, and personally interested in, and derived economic advantage from, the establishment of the new system."[6]

It is true, as we have already seen, that under the Articles of Confederation and its very weak central government, commercial and shipping interests were being hurt by state trade barriers, Indian raids on the frontier, and foreign and piracy threats on the high seas. In addition, some of the state legislatures, under the influence of small, often debt-ridden farmers, were enacting laws that worked to the disadvantage of the money-lending and land-holding interests. It is also true, as Beard fully documents, that most of the delegates to the Constitutional Convention were from the landed, commercial groups of the day—not from the small farmers, laborers, and debtors. It cannot be denied that the new Constitution marked a departure from the weak legislature-dominated government set up by the Articles of Confederation. It created a strong central government with a strong chief executive. Article I, Sections 8 and 10 particularly contain many explicit provisions that worked to the advantage of the commercial and landed interests of colonial days.

Having acknowledged all this, however, Beard's argument that the authors of the Constitution acted out of pure economic self-interest has yet to be proved. The evidence is circumstantial, not direct. Neither Charles Beard nor anyone else can peer directly into the personal motives of men who have been dead for 150 years—all we can do is make intelligent guesses. It is also well to remember that groups of persons are virtually always motivated by a variety of interests rather than by only one. We can assume that the authors of the Constitution were influenced by an intertwined complex of factors: some economic, others theoretical; some selfish, others magnanimous. Which ones were predominant no doubt varied with individual members of the convention.

The Constitution as a Document

As the delegates to the Constitutional Convention gathered in the city of Philadelphia in the summer of 1787, they brought with them their experi-

6. Charles A. Beard, *An Economic Interpretation of the Constitution* (New York: Macmillan, 1913), p. 324.

ences under colonial charters, their impressions left over from the struggle for independence, their reactions to the Articles of Confederation, their reflections on the writings of political theorists, and their own economic self-interests. But this did not mean that the delegates—with their similar backgrounds and experiences—came with a clear-cut idea of the exact nature and form of the government they were to create. The differences of opinion were sharp and the usually cordial relationships were sometimes strained.

Two factors proved to be particularly divisive. First was the dual question of how strong the central government should be and how its power should be distributed among the executive, legislative, and judicial branches. Some delegates recalled the struggle for independence and the problems the colonists had had with the British Crown and therefore feared a strong central government and a strong executive within that government. Other delegates remembered the problems brought about by the weak central government created by the Articles of Confederation and feared a departmentalized government and an overly weak executive within it.

The second factor that proved particularly troublesome was the conflicting interests of the various states. The large states were unwilling to join a union in which they would not have power in proportion to their size; the small states were unwilling to join a union in which they would be overwhelmed by the large states. In addition, the southern states split with the northern states over a number of issues. Slavery was one such issue, because the southern states feared that a strong government might take steps against slavery. Tariff policies were another such issue, because the southern states feared a strong government might impose high tariffs that, while helping the development of northern industries, would hurt southern trade with foreign nations, on which they were heavily dependent.

These divisive factors proved troublesome for the Convention because, obviously, the issues divided the delegates themselves. But they also proved troublesome because the delegates realized that if their efforts were to bear fruit, the new Constitution would have to be approved by the states.[7] Thus, merely to secure agreement among the delegates was not enough—they had to be able to win the support of influential persons back in the individual states, a task that posed many difficulties. The delegates at the Convention as well as the leaders in their home states had to be largely satisfied with the document. Given the divisions in the Convention and within and among the states, this was no mean task! The task was successfully completed, however, by a series of compromises. Thus, the Constitution may be accurately analyzed as a bundle of compromises.

7. For a helpful discussion of this point as well as a good analysis of the compromises effected at the Constitutional Convention, see John P. Roche, "The Founding Fathers: A Reform Caucus in Action," *American Political Science Review,* 55 (1961), 799–816.

Centralization of Power   There was wide agreement among the delegates to the Constitutional Convention that there should be a balance between the power of the central government and the power of the state governments. This, the delegates felt, was a key to the means by which a large political system—in distinction from the very small political units for which many of the earlier democratic theorists had argued—could be established. This large political system would, in turn, make it more difficult for a selfish faction to seize power.[8]

There were differences of opinion, however, on what the exact distribution of power between the central and state governments should be. Thus a number of compromises dealing with the power of the central government were entered into. These attempted to strike a balance between the power of the states and the rights of the people, on the one hand, and the power of the central government on the other hand. The new Constitution strengthened the central government by providing not for a simple confederation of individual states, but for a union of the *people* of those states in a new government. The Preamble to the Constitution begins, "We, the People of the United States. . . ." Thus, the powers of the new central government were conceived as having been derived from the people, and not from the individual states. In addition, this new central government was specifically given the power to raise taxes, regulate interstate commerce, and adjudicate constitutional questions concerning the nature of the new government. The people were to elect representatives to the lower house of the national legislature.

On the other hand, the central government was strictly limited in the extent of its powers. It was to possess only specifically enumerated and implied powers, and all residual powers (those not directly or indirectly granted to the central government) were to remain with the states. Although the lower house of the national legislature was to be elected directly by the people, the upper house was to be elected indirectly through the state legislatures. Hence, the senators represented states, not people. (This was changed in 1913 by the ratification of the Seventeenth Amendment to the Constitution.) Further, there were specific prohibitions, such as the passing of bills of attainder and ex post facto laws, placed on the central government. In the debate over ratification of the new Constitution, its supporters agreed in principle to further explicit limitations on the powers of the central government, and these limitations were incorporated in the first ten amendments to the Constitution, now known to us as the Bill of Rights. Here the central government is forbidden such actions as

8. This argument is clearly developed by Madison in *The Federalist* (#10): "Extend the sphere [of the government] and you take in a greater variety of parties and interests; you make it less probable that a majority of the whole will have a common motive to invade the rights of other citizens; or if such a common motive exists, it will be more difficult for all who feel it to discover their own strength, and to act in unison with each other."

establishing a national religion; restricting freedom of the press, assembly, or speech; conducting unreasonable search and seizure; and forcing a defendant to testify against himself in a judicial proceeding.

Separation of Powers and Checks and Balances   There was wide agreement among the delegates that the legislative, executive, and judicial powers should be lodged in separate institutions. This *separation of powers* was seen as a means of preventing the abuse of power the colonists felt they had suffered under King George III and as an adjunct to the division of power between the central and state governments. This is the heart of the famous *checks and balances* idea. By the creation of separate institutions, each with its own independent base of power and all required to act together in ruling the people, power checks power and no one selfish faction is able to gain control over public policy.

But agreement was far from universal among the framers on the exact division of powers among the executive, legislative, and judicial branches —as it was on the exact base of power of each (that is, on how the officials in each branch were to be selected). Again compromises were used to reach the exact provisions. The executive was strengthened by having the President elected independently from the legislature (some proposals would have provided for his election by Congress), and by giving him a number of significant powers such as commander-in-chief of the armed forces, the appointment of numerous officials, and the veto power over legislation. But he was limited by having the power to declare war given to Congress, by being subject to impeachment and removal from office by Congress, and by the authority of Congress to override his veto. A strong, effective—yet strictly limited—presidency was created. A strong Congress, with many enumerated powers, was created. But as a result of a key compromise (discussed later) it was divided into two houses, each with its own independent base of power, and the President was given the veto power over its acts. Thus, a compromise was struck between those who feared the weakness of a government dominated by the legislature (as set up by the Articles of Confederation), and those who feared an overly powerful, tyrannical chief executive, as exemplified by the British Crown.

A strong judiciary, whose independence was guaranteed by life terms, was created. It was provided that the judges would be appointed by the President, with the approval of the Senate—a compromise between some who wanted them appointed by the President alone, and some who wanted them appointed by Congress alone. In short, there was wide agreement on the basic principle of dividing power among several independent political institutions so that the power of one would be held in check by the power of another, but many compromises were needed in order to determine the exact nature of the political institutions and the exact division of power among them.

States' Interests   A number of compromises attempted to strike a balance between the contending interests of the states. The large states originally advocated a legislature based strictly on population (a plan that would have benefited them), while the small states advocated a legislature based purely on equal representation of all states (a plan that would have enhanced their influence). A compromise was reached whereby the membership of the House of Representatives was based on population in each state and the membership of the Senate on equal representation of the states. In the process the Convention was saved from disintegration.

The slavery issue was pragmatically settled by counting slaves at three-fifths their number, both for purposes of distributing taxes and for determining a state's representation in the House of Representatives. The federal government was prohibited from banning the importation of additional slaves until 1808, but after that date it could do so. The Constitution granted the central government the power to levy tariffs, but it also required that they be uniform throughout the United States, and it forbade the imposition of duties on articles being exported.

Summary   Although there was wide agreement among the leading members of the Constitutional Convention on several basic principles and goals of government, there were also many divisions and differences on exactly how these principles and goals were to be put into practice. In addition, the delegates knew they had to write a Constitution they could sell to the states. Thus either they had to compromise or there would be no Constitution—at least no Constitution that would be ratified by the states. Faced with this choice, the majority of delegates opted for compromise—even when it led them to rather inelegant compromises with principle—such as counting each black slave as three-fifths of a person and permitting the importation of additional slaves for another twenty years.

Amending the Constitution

The writers of the Constitution provided in Article V three ways in which the Constitution can be formally amended. First, if both the House of Representatives and the Senate, by two-thirds votes, propose an amendment to the Constitution and if three fourths of the state legislatures approve it, then that amendment becomes part of the formal, written Constitution. The two alternatives to this procedure are almost totally unused: One is the calling of a special convention to propose amendments, as an alternative to Congress' doing so. Such a convention is to be called into being by Congress upon the request of two thirds of the state legislatures. This procedure has never been used in proposing a constitutional amendment in large part because of fears that if such a convention were called it might radically rewrite the Constitution. The second rarely used procedure involves ratification of a proposed amendment by special state conventions, rather than by the state legislatures. It has been used in the adoption of only one of the twenty-six amendments—the twenty-first, which repealed prohibition.

The most striking feature of the formal amendment process is the infrequency with which it has been used. Only twenty-six amendments have been adopted in almost 200 years, and ten of these constitute the Bill of Rights, adopted immediately upon promulgation of the Constitution as part of an agreement worked out during the ratification debates. The fact that four of the remaining sixteen amendments have been adopted since 1961 suggests that resistance to formal amendment of the Constitution may be less today than in the past. But it remains undeniable that most of the changes in the structures, processes, and procedures of American politics come about more from changes in customs, statutes, and applications and interpretations of the Constitution than from formal amendments to the Constitution.

The Constitution and Politics

Legitimacy and Support   The original copy of the Constitution is on display in Washington, D.C., at the National Archives, in a large, vaulted room with a cathedral-like atmosphere. The spirit of quiet and reverence in that room matches well the honor in which Americans hold the Constitution. Often an interpretation of the Constitution by the Supreme Court is attacked as foolish and pernicious, but the Constitution itself is never attacked as being foolish and pernicious. No matter how much Americans may disagree over the proper interpretation of the Constitution or the policies that should be pursued under it, they still agree that the Constitution is a great document that should be obeyed, and they take pride in the fact that it is the oldest written Constitution in the world.

As a result, the Constitution and the traditions that surround it play a significant role in creating a feeling of legitimacy and in generating support for the political system—two of the system-maintenance functions. This is true because some of the honor and respect in which the Constitution is held is transferred to the institutions and processes it has created. Thus whenever a certain action or decision can be justified as being required or permitted by the Constitution, that action or decision tends to be accorded legitimacy and given support. In addition, the Constitution generates support by serving as a symbol that unites and unifies, much as the monarchy does in Great Britain.

The Constitution and Policy Making   It is clear that the Constitution incorporates decisions that profoundly affect the way public policies are made and the relative advantages and disadvantages enjoyed by differing interests in the struggle to influence public policies. The differing, constitutionally mandated structure and composition of the Supreme Court, Senate, and House of Representatives, for example, affect the nature of the role each plays in the policy-making process. In recent years it has been generally acknowledged that the Senate has been more responsive to liberal demands than has the House of Representatives (although there is evidence that this is now changing). And in the 1950s the Supreme Court was able to respond to demands for equal opportunities for the black minority at a time when neither the Senate nor the House of Representatives was at all responsive to these demands.

But it is easy to exaggerate the extent to which the Constitution in and by itself affects the public policy making processes. For the constitution, as seen earlier, is more than the formal Constitution. The formal document and its amendments are supplemented by a multitude of additional laws, decisions, and customs. In the process the governmental structure provided by the Constitution—and thereby also the advantages and disadvantages enjoyed by differing interests in the policy-making processes—is frequently and significantly modified. For example, the constitutionally specified electoral college method of selecting the President has been changed by the custom of each state's voters choosing electors pledged to vote for a particular candidate previously nominated by a political party. As will be seen shortly, the interstate commerce clause of the Constitution has been interpreted by the Supreme Court to give powers to Congress that the authors of the Constitution never dreamed of. And Congress by legislative action has created a number of independent regulatory agencies never envisaged by the Constitution.[9]

Particularly important, however, in determining the actual role played by the Constitution in the political system are the numerous applications and interpretations given the provisions of the Constitution. In writing the Constitution the authors were, in effect, engaging in *rule initiation.* They established certain general rules that have to be applied and interpreted. And the Constitution leaves a great deal of room for a variety of applications and interpretations.

This is true in part because the Constitution is ambiguous to a degree unrecognized by most Americans. Article IV of the Bill of Rights provides: "The right of the people to be secure in their persons, houses, papers, and effects, against unreasonable searches and seizures, shall not be violated. . . ." But what is an *unreasonable* search and seizure? What is reasonable to one person may be totally unreasonable to the next. This is not an isolated example of constitutional ambiguity. Article I, Section 8, provides: "The Congress shall have power . . . to make all laws which shall

9. The Constitution declares the President shall "take care that the laws be faithfully executed" (Art. II, Sec. 2), but the independent regulatory agencies, which are partly independent from presidential control, are responsible for executing many vital laws. They are discussed further in Chapter 9.

be *necessary and proper* for carrying into execution the foregoing pow-ers."[10] Article I, Section 9, states: "The privilege of the writ of habeas corpus shall not be suspended, unless when in cases of rebellion or inva-sion *the public safety may require it.*" Article II, Section 3, reads: "He [the President] may, *on extraordinary occasions,* convene both Houses [of Congress]." And Article VIII of the Bill of Rights provides: "*Excessive* bail shall not be required, nor *excessive* fines imposed, nor *cruel and unusual punishments* inflicted." The key point to keep in mind is that, when the Constitution is not specific, which of several possible meanings is to be declared the proper one must be decided somewhere in the political system.

Even where the intention of the Constitution is apparently clear, there is still often room for a variety of alternative interpretations. Perhaps the classic example here is the interstate commerce clause. Article I, Section 8, reads: "The Congress shall have power . . . to regulate commerce . . . among the several states." Apparently the intention of the authors was to allow the new central government to regulate the actual movement of goods from one state to another. Yet a statement as clear-cut as this can give rise to a host of questions. What is commerce? Are goods that *will be* shipped to another state interstate commerce and therefore within the province of Congress? What about goods that *have been* shipped from another state? After a long struggle and a process of development, the Supreme Court declared that Congress, under the powers given it by this clause, could regulate certain goods that were never even intended for interstate transportation.[11]

In short, the Constitution is such that a number of conflicting interpreta-tions can be made of many key provisions. This simple but frequently ignored fact is crucial, for it means that to a large degree the governmental structure and the public policy-making processes found in the American political system today have been determined not by the Constitution itself, but by the decisions of the political system. Sometimes these decisions evolve over a period of time in the form of customs and traditions. Some-times they take the form of acts passed by Congress or of formal decisions by the President or certain bureaucratic officials. But most often they take the form of Supreme Court interpretations, because the Constitution is sufficiently ambiguous and sufficiently open to a variety of alternative applications that many disagreements are bound to arise over the proper application of particular provisions of the Constitution. The Supreme Court is then called upon to decide which of the conflicting applications is correct—it is thereby engaged in *rule interpretation.* This question of

10. In each of the following cases the italics are added to emphasize the ambiguous word or phrase.
11. See *Wickard v. Filburn* 317 U.S. 111 (1942).

interpretation is explored fully in Chapter 10, which deals with the judiciary.

Civil Liberties

The Nature of Civil Liberties

Government and politics—as we saw in Chapter 1—mean authority and rules. Consequently, they mean—in a certain sense—the limiting of human freedom. This is true in the sense that under a political system everyone in a society is no longer free to do whatever he or she wishes to do. Someone may wish to drive eighty miles an hour through a residential area, defraud his neighbors of their money, and publicly and maliciously write against someone else. The political system says he may not do any of these. The whole rationale for even having a government rests on the fact that by the authoritative regulating of society all persons have a greater opportunity to develop themselves and pursue their own ideals. Absolute freedom (everyone doing whatever he or she pleases) means no freedom. Chaos and the law of the jungle would rule, and the order necessary for persons to live together in a civilized society would be absent.

But—and this is crucial—a balance must be maintained. Just as absolute freedom destroys freedom, so also total regulation of society destroys freedom. There is little liberty in either an anarchy or in a Nazi Germany. Thus the need to strike a balance between anarchy and tyranny arises: establishing sufficient authority that the order necessary for man to exist in society is maintained, and establishing sufficient limitations on authority that man's liberties are not suffocated. As Abe Fortas, a former justice of the Supreme Court, has written: "The achievement of liberty is man's indispensable condition of living; and yet, liberty cannot exist unless it is restrained and restricted."[12] To strike the proper balance is not easy. History is strewn with the wreckage of such attempts.

From the point of view of an individual member of society, the freedom-authority balance is a balance between rights and obligations. One has certain rights that help safeguard his liberty. These rights define areas on which neither the government nor his fellow members of society may tresspass. One is assured, for example, that government will not stop him from speaking his mind or imprison him without following certain prescribed procedures designed to give him a full opportunity to exonerate himself; and one is also assured that some other member of society will not try to stop him from speaking his mind (perhaps by threatening physical

12. Abe Fortas, *Concerning Dissent and Civil Disobedience* (New York: New American Library, 1968). On this point also see Leslie Lipson, *The Democratic Civilization* (New York: Oxford University Press, 1964), chap. 16.

violence) or hold him in involuntary servitude. Every person is guaranteed certain rights upon which neither the government nor any individual may trespass.

But one person's rights are another person's obligations. One person's right to life is guaranteed by the next person's obligation not to resort to violence. Thus every person has many obligations to fulfill that limit what he may and may not do. One may not throw his garbage out into the street (thereby safeguarding his neighbors' right to a clean, healthy neighborhood), one may not discriminate in his hiring practices on the basis of sex (thereby protecting a person's right to employment regardless of sex), and if one breaks his neighbor's window he is liable for damages (thereby protecting his neighbor's right to private property). By the enforcement of such obligations as these on the public the political system creates the order necessary for human society and for personal freedom. It should be recognized that the government also has certain obligations toward its citizens. Thus the government has an obligation not to engage in such actions as establishing a religion, interfering with free speech, or holding a person in prison without bringing charges against him.

Civil Liberties and Public Policy Making

The balance between liberty and authority, between rights and obligations, constitutes a crucial aspect of the legal context within which the political system operates. The rights guaranteed citizens not only help create a situation in which they can live their private lives in peace and freedom, but also help assure their freedom to make demands upon the political system. The authority that has been established—the obligations placed on both government and individuals—helps assure that individuals will possess the opportunity to petition the government, to criticize it, and, through prescribed channels, to work to change and replace it. And the obligation the government has toward its citizens limits what the government may and may not do. The political system may not do whatever it wishes; instead, the Constitution places certain limitations on what it may do. The political system may not deny persons the right to vote because of race or sex, it may not limit the freedom of the press, and in taking actions it must follow certain definite procedures (all laws levying taxes, for example, must be passed by both houses of Congress and must originate in the House of Representatives). Thus both the permissible outputs and the way in which the outputs are arrived at are limited by the obligations placed on the political system by the Constitution.

All this does not mean, however, that civil liberties and the dual liberty-authority, rights-obligations balance on which they depend constitute a certain and fixed element in the political system's environment. Rather, the exact nature of that balance is constantly shifting, and what constitutes a proper balance is frequently in dispute. As a result the civil liberties currently enjoyed by American citizens are largely a product of the political system's own policy-making processes.

To see why this is the case it is necessary, first of all, to see that widely different interpretations can be given those parts of the Constitution relating to civil liberties. At one time separate and equal services and facilities for blacks and whites were held to be constitutional, now they are not;[13] at one time children could be forced to pledge allegiance to the flag in school exercises, now they cannot;[14] at one time states could outlaw abortions, now they cannot.[15] All these changes came about not by constitutional amendments or by changes in statutes passed by Congress, but by new and different interpretations of the Constitution accepted by the Supreme Court. That what makes up constitutionally guaranteed civil liberties —what is the proper balance between liberty and authority, rights and obligations—changes over time can also be illustrated by apparent abuses of civil liberties condoned by the political system. During World War I a pacifist was convicted for urging resistence to the draft,[16] and during World War II large groups of West Coast citizens of Japanese ancestry were forced out of their homes and jobs and moved to camps in Nevada and Utah.[17]

Thus the Bill of Rights, other parts of the Constitution guaranteeing basic civil liberties, and statutes relating to civil liberties certainly are all parts of the legal context within which the political system acts, within which public policy making goes on. But that legal context is a shifting, flexible context, with the political system itself—through the various governmental institutions and especially the courts—determining exactly what balance between liberty and authority, rights and obligations, should be struck, thereby determining the exact content of the civil liberties guaranteed in the United States.

Federalism

A crucial feature of the political system provided for by the Constitution is a federal structure. The Constitution created a central or federal government with certain independent powers, but at the same time it left the state governments intact, also with certain independent powers. That is, the

13. See *Plessy v. Ferguson* 163 U.S. 537 (1896) and *Brown v. Board of Education* 347 U.S. 483 (1954).
14. See *Minersville School District v. Gobitis* 310 U.S. 586 (1940) and *West Virginia State Board of Education v. Barnette* 319 U.S. 624 (1943).
15. See *Doe v. Bolton* 410 U.S. 179 (1973) and *Roe v. Wade* 410 U.S. 113 (1973).
16. See *Schenk v. United States* 249 U.S. 47 (1919).
17. See *Korematsu v. United States* 323 U.S. 214 (1945).

state governments do not hold their powers at the sufferance of the central government, nor does the central government hold its powers at the sufferance of the state governments. Each holds its powers as a right, and this is constitutional *federalism*—at least this is the claim traditionally made. (A serious qualification should and will be made to this claim.) Clearly, the nature of American federalism has significance for the political system.

The Nature of American Federalism

Dual Federalism and Cooperative Federalism   Lord Bryce, a British student of American government at the turn of the century, once described the national and state governments as "each . . . doing its own work without touching or hampering the other."[18] This view of federalism is called *dual federalism*. It sees each level of government with its own sphere of activity, each making public policy in separate and distinct policy areas. The concept of federalism discussed in the previous paragraph, which stresses the independence of the powers of the state and national governments, has encouraged this view.

Cooperative federalism, on the other hand, says that instead of one level of government making policy in one policy area and another level in another area, all three—national, state, and local—share in making policy in almost all policy areas. As Daniel Elazar has written: "From public welfare to public recreation, from national defense to local police protection, the system of sharing has become so pervasive that it is often difficult for the uninitiated bystander to tell just who is doing what under which hat. . . . Under this cooperative system, the federal government, the states, and the localities share the burden for the great domestic programs."[19]

The accuracy of Elazar's statement cannot be denied. The FBI, state police, county sheriffs, and municipal police are all involved in law enforcement; the need for parks and recreation areas is met by parks and campgrounds provided from the national, state, and municipal levels. Thus in the United States today the three levels of government are marked by an intermingling of activities and the sharing of responsibilities. Cooperative federalism, not dual federalism, is the prevailing pattern.

Cooperative Federalism and the Constitution   The writers of the Constitution in 1787 attempted to divide power between the new federal government and the state governments. The federal government was given

18. James Bryce, *The American Commonwealth,* vol. I (New York: Macmillan, 1911), p. 324.
19. Daniel J. Elazar, *American Federalism: A View from the States,* 2d ed. (New York: Crowell, 1972), p. 47. For descriptions of the sharing of responsibilities by the three levels of government in providing police protection and recreation facilities see Merton Grodzins, *The American System* (Chicago: Rand McNally, 1966), chaps. 4 and 5.

certain explicitly stated powers, certain powers were explicitly denied the states, and the states were given all powers not given the federal government or denied to the states.[20] All appears neat and clear. Dual federalism, the traditional conception of federalism described in the first paragraph of this section, was followed: neither the federal nor state government owed its power to the other—each held certain powers as a right—and each was assigned its separate policy areas in which to be active.

But this is not the whole story. The Constitution already provided for some sharing of activities between the federal and state governments. It provided in Article I, Section 10, for example, that states could, with the consent of Congress, levy certain import or export duties, the money thereby collected going to the federal treasury. And the sharing of activities has increased greatly since the writing of the Constitution. At an earlier point in American history there were a number of significant policy areas almost exclusively in the hands of either the federal government or the state or local government. But as we have seen this is no longer the case: increasingly, both national and state governments have become involved in more and more of the same policy areas. American federalism has gradually moved from being largely a system of dual federalism to being one of cooperative federalism.

Two features of this movement toward cooperative federalism should be noted. First, this intermingling has usually occurred as the federal government became involved in areas that previously were the exclusive domain of the states and localities. Second, most of the expansion of federal activity has not come by way of formal amendments to the Constitution but by way of changes in its applications and interpretations, because the division of powers between the federal and state governments made by the Constitution is not firm and immovable. Instead, decisions that apply or interpret particular constitutional provisions can expand or contract the powers of the federal or state governments. Thus the situation here is the same as it is in regard to civil liberties: the Constitution has initiated certain rules, but it is up to the political system, by applying and interpreting them, to determine their exact meaning.

More specifically, the federal government has expanded its areas of concern, first, by way of constitutional applications and interpretations that opened the way for direct regulation by the federal government. The interstate commerce clause, for example, has been interpreted—as we saw earlier in this chapter—to allow federal regulation of wide range of economic activities.

The federal government has also expanded its areas of concern by a large number of grants-in-aid programs. Grants-in-aid are funds given by the federal political system to state and local political units, contingent upon their participating in certain specified programs and meeting certain

20. The last provision was implied in the original Constitution and was made explicit in the tenth amendment which was adopted immediately after the ratification of the Constitution.

specified conditions. There is a large number of highly specific grant programs that Congress has established over the years and continues to fund, close to 500, the total number depending on the definition of a grant program.

Most grant-in-aid programs are designed to serve one or both of two particularly important purposes. One is to stimulate the receiving units— state or local—to begin a new activity, expand an existing one, or experiment with a new approach or technique. A second aim in some grant-in-aid programs is to help equalize the fiscal capacity of the recipients to carry on essential activities and thus partially overcome their differences in wealth. This is based on a philosophy similar to that supporting the progressive income tax: the redistribution of wealth from those with more to those with less. In this case, whole states are the donors and receivers. Some programs distribute relatively more money to low-income states than to those with higher incomes.

In late 1972 a revenue-sharing program was established by the national political system, and has been funded at increasingly higher levels since then. Revenue sharing differs from grants-in-aid in that under it money is not given to states and localities for specific programs with required standards—it is given with almost no strings attached. But it is similar to grants-in-aid in that federally collected revenues are given to the states and localities and an equalization formula is used which gives more money per person to the poorer states and localities than to the wealthier ones.

What it is important to note is that the final determinator of the interpretations of the Constitution which have made possible the expansion of the federal government into policy areas previously exclusively state concerns, is the federal political system itself. If a dispute breaks out between the federal government and a state over whether or not the federal government has the power under the Constitution to take a particular action it is the federal Supreme Court that makes the final decision—the final interpretation of the Constitution. It is the federal Supreme Court that approved broadening the scope of federal power under the interstate commerce clause, and it is the federal Supreme Court that held grants-in-aid to be constitutional.[21]

Federalism and Public Policy Making

As just seen in the previous section, the existence of cooperative federalism means that it is difficult to find policy areas that are the exclusive domain of any one level of government. Typically all three levels of government—federal, state, and local—are directly engaged in making author-

21. See *NLRB v. Jones & Laughlin Corporation* 301 U.S. 1 (1937), *Wickard v. Filburn* 317 U.S. 111 (1942), and *Massachusetts v. Mellon* 262 U.S. 447 (1923).

itative policies for the entire American society, which, as Chapter 1 points out, is the characteristic that units need to possess in order to be considered parts of a political system. Rightly speaking, the federal political system is only one of the many subsystems in the American political order, although it is clearly the dominant one. The focus of attention in this book is, of course, the federal political subsystem and the contributions it makes to the total public policy-making processes. Thus, the state and local subsystem will be viewed as part of the context, or environment, in which the federal subsystem operates.[22]

Some Exploratory Questions

1. To the extent the Constitution has proved to be effective (and the Civil War is one testimony to the fact it has not always proved effective), can its success be better explained by strengths written into the document by the authors or by the wisdom and ability of American society and the men and women throughout history who have made it work?

2. Does the fact that the exact balance between authority and freedom that determines the actual content of civil liberties depends on the political system and its policies rather than on unchanging, rigidly fixed constitutional provisions mean that civil liberties are in constant jeopardy, or does it mean that they are protected from irrelevancy and impracticality?

3. Would the political system achieve less bureaucratization and greater flexibility and responsiveness if it went back toward dual federalism, reserving to the states whole policy areas in which each could develop its own policy and with its own resources?

Bibliographical Essay

For studies on the basic nature of constitutions, see William G. Andrews, *Constitutions and Constitutionalism* (Princeton, N.J.: Van Nostrand, 1961); Edward S. Corwin, *The "Higher Law" Background of American Constitutional Law* (Ithaca, N.Y.: Cornell University Press, 1955); and Herbert T. Spiro, *Government by Constitution* (New York: Random House, 1965).

On the origins of the American Constitution, see the classic by Charles A. Beard, *An Economic Interpretation of the Constitution* (New York: Macmillan, 1913). Then compare Beard's position with those of Robert E. Brown, *Charles Beard and the Constitution* (Princeton, N.J.: Princeton University Press, 1956) and Forrest McDonald, *We the People: The Economic Origins of the Constitution* (Chicago: University of Chicago Press, 1958). Also see Paul Eidelberg, *The Philosophy of the American Constitution* (New York: Free Press, 1968). For helpful works that discuss the changing interpretations given the Constitution, see Edward S. Corwin

22. For clarity's sake, I will use the term *political system* to refer only to the federal subsystem. When I mean to include the state and local units as well, I will explicitly say so.

and Jack W. Peltason, *Understanding the Constitution,* 4th ed. (New York: Holt, Rinehart and Winston, 1967) and C. Herman Pritchett, *The American Constitution,* 2d ed. (New York: McGraw-Hill, 1968).

A number of good books deal generally with the topic of civil liberties. One of the best is Henry J. Abraham, *Freedom and the Court,* 2d ed. (New York: Oxford, 1972). Also see Milton R. Konvitz, *Expanding Liberties* (New York: Viking, 1967) and H. Frank Way, Jr., *Liberty in the Balance,* 2d ed. (New York: McGraw-Hill, 1967).

On American federalism, see Richard Leach, *American Federalism* (New York: W. W. Norton, 1970), Daniel Elazar, *American Federalism: A View from the States,* 2d ed. (New York: Thomas Y. Crowell, 1972), and Morton Grodzins, *The American System* (Chicago: Rand McNally, 1966). More comprehensive is W. Brooke Graves, *American Intergovernmental Relations* (New York: Charles Scribner's Sons, 1964). On state-federal relations on the administrative level, see Arthur W. McMahon, *Administering Federalism in a Democracy* (New York: Oxford University Press, 1972).

Several works offer the reader a comparison of American federalism with other federal systems, including Ivo Duchacek, *Comparative Federalism* (New York: Holt, Rinehart and Winston, 1970), William Riker, *Federalism: Origin, Operation, Significance* (Boston: Little, Brown, 1964), and K. C. Wheare, *Federal Government,* 4th ed. (New York: Oxford University Press, 1964).

Many recent works have been addressed in whole or part to the intergovernmental sharing of responsibilities. On grants-in-aid generally, see Deil Wright, *Federal Grants-in-Aid: Perspectives and Alternatives* (Washington, D.C.: American Enterprise Institute for Public Policy Research, 1968). On the relationships found in specific programs, see, for instance, Roscoe Martin, *The Cities and The Federal System* (New York: Atherton Press, 1965) and James Sundquist, *Making Federalism Work* (Washington, D.C.: Brookings Institution, 1969).

The American People and Politics

The Input Channels

Part Two

Introduction
to Part Two

Among the dreams man has dreamed, few have been as compelling and as lofty as the democratic dream—the dream of human beings governing themselves in a free society. Many societies have had this dream; few have attained it. The many failures of democracy in eastern Europe between the two world wars and in many Asian and African countries since World War II are testimonies to the difficulty of building truly free, democratic societies. The problems are many and the successes few.

Stripped to its bare essentials, democracy means that the general public has a significant degree of influence over the authoritative policies made by the political system. To achieve this influence, the interests given representation in the political system must reflect the demands being made in the population as a whole. For this to be possible, the society must be free—criticism, dissent, and discussion must be fully permitted. Without this freedom, ideas and points of view present in the population could not be expressed—and therefore could not flow into the political system except under the control of the system itself. In such circumstances the political system would become closed, determining for itself which inputs it would allow and which it would exclude. The system would become a law unto itself.

A democratic political system, on the other hand, must operate in a free society where the system cannot determine for itself the demands to which it will react. Only then can the public have a significant influence over the public policies adopted by the system.

This conception of democracy assumes—as was stressed in Chapter 1—that 200 million Americans, or any other large number of people, cannot rule themselves directly. The actual policy decisions of the political system must be made by a select, elite group of persons, drawn from out of the society—not by the society itself. Thus democracy is not defined here in terms of rule by the people, but in terms of an elite that rules—under the significant influence of the general public. To go beyond this and to insist that democracy requires either that the people must rule themselves directly or that the demands present in the population must be reflected perfectly in the political system is to say that democracy requires the unattainable. But if a system is to be considered democratic, there must be at least an approximate correspondence between the demands present in the society at large, the interests represented in the political system, and, ultimately, the policy decisions of the political elite that constitutes the political system.

Part Two focuses on the processes and organizations in the American political system that must play the crucial role if demands present among the general public are to be represented in the political system—and represented in an insistent, compelling manner. Therefore, it focuses on the processes and organizations that must play the crucial role if a democratic political system is to be attained. If they fail, democracy fails.

Chapter 4

Public   Mass Politics
            Opinions
            and Voting
            Behavior

Vox Populi, Vox Dei—"The voice of the people is the voice of God." This motto has given expression to democratic man's almost mystical faith in both the wisdom and the power of the public. But if the voice of the people is the voice of God, in the present-day United States, the traditional God has become a god that speaks with an uncertain voice—often contradicting itself and often barely audible.

Even though we sometimes like to pretend that public opinion is a god, that it is a single entity that makes pronouncements on the issues of the day—"Public opinion turned against President Nixon during 1973"— there really is no such entity. When can we conclude that the god public opinion has spoken? When 51 percent of the people agree on an issue? or 75 percent? or 90 percent? And when 40 percent of the people feels very intensely one way on an issue and the other 60 percent feels the opposite way, but in a lukewarm manner, what has public opinion said? And who are the people? All the citizens? All the eligible voters? All the actual voters? The questions can go on and on, but the point is clear— public opinion as a mystical, godlike entity that speaks with one voice on questions of the day is nonexistent. A more realistic and more precise conception of public opinion is needed.

Some Definitions and Distinctions

Opinions Perhaps we can develop a realistic conception of public opinions by first of all thinking through what an opinion—any opinion—really is. For our purposes *an opinion* can be defined as a self-conscious position one takes on an issue.[1] According to this conception of an opinion, some debatable *issue* or question must be present. We do not have opinions on

1. For a good, brief consideration of what opinions are and how they can be described, see Robert E. Lane and David O. Sears, *Public Opinion* (Englewood Cliffs, N.J.: Prentice-Hall, 1964), chap. 2.

straight-forward, incontestable facts. When someone looks out the window, sees that it is snowing heavily, and says, "It is snowing," he is making a factual statement, not expressing an opinion. If, on the other hand, he says, "It is good that it is snowing, for this means I shall be able to go skiing tomorrow," he is expressing an opinion. Here there is an issue: Is snow at this time desirable? Being a skier, he says it is; others who have to shovel out their driveways may disagree.

An opinion also is a *self-conscious* position, that is, the person who holds it is aware of having that position. This does not necessarily mean that such people have carefully considered all the alternatives and given the issue a great deal of thought; it merely means that they are aware of holding a certain position. Nor does this necessarily mean that they have articulated or communicated the opinion to others. They may have a definite opinion and yet never communicate it to others.

Public Opinions   What makes an opinion a *public* opinion? Political and other social scientists have formulated many different definitions of public opinions, but most of them stress—to a greater or lesser degree—three crucial elements in a *public opinion:* (1) the issue in question must be one of general or widespread importance; (2) the opinion must be expressed; and (3) the persons holding it must be capable of producing some effect, even if only to the extent of being noticed.[2]

The rationale behind the first of these conditions is fairly clear. There may be strong opinions on a university campus about where to hold a homecoming dance, but few would claim that these opinions constitute public opinions because of the narrow scope of the issue in question. Its impact will hardly go beyond the campus, and it is of limited and passing importance even on the campus.

The opinion must also be expressed—orally, in writing, or even by gestures or actions. If an opinion is not expressed it remains merely a private opinion or thought, and the third condition cannot be fulfilled. For an opinion must also have some sort of effect or impact before it can be considered *public.* Its impact may be a matter of the newspapers taking note of it, or persons with opposing opinions speaking out against it, or governmental decision makers worrying about it. In other words, there needs to be some sort of reaction to it. To meet this third condition, the persons holding the opinion must be numerous or influential enough or must feel so intensely that they work hard enough to make themselves noticed. An opinion held by only a few persons is unlikely to have any

2. This conception draws from the definitions of public opinion put forward by Floyd H. Allport, "Toward a Science of Public Opinion," *Public Opinion Quarterly,* 1 (1937), 7–23; Bernard C. Hennessy, *Public Opinion,* 2d ed. (Belmont, Calif.: Wadsworth, 1970) chap. 1; V. O. Key, *Public Opinion and American Democracy* (New York: Knopf, 1951), pp. 216–222.

impact, but as the number, importance, and fervor of the persons holding the opinion go up, the probability that they will have an impact—and their opinion can be classified as public—also goes up.

This chapter explores the nature and effects of opinions that are public in character, that is, opinions that meet the three essential criteria. But first we must distinguish opinions from attitudes—a closely related concept— and briefly indicate the relationship between public opinions and voting behavior.

Attitudes *Attitudes* are general predispositions to act or think in a certain manner.[3] Attitudes can be distinguished from opinions in that attitudes deal with general situations, and opinions are responses to specific situations; attitudes are tendencies or leanings, whereas opinions are definite conclusions; attitudes may be unconsciously held, whereas opinions are self-consciously held. A person has an attitude of suspicion and distrust toward labor unions, but his position that a "right to work" law should be adopted in his state is an opinion; he has an attitude of distrust toward foreign nations and great confidence in the supremacy of the United States, but his position that the United States should stop all foreign aid is an opinion. As is the case in these examples, attitudes often underlie opinions. Thus the study of public opinions is incomplete without a consideration of the attitudes that underlie and influence the more specific opinions.

Public Opinions and Voting What is the relationship between public opinions and voting behavior? In one respect they are quite different. *Voting* is an overt act: it is going to the polls (or alternatively, not going to the polls) and by a physical act casting a ballot for one person or another. Public opinions, on the other hand, are, as we have already seen, a matter of thoughts, views, and positions. But the two are related in that an election is, in effect, a public opinion poll. In voting a person is formally indicating his or her opinion of the candidates. Voting is one of several means of measuring public opinions. Thus public opinions and voting behavior are distinguishable, but closely related, concepts.

Public Opinion Holding and Voting

Most of us like to think of the backbone of American democracy as the free, hard-working, common person, a man or woman not marked by much learning and sophistication, but nonetheless having good common

3. For good, brief discussions of attitudes and how they can be distinguished from opinions, see Allport, "Toward a Science of Public Opinion," pp. 7–23: and Hennessy, *Public Opinion,* pp. 209–210.

sense and a deep interest in the nation and its welfare. The opinions of such persons are based on careful thinking, and they consciously cast their votes for the candidates they have concluded are the most qualified.

But the extent to which this picture of the model citizen actually conforms to reality is a source of constant investigation and debate, especially among political scientists. It is clear that very few Americans fully measure up to the demands made on them by this picture of democratic human beings, but the extent to which most Americans do approach the ideal is not so easily determined. The evidence is mixed, and uncertainty abounds. This section of the chapter sorts out what we do and do not know about the broad nature of opinion holding and voting in the United States.

The Role of Party

It is a basic fact of human behavior that we all are heavily influenced in our attitudes and behavior by certain identifications and loyalties we have developed over the years.[4] Thus, in the area of religion, a person who belongs to and identifies strongly with the Catholic Church is much more likely to be influenced by a statement of the pope or some other Catholic leader than is someone of the Jewish faith. In similar ways we all are influenced by the persons, organizations, groups, and movements with which we identify. Because we can identify with (that is, have a sense of loyalty to and a feeling of belonging to) churches, labor unions, ethnic or racial groups, business associations, sports teams, popular entertainers, and many other things, we are often heavily influenced by them, and we try to bring our attitudes and opinions into line with them.

Political scientists have found that the sense of identification that most persons have with one or the other of the political parties has a heavy influence on how each person votes and how he or she reacts to other partisan-tinged aspects of the political world. Two basic facts stand out: (1) most Americans identify with one or the other of the two major parties; and (2) that identification affects their voting and some of their political attitudes.

Table 4.1 shows that most people can state their party identification when asked to do so and that the party identification is very stable. From 1952 to 1974 there was little change in the proportions of the population identifying with the two parties. Even the subcategories of strong, weak, or "independent" identifiers were remarkably stable. In recent years there has been a small, but discernible trend toward greater independence. The proportion in the independent category has tripled from 1952 to 1974 and

4. See the discussion in Angus Campbell, Philip Converse, Warren Miller, and Donald Stokes, *The American Voter* (New York: Wiley, 1960), chap. 12, and many of the selections in Dorwin Cartwright and Alvin Zander, eds., *Group Dynamics,* 2d ed. (Evanston, Ill.: Row, Peterson, 1960).

Table 4.1   Percentage feeling sense of party identification

	Strong Dem.	Weak Dem.	Ind. Dem.	Ind.	Ind. Rep.	Weak Rep.	Rep. Strong	Other
1952	22%	25%	10%	5%	7%	14%	13%	4%
1954	22	25	9	7	6	14	13	4
1956	21	23	7	9	8	14	15	3
1958	23	24	7	8	4	16	13	5
1960	21	25	8	8	7	13	14	4
1962	23	23	8	8	6	16	12	4
1964	26	25	9	8	6	13	11	2
1966	18	28	9	12	7	15	10	1
1968	20	25	10	11	9	14	10	1
1970	20	23	10	13	8	15	10	1
1972	15	25	11	13	11	13	10	2
1974	18	21	13	16	8	14	8	2

Source: Center for Political Studies, Institute for Social Research, University of Michigan, 1975.

Table 4.2   Percentage voting Democratic for President, by party identification

Party Affiliation	1952	1956	1960	1964	1968[a]	1972
Strong Democrats	84%	85%	91%	95%	84%	73%
Weak Democrats	62	63	72	82	58	49
Independents	34	27	46	66	26	34
Weak Republicans	6	7	13	43	10	9
Strong Republicans	1	1	2	10	3	3

[a] Because of the strong third-party showing of George Wallace in 1968, the Republican vote is not the obverse of the Democratic vote. Wallace received the vote of 8% of the strong Democrats, 15% of the weak Democrats, 17% of the independents, 8% of the weak Republicans, and 2% of the strong Republicans.

Source: Center for Political Studies, Institute for Social Research, University of Michigan, 1969, and Gerald Pomper, *Voters' Choice* (New York: Dodd, Mead, 1975), p. 75.

shows an increase from 8 percent to 16 percent in the ten years between 1964 and 1974. And from 1964 to 1974 the proportion of the public that is either in the category of independent or in the category of independent but leaning toward one of the parties (Independent Democrat or Independent Republican) has increased from 23 to 37 percent.

That party identification affects voting is supported by Table 4.2.: there is a strong tendency for people to vote for the presidential candidates of the party with which they identify. Admittedly there are defections. Note the tendency of many Democrats to cross over and vote for Eisenhower in 1952 and 1956 and of many Republicans to cross over in 1964 and vote for Johnson. In 1968 and especially in 1972 many Democrats crossed over to vote for Nixon. Nevertheless, most persons vote in accordance with party identification. In nonpresidential elections, the tendency to vote according to party identification is, if anything, even stronger than in presidential elections.[5]

Party affiliation, however, is becoming somewhat less important in determining the public's voting choices. Table 4.2 shows more defections from party affiliation since 1964 than in previous elections. These defections reached a high in 1972 when 42 percent of the Democratic identifiers voted Republican.[6] Figure 4.1 gives added support to the contention that party identification is becoming less important to voting behavior: it demonstrates the recent increase in *ticket splitting* (voting for candidates of different parties in the same election). The proportion of congressional districts that voted for one party's presidential candidate and the opposite party's congressional candidate has increased sharply in recent years, reaching a new high in 1972. One study showed that the percentage of persons voting the straight party ticket declined from about 75 percent of the electorate in the 1950s to 50 percent in the late 1960s.[7]

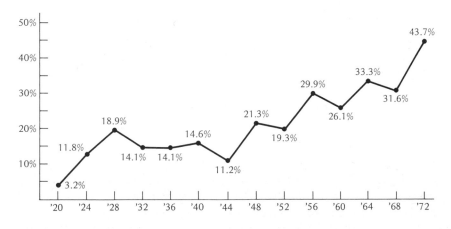

Figure 4.1   Congressional districts with split results, 1920–1972[a]

[a] Congressional districts in which a majority of the electorate voted for the presidential candidate of one party and for the congressional candidate of the other party.

Source: From data found in Walter De Vries and V. Lance Tarrance, *The Ticket-Splitter: A New Force in American Politics* (Grand Rapids, Mich.: Eerdmans, 1972), p. 30. The 1972 election data were added by the author.

5. See Warren E. Miller and Donald E. Stokes, "Constituency Influence in Congress," *American Political Science Review,* 57 (1963), 54.

6. Arthur Miller, Warren Miller, Alden Raine, and Thad Brown, "A Majority Party in Disarray: Policy Polarization in the 1972 Election," paper given at the 1973 annual meeting of the American Political Science Association, p. 5. That the party is becoming less important in structuring voters' reactions to senatorial candidates was found by Warren Lee Kostroski, "Party and Incumbency in Postwar Senate Elections: Trends, Patterns, and Models," *American Political Science Review,* 67 (1973), 1213–1234.

7. See Walter D. Burnham, *Critical Elections and the Mainsprings of American Politics* (New York: Norton, 1970), p. 120.

The trends toward less identification with one of the two major parties, more defections from party identification when voting, and more ticket splitting indicate that political parties play a weaker role in structuring the voter's view of the political world and in guiding the casting of his vote. Nevertheless, party identification still has a significant role. Most people still vote in keeping with their sense of party identification most of the time.

The relationship between party identification and attitudes and opinions is mixed. Table 4.3, for example, shows the views of Democratic and Republican identifiers in four different policy areas. Only in the area of social welfare—where differences between parties are long-standing—are there significant differences between the identifiers with the two parties. That party identification does have an effect on evaluations of presidential performance is revealed by Figure 4.2. The Democratic Johnson was judged much more favorably by Democrats than by Republicans, and the Republicans Nixon and Ford were judged much more favorably by Republicans than by Democrats.

Although the exact nature and extent of the impact that party identification has on voting behavior and on political attitudes vary, depending on the situation and the times, yet party identification continues to have a wide-ranging, pervasive impact. Any analysis of political attitudes and voting behavior must begin with the fact of party identification and its subsequent influence on attitudes and voting.

Absence of an Integrating Ideology

Political scientists, newspaper reporters, and others often refer to a person as a liberal or a conservative, as an internationalist or an isolationist, as a libertarian or a nonlibertarian. Terms like these assume that a person holds a series of interrelated opinions and attitudes that put him in a certain category. A person holds such a series of opinions and attitudes because he has a basic ideology or social philosophy that integrates them into a consistent pattern. Having adopted a certain basic ideology, he then uses it to interpret and respond to specific, day-to-day situations and questions. He views the political world through the framework of that ideology. Thus a person may consider himself a conservative: he believes a large, centralized government poses dangers of overbureaucratization and wasteful management. Therefore his more specific opinions might include: the government ought not to establish a comprehensive program to pay citizens' medical expenses, the government should not set wage and price controls, revenue sharing strengthens the state governments and thus is a good idea, and only small modifications are needed in the present welfare system. His specific opinions form a logical and consistent whole because they all are derived from his basic conservative ideology.

However, research by political scientists has shown that although this

Table 4.3   Party identification and opinions on issues, 1968

Issues	Democrats	Independents	Republicans	Difference Between Dems. and Reps.
Social welfare				
Medical help (% in favor)	76%	55%	41%	35
Job & living guarantee (% in favor)	46	27	25	21
Gov't. too powerful (% saying yes)	42	60	72	30
Racial equality				
Job equality (% for)	52	38	35	17
School integration (% for)	51	38	35	16
Blacks pushing too fast (% agreeing)	58	72	69	11
Foreign policy				
Foreign aid (% for)	48	42	45	3
Isolationism (% for staying home)	25	19	25	0
Vietnam (% saying U.S. involvement a mistake)	62	59	66	4
Law and Order				
Urban riots (% for use of force)	25	34	31	6
Demonstrations (% against)	53	52	56	3

Source: Richard E. Dawson, *Public Opinion and Contemporary Disarray* (New York: Harper & Row, 1973), pp. 162–163.

structured type of thinking is done by a minority of the population, the majority of Americans react to issues on an issue-by-issue basis—not in terms of some over-all ideology.[8]

Simply asking people what they like or dislike about the two parties and the presidential candidate of each should reveal whether or not they are thinking in ideological terms. If they are, they can be expected to speak of liberalism, conservatism, a middle-of-the-road philosophy, and so forth.

8. See Robert Axelrod, "The Structure of Public Opinion on Policy Issues," *Public Opinion Quarterly,* 21 (1967), 51–60; Campbell et al., *The American Voter,* chapter 9; and Philip E. Converse, "The Nature of Belief Systems," in David E. Apter, *Ideology and Discontent* (New York: The Free Press, 1964), pp. 206–261.

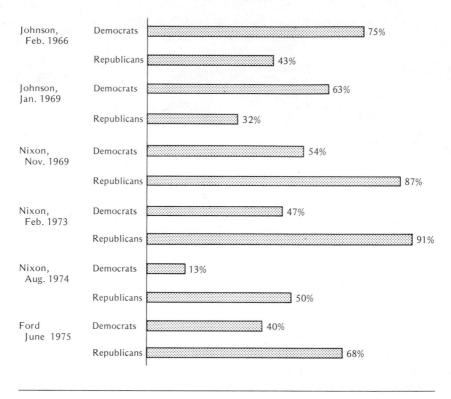

Figure 4.2   Presidential approval, by party[a]

[a] That is, the percentage of Democratic and Republican identifiers who answered yes to the question "Do you approve of the way President _____ is handling his job?"

Source: Constructed from data found in *Gallup Opinion Index* (appropriate 1966–1975 issues).

One person would like the Democrats because they are more liberal than the Republicans and would dislike President Ford because he is too conservative. Or, alternatively, he would like Ford because he is more middle-of-the-road, not so "radical," and would look askance at the "radicalism and welfarism" of Edward Kennedy. However, it has been shown that at most only about one third of the public uses ideological terms or ideas like these in describing their feelings toward the parties and their candidates.[9] Most speak of a candidate as a good man or as experienced; and they may say one party favors the common man or the other party favors big business too much.

9. See John C. Pierce, "Party Identification and the Changing Role of Ideology in American Politics," *Midwest Journal of Political Science,* 14 (1970), 25–42, and John O. Field and Ronald E. Anderson, "Ideology and the Public's Conceptualization of the 1964 Election," *Public Opinion Quarterly,* 33 (1969), 380–398.

After an intensive study of a small group of working-class men, Robert Lane concluded there was a strong tendency for the men to "morselize"; that is, they saw the political world in segmented, discrete parts instead of grouping specific political events in a broader context of ideas and events.

This treatment of an instance in isolation happens time and again and on matters close to home: a union demand is a single incident, not part of a more general labor-management conflict; a purchase on the installment plan is a specific debt, not part of a budgetary pattern—either one's own or society's. The items and fragments of life remain itemized and fragmented—at least at the conscious level.[10]

This tendency to "morselize," to see the political world in segmented pieces rather than in the framework of some integrating ideology, does not necessarily mean that the public is hopelessly confused or unable to view and react to the political world in a rational manner. "Scholars and political observers who have grown accustomed to analyzing politics in terms of the liberal-conservative continuum or other theoretical constructs, should not assume the public to be ignorant or confused because they do not conceptualize politics in these abstract terms."[11]

The level of knowledge and the awareness with which most persons evaluate the political world and make their voting decisions is considered in the next section.

Knowledge and Awareness of Issues

How knowledgeable is the American electorate? Does the average American citizen form opinions and vote in a rational, knowledgeable manner? Or does he or she vote and form opinions guided by unthinking prejudices and without knowledge or forethought? There is still much uncertainty in this area, but several conclusions are clear.

On the negative side is recurring evidence that Americans have great difficulty in remembering the names of the officials who represent them in Congress. A recent study showed that only 59 percent of the public could name one of their two United States Senators and only 39 percent could name the second Senator.[12] Less than half—46 percent—could name their United States Representative. Even more difficulty was encountered when persons were asked to name the party to which their Senators and Representatives belong—a piece of information that could well be considered minimal. Only 53 percent knew the correct party of one Sena-

10. Robert E. Lane, *Political Ideology* (New York: The Free Press, 1962), p. 353.

11. David E. RePass, "Levels of Rationality Among the American Electorate," paper given at the 1974 annual meeting of the American Political Science Association, p. 51.

12. These and the following figures are from United States Senate, Committee on Government Operations, *Confidence and Concern: Citizens View American Government* (Washington, D.C.: GPO, 1973), pp. 245–249.

tor, 36 percent knew the correct party of both Senators, and 41 percent knew the correct party of their Representative.

The levels of citizen information are even lower when, during research studies, persons are asked to identify the specific policy positions of Congressmen and candidates for Congress—presumably a minimum of information about their political representatives and essential for intelligent voting. In a recent survey only 21 percent of a cross section of the population knew how their congressman had voted on *any* bill that year.[13] In 1958, almost half the voters in 116 congressional districts reported that they voted without having heard or read *anything* about either of the candidates in their district. In addition:

Just how low a hurdle our respondents had to clear in saying they had read or heard something about a candidate is indicated by detailed qualitative analysis of the information constituents *were* able to associate with congressional candidates. Except in rare cases, what the voters "knew" was confined to diffuse evaluative judgments about the candidate: "he's a good man," "he understands the problems," and so forth. Of detailed information about policy stands not more than a chemical trace was found. Among the comments about the candidates given in response to an extended series of free-answer questions, . . . only about three comments in every hundred had to do with legislative issues of *any* description.[14]

On the other hand, there is mounting evidence that the American people are not so ignorant or so irrational in their voting and public opinions as the above figures seem to suggest.[15] First, there is abundant evidence —at least on the presidential level—that a voter's beliefs on issues are highly related to the way that person votes. Table 4.4 shows the positions taken on seven key issues in 1972 by all McGovern and all Nixon voters and by Democrats voting for McGovern and Nixon. Two basic facts stand out: McGovern and Nixon voters differed sharply in terms of their positions on issues, and their differences tended to coincide with those between McGovern and Nixon. On Vietnam, for example, McGovern voters were much more in favor of withdrawal than were the Nixon voters, matching the actual policy differences between McGovern and Nixon. Also of great significance is the fact that the Democrats who voted for McGovern and the Democrats who went against their normal party preference to vote for the Republican Nixon differed sharply on all seven issues. The conclusion that the Democrats who defected to the Republican candidate in 1972 were doing so because of their concerns about issues seems inescapable.

13. *Gallup Opinion Index* (October 1970), p. 12.

14. Miller and Stokes, "Constituency Influence in Congress," p. 54.

15. See RePass, "Levels of Rationality"; Miller et al., "A Majority Party in Disarray"; Gerald M. Pomper, "From Confusion to Clarity: Issues and American Voters, 1956–1968," *American Political Science Review,* 66 (1972), 415–428; and the able discussion in Robert S. Erikson and Norman R. Luttbeg, *American Public Opinion* (New York: Wiley, 1973), pp. 223–249.

Table 4.4   Policy positions of Nixon and McGovern voters, 1972

Policies	All McGovern voters	All Nixon voters	Democrats voting for McGovern	Democrats voting for Nixon
Favoring Vietnam withdrawal	69%	29%	69%	30%
Favoring amnesty	54	15	49	18
Favoring reduced marijuana penalties	37	17	30	10
Favoring conciliation for campus unrest	43	11	40	12
Favoring government aid to minorities	52	25	50	25
Favoring busing for desegregation	22	3	23	2
Favoring government guaranteeing standard of living	50	18	53	21

Source: Arthur Miller, Warren Miller, Alden Raine, and Thad Brown, "A Majority Party in Disarray: Policy Polarization in the 1972 Election," paper delivered at the 1973 annual meeting of the American Political Science Association, p. 10.

Tables 4.5 and 4.6, based on data at the senatorial level, throw additional light on the question of issue voting. Table 4.5 shows that those favoring federal governmental involvement in school desegregation efforts tended to vote Democratic to a stronger degree than did those opposed to federal governmental involvement. But, more significantly, Table 4.6 shows that when the voters' understanding of the positions that the parties took on this issue is taken in account, the relationship between the voters' position and their vote increased sharply. Of those voters who favored desegregation and who also thought the Democratic party favored desegregation, 87 percent voted for the Democratic candidate for United States Senator; of those voters who opposed desegregation and thought the Democratic party opposed desegregation, 91 percent voted for the Democratic candidate. Voters appeared to be trying to vote their policy views, but they differed about what position the parties were taking (these differences in perception being, perhaps, accurate reflections of the real world, because within each party there were differences on this issue from one section of the nation to another).

One of the most careful studies of voter rationality and nonrationality was made by political scientist David RePass using the 1964 presidential election. He carefully analyzed the comments of a national cross section of voters on a series of questions concerning their understanding of the issues in the 1964 campaign and what they liked and disliked about the candidates. He ranked each respondent, depending on the sophistication of his or her evaluations of the candidates and on awareness of issues and

Table 4.5   Attitudes toward school desegregation and vote for Senator, 1970

Voted for	Favor	Oppose
Democratic Candidate	65%	54%
Republican Candidate	35	46
Total	100%	100%
N	255	196

Source: H. T. Reynolds, *Politics and the Common Man* (Homewood, Ill.: Dorsey, 1974), p. 185. Based on data gathered by the Center for Political Studies, University of Michigan.

Table 4.6   Attitudes towards school desegregation, perceptions of party differences, and vote for Senator, 1970

	Voters favoring desegregation			Voters opposing desegregation		
	Voters believe					
Voted for	Democrats are in favor	No difference	Republicans are in favor	Democrats are opposed	No difference	Republicans are opposed
Dem. Candidate	87%	50%	36%	91%	57%	19%
Rep. Candidate	13	50	64	10	43	81
Total	100%	100%	100%	100%	100%	100%
N	107	118	22	21	122	37

Source: H. T. Reynolds, *Politics and the Common Man* (Homewood, Ill.: Dorsey, 1974), p. 185. Based on data gathered by the Center for Political Studies, University of Michigan.

ability accurately to link issue stances with candidates, in one of several "levels of rationality." He found 25 percent of the voters were basically nonrational.[16] Those repondents knew little or nothing about either the candidates or the issues and what information they did have was confused or inaccurate. But 37 percent of all his respondents were high in rationality, displaying the sort of knowledge and accuracy needed to cast an informed, rational vote. RePass describes them as "those who have a fairly sound awareness and comprehension of the elements of politics. They are voters who base their decisions on fairly full and accurate cognitions rather than on misinformation, oversimplification, affect, emotion, or a blind support of party."[17] The remaining 38 percent of the voters showed varying mixtures of rationality and irrationality, informed views and ignorance.

All in all RePass's findings present a fairly favorable view of the rationality of the American electorate. Almost 40 percent of the electorate fell into the fully rational category. Only one fourth clearly had no basis for rational voting. One must remember that RePass's study was on the presidential level, however, where voter awareness and information are highest. No doubt voter rationality is less on the congressional, state, and local levels.

16. This and the following figures are from RePass, "Levels of Rationality," p. 42.
17. RePass, "Levels of Rationality," p. 3.

What is the composite picture of the American public that emerges from all this? It is a public with clear party affiliations, but affiliations that, although still significant in their effects on voting and some opinions, are becoming less of a force in determining those votes and opinions. It is a public without a great deal of sophistication, especially when it comes to thinking in theoretical or ideological terms. Much of the political world revolves around a public barely aware of it. Yet particularly at the level of presidential elections and other major, long-lasting political events and issues, a significant proportion of that public attains a fairly high level of awareness and rationality. The picture that emerges falls far short of 210 million fully rational, well-informed, deeply involved Americans; but it also is far removed from 210 million irrational, totally ignorant, completely uninvolved Americans.

The Classification of Elections

The fact that most people identify with one of the two major parties and tend to vote in keeping with this sense of identification has given rise to a system of classifying elections. At the heart of this classification scheme is the concept of the normal vote, that is, the vote that would result if everyone voted in a given election in keeping with his or her feeling of party affiliation. No election is ever marked by a normal vote in the absolute sense; there are always certain short-term factors, such as current issues and the personal appeal of the rival candidates, which cause shifts away from the normal vote and toward one party or the other. Table 4.1 shows clearly that in 1974 a majority of the people identified with the Democratic party, and thus on the national level a normal vote would mean a Democratic victory. The only way the Republicans can win is by attracting many independent and Democratic voters to their candidate— a feat the Republicans have performed in four of the six presidential elections since 1952.

On the basis of the concept of the normal vote, elections can be classified into one of four types.[18] The first is a *maintaining election.* In it the majority party (in terms of party affiliation) remains in power because there is not enough deviation from the normal vote for the minority party to win. The election of 1964 was of this type. Second, there is *a deviating election.* Here the minority party is able to get enough votes from the majority party's adherents to win the election, but the basic party affiliation of the vast majority remains undisturbed. The elections of 1952, 1956, 1968, and 1972 are examples. Third, is *a reinstating election.* Here the majority

18. See Campbell et al., *The American Voter,* pp. 531–538 and Philip Converse, Angus Campbell, Warren Miller, and Donald Stokes, "Stability and Change in 1960: A Reinstating Election," *American Political Science Review,* 55 (1961), 279–280.

party—having been out of power because of an earlier deviating election —is returned to power because enough of its identifiers who had defected to vote for the minority party in the prior deviating election return to the fold and give it victory. The election of 1960 is an example. Finally, there is *a realigning election.* In this type, enough people not only vote for the minority party but also switch their basic allegiance to it, so that it becomes the new majority party. The 1932 and 1936 elections were realigning elections. As a result of the Great Depression and Roosevelt's New Deal, many Republicans not only switched over and voted for Roosevelt but also changed their basic party identifications from Republican to Democratic.

There is some evidence that at the present time the United States may be entering a period of realigning party affiliations.[19] The fact that some of the most salient issues in the mid 1970s—defense spending, law and order, race relations, and political protest—divide Americans but not along current party lines may be a precursor to a basic shift in party loyalties.[20] And the trends (noted earlier) toward the increase of independents and the weakly affiliated together with the decrease in the number of those voting in keeping with their party affiliations may be an indication of an emerging party realignment.

The Democrat's 1972 nomination of George McGovern for President may have had the effect of encouraging a realignment, with some of the more conservative elements of the Democratic party (conservative in terms of foreign policy, race, and law-and-order issues) moving toward the Republican party, and some of the more liberal elements of the Republican party moving toward the Democratic party. McGovern was perceived by many as taking clear-cut stands on foreign policy, race, and law and order that were appealing to many liberal Republicans and unattractive to many conservative Democrats. (The refusal of George Meany, president of the AFL-CIO, to endorse McGovern is an indication of the hostility aroused by the McGovern candidacy in some of the more traditional segments of the Democratic party.)

But it may be that the Watergate scandal of the Nixon administration killed whatever chances there were for a move away from the Democrats to the Republicans. In the aftermath of Watergate, Republican party fortunes, in terms of the proportion of the population identifying with the party, hit a new low.[21] At the present time it appears likely that the

19. This is one of the conclusions reached by a careful study of the 1968 election and its personalities. See Herbert F. Weisberg and Jerrold G. Rusk, "Dimensions of Candidate Evaluation," *American Political Science Review,* 64 (December 1970), 1167–1185. On this point, also see Burnham, *Critical Elections,* especially chap. 6.

20. For evidence of this, see Richard E. Dawson, *Public Opinion and Contemporary Disarray* (New York: Harper & Row, 1973), especially chap. 7.

21. The October 1974 Gallup Poll showed 23 percent of the population identifying with the Republican party, down from a percentage of 27 early in 1973 when the Watergate scandal first started breaking open. See *Gallup Opinion Index* (June 1975) p. 22.

Democratic party will maintain its sizeable majority within the population. But (as noted earlier) it also appears likely that those who identify with either party will continue to hold that identification more loosely, often voting for candidates of the opposite party. Thus the Democratic-majority position and the Republican-minority position mean less in terms of likely election results than they would if the voters' party loyalties were stronger.

Public Opinions and Voting as Input Channels

Public opinions and voting have long been considered the vital means by which the general public is able to control the decision-making elite—and thereby able to control the public policy-making process. Here one expects to find the heart of the democratic process. The public speaks—by marching to the polls or by indicating its opinions in a variety of other ways —and the decision makers listen or, at their peril, fail to listen.

It was long assumed that for public opinions and voting to so operate most persons would have to be deeply interested and concerned about political events and issues. They would therefore pay attention to the political world, study candidates and issues, and formulate informed, coherent opinions. The citizens would then be ready to express their opinions —to make their demands—by voting, by writing letters, or by engaging in other forms of political activity. They would thus force the decision-making elite to listen and to enact their policy preferences.

But we have seen how spottily the electorate meets the requirements that this conception of the democratic process demands. On the presidential level, about half the electorate may come close, but of course there is the other half, not meeting the requirements. And below the presidential level, it is clear the vast majority of the electorate does not meet the demands of this conception of democracy.

The crucial question is simply this: How can a public such as this ever control the governmental decision-making elite—and, through them, public policies? The legislator's vote on Bill X is supposedly influenced by the people back home because the active, alert citizenry will desert him at the polls if he does not vote in keeping with their demands. But how can this be when 95 to 99 percent of the people in his constituency do not have the vaguest idea how he votes on the bill? In fact, half probably do not even know who he is! Much of what even the President does passes by most of the public without notice.

There is another element to the question. Most decision makers act as though public opinions and elections make a difference. Even members of Congress—who, because of distance, would presumably have the least to worry about in terms of voter reaction to their deeds—seem to act as though they are in constant danger of the public's turning on them for the slightest mistake. One study found that 85 percent of 116 congressmen interviewed believed their personal record and stances were either very important or quite important in determining their re-election.[22] Former Senator J. William Fulbright of Arkansas, an intelligent, tolerant, and liberal-minded man by almost every standard, voted against virtually every major piece of civil rights legislation that came before the Senate—legislation that would merely help guarantee basic liberties to all Americans. He did so out of fear of the reaction of the Arkansas voters if he should take a pro-civil-rights position. In sum, the conditions presumed necessary for effective public opinions are not present; yet public opinions appear to be effective.

The explanation of this paradox lies in the wrongness of the assumptions about the means by which public opinions and voting are made effective. Clearly a revision of the role played by opinions and elections as channels for inputs—and especially demands—into the political system is needed, a revision that takes into account the true nature of opinion holding and voting. The following discussion assigns public opinions a more modest—and a more realistic—role, but at the same time it shows how and why public opinions have an effect on the decision-making elite. The effect is less than absolute control over their detailed decisions—it is closer to an influence over the broad trends of their decisions, but still it is present and must be reckoned with.

The Rule of Anticipated Reactions

Once upon a time a man, disturbed over a rash of burglaries in his neighborhood, bought the most vicious looking watchdog he could find. After that, he slept soundly, trusting his expensive watchdog to guard him and his possessions. Then one night the thieves struck. They were so expert and so stealthy that the supposed watchdog never even woke up! The thieves carefully tiptoed about the house, taking some cash from a drawer, seizing some valuable jewelry, and even removing a prized painting from the living-room wall. They then stepped carefully over the sleeping watchdog and slipped out the side door.

In the morning, the man and his dog awoke to discover the disaster. When the man had recovered from his initial shock, his wrath turned on the erstwhile watchdog and the man who had sold it to him. He stormed over to the seller and demanded his money back. "This mutt is totally worthless as a watchdog; he didn't even wake up while I was being stolen blind," he raved on and on.

"Oh, but you are mistaken, my good friend," replied the seller. "This noble animal has more than repaid the modest price I asked for him. If it

22. See Donald E. Stokes and Warren E. Miller, "Party Government and the Saliency of Congress," *Public Opinion Quarterly,* 26 (1962), 542.

hadn't been for this sleeping beast, the thieves no doubt would not have stopped with taking your money, jewelry, and painting, but would have also taken your larger, even more valuable possessions. It was no doubt fear of awaking this vicious looking beast that prevented them from removing your stereo, color television set, and automatic washing machine and dryer. Instead of berating me and this loyal dog, you owe both of us your deepest gratitude."

This fable illustrates the rule of anticipated reactions.[23] The thieves, anticipating the reactions of the sleeping watchdog should he wake up, restricted their activities so as to assure that the dog would not wake up. In that sense the dog, sound asleep, was able to influence the actions of the thieves. This influence of the watchdog rested on his potential—his ability to bark and possibly to attack if awakened. In this sense, he acted as a potential force and was thereby able to modify the actions of the thieves.

The public and its opinions can be viewed in a similar light. To some degree they are sleeping. Much—even most—of the political world passes by without arousing the public's notice. Issues of momentous importance —antiballistic missile systems, arms-reduction negotiations, health plans, and more—are debated in Congress and in the mass media without the public's paying much attention, with most persons not even knowing the names of the participants in the struggles and surely not linking up particular officeholders with particular stances on the issues.

Yet there are conditions under which the public can become very much aware of what their elected representatives are doing, and that awareness can lead to a sharp loss in votes for these officials. The *rule of anticipated reactions* says that the public officials, realizing that certain actions can lead to a loss of votes, will act so as to prevent such a situation from ever arising—they will act so as not to awaken the sleeping watchdog. An examination of the two conditions under which the public is most likely to react negatively to elected officials will help clarify the operation of the rule of anticipated reactions.

Perceived Failures   One set of conditions that can cause even an uninterested and apathetic public to take notice is an event or a series of events that results in severe disadvantages or distress for a large portion of the population. War, inflation, depression, recession, overseas reverses, domestic unrest, and riots are all events that, if serious enough, may result

23. The term *rule of anticipated reactions* was first coined by Carl J. Friedrich. For a careful explanation of it, see Carl J. Friedrich, *Man and His Government* (New York: McGraw-Hill, 1963), chap. 11. In addition to Friedrich, the following discussion is largely based on Campbell et al., *The American Voter*, pp. 552–558; V. O. Key, *The Responsible Electorate* (Cambridge, Mass.: Harvard University Press, 1966), pp. 63–79; Key, *Public Opinion and American Democracy*, pp. 552–553; and Miller and Stokes, "Constituency Influence in Congress," p. 55.

in public awareness and negative reactions against the party or presidential administration in power. As long as all is well, as long as no catastrophe hits the nation, public opinions remain fairly quiet and most persons will vote in keeping with their basic party affiliation. Great gains may even be made without much public notice. But when disaster strikes—when a recession sets in, when riots break out in major cities, or when the nation becomes bogged down in a drawn-out war—the incumbent political leaders suddenly face negative opinions: their ratings in the Gallup poll start to slip, their political opponents' prestige goes up, and electoral defeat is in the wind.

As long as public affairs go well, there is little to motivate the electorate to connect events of the wider environment with the actors of politics, and the successes of an administration are likely to go virtually unnoticed by the mass public. But when events of the wider environment arouse strong public concern the electorate is motivated to connect them with the actors of politics, typically, with the incumbent party. An economic or military or other form of calamity can force events across the threshold of political awareness, to the detriment of the administration party.[24]

Examples of this pattern are easy to find: The Roosevelt victory in 1932, following the depression of the Hoover administration; the Eisenhower victory in 1952, following the Korean conflict and other problems of the Truman administration; and the 1968 Nixon victory in the face of a frustrating and seemingly interminable war in Southeast Asia, growing unrest and frequent demonstrations at home in reaction to the war, and serious riots in many urban black ghettoes. Most recently, the sharp gains scored by the Democrats in the 1974 midterm elections can be viewed as a result of voter reaction to the Watergate scandal of the Republican Nixon administration.

The point is simple: Although public awareness is normally very low, when the leaders in power get into major difficulties (either because of their own muddling or because of events they cannot control) public awareness increases, negative reactions toward the leaders set in, and the chances of major deviations from the normal vote increase.

The significance of all this lies in the fact that the perceptive decision maker—following the rule of anticipated reactions—realizes this merciless reaction of the public to catastrophes and does everything in his power to avoid them. He tries to head off trouble before it arrives. The President, as the most visible of the decision makers, is likely to receive the heaviest impact of the condemnation when things go wrong. However, most of his party colleagues in Congress will suffer loss of votes along with their leader and thus also have a vested interest in preventing disastrous events. This factor hardly indicates that public opinions and elections result in *control* by the general public over governmental officials, but it does indicate that

24. Campbell et al., *The American Voter*, p. 556.

they have *indirect and limited influence* over them despite the public's general lack of awareness and information.

Violations of Strongly Held Opinions   On a more specific level, the public will react negatively if an elected official violates certain strongly held opinions of the voters, particularly if there is an emotional quality to the opinions. If an elected official advocates some highly unpopular cause such as unilateral disarmament, discontinuance of the social security program, or legalization of marijuana, the public in his home district may suddenly become very much aware of him—the watchdog is awakened —and voters can be expected to desert him in droves at the next election. Thus, public opinions set the broad limits within which governmental discussion and activity can take place. Any straying by an official outside these limits causes public awareness and resulting sanctions (a deviation from the normal vote in the next election in favor of his opponent). In 1972 George McGovern apparently lost votes by favoring amnesty for Vietnam draft evaders and busing for purposes of integrating schools—both of which were unpopular stances on highly emotional issues.

One may feel that this does not place a very severe limitation on governmental officials, but actually in certain policy areas, in certain constituencies, and at certain times the limits can be fairly narrow. To attack labor unions in a district with many union members, to support the Arabs against Israel in a strong Jewish district, to advocate federal protection of civil rights of blacks in a Mississippi Delta district, or to advocate integrated housing or busing to achieve racially integrated schools in an all-white working-class suburb—all violate strongly held, emotionally incited opinions. All are likely to stir up a previously apathetic electorate, and all are likely to result in sanctions being taken against the advocates of the policies. And they are just a sample.

The conclusion here, as it was in the case of reactions to perceived failures, is that the public official will anticipate the negative reactions of the public and will attempt to avoid taking stands that are highly unpopular among his constituents. In the process, the voters, even while they remain apathetic and uninformed, are nonetheless influencing the actions of the public officials.

The Role of Opinion Leaders

To this point it has been assumed that the relationship between the decision-making elite and the general public is direct, without intervening persons or institutions. But this is not always the case. In Chapters 5 and 6 we shall consider two organized institutions—the political party and the interest group—that serve as formal intermediaries between the public and the decision maker, both influencing and being influenced by the public and its opinions, and both in turn influencing the decision makers. In addition, there are certain individuals, called opinion leaders, who also play the role of intermediary between the general public and the decision makers.[25]

An *opinion leader* is any person who pays close attention to political affairs—even more so than the interested minority—*and* attempts to influence others to adopt his or her opinions. Such a person approximates the active, rational citizen discussed earlier: he is deeply interested in political affairs, he follows political events and election campaigns closely in the papers and on TV, he has strong opinions that are backed by information, and he has some underlying philosophy or ideology integrating his observations. He may be the man up the street who follows politics as avidly as others follow football. He holds no official position in a political or interest group and he has never held a public office, but he does button-hole his friends and tries to persuade them to his point of view. Or the opinion leader may be a person occupying an official position in some interest group or a political party. She may be a country chairwomen of one of the parties or president of one of the union locals. He may be an editor of a local newspaper—or of *The New York Times.* But in all cases these persons have two characteristics in common: they are interested and knowledgeable in political affairs, and they try to influence the opinions of others.

Recent research has indicated that these opinion leaders play an important role making public opinions a significant influence on decision makers. The opinion leaders are aware of what the decision makers are doing. They know their Senators and Representatives and how they vote on various issues, they know the components of the President's foreign policy toward Africa (and what alternatives he has rejected), and they know the implications of the latest Supreme Court decision. They also pass this information on to the general public in a simplified, generalized form. They pass on to their friends—or group members or readers—very general ideas and evaluations, not the detailed policy stands of decision makers or other specifics of the political world.

Thus the pollster calls at the home of the typical citizen and asks him his opinion of Senator X, who is up for re-election. Our citizen speaks vaguely of the Senator as a good man with much experience, using good judgment, and so forth, but when pressed he is unable to say anything

25. The discussion here is largely based on Key, *Public Opinion and American Democracy,* chap. 21; Elihu Katz and Paul F. Lazarsfeld, *Personal Influence* (New York: The Free Press, 1955); John W. Kingdon, "Opinion Leaders in the Electorate," *Public Opinion Quarterly* 34 (1970), 256–261; Paul F. Lazarsfeld, Bernard R. Berelson, and Hazel Gaudet, *The People's Choice* (New York: Duell, Sloan & Pearce–Meredith Press, 1944), p. 151; and Miller and Stokes "Constituency Influence in Congress," p. 55.

about the Senator's specific policy stands. The pollster leaves, wondering how democracy manages to survive in the face of such ignorance. But one of this person's co-workers follows political affairs closely, has frequently spoken of the good work Senator X is doing representing the workingman, and has urged this typical citizen to vote for him. Thus the citizen, in having a favorable opinion of the Senator, is reflecting the opinions of his informed co-worker. What has happened here is that the record of Senator X has been communicated, in a simplified and generalized form, to the ordinary citizen by a two-step process. The interested person (the opinion leader) followed the activities of the Senator closely, decided that he was acting to the advantage of the workingman, and communicated this fact to his fellow workers. If the Senator had switched his votes on several key issues and had voted against bills favorable to the working class, the opinion leader would have communicated a far different message, and the ordinary citizen would have given a different response to the pollster.

The decision makers are being watched by the opinion leaders, and the opinion leaders in turn influence the general public. Thus by an indirect, two-step process the actions and decisions of the governmental officials have a very real impact on the public and its opinions. Thus the deviations from the normal vote that appear are in part the result of these opinion leaders. This in turn causes the public official to weigh the likely repercussions of various courses of action on public opinions (via the opinion leaders) before making his decisions. In short, public opinions are having an indirect and limited influence, but an influence nonetheless.

The Interested Minority

Although the electorate as a whole falls short of the fully rational, deeply interested citizenry that the traditional view of the democratic process demands, there exists a minority of voters—and a very sizeable minority on the presidential level—who possess a fair amount of knowledge and interest. These are the voters who have a general knowledge of the candidates and their stances on one or more issues and whose votes are affected by their views of the candidates and issues.

This group of interested, rational voters is large enough, especially on the presidential level, but also on lower levels, to be a force to be reckoned with. Candidates for lower-level offices—and even presidential candidates —can assume that the majority of voters will not pay attention to their actions and stances, but they know that there are always some who do. In the previous section we saw that this minority can be important when its members act as opinion leaders. But it can also be a significant force because of its own numbers, particularly because of the situation described in the next section.

Uncertainty and Margins

Underlying all three of the previously discussed elements that make public opinions an effective influence on elected officials are two facts of the political life of all elected officials: uncertainty and margins. The elected official is, first of all, never certain exactly what results a contemplated action of his will have on the electorate. He can never be certain whether a contemplated vote will arouse the electorate back home, or whether a contemplated action will adversely affect the interested minority's or the opinion leaders' assessment of him. Often it is only by hindsight that he can conclude whether or not a particular action was damaging in terms of votes lost. In the face of this *uncertainty* the very natural tendency of elected officials is to err on the side of safety—to play it safe by taking the stance they perceive is most in keeping with public opinions.

Compounding this tendency is the fact that elected officials are dealers in margins. For most officeholders to lose the next election, it is not necessary to alienate 30 or 40 or 50 percent of the voters—only 5 to 10 percent will do. Even a shift in a small number of voters can be disastrous. That 4 or 5 percent of votes that marks the *margin* of victory is all important. With it he is a public officeholder with influence and recognition; without it he is just another private citizen.

If one combines the uncertainty inherent in many of the choices elected officials must make with the often small margin of votes on which their political lives depend, one can better understand why the rule of anticipated reactions, the interested minority, and the opinion leaders are such important constraining influences on elected officeholders. The basic point is not that public opinions constitute an all-pervasive, all-controlling force that determines every move of elected officials. Rather, the point is that public opinions constitute a highly significant force that must be taken into account by elected officials, a force that frequently has an influence on the decisions they make.

Public Opinions and Voting: Formation and Change

That there is an extreme diversity of opinions in the United States is obvious: some people are Democrats, others Republicans; some favor one presidential candidate, others the opposition candidate; some favor an increased role for the federal government in meeting the problems of large cities, others fear the "encroaching power of the federal octopus." Why is one person thoroughly convinced that Democrats are misguided and selfish and Republicans perceptive and public-minded, while his next-door neighbor is equally convinced that it is the Republicans who are misguided and selfish and that it is the Democrats who are perceptive and public-minded? This section of the chapter explores the question of why persons hold to the opinions that they do.

Family, School, and Peers

It is clear that when a person enters the adult political world of voting and opinions, he does not do so with his mind a blank tablet ready to start receiving political observations and impressions. He does not decide that he is now going to start observing the political world and then proceed to form his basic attitudes and more specific opinions without bias or prejudice. Instead, he approaches the political world with a fairly well-developed set of basic attitudes and opinions—and it is from this base that he views the political world. These attitudes and opinions evolve naturally out of a person's life experiences, from infancy to childhood to adolescence to young adulthood. Among the life experiences that play a dominant role in shaping political attitudes and opinions three are of particular importance: *family, school,* and *peers.*

Family

By fourth grade more than six out of ten of the New Haven children were able to state whether their party preference was Republican or Democratic. . . . The prevalence of party identifications among nine-year-olds is especially striking when we realize that the proportion of adult Americans who identify with parties (75 percent) is not much greater. . . .

The source of these performances is, as often has been noted in the voting literature, the family. Only a handful of children in the entire sample indicated that their own party preferences differed from those of their parents. In interviews children explicitly speak of party as an attribute of the family. (Judith says, "All I know is we're not Republicans.")[26]

This is the conclusion that Fred I. Greenstein reached on the basis of a study of grade-school children in New Haven, Connecticut. If children have already adopted party preferences by the fourth grade, they clearly are forming partisan attachments and attitudes before they are in a position to observe and evaluate the relevant political information.

These partisan attitudes learned as children are not merely passing fashions that are left behind as a person enters adult life. One study found that about 70 percent of all adult voters have the same party affiliation as their parents did (in cases in which both parents identified with the same party).[27] The great stability of party affiliation revealed by Table 4.1 helps confirm the fact that party affiliations learned as a child are not often abandoned after a person enters adult life.

Although the family clearly plays the dominant role in determining a person's party affiliation, it is less clear how pervasive its influence is in

26. Fred I. Greenstein, *Children and Politics* (New Haven: Yale University Press, 1965), pp. 71–73. Another study has found that when the parents of high school seniors agreed in their party affiliation 76 percent of the students agreed with them. See Kenneth P. Langton, *Political Socialization* (New York: Oxford University Press, 1969), p. 59.

27. Campbell et al., *The American Voter,* p. 147.

determining other types of attitudes and opinions. On the one hand, the importance of the family is supported by a study that found that children who see their fathers as being dominant possessed more political interest and were better informed than children who saw their mother as being dominant.[28] Another study found parents had a significant impact on their children's attitudes *if* the parents thought the issue was important and the children correctly perceived their parents' position.[29]

On the other hand, a recent study of the opinions of high school seniors and their parents showed very weak correlations in many areas between the opinions of the students and those of their parents. The amount of agreement was found, however, to be somewhat higher on issues of relative immediacy and importance to the parents and the students, for example, school integration and prayers in school. The authors conclude: "In spite of what appear to be powerful forces pushing in the direction of homogeneity, parent-student pairs resemble each other moderately only when issues are especially prominent."[30]

Thus the evidence indicates that what an individual receives from one's family background is not a set of detailed opinions and attitudes covering the whole political-social spectrum, but certain very basic identifications (such as party affiliation) and more specific opinions on issues that are especially immediate and concrete or are highly partisan.

To the extent that children reflect family attitudes and opinions it should not be thought that they do so because they are consciously taught them by their families. Rather, children gradually adopt the norms and attitudes that surround them, in much the same way that they adopt words and expressions used by their families.

School   A second factor playing a major role in the life experience of a growing child is school. From age five to seventeen most people spend a major portion of their waking hours at school. Adding to the likelihood that experiences in school will have a major effect on the development of political attitudes and opinions is the significant emphasis given to political and politically related topics in American classrooms. Politically relevant symbols such as the flag and pictures of present and past Presidents are

28. Robert D. Hess and Judith Torney, *The Development of Political Attitudes in Children* (Chicago: Aldine, 1967), pp. 101 and 217. However, in general this study found that the influence of the family on the shaping of political opinions and attitudes is limited; see pp. 95–101. For another study that found that whether the father or the mother is dominant affects the development of political attitudes of the children, see Langton, *Political Socialization,* pp. 42–49.

29. Kent L. Tedin, "The Influence of Parents on the Political Attitudes of Adolescents," *American Political Science Review,* 68 (1974), 1579–1592.

30. M. Kent Jennings and Richard G. Niemi, *The Political Character of Adolescence: The Influence of Families and Schools* (Princeton, N.J.: Princeton University Press, 1974), p. 79.

found in almost all classrooms, and patriotic rituals such as the pledge of allegiance to the flag are part of the daily ritual in most classrooms. Teachers of grades two through eight have reported they give large amounts of time to discussions of political leaders.[31] Over two thirds of American high school students take at least one governmental or civics course.[32]

Although it is easy to document the emphasis given political education in the formal curriculum of the schools, it is very difficult to determine the amount of influence this emphasis actually has upon the development of children's political attitudes and opinions. The available evidence suggests that what influence the schools do have is exercised on the elementary, rather than high school level. One study found that it made almost no difference in political interest, knowledge, or attitudes whether a high school senior had had one, two, or no civics courses.[33] High school teachers have been shown to have little impact on the political views of their students.[34]

In summary, the degree of influence the schools exert upon children's political attitudes and opinions remains in doubt. The heavy emphasis on political rituals and citizen education in the elementary grades favors, however, the presumption that the child's school experiences do in fact play a significant role in shaping political views and orientations—especially in the lower grades. Most of these views and orientations probably deal with basic attitudes toward the political system on which society is generally agreed, rather than specific opinions on subjects of controversy. Schools tend to avoid the more controversial areas and to emphasize things such as one's obligations as a citizen.[35]

Peers   In addition to experience in the family and at school, a large part of a child's life experiences revolves around friends and associates he or she meets in the neighborhood and through school, church, and other associations. Especially among younger adolescents, peer group standards possess a powerful influence on persons' standards and behavior, according to the findings of developmental psychologists.[36] Thus peer group standards may play a significant role in molding political attitudes and opinions.

31. Hess and Torney, *The Development of Political Attitudes in Children,* pp. 108–109.
32. Langton, *Political Socialization,* p. 91.
33. Langton, *Political Socialization,* pp. 97–100. On the lack of an impact by the high school curriculum on students' political views and orientations, also see Jennings and Niemi, *The Political Character of Adolescence,* chap. 7.
34. See M. Kent Jennings, Lee H. Ehman, and Richard G. Niemi, "Social Studies Teachers and the Pupils," in Jennings and Niemi, *The Political Character of Adolescence,* pp. 207–227.
35. See Hess and Torney, *The Development of Political Attitudes in Children,* pp. 110–111, 218.
36. See, for example, Erik H. Erickson, *Identity: Youth and Crisis* (New York: Norton, 1968).

The authors of probably the most careful study in this area conclude: "In sum, the friendship group plays a consequential role in the development of youthful political orientations."[37]   Table 4.7 shows that when parents and friends are in agreement, the students are very likely to adopt the same view; but when parents and friends disagree, students sometimes go along with their parents and sometimes with their friends. Both family and peers have a distinct, measurable influence.

In summary, young adults enter the world of political opinions and activities, not with minds open and ready to start observing and reaching conclusions, but with an already determined set of basic identifications and opinions with which they view the political world. The source of these identifications and opinions lies in the formative years of childhood and adolescence. No doubt an intertwining maze of innumerable life experi-

Table 4.7   Agreement between high school students and their friends and parents

	Party identification	1964 Presidential vote	Political trust	Political efficacy	18-year-old vote
Overall agreement with					
Friends	52%	78%	62%	72%	66%
Parents	72	83	66	57	55
	(240)	(230)	(237)	(239)	(238)
Agreement when friends and parents agree	76	93	72	77	69
	(151)	(164)	(178)	(126)	(142)
When friends and parents disagree, agreement with					
Friends	12[a]	42	46	65	62
Parents	64	58	54	35	38
	(89)	(66)	(109)	(113)	(96)

[a] This pair of figures will, unlike the others in these two rows, equal less than 100 percent. This is because party identification was not treated as a dichotomous variable, whereas the others were.

Source: Suzanne Koprince Sebert, M. Kent Jennings, and Richard G. Niemi, "The Political Texture of Peer Groups," from M. Kent Jennings and Richard G. Niemi, *The Political Character of Adolescence* (Princeton: Princeton University Press, 1974), p. 246.

37. Suzanne Koprince Sebert, M. Kent Jennings, and Richard G. Niemi, "The Political Texture of Peer Groups," in Jennings and Niemi, *The Political Character of Adolescence*, p. 247. Further support for this conclusion can be found in Hess and Torney, *The Development of Political Attitudes in Children*, pp. 120–125, and Langdon, *Political Socialization*, pp. 120–139.

ences determines each person's particular constellation of attitudes and opinions. Probably the single most important type of life experience centers in the family, with schools and peers playing crucial subsidiary roles. Additional research needs to be done before we can speak with greater certainty.

People's basic identifications and opinions—even though they have a continuing influence throughout their lives—do not, however, remain static. They change and develop as people move into adulthood and undergo changing circumstances and influences. It is to the factors that change and mold the identifications and attitudes taken into the adult political world that we now turn.

The Mass Media and Opinion Change

The mass media—television, radio, movies, and the printed word—are constantly bombarding the public in an attempt to influence public opinions. The newspaper editor with his editorials and sometimes slanted news stories, the TV news commentator with his interpretations of the news, and the political candidate with his campaign literature and TV spot announcements are all using the mass media in an attempt to change public opinions. From the amount of money and effort that is expended on attempting to influence opinions via the mass media, one would conclude that they must indeed be potent weapons of influence. Yet study after study points to the very opposite: the mass media are a relatively ineffective means of changing public opinions.

The Ineffectiveness of the Mass Media   V. O. Key reported a classic case of failure of the mass media to change opinions:

In the summer of 1940 the Cleveland *Plain Dealer,* the paper with the largest circulation in Erie County, Ohio, splashed on the front page an announcement in support of Willkie; it followed up during the campaign with daily front-page editorials. In September, 59 percent of a sample of Erie County did not know which candidate the *Plain Dealer* was supporting. Only about one in seven of those persons with a Democratic predisposition—those who would have to be converted if the paper was to have influence—knew the paper's editorial position.[38]

In 1958 Republican William F. Knowland was fighting for his political life against Democrat Edmund Brown for the governorship of California. In a dramatic, last-minute move to capture votes he conducted a statewide, marathon television program lasting 20 hours in which he answered questions phoned in by the audience. Knowland headquarters enthusiasti-

38. Key, *Public Opinion and American Democracy,* pp. 352–353. On the normal ineffectiveness of the mass media in changing opinions, also see Joseph T. Klapper, *The Effects of Mass Communications* (New York: The Free Press, 1960).

cally reported that some 7,000 calls poured in. The then Vice President, Richard Nixon, added to the optimism of the Knowland camp, when, in a telegram read on the air, he was quoted "as saying that he had 'glowing reports' of the telethon, and was confident that it would 'make thousands of new friends not only for your election as Governor but for the entire Republican slate in California."[39]

But a far different picture was painted by a survey conducted by the Stanford Institute of Communications Research immediately after the telethon. Of 563 persons who were interviewed, only 65, or 11.5 percent, reported watching any part of the program. The results in terms of changed votes were practically nil: "Two of the 65 viewers said it helped them make up their minds: one to vote for, one against Knowland. One Republican said it changed his mind; from having tentatively decided to vote for Brown, he returned to the party fold and decided to vote for Knowland."[40]

A study of the impact of television network newscasts on the voters during the 1972 presidential election concluded that the newscasts had a minimal impact.[41] The authors found very little relationship between exposure to new stories and changes in voter opinions.

In short, prodigious efforts in using the mass media to change public opinions normally result in microscopic changes in the opinions of the general public. There are some exceptions, however, as will be noted later.

Personal Influence and Opinion Change

In contrast to the normal lack of influence by the mass media on the general public, many studies have demonstrated the importance of personal influence in changing opinions. *Personal influence* is influence arising from the face-to-face, informal contacts that one has with other persons on a day-to-day basis. Spouse, relatives, friends, roommates, and co-workers are all examples of possible sources of personal influence, and all have been demonstrated to be potent sources of opinion influence.[42]

One of the surest ways to ensure that the party identification a person has received from his or her family will undergo change is marriage to someone from the opposition party. A study conducted in the Minneapo-

39. Wilbur Schramm and Richard F. Carter, "Effectiveness of a Political Telethon," *Public Opinion Quarterly,* 23 (1959), 121–127.

40. Schramm and Carter, "Effectiveness of a Political Telethon," p. 125.

41. Robert D. McClure and Thomas E. Patterson, "Television News and Voter Behavior in the 1972 Presidential Election," paper given at the 1973 annual meeting of the American Political Science Association.

42. The literature is large, but especially see Lazarsfeld, *Personal Influence;* Lazarsfeld et al., *The People's Choice;* and Bernard Berelson, Paul Lazarsfeld, and William McPhee, *Voting* (Chicago: University of Chicago Press, 1954); and Herbert McClosky and Harold E. Dahlgren, "Primary Group Influence on Party Loyalty," *American Political Science Review,* 53 (1959), 757–776.

lis-St. Paul area found the following: "When both the spouse and parents favor the same party, the chances are overwhelming (93 percent) that a voter will also favor that party; when, however, their political outlooks are diverse, the probability that a voter will remain loyal to his parents' party falls to only 28 percent.[43]

Table 4.8 shows that the relationship between the candidate preference of friends and co-workers and the actual vote of the persons interviewed is extremely strong. These relationships are probably not entirely the result of the influence of the friends or co-workers on the persons interviewed, because to a considerable degree persons of similar backgrounds and therefore of similar political views form friendships and are put together in work situations. Yet the presumption is strong that personal influence has its effect.

The Mass Media and Personal Influence

The basic reason why personal influence is so much more effective in changing opinions than are the mass media rests on the fact that the

Table 4.8   Relationships between group memberships and voting, 1968

(a)

Respondent voted for	Number of respondent's friends who voted for Humphrey				
	All	Most	Some	A few	None
Humphrey	92%	87%	42%	21%	7%
Nixon or					
Wallace	8	13	58	79	93
Total	100%	100%	100%	100%	100%
N	(279)	(1,080)	(1,685)	(1,120)	(477)

(b)

Respondent voted for	Number of respondent's coworkers who voted for Humphrey				
	All	Most	Some	A few	None
Humphrey	85%	76%	43%	23%	17%
Nixon or					
Wallace	15	24	57	77	83
Total	100%	100%	100%	100%	100%
N	(78)	(423)	(747)	(374)	(194)

Source: H. T. Reynolds, *Politics and the Common Man* (Homewood, Ill.: Dorsey, 1974), p. 154.

43. McClosky and Dahlgren, "Primary Group Influence on Party Loyalty," p. 770.

defense mechanisms by which we all resist opinion change can operate much more effectively with the mass media than with friends, co-workers, spouses, and others with whom we are in personal contact. Most overt attempts—such as campaign brochures and television commercials—via the mass media to change our opinions are written off by the public as highly untrustworthy because they are obviously self-interested. During election campaigns, most persons consider even straight news stories highly suspect. Their defense mechanisms are up.

In contrast, personal influence can operate over a long period of time in many subtle, unconscious ways. The social pressure of a group and our ever-present desire for approval act as constant gentle persuaders to conform to those with whom we are in frequent, direct contact.

But this does not mean the mass media can never be effective in changing attitudes and beliefs. The mass media can be highly influential when their influence can operate over a long period of time and when they have an objective rather than a propagandistic aura. Most of us are immediately suspicious of an obvious piece of propaganda but tend to let our guard down when we are reading or watching purportedly objective reporting. Thus long-term exposure to a particular point of view when that point of view is presented in the form of a newscast or some other kind of objective reporting can have an influence that more limited and more clearly propagandistic appeals do not have.

In addition, the mass media are no doubt more effective in shaping the opinions of the opinion leaders mentioned earlier. Thus the mass media may have an indirect impact, with the media affecting the opinions of the leaders and the opinion leaders in turn affecting the opinions of the general population.

Finally, one should note that in an election campaign just a small change in public opinions can have highly important results. An election campaign, which spends millions of dolars to influence opinions by means of the mass media, may change only 5 to 10 percent of the voters—thereby indicating that all the efforts and dollars never changed the vast majority of the population—yet that 5 to 10 percent shift can make the difference between election and defeat, thereby justifying all the effort and expenditure.

Patterns of Public Opinions and Voting Behavior

To this point we have considered the general nature of opinion holding and voting, the ways in which they serve as channels for inputs into the political system, and the formaton of opinions. We have not yet considered what persons hold what opinions and vote in what ways. This question is interesting because of our natural curiosity, and it is significant because of its importance to understanding of the inputs that different groups within the population channel into the government.

Voting Turnout

That many Americans do not exercise their right to vote at the polls is a well-known fact. Registration procedures and residency requirements often serve effectively to disenfranchise a sizeable portion of the total potential electorate. But even when these factors are taken into account, we find that certain groups of persons have significantly higher rates of nonvoting than do other groups.

In other words, some groups use voting as an input channel to a lesser degree than do some other groups. Table 4.9 shows the rate of nonvoting of various groups within the population.[44] Men tend to vote more often than women, the middle-aged more than the young and the old, Catholics and Jews more than Protestants, whites more than blacks, the highly educated more than those with little education, those in skilled occupations more than those in unskilled occupations, those with high incomes more than those with low incomes, and non-Southerners more than Southerners.

However, these findings do not necessarily mean that the characteristic shared by the persons in these categories is *causing* their voting or nonvoting.[45] Protestantism does not necessarily cause nonvoting, nor does low income necessarily cause nonvoting. Third factors or several factors working together may cause the nonvoting. The high rate of nonvoting among blacks, for example, is caused in part by the legacy of legal and procedural maneuvers that were used in many areas of the South to disfranchise the black. And blacks are also disproportionately represented in the unskilled and lower-income groups, groups also marked by low voter turnout. Protestantism is especially strong in the South—a high nonvoting area—and this may in part explain the high nonvoting ratio among Protestants.

Voting Choice

The vote in any given election and the shift in votes from one election to the next are far from uniform among the various demographic groups. As Table 4.10 shows, some persons tend to vote Democratic (Catholics, Jews, blacks, the young, and working-class members); others vote Republican (Protestants, the college educated, and professionals and businessmen).

44. It should be kept in mind that these figures are all for presidential elections, where interest and turnout tend to be the highest. Comparable nonvoting figures for nonpresidential elections would be considerably higher.
45. This is the case not only with regard to nonvoting, but also with regard to the other patterns to be discussed.

Table 4.9   Demographic groups and nonvoting, 1948–1972

	1948[a]	1952	1956	1960	1964	1968	1972
			Percentage of persons not voting				
Sex							
Male	31	20	20	16	19	22	24
Female	41	31	32	25	24	26	30
Age							
Up to 35	45	32	37	28	32	33	34
35–44	34	25	25	21	16	21	21
45–54	25	21	22	13	18	15	19
55–64	33	19	19	20	17	22	24
65 and over	41	27	24	21	22	28	31
Religion							
Protestant	42	29	30	23	24	25	30
Catholic	21	15	19	13	16	21	21
Jewish	20	8	5	15	5	6	9
Race							
White	34	22	24	19	21	24	26
Black	63	67	65	47	35	36	35
Education							
Grade school	45	38	40	33	32	40	42
High school	33	20	26	19	22	22	30
College	21	11	10	10	11	16	13
Income							
Lower	54	47	45	36	36	40	40
Lower-middle	39	27	28	22	24	27	36
Upper-middle	26	16	21	18	18	17	27
Upper	21	9	14	11	12	12	13
Occupation of family head							
Professional and managerial	25	12	17	12	14	15	16
Other white-collar	18	19	21	18	15	14	24
Skilled and semiskilled	29	26	28	24	26	30	33
Unskilled	51	40	47	31	32	34	41
Farm operators	58	33	27	18	19	24	14
Region							
Northeast		16	17	10	13	21	22
Midwest		15	21	14	19	19	23
South		51	45	32	33	33	37
West		23	23	29	20	24	23

[a] Because of the small number of persons on which the 1948 figures are based, they may not be completely accurate.

Source: Center for Political Studies, Institute for Social Research, University of Michigan.

These patterns can be explained largely on the basis of certain voting predispositions being communicated from one generation to the next and on the basis of the different personal contacts a person has, depending on membership in different demographic groups.

Table 4.10 shows that even when a party's over-all vote does not fluctuate very much from one election to the other, its vote within certain groups may fluctuate greatly. From 1956 to 1960 the total Democratic vote went up 8 percentile points, but the Democratic vote among Roman

Table 4.10   Demographic groups and voting choice, 1948–1972

	Percentage voting Democratic						
	1948[a]	1952	1956	1960	1964	1968[b]	1972
Sex							
Male	53	42	43	51	64	36 (15)	30
Female	49	40	37	46	68	42 (8)	37
Age							
Up to 35	57	45	41	52	71	40 (14)	43
35–44	57	45	41	50	67	44 (9)	32
45–54	44	42	39	54	68	36 (12)	31
55–64	40	34	32	43	68	37 (11)	26
65 and over	46	36	43	37	53	40 (8)	29
Religion							
Protestant	43	36	35	36	61	32 (13)	30
Catholic	62	51	45	82	79	54 (7)	37
Jewish	100	71	77	89	89	85 (3)	66
Race							
White	50	40	39	47	63	35 (12)	30
Black	50	79	63	66	98	94 (0)	84
Education							
Grade school	63	48	41	54	78	48 (15)	38
High school	51	43	43	52	68	40 (13)	32
College	22	26	31	35	53	33 (7)	36
Income							
Lower	61	42	45	47	72	44 (13)	41
Lower-middle	62	46	42	46	69	38 (13)	38
Upper-middle	46	42	40	53	71	41 (9)	34
Upper	36	26	35	46	55	36 (10)	30
Occupation of family head							
Professional and managerial	19	31	31	44	57	34 (9)	31
Other white-collar	47	35	39	48	63	38 (11)	32
Skilled and semiskilled	72	51	44	57	76	43 (14)	35
Unskilled	67	67	47	59	80	53 (9)	55
Farm operators	59	37	46	33	63	34 (17)	31
Region							
Northeast		41	32	49	73	46 (4)	39
Midwest		39	40	44	65	39 (9)	33
South		51	48	49	64	36 (23)	32
West		38	42	54	64	36 (6)	32

[a] Because of the small number of persons on which the 1948 figures are based, they may not be completely accurate.

[b] The vote for George Wallace is given in parentheses.

Source: Center for Political Studies, Institute for Social Research, University of Michigan.

Catholics went up 27 percentile points. This change was probably caused by the return of many Catholics to their normal Democratic party identification because the popular Eisenhower was no longer on the Republican ticket, and because the Democrats had nominated for the presidency a Catholic who was being attacked because of his religion.

The ratification of the Twenty-sixth Amendment to the Constitution in 1971, which lowered the voting age to 18, substantially increased the size of the total electorate and increased the importance of the youth vote in national elections. Table 4.10 shows, however, that age is not as closely related to voting choice as are several other demographic groups such as religion, race, and education. Thus, the newly enfranchised eighteen- to twenty-year-olds do not constitute a separate, distinguishable voting bloc, but vote in keeping with the religious, regional, and socioeconomic groups of which they are members.

We saw earlier in the chapter that persons normally vote in keeping with their basic sense of party affiliation (see Table 4.2). In fact, a person's party affiliation is a better predictor of how he or she will vote than any of the demographic groups listed in Table 4.10.

Opinions

Opinions on political issues also vary among the demographic groups. Table 4.11 demonstrates the differences of opinion in three policy areas —social welfare, foreign affairs, and civil rights. The sharpest differences

Table 4.11   Demographic groups and opinions, 1968

	Favoring gov't help in paying medical bills	Favoring foreign aid	Favoring school integration
Occupations:			
Professional	50%	58%	46%
Business	57	51	42
Clerical and sales	50	48	40
Skilled workers	58	40	32
Nonskilled workers	76	42	59
Farmers	44	33	23
Region:			
Northeast	66	49	50
Midwest	54	46	42
South	65	47	35
West	63	40	50
Race:			
Whites	58	44	37
Blacks	94	62	90
Age:			
Under 30	57	48	49
30 to 49	59	50	46
50 and over	67	40	37

Source: Compiled from data found in Richard E. Dawson, *Public Opinion and Contemporary Disarray* (New York: Harper & Row, 1973), pp. 91, 94, 97, 112, 118, and 126. Data originally from Center for Political Studies, Institute for Social Research, University of Michigan.

are found between blacks and whites, with blacks tending to take more liberal stances in all three policy areas. The regional differences are not as sharp and clear as most people would probably expect.

Among the occupational groups, farmers were the most conservative in all three policy areas. The higher-status occupations—professional and business—tended to be more conservative than the other groups on the social welfare item and more liberal on the foreign policy and civil rights items. (Much less liberal on school integration are the nonskilled workers, if blacks, who tend to be concentrated in this group, are removed.) Young people, as compared to the older groups, are more liberal on civil rights and foreign policy matters and more conservative on social welfare. Thus to speak simply of a liberal or a conservative is an oversimplification; many persons are "liberal" in some areas and "conservative" in others.

With this we come to an end of our consideration of public opinions and voting behavior. We have seen the general nature of public opinions and voting and how and why they can have a significant effect on the decision makers. We have also looked at the complicated, and sometimes surprising, process by which opinions are formed and changed—especially noting the importance of the family and personal contacts. Finally, we have looked at certain general patterns of opinion holding and voting in the United States, noting how various demographic groups differ in their opinions and voting.

Some Exploratory Questions

1. What would be the effect on the responsiveness of elected officials if the electorate were better informed and more attentive?

2. If the current trends toward less party affiliation and less party voting continue, are the results in the long run likely to be beneficial or harmful for the political system?

3. The strong impact of families on their children's political attitudes is a conservative force, because it tends to perpetuate existing attitudes from one generation to the next. Would the weakening of family influence and the strengthening of other influence sources be desirable in that this would make it easier to change outdated, undesirable attitudes? Or would it be undesirable in that this would make it easier for popular attitudes to be manipulated by malevolent individuals and groups?

Bibliographical Essay

Two textbooks that survey the current state of research in the field of public opinion and voting behavior and give very good overviews of the field are Robert S. Erikson and Norman R. Luttbeg, *American Public Opinion* (New York: Wiley, 1973) and

Bernard C. Hennessy, *Public Opinion,* 2d ed. (Belmont, Calif.: Wadsworth, 1970). For an excellent collection of readings covering the entire field of public opinion and voting, see Dan D. Nimmo and Charles M. Bonjean, eds., *Political Attitudes and Public Opinion* (New York: McKay, 1972). Also broad in its scope, but giving special emphasis to opinions and attitudes conducive to stable democracy is V. O. Key, *Public Opinion and American Democracy* (New York: Knopf, 1961). Seymour M. Lipset, in *Political Man* (Garden City, N.Y.: Doubleday, 1960), develops many theories concerning the relationship between attitudes, political behavior, and political institutions. Lester W. Milbrath, *Political Participation* (Chicago: Rand McNally, 1965) explores the nature and extent of political involvement in the United States. Also concerned with political involvement, but concentrating more on the results of political involvement for the political system is Sidney Verba and Norman H. Nie, *Participation in America* (New York: Harper & Row, 1972).

A number of books deal more specifically with the topic of voting behavior. The basic work in this field is Angus Campbell, Philip E. Converse, Warren E. Miller, and Donald E. Stokes, *The American Voter* (New York: Wiley, 1960). This book is also available in an abridged, paper-back edition (New York: Wiley, 1964). For an able, comprehensive study of recent trends in voting behavior, see Gerald Pomper, *Voters' Choice* (New York: Dodd, Mead, 1975). Two earlier, pioneering books on voting behavior are still very helpful: Paul F. Lazarsfeld, Bernard R. Berelson, and Hazel Gaudet, *The People's Choice* (New York: Duell, Sloan & Pearce, 1944), and Bernard R. Berelson, Paul F. Lazarsfeld, and William N. McPhee, *Voting* (Chicago: University of Chicago Press, 1954). V. O. Key, *The Responsible Electorate* (Cambridge, Mass.: Harvard University Press, 1966), argues that the voter is more rational in casting his vote than some researchers have found him to be. Walter D. Burnham, *Critical Elections and the Mainsprings of American Politics* (New York: Norton, 1970), considers the nature of realigning elections and whether the United States is presently in a realigning era.

An interesting, helpful book that gives insight into how people form political attitudes and react to the political world is Karl Lamb, *As Orange Goes* (New York: Norton, 1974), which intensively studies twelve families in Orange County, California. Helpful in giving insight into the different opinion groupings present in American society are Richard E. Dawson, *Public Opinion and Contemporary Disarray* (New York: Harper & Row, 1973), and Richard Hamilton, *Class and Politics in the United States* (New York: Wiley, 1972).

Many books concentrate on the learning and changing of opinions. On the early learning process, see Dean Jaros, *Socialization to Politics* (New York: Praeger, 1973); Robert Hess and Judith Torney, *The Development of Political Attitudes in Children* (Chicago: Aldine, 1967); and Kenneth P. Langton, *Political Socialization* (New York: Oxford University Press, 1969). The most thorough study of the political attitudes of high school students is reported in M. Kent Jennings and Richard G. Niemi, *The Political Character of Adolescence: The Influence of Families and Schools* (Princeton, N.J.: Princeton University Press, 1974). Elihu Katz and Paul F. Lazarsfeld's *Personal Influence* (New York: Free Press, 1955) is helpful in understanding opinion change, although it is not concerned specifically with political opinions. Helpful in analyzing the role played by the mass media in opinion change is Joseph T. Klapper, *The Effects of Mass Communication* (New York: Free Press, 1960). An excellent source of essays on opinions and voting is the journal *Public Opinion Quarterly,* which has been published quarterly since 1937. Also of interest are the *Gallup Opinion Index,* a monthly report of opinions on a variety of current issues, and *The Harris Survey Yearbook of Public Opinion,* a yearly volume published since 1970, which summarizes current public opinions on a whole variety of issues.

Chapter 5

Political Parties   Organized Politics

The Constitution never mentions political parties, and George Washington, in his famous farewell address, warned of "the baneful effects of the spirit of party." In spite of this inauspicious beginning, political parties have flourished; in fact, they have been a crucial part of the American political system throughout almost all its history. But today political parties are under an attack as sustained as there has ever been. Many observers—to the dismay of few—are writing about the disintegration of the parties and foreseeing their early demise.[1] From the streets of Chicago during the 1968 Democratic national convention to the 1972 re-election campaign of Richard Nixon, which was almost wholly independent of the Republican party organization, the parties are under attack and, perhaps more seriously, are being ignored as irrelevant.

To understand these criticisms, to evaluate the predictions of an early demise, and to judge the effectiveness of the parties in today's political system, we need to know the role of the parties in the policy-making processes and the forces that are pressing in on them.

Political Parties: Nature and Functions

Political Parties as Organizations

If any fact concerning the two major American political parties is clear it is that they are not tightly knit organizations, with centralized power flowing from the top down. This much is revealed by the simple observation that several Southern Democratic congressmen have refused to support their party's presidential nominee in every presidential election since 1960, or by the simple fact that such widely different individuals as Senators Strom Thurmond of South Carolina and Jacob Javits of New York coexist in the Republican party.

1. See, for example, the book by David Broder, *The Party's Over* (New York: Harper & Row, 1972).

Some observers have suggested that in reality each of the major parties is a loose coalition of fifty state party organizations that come together every four years to nominate and elect a President. But even this position is open to challenge on the grounds that it presupposes that each of the state parties is an organization, whereas in fact "most state party organizations are merely federations—and loose confederations at that—of semi-autonomous or autonomous local political baronies and baronial county chairmen."[2]

It is not true, of course, that *no* organizations are found within the parties. They are. County committees, campaign committees, Democratic or Republican clubs, and the Senate and House campaign committees are all examples. In fact, both parties consist, to a large extent, of many organizations. Thus the subtitle of this chapter: "Organized Politics." The key point is that these organizations are autonomous and semi-autonomous, often competing or conflicting with each other, instead of being organizations united into one or several over-all organizations.

Having said this much, we might be tempted to conclude that Republican and Democratic are mere titles referring to two categories of persons, much as the terms Protestant, farmer, or college graduate refer to categories of persons and not organized groups. Are the party labels no more than that—labels referring to categories of individuals and nothing more?

Clearly not. The major American parties meet the requirements of a system set down in Chapter 1: *differentiation* and *integration*. The differentiated units of the party subsystem take many different forms: individuals, small groups and cliques of individuals, more formal organizations, and on the highest level the major parties. At first, the conflict and division that mark the parties would appear to preclude integration. But conflict and clash do not necessarily prevent the joint accomplishment of certain functions. The determinative factor is whether the parties jointly perform certain functions in such a way that to remove one of the units would affect the other units. The next section discusses a number of such functions.

Activities and Functions of the Party Subsystem

Party Activities   The contesting of elections in the hope of placing party members in political office is the key *activity* of American political parties, as a majority of political scientists agree.[3] This activity actually involves two distinct activities: nominating candidates and working for their election. Thus parties are distinguished from interest groups (to be discussed in the following chapter) in that interest groups are not primarily involved

2. Frank J. Sorauf, *Party Politics in America,* 2d ed. (Boston: Little, Brown, 1972), p. 81.
3. See Sorauf, *Party Politics in America,* pp. 12–14, and Austin Ranney and Willmore Kendall, *Democracy and the American Party System* (New York: Harcourt, Brace, Jovanovich, 1956), pp. 84–87.

in nominating candidates or in attempting to ensure their election. A third important activity of parties is helping to organize the institutions of the political system, such as Congress and the bureaucracies. Because of their extreme decentralization (which is discussed soon), American parties engage in this activity unevenly and sporadically. But they are involved in it to some extent. All three party activities are discussed at length later in the chapter.

Interest Representation   The functions performed by the parties emerge out of these three activities. The key one is the first of the conversion functions—*interest representation*, that is, channeling demands and supports into the political system, thereby determining the policy alternatives to be considered and the conditions under which policy decisions are made. Each of the three activities of the parties contributes to the performance of this function. First, in nominating candidates, parties are in effect representing interests. Different candidates reflect different interests, or at least different priorities among interests. Thus when the Democrats nominated George McGovern instead of Hubert Humphrey in 1972, they were selecting not only one person over another person, but one complex of interests rather than a somewhat different complex. And every party organization does the same whenever it nominates a candidate—whether it is a national convention nominating a presidential candidate or a group of local party leaders selecting someone to run for the state legislature. When a party nominates a slate of candidates—as, for example, the presidential and vice-presidential candidates on the national level—it can broaden the interests represented by nominating a "balanced ticket," composed of two candidates, each of whom represents somewhat different interests.

Parties also engage in interest representation through conducting election campaigns. Typically a candidate for public office and his or her party are confronted by a public with many concerns—a host of difuse and semi-articulated demands—out of which they then select those to emphasize in the campaign. In so doing they are helping to determine which policy alternatives will be drawn into the political system. The candidate and party that are able to stimulate public support for their policy alternatives—or are able to guess successfully which policy alternatives the public will respond to—are helping to insure that those alternatives will indeed have to be reckoned with by the policy makers.

Finally, parties also represent interests by their activity of organizing the government. When officeholders, acting in their roles as party members, organize the government and work together for certain programs, they are representing interests. This is less clearly a case of the parties' engaging in interest representation, however, than are the nominating and campaigning activities. This is true because of the frequent lack of cooperation among officeholders of the same party and because of the difficulty of disentangling officeholders acting as party members from officeholders acting in their other roles.

Even in a dictatorial political system, the function of interest representation is performed, but there is no guarantee that the interests represented incorporate the demands present among the general population. Instead, the demands may very well be those of the military elite, a few wealthy landowners, or some other small segment of the population. If a system is to be considered democratic, the demands that are channeled into the political system must be those of the general public—not certain subsections of it. Not that every demand present in the society will be given representation in a democracy. This would be impossible. Yet if a system is to be considered democratic, demands made by significant segments of the public must be represented in the policy alternatives from which the political system's decision-making elite makes the authoritative policies. If this representation is to be accomplished in the American political system, the political parties presumably have to play a key role by drawing demands within the general public into the political system. Thus one of the crucial questions this chapter explores is whether or not the American parties perform the interest representation function in such a way that the major demands present in American society are reflected in the interests represented by the parties.

System-maintenance Functions   The political parties also significantly aid in performing two of the *maintenance functions* of the political system: *conflict resolution* and *generation of support.* Conflict resolution is an especially important function of the parties, for in interest representation a transformation process is going on. More particular, narrow, and perhaps even somewhat conflicting interests are combined into complexes, or aggregates, of interests. Many different interests are combined into a single program, which individuals—whether voters or party workers—can support or reject. The aggregates or complexes usually take the form of candidates and the issue stands they represent and advocate. And as these aggregates of interests are put together, conflicts are being resolved. Persons having particular interests are not obtaining exactly what they wanted, but many are obtaining something of what they wanted. Often slates of candidates and party platforms are masterpieces of compromise.

The parties—because of the tarnished reputation they and their activities possess in the American political culture[4]—have difficulty generating support and creating legitimacy. In fact, they play only a minor role in creating legitimacy. They are, however, able to play a significant role in generating support in spite of their tarnished reputations because of their strong, explicit support of democracy and the American form of government.

4. This fact was noted in Chapter 2. See pp. 25.

Especially during election campaigns, they draw public attention to the political process, heap praise upon it, and give the voters a sense of participation in it. In addition, giving a wide variety of interests a feeling that their points of view and needs are being represented is helpful in increasing support for the political system.

The next three sections of this chapter explore the basic characteristics that mark the American political parties; the rest of the chapter then considers how the parties, in the light of these characteristics, carry on their activities and functions.

The Two-party System

Probably the most obvious distinction among the party systems of different countries is the number of parties competing for office. The Netherlands has six, Switzerland five, West Germany three, and Britain two. The United States has been marked throughout its history by two major parties. A stable two-party system is so much a part of American political life that Americans tend to take it for granted. But the existence of a two-party system is far from pre-ordained. This section examines the nature, causes, and significance of a two-party system.

Minor Parties

There are, of course, American political parties other than the two major ones.[5] The American Independent, Socialist, and Socialist Labor are all examples. Yet the American party system should be considered a two-party system because only two parties have sufficient strength to compete for political offices with any realistic chance of success. Most minor parties belong to one of two types: the ideological parties, and the protest parties.

The *ideological parties,* such as the Prohibitionist and the Socialist Labor, are committed to rigid, well-worked-out ideologies. They regularly nominate candidates for the presidency and frequently for state offices, but they virtually never elect anyone—and have no realistic hope of doing so. In fact, in functions they resemble interest groups more than political parties. Their chief aim is to propagate their ideas and to influence opinions, not to win elections. Their leaders would rather go on losing elections than alter ideological commitments.

A somewhat different type of minor party is the *protest party,* a party that seizes on some interest or concern that is not being adequately repre-

5. For helpful discussions of the minor parties see Daniel A. Mazmanian, *Third Parties in Presidential Elections* (Washington, D.C.: Brookings Institution, 1974) and V. O. Key, *Politics, Parties, and Pressure Groups,* 5th ed. (New York: Thomas Y. Crowell, 1964), Chapter 10.

sented by either major party. Often it splits off from one of the major parties after its point of view has been rejected by those in control of the major party. Protest parties normally contest only one or two elections (often with a degree of success) and then quickly fade away. The Populist party of the 1890s, the Progressive party of the 1920s, and George Wallace's American Independent party of the late 1960s are all examples. But throughout American history, no protest party has been able to displace one of the major parties. These protest parties, however, sometimes pose a greater problem than the smaller, more permanent ideological parties, for they may occasionally get enough votes in a certain election to affect its results. Thus the major parties sometimes alter their programs in order to forestall or undercut protest parties. After the 1968 election, in which George Wallace obtained 13 percent of the vote, Wallace complained that he should have copyrighted his speeches, because various officials in the Nixon administration were saying the same things he had said throughout the campaign! And, in fact, President Nixon's alleged "Southern Strategy" was to take certain actions that would give a more conservative, southern cast to this administration.

Why a Two-party System

In spite of the simple, obvious fact of a two-party system, political scientists have no fully satisfactory explanation of why additional parties have not arisen in the United States. In view of the wide regional, ethnic, and economic differences present in the United States, we might suppose that a number of parties would arise, each based on a particular grouping of the population. That this is not so was attributed by V. O. Key to three factors.[6] The first is the "persistence of initial form." Key writes: "The circumstances that happened to mold the American party system into a dual form at its inception must bear a degree of responsibility for its present existence."[7] He notes that the debate over the new Constitution divided the country into two camps and suggests that this initial division has been perpetuated.

A second reason for the two-party system offered by Key is the impact of institutional factors. Key suggests that "certain features of American institutions are congenial to two-partyism and certainly over the short run obstruct the growth of splinter parties."[8] The chief such institutional feature is *plurality elections* in which the winner—no matter how narrow his margin—takes all, instead of *proportional representation elections,* in

6. Key, *Politics, Parties, and Pressure Groups,* pp. 205–210. Also see the helpful discussion by Sorauf, *Party Politics in America,* pp. 36–40.
7. Key, *Politics, Parties, and Pressure Groups,* p. 207.
8. Key, *Politics, Parties, and Pressure Groups,* p. 208.

which parties with less than a plurality receive some representation.[9] With plurality elections, unless a new third party can muster more votes than the major parties—not a very likely happening—it receives no seats in the legislature (or in the case of the presidency and the electoral college, no electoral votes). This, it is argued, discourages minor parties and their potential supporters.

Key also lists "systems of beliefs and attitudes" as possible causes of the dual-party system. He stresses "the absence of groups irreconcilably attached to divisive or parochial beliefs" and "a popular consensus on fundamentals." [10]

A fourth possible explanation, and one not mentioned by Key, for the perseverance of the two-party system is the flexibility and pragmatism of the two major parties. Often a third party has started to gain strength only to find one of the major parties taking over much of its program. The third-party thunder is effectively stolen, and it loses the support it had started to gain. But plausible as these four explanations may be, one must still agree with Key that they "remain unsatisfactory." At this time, a complete answer is not possible.

Significance of the Two-party System

The chief significance of the two-party system lies in its encouragement of broadly based parties. When a nation has a multiparty system, the different parties appeal to certain groups within the population: workers, businessmen, farmers, Catholics, and Protestants are the usual ones. Each party largely strives to win the votes of all the members of the group it is based on—not to win the votes of other groups. But in a two-party system no party can win an election by appealing only to Catholics, or only to workers, or only to businessmen. With only two parties competing, a party must gain over 50 percent of the votes to win, and these several groups do not constitute majorities. Thus both the Democrats and the Republicans must appeal to a variety of occupational, ethnic, and religious groups. This, in turn, encourages moderate stands, a blurring of issues, and a pragmatic flexibility. In representing interests, each party must take into account the demands of a wide variety of groups.

Party Centralization: Unity and Disunity

"Decentralization of power is by all odds the most important single characteristic of the American major party; more than anything else this trait

---

9. For two opposing views on the significance of plurality elections in causing two-party systems, see Maurice Duverger, *Political Parties,* trans. by Barbara and Robert North (New York: Wiley, 1954), pp. 207–255, and John G. Grumm, "Theories of Electoral Systems," *Midwest Journal of Political Science,* 2 (1958), 357–376.

10. Key, *Politics, Parties, and Pressure Groups,* p. 210.

distinguishes it from all others. Indeed, once this truth is understood, nearly everything else about American parties is greatly illuminated." [11] This is a basic thesis E. E. Schattschneider articulated in his classic work, *Party Government,* a thesis still generally accepted by students of the American party system. At the same time, it is clear that there is a minimal degree of coordination within the two major parties. After all, they nominate presidential and vice-presidential candidates every four years—often even without bitter fights—and usually almost all segments of each party support their party's nominees. And the parties in the different states are normally able to accomplish the same for statewide offices.

Thus the basic questions for us to explore are these: Why are American parties essentially decentralized? And why do they still manage to maintain a minimal degree of coordination? The answer to these questions is found in the push and pull of certain forces. The outcome of this interplay of forces goes a long way toward determining how parties perform their interest representation, conflict resolution, and support-generating functions. This section of the chapter therefore explores three factors that have —in varying degrees—uniting and disuniting properties.

Party Structure

No where is the fact that the United States is made up of 50 separate, viable states seen more clearly than in the structure of the two parties. The influence of the states is seen both in the 50 different state party structures found within each party and in the national party structure, which is largely made up of representatives from the state party organizations. Thus, we must consider the state, local, and national party structures and their uniting and disuniting qualities.

State and Local Party Structures   Every state except South Carolina regulates by statute the internal operations of the parties by establishing and regulating a welter of committees, councils, and conventions. As though deliberately working to confuse, each state has created somewhat different —and sometimes radically different—party structures and procedures.[12]

The reason for the detailed state regulation of the parties lies in the American political culture's deep distrust of politicians and parties. Thus the belief has arisen that parties must be carefully regulated, and regulated in such a manner that no "boss" or "machine" can dominate them. This is done by creating a large number of different party councils and organiza-

---

11. E. E. Schattschneider, *Party Government* (New York: Holt, Rinehart and Winston, 1943), p. 129.

12. For good summaries of the formal local and state party organizations, see Thomas W. Madron and Carl P. Chelf, *Political Parties in the United States* (Boston: Holbrook, 1974), pp. 101–115; Sorauf, *Party Politics in America,* chap. 3, and Hugh A. Bone, *American Politics and the Party System,* 4th ed. (New York: McGraw-Hill, 1971), pp. 131–159.

tions and then dividing power among them in the hope that by this splintering of power no one person or group can seize control. With only a few notable exceptions, these state regulations have succeeded beyond their authors' fondest hopes—most state parties remain unbelievably fragmented.

Among the basic party structures usually found in states and localities are *precinct committeemen,* often elected in primary elections, who supposedly head up party activities in the precincts (the small voting districts of 400 to 2,000 voters). *County committees* and *chairmen* (usually named by the precinct committeemen) are also normally found on the local level. On the statewide level *state conventions,* a *state executive committee,* and a *state chairman* are normally found. Their make-up and selection varies from state to state. Typically they grow out of local party organizations in that they are either made up of or named by representatives from the local organizations throughout the state. Although the party organizations may look forbidding on paper, they are often in practice skeleton-thin, with many of the available positions—especially the precinct committeemen posts—going unfilled because of lack of interest.

Outside the regular, legally provided party structures are a variety of extralegal organizations, such as partisan clubs and campaign organizations for individual candidates. These are not established by state law, but sometimes they overshadow the regular party structures in power and significance. Especially important are candidate organizations, because candidates for a variety of reasons often prefer—or are forced—to work through their own organizations, instead of through the regular party organization.

National Party Organizations Each party has a *national committee.*[13] The Republican national committee is made up of two persons, a man and a woman, from each state, plus the state chairmen of states that voted Republican in one of several specified, recent elections. Recently the Democratic national committee was expanded to over 300 members, in an attempt to represent a broader range of party elements.[14] In form, most of the members of the national committees are elected for four-year terms by the national conventions. In practice, however, they are named by the state parties (using a bewildering variety of procedures) and then merely ratified by the national conventions.

13. For more complete descriptions of the national party organizations, see Bone, *American Politics and the Party System,* pp. 160–191; Sorauf, *Party Politics in America,* chap. 5; and Cornelius P. Cotter and Bernard C. Hennessy, *Politics Without Power: The National Party Committees* (New York: Atherton, 1964).

14. For a copy of the permanent charter of the Democratic party adopted in 1974, which creates a larger national committee more representative of the various elements in the party, see *Congressional Quarterly Weekly Report* (December 14, 1974), pp. 3334–3336.

The national committees play a minor role in the parties. The very fact that they are large (more than a hundred members) and are composed of members geographically dispersed and meeting infrequently indicates the problems they would have in functioning as ongoing policy-making and policy-directing bodies. Thus Cotter and Hennessy are not inaccurate when they write that "the national committees themselves are large groups of people variously selected, representing different amounts and kinds of local political interests, who come together now and then to vote on matters of undifferentiated triviality or importance, about which they are largely uninformed and in which they are often uninterested." [15] Recently there have been attempts by both parties—and especially by the Democrats—to make the national committees more representative and effective. Whether they will succeed, however, remains doubtful.

Each party has a *national chairman*. In form, he is the head, the apex, of the party organization—but, in fact, he is largely a head without a body. In no sense of the word is the national chairman the "boss" of his party. In form, the national chairman is elected by the national committee. In fact, immediately after the national convention the national committee names as chairman the person designated by the party's presidential nominee. If a vacancy occurs during the four years between national conventions and if the party is in power, the President designates the national chairman. If a vacancy occurs in the party out of power, the national committee has discretion in electing a new chairman. National chairmen most frequently are either members of Congress (this is especially true of the Republicans) or experienced party leaders from the state level.

Cotter and Hennessy list five roles played by the national chairman: image-maker (projecting a favorable image of the party to the public), hell-raiser (stimulating partisan loyalty and enthusiasm among the party faithful), fund raiser, campaign manager (managing the presidential campaign), and administrator (overseeing the staff of the national headquarters).[16]

What Cotter and Hennessy could not include in this list of roles is as significant as what they could list. Two particularly significant roles had to be left out: policy maker and coordinator. Conceivably the office of national chairman could have developed into a significant policy-making and policy-articulating institution or into one coordinating the disparate institutions and individuals within the party. After all, the national chairman is elected by the national committee, which in turn is elected by the national convention. Thus he would seem to be the focal point of the party, with the authority to exert real leadership. But this has not occurred. The few chairmen who have attempted to move toward such a role have met with

15. Cotter and Hennessy, *Politics Without Power*, p. 3.
16. Cotter and Hennessy, *Politics Without Power*, pp. 67–80.

failure. The basic reason is the absence of any effective sanctions they can take against uncooperative party members or organizations. Whatever influence a chairman has rests largely on his ability to cajole the various elements in the party to do what he wants them to do by way of bargaining and negotiating.

Every four years each party holds a *national convention* that meets to adopt a platform, to nominate presidential and vice-presidential candidates, and, as already seen, to elect the national committee. The politics of the conventions' nominating and platform-writing activities are discussed later, but here we should note how convention votes are apportioned among the states and how delegates are selected. Unbelievably complex formulas are followed by the two parties in determining the number of convention votes each state will have. Fundamentally, they award each state a set number of votes, give additional votes in proportion to the number of congressional seats each state has, and then give additional votes to those states that voted for the party in certain designated, recent elections.

Delegates to the national conventions are chosen in many and very different ways. Because since 1968 the number of states with presidential primary elections has increased, these primaries have some part in the selection of a majority of both parties' delegates (although the exact part varies widely from one state to another). Many states still select delegates through their party organizations, using a combination of congressional district conventions or caucuses and state conventions. The Democratic party—first in the rules governing its 1972 convention and then in its permanent charter adopted in 1974—has attempted to assure that delegates will be selected by processes that are open to grass-roots Democrats (not just to established state and local party leaders) and encourages the selection of women, youths, and minorities in proportion to their numbers in the electorate.[17]

The remaining formal organizations on the national level are the four *Senate and House campaign committees,* each party having one in each house of Congress. Members of each of the parties in the House and in the Senate select committees from their own membership to help elect members of their party to the House or Senate. Their activities include fund raising, furnishing speakers, distributing literature, and so forth. For the most part, they operate independently from the national committees, the national committees and chairmen being more concerned with presidential elections. The extent to which congressional committees cooperate with the national committees and state and local committees depends on shifting circumstances.

17. For a copy of the permanent charter of the Democratic party and an account of the controversies surrounding its adoption see *Congressional Quarterly Weekly Report* (November 30, 1974), pp. 3209–3214 and (December 14, 1974), pp. 3330–3336.

There are also extralegal committees and organizations on the national level, just as there are on the state and local levels. Especially important are the campaign organizations set up by presidential candidates. The increasingly common pattern is for these campaign organizations to operate independently from the formal party organizations.

Figure 5.1 shows the basic party structure in schematic form. No lines of responsibility or authority have been drawn between the various organizations because, when they exist at all, they are generally extralegal and transitory.

Party Structure: Consequences   The formal party structures act more as disuniting than as uniting forces, although they do of course establish organizations with at least some potential for coordination. But two divisions are found within each of the parties—divisions that the parties'

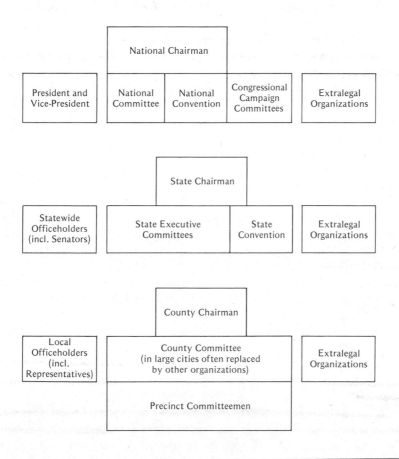

Figure 5.1   The formal party structure

structures, by their nature, have encouraged. The first is a division between the three levels of the parties—national, state, and local—as is shown in Figure 5.1. At first glance the parties' organizational structures appear to be in the form of a hierarchy, or pyramid. Starting with the precinct committeemen at the bottom we move up to the county committees and the county chairmen. The county organizations are bound together into state organizations, and the state organizations are in turn bound together into a national organization. But to have a true hierarchy those persons and organizations higher in the hierarchy must have some means by which they can control—or at least significantly influence—those lower in the hierarchy. Thus in political parties the persons higher in the hierarchy could possibly exert a certain degree of control over the lower levels by dispensing (or withholding) campaign funds, by possessing the right to approve candidates nominated for public office by the lower levels, or by expelling members from the party. These and other powers are frequently possessed by party leaders in other democracies, but not in the United States. The appearance of hierarchy is misleading.

In actuality, the party structure provided for by state statutes and the party structure that has developed is such that the three levels operate largely independently of each other. Party organizations on the three levels are pretty well free to do as they please—to nominate the candidates they wish, to adopt the policy stands they feel proper, and to support or not support candidates nominated by other party organizations. Sometimes local parties nominate candidates at variance with the state party leadership, sometimes state party leaders publicly oppose policies the national party supports, and sometimes state parties refuse to endorse their own party's presidential nominees. John Fenton, after observing the Ohio Democratic party in the early 1960s, concluded: "there was, in fact, no statewide Democratic party in Ohio. The state's Democratic party was an aggregation of city machines which had little or no interest in statewide elections unless the candidate was from their city. Ray Miller, the Cuyahoga County (Cleveland) boss, explicitly maintained that his organization was an independent entity with neither legal nor moral ties with a state Democratic party."[18] Such situations are far from unusual.

In short, the formal party structure provides for next to no hierarchical control, and party leaders have generally been unsuccessful in developing informal, extralegal controls. As a result, the parties, on both the state and national levels, largely consist of autonomous and semi-autonomous organizations.

A second division that the formal structure of the parties has encouraged is a split between the party organizations and the elected officeholders. The formal structure provides no means by which the party organizations

18. John Fenton, *Midwest Politics* (New York: Holt, Rinehart and Winston, 1966), p. 137.

can control their elected officeholders—and, for that matter, no means by which officeholders can control the party organizations. For the most part, both exist independent of the other. The extent to which they are interdependent is a result of factors other than the formal structure. In recent years candidates have increasingly relied on professional campaign consultant firms to give advice and even to run their campaigns (a trend to be discussed more fully later). This trend has worked to make candidates even less dependent on party organizations, both for workers and for advice, than they were previously. Thus Figure 5.1 shows the party's officeholders separate from the party organization.

Party Activists, Motivations, and Party Centralization

When we speak of party unity and disunity, we are of course speaking of individual persons who are either willing or unwilling, able or unable, to work together in a unified, cohesive manner. Thus to understand party unity—and its absence—we must understand something about the nature and motivations of the persons who make up the parties.

Issues One motivation that leads some persons to become politically active is a concern about issues. Their concern is which public policies will be adopted. They enter the arena of party politics in order to work for the victory of the policy principles and issue positions to which they hold.

Within the parties, the existence of large numbers of persons who are issue-motivated can either help or hinder the creation of unity and cohesion. Unity is hindered when persons with conflicting issue positions are thrown together, a situation easily documented. President Ford's economic and energy policies in the mid-1970's were opposed by many congressmen of his own party. During the latter half of the 1960s much of the debate over the Vietnam conflict took place within the Democratic party. Merely juxtaposing the names of Senators James Eastland of Mississippi and Edward Kennedy of Massachusetts reveals deep issue differences in the Democratic party. And what is obvious in the case of public figures such as these is equally true of the less publicized party workers and leaders.

The key fact to remember is that whenever strong-minded individuals have deep divisions over issues or ideology, it is difficult for them to work together. The inability of George McGovern to patch up completely the split between himself and some elements of organized labor in the Democratic party during his 1972 presidential campaign is testimony to the often divisive effect of issues on parties. Certainly anyone might hesitate to subject himself to an authority that might have different policy views. If there were general agreement on issues within each of the parties, the factions, organizations, and individuals that comprise them would guard their autonomy less jealously, because they would have less to lose by submerging some of their autonomy under a central authority.

On the other hand, the divisions on issues are greater, on the average, between the two parties than within the parties. This is illustrated by Table 8.1 (page 236), which shows the much more liberal voting record of Democratic congressmen as compared with that of the Republican congressmen.

Further evidence indicating there are significant issue differences between the two parties was found by a study of the issue positions of the delegates to the parties' 1968 national conventions. As Table 5.1 shows, on all but one of the issues the Democratic delegates were significantly more liberal than the Republican delegates. The authors of this study

Table 5.1 Issue differences between Democratic and Republican party activists[a]

	Democrats, % Liberal Responses	Republicans, % Liberal Responses	Difference
1. Public employees should not have the right to strike for higher wages. (Liberal-disagree)	69% (N = 185)	28% (N = 165)	40%
2. The best way to deal with people who break the law is to punish them so they fear the consequences of breaking it again. (Liberal-disagree)	49% (N = 185)	18% (N = 165)	31%
3. Law enforcement agencies should be allowed limited eaves-dropping by wiretapping and other devices. (Liberal-disagree)	50% (N = 187)	21% (N = 166)	29%
4. The U.S. should give help to foreign countries even if they are not as much against communism as we are. (Liberal-agree)	79% (N = 185)	52% (N = 159)	27%
5. People who advocate radical changes in our way of life are over-protected by our laws. (Liberal-disagree)	63% (N = 185)	39% (N = 166)	24%
6. School children should be bussed to achieve racial balance in elementary and secondary schools. (Liberal-agree)	33% (N = 179)	10% (N = 168)	23%
7. Communism today has changed greatly and we must recognize that most wars and revolutions are not communist inspired. (Liberal-agree)	38% (N = 184)	17% (N = 169)	21%
8. One has a moral responsibility to disobey laws he believes are unjust. (Liberal-agree)	17% (N = 186)	4% (N = 169)	13%
9. Vietnam is historically and geographically an Asian country and should be allowed to develop autonomously within the Asian sphere of power. (Liberal-agree)	64% (N = 181)	71% (N = 155)	−7%

[a] Delegates to the 1968 national conventions.

Source: John W. Soule and James W. Clark, "Issue Conflict and Consensus: A Comparative Study of Democratic and Republican Delegates to the 1968 National Conventions," *Journal of Politics*, 33 (1971), 78.

concluded "that substantial ideological differences do exist between the Democratic and Republican delegates to the 1968 National Conventions."[19]

The sharp issue differences between the two parties and the degree of agreement on issues within them are significant because they enable issues to serve as a force drawing the elements of a party together. This is true for two reasons. First, the intraparty agreement can serve as a basis for the development of a sense of belonging and loyalty on the part of those active in the parties. Thus appeals for party unity can be based on the activists' shared sense of commitment to the party. Second, it is only by electing persons to office that party activists will see their issue positions, instead of those of the opposite party, translated into public policies. Thus electoral victory is essential for the issue-motivated person or organization to achieve its goal of the adoption of public policies in keeping with its beliefs. The key point to be remembered is this: *a common desire for victory at the polls is a powerful unifying force.* It opens the way for winning the cooperation of a party organization or leader by the argument, "Look, if we do not stick together, we will surely lose the election." The skillful party leader—whether he or she be a county chairman, a state chairman, a national chairman, or a candidate running for office—can sometimes win the cooperation of party elements by appealing to their sense of loyalty to party principles and stands on issues. And he or she can raise the specter of victory for the opposite party if they do not cooperate. At least a measure of coordination can sometimes be achieved by this means.

Personal Ambitions

Personal ambitions, as well as concern over issues, may motivate an individual to become active in a political party. These personal ambitions may take the form of hoping to obtain a patronage job, such as that of a federal marshal or a township clerk, to influence the awarding of certain contracts, to run for elective office sometime in the future, or simply to experience the prestige and enjoyment of holding and exercising political power within the party. But whatever form a particular individual's ambitions may take, he is weighing different alternatives in terms of how they will affect his personal ambitions.

As is true of concern with issues, personal ambitions can act as either a cohesive or a disruptive force, depending on the circumstances. They act as a cohesive force when persons conclude that their ambitions are best served by working with other party leaders and organizations. A county

19. John W. Soule and James W. Clarke, "Issue Conflict and Consensus: A Comparative Study of Democratic and Republican Delegates to the 1968 National Conventions," *Journal of Politics,* 33 (1971), 88.

chairman may cooperate fully with a gubernatorial candidate, hoping to influence the letting of highway contracts at a later date. Or a state chairman may work closely with the party's presidential candidate, hoping to be in a position to distribute federal patronage if the candidate wins. Or a precinct committeeman may work with the county chairman, hoping to win the nomination for a state legislative post. Thus persons often perceive their self-interest as best served by working with other party organizations or leaders.

The old-time urban bosses maintained their power by the skillful use of rewards of this type, with which they put people in their debt and paid off past obligations. They have faded in the last thirty to forty years as patronage jobs have diminished and as state and federal welfare programs have undercut the dependence of the public on their favors.[20]

In addition, the desire to win acts as a unifying force and is as relevant here as it is with issues. As long as one's party wins no election most personal ambitions are likely to go unfulfilled. A defeated party dispenses no patronage, lets no contracts, and offers little prestige to its leaders. Thus personally ambitious individuals and organizations within a party can be approached with the argument that cooperation with other party elements is necessary for victory—and the desired rewards.

But these same ambitions can lead people not to cooperate with other elements of their party. To oppose the President, even though he is of the same party, may be helpful to a Senator in his re-election bid. Or a county chairman, by defying the state central committee, may gain favor with the county committee. And persons who currently possess influence within the party structure would tend to lose it if any centralizing movement succeeded. The county chairman would no longer have as much control over local nominations, the state chairman would no longer be free to choose whether or not to cooperate with the party's presidential nominee, and the Senator would face the threat of not being renominated if his voting record were contrary to party policy. Thus people having a great deal of influence within their parties would tend to lose some of their influence, and so—with an eye on their personal stakes—they tend to oppose centralizing efforts. And since their influence is still great, they are in an excellent position to block such efforts. In short, those with the most to lose from the centralization of power are the very ones in the best position to block it.

---

20. For a helpful account of the bases of the bosses' power and the reasons for their decline, see Elmer E. Cornwell, Jr., "Bosses, Machines and Ethnic Groups," *The Annals of the American Academy of Political and Social Science,* 353 (1964), 27–39. Also see the highly interesting, personal account of what has probably been the most tightly knit party organization in the United States today (and one largely held together by material rewards)—the Democratic organization of Richard J. Daley in Chicago: Mike Royko, *Boss* (New York: New American Library, 1971).

Amateurs and Professionals   Party cohesion, and its problems and prospects growing out of the nature and motivations of party activists, are clarified by a basic distinction made by political scientists between what have been called *amateur activists* and *professional activists.* [21] Amateur activists are issue-oriented activists with the added characteristic of a certain missionary fervor. They tend to see politics as a struggle between good and evil and their involvement in politics as a holy crusade. Professional political activists, on the other hand, take a more detached approach to their politics. They may be motivated by either issue concerns or personal ambitions, but they are committed to winning elections and are normally willing to make the compromises and concessions necessary for victory. Politics is seen by them as a struggle among contending forces, no one of which is the repository of all wisdom and virtue. James Wilson drew the distinction this way: "The ideal amateur has a 'natural' response to politics; he sees each battle as a 'crisis,' and each loss as a defeat for a cause. The professional tends, by contrast, to develop a certain detachment toward politics and a certain immunity to its excitement and its outcomes." [22] In a helpful footnote Wilson goes on to explain: "A politician develops a professional attitude toward politics in the same way that a mortician develops a professional attitude toward death, a scholar a professional attitude toward knowledge, and a prostitute a professional attitude toward love." [23]

Recent studies have been able to classify delegates to national conventions as amateurs of professionals. Table 5.2 shows the percentage of amateurs and professionals at the 1968 and 1972 Democratic conven-

Table 5.2   Amateurs   and   professional,   1968–1972 Democratic   national conventions

Year	Amateurs	Semi professional	Professionals	Total
1968 (N = 188)	23%	61%	16%	100%
1972 (N = 314)	51	22	27	100%

Source: John W. Soule and Wilma E. McGrath, "A Comparative Study of Presidential Nomination Conventions: The Democrats 1968 and 1972," *American Journal of Political Science,* 19 (1975), 511.

21. It should be noted that the terms *professional* and *amateur* are *not* used to distinguish between political activists who are active on a full-time, paid basis from those who are active as a hobby or avocation. Amateurs and professionals—as the terms are being used here— are found in both these two groups. On the distinction, see James Q. Wilson, *The Amateur Democrat* (Chicago: University of Chicago Press, 1962); James Q. Wilson, "The Amateur Democrat in American Politics," *Parliamentary Affairs,* 16 (1962–1963), 73–86; John W. Soule and James W. Clarke, "Amateurs and Professionals: A Study of Delegates to the 1968 Democratic National Convention," *American Political Science Review,* 64 (1970), 888– 898.
22. Wilson, "The Amateur Democrat in American Politics," p. 75.
23. Wilson, "The Amateur Democrat in American Politics," p. 75.

tions. A study of the delegates to the 1972 Republican national convention found 13 percent were strong amateurs, 29 percent qualified amateurs, 45 percent qualified professionals, and 13 percent strong professionals.[24]

The significance of this distinction is that professional activists—with their willingness to compromise and their desire for electoral victory—form a better basis for building party unity than do amateurs. Whether such individuals are largely motivated by issue concerns or by personal ambitions, the appeals to party loyalty and the need to win elections to gain their goals (and therefore the need to compromise with other elements in the party to gain the cohesion and cooperation needed for victory) are likely to be effective. The amateurs, on the other hand, put commitment to their issue positions—to their cause—above loyalty to party or concern for victory. Compromise is immoral, and working with other party elements is selling out. Typical is the attitude revealed in an account of the McGovern delegation from California to the 1972 Democratic national convention:

McGovern's campaign staff in California had recommended adding [Senator John] Tunney, an early Muskie backer, to the delegation. . . . The final speech for Tunney, itself symbolic of the campaign's difficulties, was delivered by Assemblyman Willie L. Brown, Jr., one of the leading black politicians in the state and later chairman of the California delegation. The flamboyant Brown proceeded to castigate Tunney in the most vitriolic manner for fully 10 minutes—each insult receiving louder cheers. Brown concluded by saying: "John Tunney is a devil. But the book says that we have to give the devil his due. What the devil is due on this delegation is one seat—and who better to sit on His seat than John Tunney."[25]

Clearly attitudes such as these make party unity more difficult to achieve. The fact that the studies cited above show both amateurs and professionals to be present in large numbers—at least at the national convention level—means that there is a base for unity among the professionals, even though the presence of the amateurs creates problems. Although there is no firm evidence that it is a continuing, long-term trend, there is scattered evidence that the proportions of amateurs to professionals in the parties is growing. Table 5.2 shows that the percentage of amateurs at the Democratic convention more than doubled from 1968 to 1972, reflecting the fact that McGovern's movement was largely an amateur movement. Nixon's Committee to Reelect the President also had a significant number of amateurs in it. If in fact more amateur activists are becoming politically involved, then the parties are likely to have more difficulty maintaining unity in the future than they have had in the past.

24. Thomas Roback, "Amateurs and Professionals Among 1972 Republican National Convention Delegates," paper given at the 1973 annual meeting of the American Political Science Association, p. 5.

25. William Cavala, "Changing the Rules Changes the Game: Party Reform and the 1972 California Delegation to the Democratic National Convention," *American Political Science Review,* 68 (1974), 41.

In summary, because of their formal structure, their ideological divisions, their conflicting personal ambitions, and a probable increasing proportion of amateur activists, the American parties are largely decentralized. Each party is composed of uneasy coalitions of numerous autonomous and semi-autonomous organizations; yet a minimal degree of coordination and cooperation is achieved on the basis of issues and personal ambitions—especially when they are combined with a preponderance of professional activists. There is sufficient unity and cohesion within each of the parties to consider them distinct, identifiable units. In spite of all their divisions, the parties normally manage every four years to gain the support of almost all their segments for their presidential and vice-presidential candidates, and party ties do provide a basis for congressional cooperation, helping bridge the presidential-congressional and other institutional gaps. Divisions and fissures are present within the parties; but a minimal level of cohesion is also present.

Party Centralization and Party Functions

The basic decentralization, intertwined with some cohesive ties, that characterizes the parties affects their performance of the interest representation and system-maintenance functions. To the extent the parties are marked by decentralization, they represent very specific, particularistic interests. The interests of particular groups are able to find expression through individual party organizations or through individual candidates and party officials, all of which give voice to and work for their own points of view. This pattern can be seen when a local party organization falls under the domination of a particular group or point of view (perhaps it is captured by organized labor or perhaps by conservative extremists) and then espouses that interest's point of view through the candidates it supports and the pronouncements it makes.

On the other hand, to the extent the parties are marked by unity and cohesion, they represent broader aggregates or combinations of interests. Local party organizations and key party leaders who may be dominated by a particular interest are forced to reconcile their particularistic points of view with other party leaders and other party organizations who are dominated by different interests. As a result, the total party ends up representing an amalgam of interests that reflect—partially, not fully—the points of view of a number of interests. The American parties, because of their particular balance of decentralization and cohesiveness, to a large degree represent many specific, particularistic interests, but to a limited degree they also represent broader aggregates of more particularistic interests.

To the extent the parties represent broad aggregates of interests, they are also engaged in conflict resolution. In constructing these aggregates out of the more particularistic interests, those who hold to these specific interests are being persuaded to accept something less than they originally wanted in order to find a common ground. Conflicts are thereby being resolved.

Support is also generated, as the parties allow particularistic interests to have a say in the construction of broader aggregates and as the particularistic interests themselves are often given representation. In both cases persons are given the feeling that they are having an impact on the parties and —through them—on the political system. Increased support is the likely result.

Parties in the Government

The Responsible Party Model

The American political system has been aptly described as one of "separated institutions sharing powers."[26] As will be seen more fully in Part Three, the Senate, the House, the presidency, the executive departments, the independent regulatory commissions, and the judiciary are separate institutions, each with its own legal basis, but all take part in the policy-making process. The actions of one affect the others.

Some observers—especially a number of political scientists—would like to have the parties play an organizing role within and among the formal institutions of the political system. The Constitution has divided decision-making power among a number of institutions; parties should act as a unifying force, coordinating these divided institutions. If, for example, the Democrats won a presidential election and carried both houses of Congress, the Democratic party would be in a position to coordinate all of government. For Congress would be controlled by Democratic leaders, the President would be a Democrat, he would appoint Democrats to other positions in the presidency, the bureaucracy, and the judiciary. The Democratic party would then be in a position to coordinate the activities of the different institutions of the political system as they worked together in putting the Democratic program into effect. Then, at the next election, the public could either decide that it liked what the Democrats had been doing and return them to office or decide that it did not and replace them with the Republicans. In that event, the Republicans would have the opportunity to run the government. This is the *responsible party model:* one or the other of the parties is entrusted with organizing and running the government, and it is held responsible by the electorate for its performance. The model is largely inspired by the role that parties play in Britain's political system.

American Parties and the Responsible Party Model

For the responsible party model to operate, two conditions need to be present: each party must have a reasonably clear program, and each party

26. Richard E. Neustadt, *Presidential Power* (New York: Wiley, 1960), p. 33.

must have some centralized authority. American parties have neither.[27] Although each American party occupies a somewhat different general position on the political landscape, it would not be accurate to say that each has a clearly defined program that it is eagerly waiting to put into effect. Thus whenever a party wins a national election (that is, wins the presidency and both houses of Congress), it is difficult to say exactly what its mandate is. A very general mandate is usually discernible, but it is bound to be general and vague, not explicit, when the winning party contains a wide variety of points of view.

Even more serious is the absence of centralized authority in the parties. Conceivably there could be some institution at the apex of the formal party structure that would determine policy priorities and strategies and coordinate the activities of the party members in government. But as we have already seen, there is no institution even remotely resembling such a one in the American parties. The President or the party leaders in Congress could conceivably play that role, but, as we will see in Part Three, their powers are limited and they have no real control over their fellow party members in government. In short, American parties—for good or bad—do not have the discipline, centralization, and programmatic unity needed to meet the responsible party model.

The Actual Role of Parties in Government

If American parties do not meet the requirements of the responsible party model, what role do they play in organizing the government? In brief, parties do have a coordinating, organizing role, but they fulfill it with uneven success and they are only one of several forces working toward coordination in the government.[28]

Parties are very prominent when Congress organizes itself at the start of a new session. Committee chairmanships and the elected leadership positions are decided on the basis of party. Parties are also important factors in the general legislative process in Congress. Party considerations are also very much in evidence in presidential appointments to the judiciary and the bureaucracy. As noted in Chapter 9, the fact that the top-level bureaucrats are usually of the same party as the President helps communication and coordination. The members of the President's party in Congress form

27. Much has been written on whether American parties should approximate the responsible party model. Two works arguing that they should not are Ranney and Kendall, *Democracy and the American Party System,* especially Part VI; and Pendleton Herring, *The Politics of Democracy* (New York: Norton, 1940). Two works arguing that they should are Schattschneider, *Party Government,* and Committee on Political Parties of the American Political Science Association, *Toward A More Responsible Two-Party System* (New York: Holt, Rinehart and Winston, 1950). For a helpful critique of the latter study, see Evron M. Kirkpatrick, "*Toward a More Responsible Two-Party System:* Political Science, Policy Science, or Pseudo-Science?" *American Political Science Review,* 65 (1971), 965–990.

28. For a helpful discussion of the role of parties in the government, see Key, *Politics, Parties and Pressure Groups,* Chapters 24 and 25.

a natural starting point for his attempts to influence Congress. He has certain arguments and sanctions he can use in gaining their support that he does not have with the members of the opposing party. Normally the majority of support for his program comes from his own party members.

Thus party is clearly a factor that helps to bind the disparate formal institutions of the political system together. Yet to say that it does so effectively and completely, or to say that it is the only factor doing so, or to say that it is clearly the major factor doing so, is not warranted. Often persons jump the party traces and work at cross-purposes with their fellow party members. This occurs within Congress, within the bureaucracy, between Congress and the President, between the President and the bureaucracy, and on and on. Much of Part Three is documentation of this fact. The President, in his general leadership role, is a greater coordinating and organizing force than the parties. Much the same can be said for the basic values and rules of the game held to by persons in government. But neither must the parties be dismissed too lightly—they are significant factors aiding in the coordination of the widespread, separated institutions of the American political system.

To the extent that the parties play a coordinating role in government they are helping to resolve conflicts and represent interests. Coordination means determining which individuals and the positions they represent are to be given priority (both in time and in importance). And this means resolving conflicts. And interests are represented whenever party members in government speak and work for certain positions.

Nominations

Although we have been forced to equivocate on the role of parties in government, there is no need to equivocate on the role of parties in the nomination of candidates. Here is the prime role of parties assigned them by tradition, the one most frequently cited as the distinguishing mark of political parties. But the extent to which the parties' role in the political system is being challenged is revealed by the fact that the parties' part in nominating candidates is under severe attack and to some degree has been successfully taken from them.

Nominations, Interest Representation, and Democracy

Two basic methods of nominating candidates for public office are in use today: primary elections and party conventions. Under the *primary system,* candidates are elected in an official election in which all the supporters of a party may vote. In the *closed primary system,* which is most frequently used, voters register either as Democrats or as Republicans and may vote only in the primary of their party. In the less frequently used *open primary system,* voters decide at the time of each primary whether to vote in the Democratic or the Republican primary. Almost all states use the primary to nominate candidates for most offices, and every state uses the primary to nominate candidates for some offices. Under the *convention system,* candidates are nominated by a gathering of party leaders and activists from lower party organizations. The convention method of nomination is used in nominating candidates for some offices in a number of states and, of course, in nominating presidential candidates.

The Goal   The elusive goal (or ideal) that democracy demands of the nomination process is the nomination of candidates who reflect the interests and demands of the general public—not those of some elite group. As we have seen the process of nominating candidates for public office is one form of interest representation. Each potential candidate represents—through his or her issue stances and group alliances—a particular constellation of interests and demands. Thus, when one particular candidate is nominated and other candidates are rejected, a certain combination of interests is being given representation and others are not. In a democracy the demands that are channeled into the political system through the interest representation function ought to be demands that are being made by large segments of the population. Thus there have been recurrent attempts in American political history to assure that the nomination process will result in candidates truly representative of popular concerns and demands.

Typically the chief danger that candidates will not be representative has been seen to lie with party bosses—or party leaders, to use a more neutral term. Strong parties have been considered the enemy of democratic interest representation, not as the means to it. This tendency has no doubt resulted from the American culture's ingrained suspicion of parties and its faith in direct popular rule, which were noted in Chapter 2. But in fact reducing and splintering the influence of party leaders over nominations is no guarantee that nominees will be representative of public demands and interests. The rest of this section explains why.

The Intraparty Route   Basically, there are two routes by which to reach the ideal of democratic interest representation: the intraparty route and the interparty route. The *intraparty route* stresses the need to make the internal party processes by which candidates are nominated as democratic as possible. One way to do this is to require that party activity be open to all persons and to enforce democratic procedures on the internal operations of the parties. But the most frequently used device has been the direct primary. The great popularity of the primary rests on the claim that it takes the all-important nomination process out of the hands of the somewhat suspect politicians and puts it into the hands of the people. Thus the candidates nominated naturally reflect the demands and interests of the general population, not those of the party leaders.

But in practice there are several problems. One basic fact of primary life has been the low turnout of voters at primary elections. Only 20 to 30 percent of the electorate turns out to vote in primary elections.[29] This low turnout means that relatively few persons determine the outcomes of primary elections. In a congressional district of 400,000 persons, about 200,000 will probably be registered voters. About 30 percent, or 60,000, will vote in any given primary election. Assuming the parties are evenly split, 30,000 vote in each party's primary. If there are two candidates in a party's primary, 15,001 votes win the monination. If there are more than two candidates even fewer votes do. Thus in a congressional district of 400,000 persons, 15,001 or fewer are normally able to determine the nomination. This basic fact of life raises two questions.

The first question asks how representative the primary voting electorate is of the population as a whole. Perhaps the 30 percent that votes in a primary (and the 8 to 10 percent that is sufficient to nominate most candidates) is no more representative of the general public's interests and concerns than is an elite group of party leaders. The evidence available on this point is mixed: studies have shown that the age, socio-economic composition, and educational levels of the primary voters differs from that of the general public, but more recent studies have also shown that this fact does not necessarily mean they differ widely in their opinions and views.[30] At the least we cannot simply assume that the primary-voting electorate's concerns and demands are those of the population as a whole. Sometimes they no doubt are; other times they no doubt are not.

A second question raised by the low voter turnout in primary elections concerns the extent to which party organizations are still able to influence the outcome of primary elections. A large percentage of the persons who do vote in primaries are the strong party loyalists, having direct and indirect ties with the party organization. Because relatively few votes are needed to win, a well-organized party that is able to get the word out to its members and followers to support a particular candidate—whether by a formal endorsement or by informal word of mouth—is likely to be successful in carrying the primary for that candidate.

In addition, primary candidates favored by the party leaders are frequently helped in numerous ways by the party leaders and their followers. Campaign advice, volunteers for canvassing, mailing lists, funds (an espe-

---

29. See Austin Ranney, "Parties in State Politics," in Herbert Jacob and Kenneth N. Vines, eds., *Politics in the American States,* 2d ed. (Boston: Little, Brown, 1971), p. 98.

30. See Austin Ranney and Leon D. Epstein, "The Two Electorates: Voters and Non-Voters in a Wisconsin Primary," *Journal of Politics,* 28 (1966), 598–616; Austin Ranney, "Turnout and Representation in Presidential Primary Elections," *American Political Science Review,* 66 (1972), 21–37; and Andrew J. DiNitto and William Smithers, "The Representiveness of the Direct Primary: A Further Test of V. O. Key's Thesis," *Polity,* 5 (1972), 209–224.

cially critical factor), and favorable contacts with the mass media and key interest groups are the type of services and advantages that candidates favored by the party leadership can be given. Primary candidates without the party leaders' favor are left to struggle for funds, volunteers, and other ingredients of electoral victory. Sometimes, especially if they have independent sources of money or the support of powerful interest groups, they may be able to do so successfully. More often they are unable to do so.

The basic situation seems to be one in which primary elections do not automatically result in the control of nominations being taken out of the hands of the parties, but primaries do present a formidable challenge to the parties' ability to nominate their own candidates. Often party leaders are able to keep control of the nomination process. But at other times party leaders clearly lose control, and candidates not wanted by them win primary elections. In 1972 George Wallace won the Democratic Michigan presidential primary, while most of the leaders of the Michigan Democratic party were insisting that Wallace was not even a genuine Democrat. Yet such instances appear to be the exception, not the rule.

Primary nominations mean that the parties are being challenged in their right to nominate candidates—a challenge they are usually, but not always, able to meet. Before drawing the conclusion that, because party organizations still frequently play a key role in determining the outcome of primary elections, public concerns and demands are not well served by the nomination process, we must consider a second route by which democratic interest representation can be achieved.

The Interparty Route   A second route by which to achieve the nomination of candidates whose interests and concerns match those of the general public is by way of strong *interparty competition.* American culture, probably because of its suspicion of the political parties and its faith in direct popular rule, is less comfortable with this route than with the intra-party route, yet it serves as a powerful force to assure democratic interest representation in the nomination process. The basic concept rests on the fact that victory at the polls in the general election is the prime goal of both political parties. Whatever motivates a party organization as a whole or individual activists within it—issue concerns, material rewards, or whatever—the goal is most unlikely to be achieved without winning elections. Winning is the name of the game. And the candidates most likely to win are the candidates most in tune with the people's sentiments and concerns. If the party leaders secure the nomination of someone pleasing to themselves but very unrepresentative of the general population and its demands, the chances are their candidate will lose the general election—and the party leaders will have nothing to show for their efforts. Thus there is indirect pressure on the party leaders to nominate people who are popular, are good vote-getters, and are thus representative of the major interests of

lation. The interests of the public, by an indirect process, are being
ited. Thus when party leaders seek to control the outcome of a
election—or are able to nominate candidates directly at a party
ation—they no doubt frequently do so not with their personal preferences uppermost in mind, but with thoughts of which candidate most
enhances the chances of victory in the general election.

But there can also be problems with this second route. If the electoral
district within which the nomination is taking place is noncompetitive—
if one party or the other is in a position of overwhelming strength—there
is not much pressure on either party organization to nominate a candidate
representative of the public. No matter what they do, the one party is
almost bound to win and the other to lose. Or if a party organization is
dominated by amateur activists, it may nominate a losing candidate representative of their beliefs and not of the public's beliefs, rather than go
against their beliefs to nominate a winning candidate in tune with the
public's beliefs.

As is often true with the real world—and especially with the real political
world—no neat and simple answer can be given to the dual question of
the actual role of parties in nominations and the extent to which the
nomination process is responsive to popular demands and concerns. Traditionally the parties have had the predominate role in nominating candidates, but primary elections—while not taking nominations completely out
of the hands of the parties as they were originally intended to do—have
challenged the parties' primacy in the nomination process. Party organizations, especially where they are fairly strong and united, are for the most
part able to control nominations; but where party organizations are weak
or divided, the ability to determine their nominees may slip away. Whether
or not the parties are dominant in the nomination process in any particular
race may or may not lead to democratic interest representation. Because
of the two routes by which to achieve democratic interest representation
and the effects of each, there is no guarantee attached to either route.

The National Nominating Conventions

The *national nominating conventions* are among the most colorful spec-
tacles American politics has to offer. Bands, cheering crowds, strategy
conferences, closely contested roll-call votes: all are there—along with
"live and in color" television coverage. In order to understand these big,
noisy, confusing—and frequently misunderstood—conclaves, it is necessary to strip away their superficial characteristics and to explore their true
nature and the actual role they play in the political system. Behind all the
noise and confusion lies the deadly serious business of selecting—as the
convention orators like to remind us—the next President of the United
States.

The Preconvention Phase   The jet airplane, the telephone, television, and public opinion polls have revolutionized the politics of presidential nominations and the role played by the national conventions.[31] Formerly, the conventions were conclaves of state and local party officials who met in order to hammer out an agreement on a presidential candidate and other matters. Long-distance communications were difficult, and the conventions provided an opportunity for the all-important negotiating and bargaining. But with New York five hours from Los Angeles and with the Oregon state chairman as easy to call as a secretary in the next room, much of the bargaining process can go on before the convention opens. Television enables the candidates to receive the nationwide publicity needed to build a successful drive for the nomination. And the polls record the rise and fall of the potential candidates' popularity. The result is that national conventions are serving more and more to ratify the decisions made during the preconvention maneuvering than to make the decisions. One has to go back twenty years and ten conventions—to 1952—to find a convention in which the nominee was not selected on the first ballot. In contrast, in only two of the six conventions from 1936 to 1952 that did not renominate an incumbent President was the nominee named on the first ballot.

The Democrats recently abolished the unit rule. (The Republicans never made as much use of it as the Democrats did.) The *unit rule* permits the candidate getting the majority support in a caucus, local convention, or primary election to have automatically all the delegate votes controlled by that caucus, convention, or primary at the national convention. This rule tends to have the effect of adding to the strength of potential nominees who are already strong. Therefore its abolition by the Democrats will make it somewhat more difficult for an aspirant with strong support to parlay this support into an insurmountable lead in delegate votes. Nevertheless, other factors still make it likely that the number of national conventions having to hammer out the presidential nomination will be few.

Successful preconvention drives for the presidential nomination consist of three distinguishable facets: public, party, and grass-roots. The *public facet* consists of an aspirant's attempts to gain and to demonstrate overwhelming popularity with the voters. He thereby hopes to pick up large blocs of delegates to the national convention by winning a series of primary elections and to impress the party leaders with the fact that he is their best chance of defeating the opposing party in November and carrying their state and local candidates into office with him. Thus an aspirant

31. On the politics of the presidential nomination process, see Paul T. David, Ralph M. Goldman, and Richard C. Bain, *The Politics of National Party Conventions* (Washington, D.C.: Brookings, 1960); James W. Davis, *Presidential Primaries* (New York: Thomas Y. Crowell, 1967); Gerald Pomper, *Nominating the President* (New York: Norton, 1966); and Nelson W. Polsby and Aaron B. Wildavsky, *Presidential Elections,* 3d ed. (New York: Charles Scribner's Sons, 1971).

normally enters many primaries, hoping that victories will bring him not only additional delegates, but also increased television coverage and higher poll standings (there is a well-established pattern of primary victories leading to better showings in the polls). The increase in the number of primaries, which occurred between 1968 and 1972, has increased the importance of the public facet—twenty-four states, with a majority of the delegate votes, now have presidential primaries of one type or another. An aspirant cannot afford to ignore them. John Kennedy in 1960, Robert Kennedy in 1968, and both George McGovern and Hubert Humphrey in 1972 relied very extensively on this approach.

The *party facet* of a preconvention campaign for the presidential nomination consists of quietly working with state and local party leaders, attempting to win their support. A variety of levers can be used in this attempt. The most common is collecting on past favors and playing on personal loyalties. Often a contender has done such favors for state and local party leaders as speaking at fund-raising dinners, campaigning in earlier elections, or interceding in the executive branch for some reason. The net result is that many state and local party leaders may feel a certain personal obligation or loyalty to the candidate, a feeling that can be transformed into pledges of convention votes.

There are other bases on which the aspiring candidate can try to win the support of state and local party leaders. The vice-presidency is a prize he may dangle in front of several governors and senators, hoping that they will jump on the bandwagon. Or there are other appointments—cabinet positions, judgeships, and ambassadorships, for example—that a candidate may trade for promises of support at the convention. These bargains are usually more implicit than explicit. He quietly lets it be known that if he wins the nomination and then the presidency, he will "take care of" certain individuals if they join his cause now. Certain weaknesses of his opponents can also be pointed out—lack of party loyalty in the past, close association with an "extreme" wing of the party, or lack of experience are possibilities. And the ideological similarities between the candidate and his potential supporters can be stressed. Both Richard Nixon and Hubert Humphrey relied extensively on this approach in 1968.

Because of the changes the Democratic party has made in the process of delegate selection, the party facet has become less important for Democratic aspirants. The reforms adopted by the Democratic party have reduced the role of state and local party leaders and increased the role of grass-roots activists in the delegate-selection process. Thus the party facet is no longer as important for Democratic aspirants as it once was and still is for Republican aspirants.

The *grass-roots facet* of a preconvention campaign for the presidential nomination consists of working within local and state party caucuses and conventions, which in turn select delegates to the national convention. The goal is to take them over, or at least to gain strong minority strength in them, so that they in turn will name delegates to the national convention who are committed to the aspirant. The new delegate-selection process of the Democratic party makes it easier for a well-organized, united group to pursue this strategy. To be successful, however, it requires a fairly large number of strongly motivated persons on the grass-roots level, because they are needed to infiltrate party organizations on the lower levels. Both Barry Goldwater in 1964 and George McGovern in 1972 used this method extensively in nonprimary states.

The three facets of a drive for the presidential nomination are not mutually exclusive, but interrelated. Underlying both the party and grass-roots facets is the public facet. If party leaders are convinced that a candidate stands little or no chance of winning the November election, the pleas of the party facet of his campaign are likely to fall on deaf ears: A defeated presidential candidate appoints no cabinet officers or judges, secures the passage of no legislation, and adds little prestige to his supporters. In addition, a strong vote-getter carries many state and local party candidates into office with him; a weak one carries many to defeat. Demonstrating to party leaders the candidate's vote-getting ability—the public facet—is thus a crucial supplement to the party facet of a campaign for the nomination. Richard Nixon—while relying extensively on the party facet in 1968 —also entered many primaries in the attempt to dispel the loser image he had attained because of his 1960 and 1962 electoral defeats.

The public facet also underlies the grass-roots facet of a campaign. A feeling that there is a ground swell of popular support for an aspirant will encourage more of his grass-roots followers to work hard in state and local caucuses and conventions to win additional delegates. A loser image will discourage his followers. Thus the public facet of a campaign complements its grass-roots facet. McGovern's early Wisconsin primary victory in 1972 was crucial, because it sent a surge of hope—and willingness to work— through his followers.

The grass-roots and party facets complement each other: Strong support in the party's grass roots can help persuade party leaders to support an aspirant, and support among party leaders can ease the way for an aspirant's grass-roots supporters to win control—or at least a strong say— in the delegate-selection process.

Although a successful campaign for the presidential nomination usually must use all three of the facets simultaneously, they do vary in the degree to which each is emphasized. The exact emphasis a contender gives to each of the three facets and the exact strategy he develops in pursuing each is largely dictated by his strengths and weaknesses. An aspirant with a very well-known name and widespread popular support tends to pursue the public facet extensively. An aspirant somewhat lacking in voter popularity but having either good contacts with many key state and local party leaders or a widespread grass-roots organization of dedicated followers tends to stress either the party facet or the grass-roots facet. But no aspirant can pursue one strategy to the total exclusion of the others. It is a matter of emphasis, with any aspirant having to stress all three facets to some degree.

In summary, aspirants for the presidential nomination, by entering a number of primaries, obtaining extensive television coverage, tirelessly crisscrossing the country, making innumerable phone calls in order to confer with party leaders, and building up grass-roots organizations, are usually able to gain sufficient strength to be nominated on the first ballot —or are outclassed and outmaneuvered by an opposing aspirant and for all practical purposes have lost the nomination before the first gavel falls at the convention.

The Convention   If the nomination has not been decided during the preconvention phase, the same type of bargaining and negotiating typical of the party facet of the preconvention phase goes on in greatly intensified form. Each proponent attempts to persuade uncommitted and wavering delegates that their man is the best qualified and the one most likely to win in November. Often implicit or even explicit bargains are entered into.

In addition to selecting a presidential nominee, the conventions make two other important decisions. They adopt a platform and they select a vice-presidential nominee. The vice-presidential nominee is the choice of the person who wins the presidential nomination, with the delegates nominating whomever the presidential candidate names. The presidential candidate normally names the person he feels will add most to his chance of victory at the polls. Thus the vice-presidential candidate is usually from a section of the country different from that of the presidential candidate, has a somewhat different background, and comes from a different wing of the party. As noted earlier, sometimes the vice-presidential nomination is used as a bargaining point in securing the nomination. Thus in 1972 the Protestant, strongly liberal George McGovern, whose ties with organized labor and some regular party elements were strained, first selected as his running mate Thomas Eagleton, a moderately liberal Catholic, who had cordial relationships with organized labor and had not been a McGovern backer before the convention. When Eagleton was forced to resign from the ticket because of earlier mental health problems, McGovern selected Sargent Shriver, another Catholic with strong ties with regular party elements.

A second important decision of the national conventions is the adoption of a party platform, in which the goals and ideals of the party for the next four years are set out. Platforms are usually masterpieces of ambiguity and fence straddling; parties attempt to write platforms that will be attractive to as large a segment of the population as possible while alienating as small a segment as possible. No mean task! By including in it planks pleasing to defeated aspirants, backers of the winning presidential candidate some-times use the platform to appease their supporters. But because the plat-form is adopted before the nominations are made, this can be done only when one candidate has won during the preconvention phase. In practice, victories—or defeats—over the platform are largely symbolic, for platform pledges are usually forgotten once the convention is over.

Finally, it should also be noted that conventions enjoy free nationwide television coverage. Thus a good part of the time and effort of the conven-tions goes to creating a favorable public image of the party and its candi-date for the television audience. Major events—such as the acceptance speech by the presidential nominee—are scheduled during prime televi-sion viewing hours and tremendous efforts are made to keep the proceed-ings lively and the speeches short.

In summary, the conventions can be described as conclaves of the party faithful, meeting to ratify the nomination of their party's presidential candi-date and only occasionally actually to decide whom to nominate. They also ratify the presidential nominee's choice for the vice-presidential nomi-nation, adopt a platform, and serve as campaign rallies. Although this is an accurate description of conventions, our understanding of them would be incomplete if no more were said. To complete the picture, the conven-tions' role in the political system must be grasped.

The Functions of the Conventions   The conventions play significant roles in interest representation and conflict resolution. In the nominating of presidential and vice-presidential candidates and to a lesser degree in the adoption of a platform and in the proclaiming of party ideals by convention orators, interests are being represented. The candidates represent an amal-gam of interests through their stands on issues and their past actions. In 1968 Richard Nixon represented a somewhat different complex of inter-ests from the one Nelson Rockefeller would have represented, and in 1972 George McGovern represented a complex different from Hubert Hum-phrey's or George Wallace's. The same holds true for the vice-presidential candidates. That interests are represented in the platform and in the speeches is even more easily seen.

It is clear that interest representation goes on in conventions, but for those of us interested in democratic politics, an additional question re-mains: Are major demands present in the general population being re-flected in the interests represented by the conventions? Sometimes the conventions have been criticized for being undemocratic because the public does not participate directly in nominating the candidates. But we saw earlier that forces can be present, even when party leaders are nomi-nating candidates, that work to assure that the persons nominated are in tune with public wishes and concerns. In fact there are forces present that normally assure—but do not absolutely guarantee—that the candidates nominated by the national party conventions reflect currently dominant interests and demands.

The popularity of a candidate among the general public is critical for his nomination. It is obviously necessary in order to win primary victories, but it is also necessary in order to pick up support from key party leaders and to motivate his grass-roots followers. Even the most cynical of party bosses —if he or she wishes help for the local ticket and subsequent jobs, influence, and prestige—must consider and weigh whether or not the aspirant he is considering backing has the popular support needed to win in November. He cannot simply nominate the person he personally might favor.

We might easily suppose that as a result of the Democratic delegate-selection reforms, candidates named by Democratic conventions will be more highly representative of the interests of the general public than was the case previously and still is for the Republicans. After all, the whole purpose of the reforms was to make the conventions more representative of the public. But this is not necessarily the case. The major result of the Democratic reforms will probably be to make it more likely that the party will be more responsive to well-organized movements among grass-roots party members and less responsive to long-term state and local party leaders. The key question is what effect this change will have on the interests given representation in future Democratic conventions.

Clearly state and local party leaders can be very unrepresentative of the general public. But it is equally true—even though less frequently recognized—that grass-roots party movements can also be highly unrepresentative of the general public. Often grass-roots movements are composed of highly educated, ideologically oriented, amateur party activists, highly unrepresentative of the general population. Amateur party activists are less likely to take the potential voter appeal of aspirants for the nomination into account than are the professional party activists, who are likely to be found among long-term state and local party leaders. The amateurs' missionary fervor says to them that it is better to lose with an unpopular candidate who is right on the issues than to win with a candidate wrong on some issues but more in tune with current popular demands and concerns. The professional activists tend to be quicker to compromise and to accept an aspirant on the basis of his or her potential for victory at the polls in November. Thus in 1964 a well-organized grass-roots movement won the Republican party's nomination for Barry Goldwater—a candidate clearly out of tune with the general public.[32] The Democrats' 1972 nomination of George McGovern also fits this pattern. McGovern won the nomination

32. On the 1964 Goldwater grass-roots movement and Goldwater's unrepresentativeness, see Theodore H. White, *The Making of the President, 1964* (New York: Atheneum, 1965), pp. 88–97, 130–138; and Philip E. Converse, Aage R. Clausen, and Warren E. Miller, "Electoral Myth and Reality: The 1964 Election," *American Political Science Review,* 59 (1965), 323–327.

with the support of a well-organized cadre of grass-roots supporters, even though he was the first choice of only 30 percent of the Democratic voters and even though 75 percent of the voters in the primaries in which he was entered did not vote for him.[33] As with Goldwater, a disastrous defeat resulted. The paradoxical conclusion is that although the Democrats' emphasis on grass-roots party movements instead of long-term state and local party leaders was adopted in order to help assure the nomination of candidates more representative of the general public and its demands, in practice it is likely to accomplish the opposite.

In performing the system-maintenance function of conflict resolution, conventions, for the most part, are successful. Given the wide ideological differences and the many personal animosities within each of the parties, it is no easy task to find candidates and programs for which the entire party membership can campaign enthusiastically. Yet, with relatively few exceptions, the party conventions achieve this very thing. The convention and preconvention maneuverings offer many opportunities for the bargaining and negotiating that are normally found at the heart of the conflict-resolution process. This process is helped by the fact that a number of advantages and favors are given out during and preceding conventions: opportunities to influence the planks in the platforms or to have a prominent place in the convention proceedings, the promise of future support or office, the vice-presidential nomination, and the greatest prize of them all—the presidential nomination. Because a number of advantages are distributed, compromises and log-rolling will be engaged in, much as in Congress.[34] In the process, conflicts are resolved.

This conflict resolution is of obvious importance to the parties in view of the coming election campaign. But by resolving conflict within themselves the parties are also making conflict resolutions easier within the political system as a whole. The conflicts are made more manageable, as many particular, narrow demands and interests are aggregated into two general positions.

Election Campaigns

Once a nomination has been made—and sometimes even before—the political parties attempt to shift into another of the major activities traditionally assigned to them: contesting elections. This final section of the chapter explores basic patterns of activities that mark election campaigns,

33. See *Gallup Opinion Index* (June 1972), pp. 9–10 and Clark MacGregor, "The Coming Nixon Victory," *Saturday Review,* 55 (July 29, 1972), 39. On the similarities between the Goldwater and McGovern candidacies, see Everett C. Ladd, Jr., and Seymour M. Lipset, *Academics, Politics, and the 1972 Election* (Washington, D.C.: American Enterprise Institute, 1973), pp. 52–61.

34. See Chapter 8, pp. 247–248.

the decreasing role of the parties in them, and the extent to which they contribute to interest representation, conflict resolution, and generating support.

Purposes of Election Campaigns

To raise the question of the purposes of election campaigns would appear to many to be a waste of time. After all, is not their purpose self-evident —to win elections by persuading voters to support a particular candidate? But three subborn facts—often overlooked by arm-chair campaign strategists and sometimes even by professionals—make the answer to the question less than obvious. The first fact is that a large majority of voters mark their ballots in keeping with their long-standing partisan affiliations. Table 4.2 showed that in presidential elections from 75 to 90 percent of the persons who identify with one of the parties vote in keeping with that party identification. And about 75 percent of the population identifies with one of the major parties. It is estimated that in congressional elections about 85 percent of the votes cast are cast by individuals voting in line with their party affiliation.[35] This fact helps to explain the second fact that affects the purposes of campaigns. Table 5.3 shows that from 55 to 75 percent of the voters in presidential elections make up their minds on how to vote even before the start of the campaign. The third fact all candidates must remember is that the majority of the public has a very limited interest in politics and pays only limited attention to election campaigns.

It is thus clear that at the start of a campaign the two opposing candidates are not faced with a neutral public, waiting to listen to them and then make up its mind. Instead, the candidates are faced with a disinterested and often apathetic public, most of whose members are habitually committed to one or the other of the parties and therefore to one or the other of the candidates. Most have already made up their minds.

Recognizing this situation, a group of social scientists concluded thirty years ago that campaigns fulfill essentially three purposes.[36] The first is *reinforcement*. A candidate must reinforce the predispositions and biases of the supporters of his own party. If he is to win, they will provide the bulk of his support, and he must be certain that they do not defect to his opponent. Many of those who vote in line with their party affiliation, or who decide for whom to vote even before the campaign starts, might defect to the other candidate if their candidate did not wage an effective campaign aimed at reinforcing their original leanings.

A second purpose of election campaigns is *activation*, that is, increasing the level of activity of one's supporters: from nonvoting to voting, and from

35. Warren E. Miller and Donald E. Stokes, "Constituency Influence in Congress," *American Political Science Review*, 57 (1963), 54.

36. Paul F. Lazarsfeld, Bernard Berelson, and Hazel Gaudet, *The People's Choice* (New York: Duell, Sloan & Pearce, 1944).

Table 5.3 Time of decision on voting choice for President, 1948–1968

Time of decision	1948	1952	1956	1960	1964	1968
Before conventions	37%	34%	57%	30%	40%	33%
During conventions	22	31	18	30	25	22
During campaign	26	31	21	36	33	38
Don't remember or NA	9	4	4	4	3	7
	94	100	100	100	101	100
Number of Cases	421	1251	1285	1445	1126	1039

Source: Compiled by William H. Flanigan, *Political Behavior of the American Electorate*, 2nd ed. (Boston: Allyn and Bacon, 1972), p. 109, from data gathered by the Center for Political Studies, Institute for Social Research, University of Michigan.

voting to more active forms of support. A candidate could have a majority of the eligible voters in his favor and yet lose the election if large numbers of supporters stay at home. Thus, a major chore of his campaign must be making sure that his supporters actually get out on election day and vote for him. This can be done by specific "get out the vote" drives among persons known to be favorable to the candidate or by so increasing enthusiasm among a candidate's supporters that they will have the motivation to vote. Activation has goals besides merely turning out the vote, however. A candidate's supporters who normally would have done no more than vote for him may have their enthusiasm so increased by the campaign that they will talk to friends and relatives about the candidate or perhaps even volunteer time or money to the campaign.

A third purpose of campaigns is *conversion,* that is, persuading persons to adopt a more favorable opinion of the candidate than their previous one. Conversion may take two forms: an undecided person decides to support the candidate, or a supporter of one candidate decides to support the other candidate. In most election campaigns only a small minority of voters are converted from one position to another, but, if the election is at all close, that minority may spell the difference between victory and defeat. Thus, conversion is an important purpose of campaigns.

Strategy and Tactics

In few areas of American politics is the folklore as rich or the number of self-appointed experts as large as in campaign strategy and tactics.[37] Terms such as "the Italian vote," "peaking too soon," and "going where the votes are" are often thrown into conversations with greater confidence

37. On campaign strategy and tactics see Lewis A. Froman, Jr., "A Realistic Approach to Campaign Strategies and Tactics," in M. Kent Jennings and L. Harmon Zeigler, eds., *The Electoral Process* (Englewood Cliffs, N.J.: Prentice-Hall, 1966), pp. 1–20; Robert Agranoff, ed., *The New Style in Election Campaigns* (Boston: Holbrook, 1972); and Dan Nimmo, *The Political Persuaders* (Englewood Cliffs, N.J.: Prentice-Hall, 1970).

than knowledge. This section cannot possibly cover all the tactics and strategies that have been used and misued, but it does suggest some most frequently used by presidential and congressional candidates.

The American way of waging election campaigns has undergone profound changes in recent years. Television and polls have revolutionized campaigning, have added greatly to their complexity and costs, and in the process have reduced the campaign role of party organizations. Formerly, the backbone of most successful campaigns was a systematic attempt by both of the party organizations to get their identifiers out to the polls. These attempts had two stages.

The first was identifying all the supporters of the candidate's party. This was done weeks or even months ahead of the election and meant that many volunteers had to spend hours telephoning and canvassing, precinct by precinct and block by block. On election day the second stage was reached when watchers were stationed at each polling place to check off the name of the party supporters as they came to vote. Then, during the latter part of the day, those supporters who had not yet voted were reached and urged to do so. Transportation to the polls was offered when needed. This tactic rested on the assumption that in most close elections the losing party had had enough voters sitting at home and not voting to have won the election if only they had been brought out to the polls to vote the party ticket.

This tactic is still a part of most campaigns for office. But it is becoming a less effective tactic than it was earlier, because it rests upon the assumption that one can identify weeks before the election which voters will vote for one's candidate. Usually this is done by way of party identification— turning out as many identifiers with the candidate's party as possible. But in a day when increasing numbers of voters are independents and increasing numbers are splitting their tickets and voting contrary to their sense of identification, it is possible to bring to the polls as many voters for one's opponent as for one's candidate. In 1972 both the Nixon and McGovern campaigns used this tactic extensively, but both attempted to identify their individual supporters and did not risk simply turning out all of their parties' identifiers—certainly a much more difficult and uncertain process now than when it was safe to turn out all the partisans.

Well-run campaigns are increasingly making use of opinion polls, largely aimed at discovering the major concerns of the voters and their reactions to the campaign as it progresses. Thus the candidate is able to tailor the campaign to meet the mood and reactions of the public. He attacks his opponent where the polls show his opponent to be weak and shores up his own image and those issues where the polls show that he himself is weak.

Television has opened up another new world of campaigning. The usual tactic is the five-minute appeal, although one-minute or thirty-second spot announcements are being used more frequently than they were. When a candidate buys a thirty- or fifteen-minute time period, only a portion is used by the candidate to address the television audience directly; the rest consists of film clips of the candidate out campaigning, relevant events, or endorsements by celebrities or supposedly ordinary folk. When television is used, all the tactics are aimed at combating public disinterest and the tendency for people to expose themselves only to candidates of their own party. A long program will probably be turned off by all but the strongest supporters of a candidate—the very people he has no need to reach—but the shorter, more entertaining programs may hold the less interested, less committed audience.

Recent studies have shown that television is not the all-powerful medium it has sometimes been assumed to be.[38] In the 1972 presidential campaigns considerably less was spent on television than in 1968.[39] Voters seem to have a certain resistance to influence from commercial-looking messages and a greater susceptibility to influence from seemingly objective messages. Thus campaigns are putting increasing emphasis on getting appearances on the evening television news shows. Much of the campaign is geared toward the pseudo event: an event staged for television, at a time convenient for the television cameras and containing a sense of excitement or action. Thus supporters are bused in to assure that an enthusiastic crowd is on hand to greet the candidate at a noon rally (noon is better than evening for it can then make the evening news shows), or a poignant scene, the candidate meeting a wounded war veteran perhaps, is arranged (before noon again, of course).

Recently campaigns have been supplementing television with additional technological tactics. For example, computerized direct mail sent to certain targeted occupation or religious groups, or a telephone campaign is mounted in which a recorded message from the candidate is played to selected persons who are called by automated equipment.

To conduct and interpret polls and to take full advantage of television and other recent campaign innovations is no job for amateurs—and increasingly is not left up to amateurs. Most campaigns are either entirely run by a campaign firm hired by the candidate or at least have the advice of professional campaign consultants. Professional campaign firms are available to conduct the entire campaign—all the way from circulating nominating petitions to arranging the victory party.

Two side effects of these changes in campaigning are clear: campaign costs have soared astronomically, and the role of party organizations in

38. See, for example, Thomas E. Patterson and Robert D. McClure, *Political Advertising: Voter Reaction to Televised Political Commercials* (Princeton, N.J.: Citizens' Research Foundation, n.d.), which suggests both the potential and the limitations of television commercials.

39. See *Congressional Quarterly Weekly Report* (May 12, 1973), p. 1135.

campaigning has decreased. Campaign costs are discussed later but here it is important to note that professional campaign consultant firms have replaced the party organization to a significant degree as the basic source of advice, know-how, and sometimes campaign workers. Now candidates, much more frequently even than in the recent past, depend on a combination of these hired consultants and their own volunteers to build up a personal campaign organization rather than relying on on-going, already existing party organizations. Party organizations usually have at least some role to play as a source of workers, "get out the vote" drives, advice, and money, but usually they are no longer dominant and at times they are almost totally eclipsed by candidates' own personal organizations.

Campaign Finance

Campaigns costs money—and never has this been more true than today. Figure 5.2 shows the sharp increase in campaign costs in recent years.[40] Most of this increase has come from the additional use of television, polls, and professional consultants.

A central fact of campaign finance is that a majority of the money raised comes from a relatively small number of large donors rather than from a large number of small donors. Table 5.4 shows the number of large contributors to presidential campaigns between 1952 and 1972. Two facts stand out: vast sums of money are given by a relatively small number of persons, and the amount of money given by large contributors has sharply increased in the last two campaigns. In addition, there is an even smaller number of persons that make extremely large contributions. In 1972 there were 27 persons who gave over one hundred thousand dollars each to one or the other of the presidential candidates—18 of them to Nixon and nine of them to McGovern.[41] In 1968 close to three million dollars was given by 12 very prominent families like the Rockefellers, DuPonts, and Mellons.[42] Part of the Watergate scandal of the Nixon administration involved the payment of large illegal contributions to the Committee to Re-elect the President.[43] Although the acceptance of (or even coercive demands for) a large number of illegal contributions was unique to Nixon's 1972 campaign, the dependence of parties and candidates on a relatively few large

40. On the increase in campaign costs, see The Twentieth Century Fund, *Voters' Time* (New York: Twentieth Century Fund, 1969); Delmer D. Dunn, *Financing Presidential Campaigns* (Washington, D.C.: Brookings Institution, 1972); Herbert E. Alexander, *Financing the 1968 Election* (Lexington, Mass.: Heath Lexington, 1971); and Herbert E. Alexander, *Financing the 1972 Election* (Lexington, Mass.: Heath Lexington, forthcoming in 1976).

41. *Congressional Quarterly Weekly Report* (October 6, 1973), p. 2656.

42. Alexander, *Financing the 1968 Election,* p. 180.

43. See Congressional Quarterly, *Watergate: Chronology of a Crisis* (Washington, D.C.: Congressional Quarterly, 1974), p. 133.

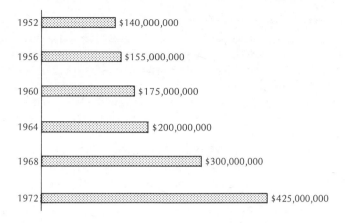

Figure 5.2 Total campaign spending in presidential election years, 1952–1972

Source: Herbert E. Alexander, *Financing the 1972 Election* (Lexington, Mass.: Heath, forthcoming in 1976).

contributions is not. How this dependence of the parties and candidates on a relatively small number of persons for ever increasing amounts of money affects the parties' interest-representation function is discussed in the next section.

In response to the Watergate scandal, Congress in 1974 enacted major legislation seeking to reform the financing of campaigns for the presidency and Congress. The act contains provisions that limit the amount of money individuals and organizations can give to candidates, limit the amount of money candidates may spend, provide for partial public financing of presi-

Table 5.4 Number of large contributors to presidential campaigns, 1952–1972

Year	Number of persons contributing over $500	Number of persons contributing over $10,000	Amounts contributed by persons contributing over $10,000
1952	9,500	110	$ 1,936,870
1956	8,100	111	$ 2,300,000
1960	5,300	95	$ 1,552,009
1964	10,000	130	$ 2,161,905
1968	15,000	424	$12,187,863
1972	51,230[a]	1,254[b]	$51,320,154

[a] This figure is derived from the same ratio used for the 1968 election, when reporting conditions were somewhat different, and thus may be inflated.

[b] This figure includes persons who contributed an aggregate of $10,000 or more to candidates and/or committees.

Source: Herbert E. Alexander, *Financing the 1972 Election* (Lexington, Mass.: Heath, forthcoming in 1976).

dential elections and primaries, require strict reporting of campaign financing, and create a Federal Elections Commission to oversee the enforcement of the act.[44] The law is comprehensive enough and tightly enough written to have a significant impact on election campaign financing. But its exact impact and the degree of the significance of its impact remain to be determined. Much depends on how the law is interpreted and enforced. In the past, campaign finance laws have often been interpreted and enforced in such a way as to favor big giving, big spending, and secrecy. It is going to be more difficult to do so with this law because of its tighter language and an independent enforcing body, but only time and experience will reveal its effectiveness in cutting down on election campaigns lavishly financed by a relatively small number of big donors.

Campaigns and Party Functions

Campaigns have often been criticized for creating more heat than light. There is a certain measure of truth in such comments. Candidates may ignore crucial but controversial issues or discuss them in an emotional, superficial fashion, public relations experts may project a false image of a candidate, and the high costs of campaigning may put the parties and candidates firmly in debt to certain special interests.

Admittedly the function of interest representation suffers as a result of the American style of campaigning. To the extent that the high cost of campaigning places individual candidates and parties in the debt of a relatively small number of large contributors, the representation of the general public's interests suffers. Those persons and organizations with large sums of money are able to have their interests better represented in the political process than those without the same financial standing, for they have a path into the political process through their campaign contributions that those without the same financial standing do not have. There is reason to hope, however, that the 1974 reform legislation will eliminate the worst of the problem. But given past ineffectiveness of campaign reform legislation a certain skepticism is not out of order.

Problems in interest representation are also posed by campaigns' tendencies to obfuscate or avoid key issues. To contribute fully to interest representation, campaigns should clarify the combinations of interests represented by the candidates. What was already known of their past records and statements would be expanded and communicated to the general public. Instead, campaigns often becloud rather than clarify. Public relations firms sometimes try to market candidates with about as much thoughtfulness and sensitivity to the public's need for information as they do when they market a new deodorant. Nevertheless, certain distinguish-

44. For more information on the provisions of the act and the events surrounding its passage, see *Congressional Quarterly Weekly Report* (October 12, 1974), pp. 2865–2870.

able, general positions of the candidates manage to emerge—perhaps in spite of rather than because of the campaign. It is generally known which interests would gain and which would lose by the victory of a particular candidate. Thus, although election campaigns marked by more clear-cut, rational discussions of issues would certainly increase the interest representation role of campaigns, interests are represented even with the present style of campaigning.

More positively, there is evidence that campaigns help increase the information voters have about officeholders and candidates. One study showed that those who had been directly reached by the parties through canvassers, phone calls, distributed literature, and so forth had more information about their Senators and Representatives than those who had not been reached and that people's interest in political affairs was increased by being approached by the parties.[45]

By increasing the information and interest of the voters, campaigns are, in effect, aiding in interest representation, for they are mobilizing masses of voters behind the policy alternatives represented by the candidates. And obtaining massive support for policy alternatives assures that these will be forcefully brought to the attention of the decision makers. Policy alternatives with little support from the public would probably be largely ignored —they would remain "out there" and not be brought into the political process as viable policy alternatives. Thus election campaigns, by mobilizing voters behind candidates and the interests they represent, are effectively helping to channel the public's demands into the political system.

Campaigns also help in resolving conflicts. The blurring of issues and the invoking of old party symbols (such as past achievements and party heroes) help bring divergent persons together in support of the same candidate. In making nominations the parties are resolving conflicts by selecting candidates or slates of candidates whom the party activists can accept: the campaign then takes these candidates and attempts to unite large segments of the public behind them. To the extent that they succeed, conflicts are being resolved—or at least mellowed. Emotional appeals, the playing down and blurring of issues, and the stress on the personal qualities of candidates can help in conflict resolution. Hard-fought campaigns, with the parties clearly and sharply divided on issues, could so divide the nation that national unity would be hard to achieve.

Campaigns can also help generate support for the political system. The invoking of such national symbols as the Constitution, George Washington, and Abraham Lincoln and the glorifying of the political system and the qualities of the American people that normally go with a campaign—all these increase support for the system. And merely going through the expected ritual of carrying the campaign to the people can help to increase

45. Samuel J. Eldersveld, *Political Parties* (Chicago: Rand McNally, 1964), po. 460, 494.

the support given to the political system. To one brought up in a democratic political culture, there is something satisfying to see even the President going out into the streets and villages of the nation, shaking hands and
joking with ordinary citizens.

Political parties have played and continue to play a vital role in the
making of public policies. At their best they serve as a bridge between the
people and their often unarticulated but deeply felt needs and desires on
the one hand and the makers of public policies on the other. But times have
been hard on the parties. Their right to perform all of their traditionally
assigned activities is under challenge. The very fact that whether or not the
political parties are disintegrating is being debated by political scientists is
revealing. But for the present—particularly in the nominating process—
parties are still alive, but not particularly well. Whether the parties will
continue to decline or whether they will experience a renaissance only the
future can tell.

Some Exploratory Questions

1. The American political culture tends to be highly critical of political parties.
Would greatly weakened parties or even no parties at all have harmful or beneficial
effects for the political system?

2. Between 1968 and 1972, in response to calls—largely from political liberals—
for greater popular participation in the presidential nomination process, several
states adopted new or strengthened presidential primaries. The first of these held
in 1972 was the Florida primary—won by George Wallace. Should this fact give
political liberals any second thoughts about expanding direct popular participation
in the presidential nomination process?

3. Is the entrance of professional public relations firms into election campaigns
likely to lead to more direct, effective communication with voters or to a blurring
of the information needed by voters to make intelligent, rational choices?

Bibliographical Essay

Three of the better works on the American party system as a whole are V. O. Key,
Politics, Parties and Pressure Groups, 5th ed. (New York: Thomas Y. Crowell,
1964); Frank J. Sorauf, *Party Politics in America,* 2d ed. (Boston: Little, Brown,
1972); and Judson L. James, *American Political Parties in Transition* (New York:
Harper & Row, 1974). On third party movements, see Daniel A. Mazmanian, *Third
Parties in Presidential Elections* (Washington, D.C.: Brookings Institution, 1974).
    For two short but very helpful discussions of the two major parties, see Ralph
M. Goldman, *The Democratic Party in American Politics* (New York: Macmillan,
1966); and Charles O. Jones, *The Republican Party in American Politics* (New
York: Macmillan, 1965). The national committees and chairmen are considered by

Cornelius P. Cotter and Bernard C. Hennessy, *Politics Without Power* (New York: Atherton, 1964). The national conventions and the presidential nominating process are fully discussed by Gerald Pomper in *Nominating the President* (New York: Norton, 1966); James W. Davis, *Presidential Primaries* (New York: Thomas Y. Crowell, 1967); and Paul T. David, Ralph M. Goldman, and Richard C. Bain, *The Politics of National Party Conventions* (Washington, D.C.: Brookings Institution, 1960), which is also available in an abridged paperback edition (New York: Random House, 1964). For brief descriptions and the voting records of each of the national conventions from 1832 to 1972, see Richard C. Bain and Judith H. Parris, *Convention Decisions and Voting Records* (Washington, D.C.: Brookings Institution, 1973). For a study of the politics of both the nomination and campaign stages of presidential elections, see Nelson W. Polsby and Aaron B. Wildavsky, *Presidential Elections,* 3d ed. (New York: Charles Scribner's Sons, 1971). For an able exploration of proposals to reform the presidential nomination and election procedures, see Alexander Bickel, *Reform and Continuity* (New York: Harper & Row, 1971).

Several books explore the politics of particular regions of the country, thereby giving many insights into the political parties on the state and local levels. See V. O. Key, *Southern Politics* (New York: Knopf, 1949); John H. Fenton, *Politics in the Border States* (New Orleans: Hauser, 1956); John H. Fenton, *Midwest Politics* (New York: Holt, Rinehart and Winston, 1966); and Duane Lockard, *New England State Politics* (Princeton, N.J.: Princeton University Press, 1959).

Helpful in analyzing the nature and motives of party activists is James Q. Wilson, *The Amateur Democrat* (Chicago: University of Chicago Press, 1962). On the nature and functions of campaigns, see M. Kent Jennings and L. Harmon Zeigler, eds., *The Electoral Process* (Englewood Cliffs, N.J.: Prentice-Hall, 1966); and Dan Nimmo, *The Political Persuaders* (Englewood Cliffs, N.J.: Prentice-Hall, 1970). Also helpful in giving insights into presidential campaigning are the very interesting books by Theodore H. White on the 1960–1972 campaigns: *The Making of the President, 1960* (New York: Atheneum, 1961); *The Making of the President, 1964* (New York: Atheneum, 1965); *The Making of the President, 1968* (New York: Atheneum, 1969); and *The Making of the President, 1972* (New York: Atheneum, 1973). On financing elections, see Alexander Heard, *The Costs of Democracy* (Chapel Hill: University of North Carolina Press, 1960); Delmer D. Dunn, *Financing Presidential Campaigns,* (Washington, D.C.: Brookings Institution, 1972) and the more polemical David Nichols, *Financing Elections: The Politics of the American Ruling Class* (New York: Franklin Watts, 1974). See Melvyn H. Bloom, *Public Relations and Presidential Campaigns* (New York: Thomas Y. Crowell, 1973) for a critical examination of the role of professional public relations in presidential campaigns.

Chapter 6   **Interest**   The Politics of
                Groups   Influence

When retiring President Eisenhower warned, in his farewell speech, of the harmful effects of an emerging military-industrial complex, he little realized this warning would be more often cited than any other he had made during his eight years as President. But the specter of huge, powerful industrial interests in league with an equally huge and powerful military establishment has caused many subsequent observers to echo Eisenhower. In the mid-1970s Watergate and its sordid world of illegal campaign contributions and secret cash funds encouraged the suspicion that not only defense industries but also other powerful special interests exert inordinate influence throughout the government.

Thus, recent years have seen the issue of interest-group politics being raised from the level of charges of petty corruption and smoke-filled rooms to a level on which the whole representativeness of the American political system is being called into question. There are those who argue that powerful interest groups and combines of interest groups—and especially business groups—have carved out for themselves so comfortable and so supportive a relationship with government that today the governmental decision makers and the nation's top corporate executives constitute a tightly knit elite, which runs the government to their mutual advantage and to the disadvantage of the vast majority of the population.

This chapter explores the nature of interest groups and their role and influence in the political system. In the process light will be thrown on the question of whether or not the specter of a government dominated by special interests has substance.

Definitions and Functions

Interests and Interest Groups

It is important to be clear from the beginning on the meaning of a number of terms associated with interest groups.[1] An *interest* is simply a concern

---

1. For helpful definitions of interest groups and related concepts, see David B. Truman, *The Governmental Process* (New York: Knopf, 1951), pp. 23–43.

shared by a large number of individuals. This concern may spring from certain perceived economic or physical needs, such as a job, health care, or protection of investments; or it may spring from certain nonmaterial beliefs and values, such as a belief in the equality of all races or fears of communist infiltration of political institutions. When only two or three, or even ten or twenty, people share a concern, it is difficult to consider it an interest. But when the concern is shared by several hundred persons, it should be considered an interest.

An *interest group* is an organization of individuals who share one or more interests and who try to influence decisions of the political system so as to promote their interests. Thus an interest group is an organization —it has a formal structure and lines of authority. But organizations composed of individuals with certain interests in common can exist without being interest groups. They become interest groups only when they attempt to influence decisions of the political system. Say that a group of individuals organizes a rod-and-gun club and attempts to promote its hunting and fishing concerns by purchasing and developing a fish-and-game-preserve. At this point it is not an interest group. But if it attempts to persuade the state conservation department to stock a lake on its preserve with trout, it then becomes an interest group, for it is attempting to influence a decision of the political system so as to promote the interests of the group.

Most persons think first of all of Congress when thinking of interest groups and lobbyists. But interest groups in fact know no institutional bounds. They attempt to influence any decisions of the political system that affect their interests, whether those decisions are made by Congress, the presidency, the bureaucracy, or the judiciary.

A *pressure group* is the same as an interest group. The term "pressure group" has certain unfavorable connotations, implying that such groups impose their will by putting some type of pressure on political officials. Therefore the more neutral term "interest group" is used in this book. A *lobbyist* is an individual hired by an interest group to represent its cause before the political decision makers. *Lobbying,* of course, is the activity of representing the cause of an interest group in the political system.

Functions of Interest Groups

Interest Representation   Interest representation—that is, channeling demands and supports into the political system, thereby determining the policy alternatives to be considered and the conditions under which policy decisions are made—is formally provided for in the American political system by way of elections and such representative bodies as Congress. And, as we saw in the previous chapter, political parties also play a vital role in interest representation.

But these largely formal, legal means of interest representation have several shortcomings. The first is that they are not adequate for representing, in all its variety and particularity, the entire spectrum of interests present in the United States. A certain amount of aggregating of interests must go on. One candidate and later one congressman or one President must reflect a whole range of interests. Thus interests must be combined as a compromise is struck between two different interests or as a small interest is overshadowed by a larger one. The problem is how specialized, particular interests are to be represented in the political system.

Interest groups, as representatives of interests, play a vital part in meeting this problem. By organizing themselves into an interest group, persons with a particular interest whose point of view might be distorted or even completely lost in the shuffle of aggregating interests are able to approach public officials directly with their demands. The net result is a representation of interests more effective than if only parties and elections were relied on for interest representation.

A second problem interest groups can help solve is that of supplying decision makers with vital information needed to make sound decisions. The formal institutional context within which the decision makers operate tends to remove them from the situations and persons for which they are making decisions. The executive in the Department of Agriculture is not a farmer, the member of the House Education and Labor Committee is not a professional educator, and the Supreme Court justice is not a criminal. This problem of information is solved, in part, through professional staffs, press reports, scholarly writings, and other means. Also contributing are interest groups. One congressman has stated that lobbyists "are frequently a source of information. If they come to your offices and explain a program or factors contributing to the need for legislation, you get a better understanding of the problems and the answers to them."[2] Interest groups can give firsthand information on how their members are likely to be affected by a proposed course of action, what circumstances currently prevail, and so forth. Again this, in effect, is interest representation—conditions, concerns, and needs in the society are being presented, sometimes with great force, to the decision makers.

Interest groups also aid in the function of interest representation by making the electoral process more effective. They play a role in informing their members of the general predispositions and past records of candidates for nomination and election. This is a factor, as noted in the discussion of opinion leaders in Chapter 4, that helps explain why public

2. Quoted in Charles L. Clapp, *The Congressman: His Work As He Sees It* (Washington, D.C.: Brookings, 1963), p. 163. On the informing role of interest groups, also see Andrew M. Scott and Margaret A. Hunt, *Congress and Lobbies* (Chapel Hill, N.C.: University of North Carolina Press, 1966), chap. 5; and Lester W. Milbrath, *The Washington Lobbyists* (Chicago: Rand McNally, 1963), pp. 305–314.

opinions are to a degree effective restraints on decision makers.

Ideally, by representing the particular demands of interests present in the population, by supplying information about these interests, and by making the electoral process more effective, interest groups help assure that the general public has a significant degree of influence on the policy-making processes. Thus interest groups can help to achieve a democratic political system. If, however, certain interests were to gain an overwhelming pre-ponderance of influence—as we know some persons believe has occurred in the United States—they would be able to ensure the translation of their demands into public policy, irrespective of perhaps equally valid demands arising from other segments of the population. The political system would then be responsive only to certain well-organized, powerful interests and not to a broad spectrum of interests. Those powerful interests would, in fact, go beyond merely giving representation to demands and would, in effect, be making actual authoritative policies. Thus in analyzing the func-tions performed by interest groups in the political system it is important to determine whether or not the field has been monopolized by a few all-powerful interests to the exclusion of other, equally significant interests.

System-maintenance Functions As a result of their interest representa-tion function, interest groups play an important role in generating support for the political system. Whenever persons are able to influence political decisions, or think they are able to influence them, they are likely to give support to the political system. The political system no longer appears to be a far-off, impersonal, unyielding object; instead, it appears to be close and responsive. Thus to the extent that interest groups give their members these feelings of greater efficacy, they are helping to generate support. Interest groups can do this by actually influencing the decisions of govern-ment, of course, but they also do it by merely giving their members the feeling of having been given their say—of having been given a fair hearing.

This may help create increased legitimacy for the political system also. If people feel they have been given access to the political system—that their interests were fairly represented—they will more quickly accord legitimacy to the system and its decisions than they will if they feel ex-cluded from the whole political process.

At first glance it may appear that interest groups play a very minor role in conflict resolution. And, in fact, many of the conflicts that the political system's other institutions and processes must handle are caused by inter-est groups as they press their particular—and often clashing—demands. Interest groups do, however, contribute often to conflict resolution by softening or moderating demands that might otherwise be more extreme in nature. They do this because there are persons of different points of view within individual groups: within a labor union, for example, one may find black NAACP members and white Ku Klux Klan members. And within both the NAACP and the KKK, on the other hand, one may find both labor union members and businessmen. Thus, all three organizations—unions, the NAACP, and the KKK—often must either altogether avoid certain issues that would divide their members or considerably moderate their stands in order to keep their own membership together. The point is that, in the process, the political system's function of conflict resolution is made easier to perform because the demands being fed into it are not as sharply divergent as they otherwise would be.[3]

A Typology of Interest Groups

Because the interest groups active in Washington vary widely—from the National Association of Manufacturers to the Upper Colorado River Grass Roots, Incorporated—the task of classifying them into meaningful categories is difficult. Nevertheless, even a rough classification of the seemingly innumerable interest groups is helpful in gaining a deeper understanding of their scope and nature. Taking the type of interest being promoted as the discriminating factor, the following discussion divides interest groups into five of their possible categories.[4]

Economic Interest Groups

If someone were to ask an average American to name several interest groups, the chances are that he or she would name economic interest groups, for in this category are found the strongest and most successful, as well as those that receive the most publicity. These groups primarily operate to protect their members' economic self-interest. Here one finds the labor unions: the inclusive AFL-CIO; major independent unions, such as the Teamsters and United Auto Workers; individual unions affiliated with the AFL-CIO; and even individual locals. Business and management interest groups form a second class within this category: the National Association of Manufacturers; the Chamber of Commerce (the national organization as well as state and local organizations); and individual trade associations, such as the National Association of Electric Companies and the United States Savings and Loan League. Many individual corporations, such as General Motors and General Dynamics, are large enough to be individual interest groups in themselves.

3. For a more complete discussion of this point, see Truman, *The Governmental Process,* chap. 6.
4. For additional information on individual interest groups, see L. Harmon Zeigler and G. Wayne Peak, *Interest Groups in American Society,* 2d ed. (Englewood Cliffs, N.J.: Prentice-Hall, 1972), chaps. 9–10, and V. O. Key, *Politics, Parties and Pressure Groups,* 5th ed. (New York: Thomas Y. Crowell, 1964), chaps. 2–5.

The farm organizers form the third large class of organizations included in this category. The American Farm Bureau Federation, the National Grange, and National Farmers Union are the three major ones. There are also organizations for specific commodities, such as the American Milk Producers and the Peanut Growers Association.

Ideological Interest Groups

The least effective interest groups are likely to be ideological interest groups—groups whose members are motivated by their beliefs and values, not by hope of gaining economic or other tangible advantages. Included in this category are groups whose concerns cover a wide range of issues. Examples are the Americans for Democratic Action and—at the opposite end of the political spectrum—the John Birch Society. Also included are groups whose interests are narrower, such as the venerable Woman's Christian Temperance Union and the American Civil Liberties Union. Another important type of interest group falling into this category are churches—either individual denominations or associations of denominations—and organizations closely associated with or sponsored by churches. The National Council of Churches and the National Catholic Welfare Conference are two good examples.

Included in this category are a number of widely respected and influential interest groups, such as the American Civil Liberties Union and some of the church groups, but one also finds, as already noted, a disproportionately large number of groups that are almost totally ineffective. This is so because persons who are strongly motivated by ideals are often willing to go on battling for lost causes, and because these organizations are frequently made up of amateurs whose enthusiasm exceeds their knowledge of political realities.

Economic-Ideological Interest Groups

A number of groups mix in almost equal parts their ideological concerns and economic self-interest. Thus they really do not fit into either one of the first two categories. Most of the professional associations belong in this category. The American Medical Association, the American Bar Association, the National Education Association, and the American Association of University Professors are all excellent examples. All certainly are concerned with the economic self-interest of their members. The National Educational Association is concerned with salaries and therefore with governmental aid to education. And it would take an especially naïve person to believe that the American Medical Association's intransigent opposition to federal health insurance programs was born purely out of a desire to protect patients. Although the more cynically inclined may regard such groups as purely economic interest groups, they do appear to have genuine ideological concerns as well. There is no reason to write off the American Bar Association's concern with the quality of judges, the National Educational Association's concern with educational standards, and the American Medical Association's concern with medical school standards as examples of pure economic self-interest.

Much the same can be said for the veterans' organizations, such as the American Legion and the Veterans of Foreign Wars. Certainly they are concerned with economic issues like veterans' bonuses and other veterans' benefits; yet they are also concerned with broader ideological questions—patriotism, defense preparedness, and, on occasion, alleged communist infiltration of the schools or government.

Minority Interest Groups

There are also interest groups whose primary aim is to protect the interests of certain ethnic, racial, or religious minorities. The best known of these groups are those concerned with obtaining equality for blacks: the NAACP, the Urban League, the Southern Christian Leadership Conference, the Student Nonviolent Coordinating Committee, and the Congress of Racial Equality. Also included in this category are several groups designed to protect the interests of Jews. Best known is the Anti-Defamation League of B'nai B'rith, although its concerns are broad enough to justify its being placed in the ideological category as well. More recently several groups devoted to protecting the interests of Indians and Spanish-speaking Americans have come into being.

Formal Governmental Organizations

The interest groups in this last category are placed there not because of the type of interest they are promoting, but because of their special organizational basis. A wide variety of offices and other organizations are found within the formal structure of the political system. And with the American political system marked by an extreme decentralization of decision-making power, it is only natural that one part of the formal government will frequently try to influence the decisions of another. This most often takes the form of the attempt of a state, a city, or some other unit of local government to influence a decision of the federal government, or the attempt of an organization in the bureaucracy to influence Congress. Many executive agencies and state and local units of government have established sections with the specific task of lobbying (although the term "lobbying" is not used) in Congress or in other branches of the government.

Interest Group Power and Its Limitations

One hundred and one lobbyists and 38 congressmen, asked about the relative importance of lobbyists, the President, Congress, executive agencies, political parties, opinion leaders, and voters on the making of public policy, gave Lester Milbrath this information:

Most important for our purposes, only one lobbyist gives first rank importance to lobbying, and only five rate it second. Congressional respondents also accord very slight importance to lobbying in making public policy: about half of them, in fact, place lobbying at the bottom of the list. ... One lobbyist struggling with this question said: "I don't know where in the world I would fit the lobbyists as a group. Some of them have been up here for years battling for lost causes. On the whole, and speaking of all lobbyists in general, I think they are a lot less effective than most people believe."[5]

Milbrath later remarks: "Most careful observers of governmental decision-making have concluded that the over-all impact of lobbying is relatively minor."[6]

In contrast Marvin Levine, deputy county counsel for Santa Barbara, after attempting to win more stringent federal regulation of offshore oil wells, stated:

When I went into this fight to save the Bay from further oil pollution, I was really naïve. I thought it was *our* government—your government and my government— and that it wouldn't lie to us and that it would try to protect the people. Why, it acts like nothing but a major stockholder in the oil companies. Federal officials, the Corps of Engineers, the oil companies operate in league. The government won't even talk to you sometimes.[7]

In the face of such widely divergent assessments of the power of interest groups as these, it is difficult—yet imperative—to unravel the tangle of claim and counterclaim in order to arrive at a realistic assessment of interest group power.

The Basic Ingredients

The starting point for a clear understanding of interest group power and its limitations is the recognition that power or influence can best be defined as the ability to cause someone to do something he otherwise would not have done.[8] Thus the power of interest groups necessarily rests on two

5. Milbrath, *The Washington Lobbyists,* p. 352.

6. Milbrath, *The Washington Lobbyists,* p. 354.

7. Quoted in Robert Sherrill, *Why They Call it Politics* (New York: Harcourt, Brace, Jovanovich, 1972), p. 211.

8. "Power" is used here synonymously with "influence," although some theoreticians make a distinction between them. See the discussion of Robert A. Dahl, *Modern Political Analysis,* 2d ed. (Englewood Cliffs, N.J.: Prentice-Hall, 1970), pp. 14–34.

factors: (1) the resources of the political decision makers who are being subjected to influence attempts—resources with which they can resist those influence attempts, and (2) the resources at the disposal of the interest groups with which they can influence the political decision makers. Whether or not an interest group is able to win the policy decision it wishes from the decision makers depends upon the relative number and strength of the resources possessed by the decision makers and the interest group. Thus it is important to understand these potential resources.

Potential Resources of the Policy Makers

The Institutional Settings   There are three basic resources that the makers of public policies may have, which—when present—can be used to withstand influence attempts of interest groups. The first is the *institutional setting.* The institutional setting of a decision maker may be such that he or she is fairly well insulated from interest group pressures—or at least from the pressures of some interest groups.[9] Particularly judges—because of their long tenure and the prohibition against informal interest group contact with them—are to a large extent insulated from group influence attempts. Individual congressmen are largely insulated from the influence of certain groups by virtue of their constituencies. A representative from the plains of South Dakota is largely insulated from influence by the NAACP because of the absence of blacks in his constituency (although he will not, of course, be insulated from certain other groups such as the American Farm Bureau Federation). Thus the extent to which a political decision maker is insulated from group influence varies with the decision maker and the type of interest group.

Countervailing Interest Groups   The ability of policy makers to withstand interest group attempts at influence is also affected by the existence or absence of *countervailing interest groups.* Sometimes the demands made upon a political decision maker by one interest group are balanced by opposing demands being made on that same person by another interest group. Labor is opposed by management, business by environmentalists, mass transit advocates by the highway lobby. The efforts of one group are cancelled by the efforts of another. Thus when a political decision maker finds the demands for certain actions by one group balanced by demands for opposite actions by an opposing, equally powerful group, his or her hand is significantly strengthened.

Public Attentiveness   Public attentiveness to the policy makers and their actions is a third potential resource that can help them withstand interest

9. By the same token, of course, certain other decision makers may be particularly vulnerable to interest group influence because of the institutional setting in which they find themselves.

group influence attempts. *Public attentiveness* brings a wide variety of countervailing forces into play beyond that of countervailing interest groups. Public attention means that the press, key community or national leaders, influential persons in the presidency or even the President himself, congressmen, and officials in the executive agencies will be concerned with what actions the political decision maker takes. The possibility of exposure and ridicule—or alternatively of commendation and praise—is present. Thus interest groups are normally most effective when they can operate under the umbrella of public apathy and disinterest. Then the only demands coming to the decision maker are those of the interest group, and he or she knows that going along with the group will bring no condemnation, and resisting the group will bring no commendation.

Potential Resources of the Interest Groups

Size   There are four particularly important resources that interest groups can have. Whenever an interest group possesses all or most of these resources, it indeed is in a powerful position. The first such resource is *size*. Such mass organizations as the labor unions, farm organizations, and veterans' groups have an advantage over smaller groups simply by reason of sheer size. Milbrath found that the Washington lobbyists he interviewed tended to believe that the large-membership organizations were the most influential in Congress.[10] Their large size, for one thing, gives them opportunities to publicize their causes. The leader of an organization of 3 million people is going to be given greater attention by the mass media than the leader of 100,000.

Large groups also have the advantage of being potentially able to affect the outcome of elections by influencing the votes of their own members. One should be careful, however, not to exaggerate the extent to which interest groups can influence the votes of even their own members. Two political scientists, after surveying several studies, concluded: "A fair assessment of the influence of groups over their members' votes is that it is zero at worst and only minimal at best."[11] Even though the ability of groups to influence votes is far from complete, organizations can, however, normally influence them to some extent—and a congressman or President under pressure from them is never certain how many votes they will be able to swing against him.

Finally, large groups sometimes are able to raise large sums of money, even when their individual members are not affluent, by raising small amounts of money from a large number of people—and financial strength is an additional source of interest group power.

10. Milbrath, *The Washington Lobbyists,* p. 348.
11. Zeigler and Peak, *Interest Groups in American Society,* p. 123.

Prestige   The *prestige*—the standing or respect—of an interest group is a second potential resource that groups may possess. A generalized prestige—prestige accorded the group by most segments of the population—is the most helpful. Professional groups, such as the American Medical Association and the American Bar Association, rank high in prestige in the eyes of most persons because of the generally high status accorded physicians and lawyers in American society. But other groups, while perhaps not ranking high in general prestige, may still have high prestige in the eyes of certain segments of the population. The NAACP, for example, does not possess a high level of general prestige, but it no doubt has a high level of prestige in the eyes of many blacks and others dedicated to racial equality.

The prestige of an organization constitutes a resource in that it can open the door of access to key political decision makers, can help it gain desired publicity in the mass media, and can aid it in influencing the opinions and votes of the public. The greater and the broader (in the sense of the number of persons by whom the group is accorded prestige) the prestige of a group, the more this factor will work to its advantages.

The Financial Strength   The *financial strength* of an interest group is also an important resource. It can be used to hire able lobbyists, to make campaign contributions and perhaps bestow other favors on key decision makers, and to gain favorable public recognition (through professional public relations). Thus a group such as the National Association of Manufacturers has a resource in its financial strength that the National Welfare Rights Organization does not have.

Unity and Motivation   Finally, the *unity* and *motivation* of an interest group are also an important resource. A highly united organization composed of members thoroughly committed to the causes promoted by the group will be in a stronger position to influence decision makers than a fragmented group, composed of members only weakly committed to the group's causes. The leaders of a united, highly motivated group will much more easily be able to mobilize their members and their resources in support of the group's goals.

Interest Group Power: Conclusions

All this leaves the question of whether interest groups are all-dominant power blocs, able to cow policy makers into meek submission, or are one of several forces acting on policy makers, able only to persuade and plead. It is impossible to give a simple answer that covers all circumstances because the answer depends on the interest group and the policy area with which it is concerned. Some groups in some policy areas are almost totally impotent; other groups in other policy areas are clearly dominant. More often, interest groups possess influence—significant influence—yet are forced to compete with other influential forces to whom they sometimes lose and over whom they sometimes win.[12]

Interest Group Weakness   The lobbyist quoted by Milbrath earlier in this chapter made reference to groups "up here for years battling for lost causes."[13] There are many groups able to attract a hard core of dedicated followers, but unable to attract wide support. Because of the hard core, they continue in existence; because of the failure to attract wide support, they are unable to build the resources needed for effective lobbying. And because they often call for sharp departures from current policies, they frequently are opposed by other interest groups—or by simple inertia. Most of these groups fall into the ideological group category: groups like the John Birch Society, World Federalists, and Committee for a New Constitution come to mind. Because these groups are almost totally devoid of resources and because the decision makers normally possess at least one or two resources, their impact on policy outcomes is negligible.

Interest Group Influence   Most frequently interest groups have sufficient influence to compel the attention of decision makers and have an appreciable impact on policy outcomes, but fall short of having enough influence to dominate policy outcomes. This is true because groups typically fall short of possessing all four of their potential resources and decision makers rarely are without at least one or two resources.

Concerning interest group resources, the most prestigious groups tend to be small groups, composed of small, but prestigious occupational groups, such as physicians, lawyers, or bankers. And many large groups do not have large sums of money to spend: sometimes (as with the NAACP and National Council of Senior Citizens) because of the low incomes of their members and sometimes (as with some of the environmental and consumer groups) because their members lack the necessary motivation to give generously. For most persons, joining a group is a fairly marginal act, so that as a group's leadership attempts to raise their demands on their members' time or money, they are likely to meet resistance.[14]

12. This is the general conclusion many researchers have reached. See Milbrath, *The Washington Lobbyists;* Scott and Hunt, *Congress and Lobbies;* Donald R. Matthews, *United States Senators and Their World* (Chapel Hill, N.C.: University of North Carolina Press, 1960), chap. 8; Raymond A. Bauer, Ithiel de Sola Pool, and Lewis Anthony Dexter, *American Business and Public Policy: The Politics of Foreign Trade* (New York: Atherton, 1963), Part IV; James Q. Wilson, *Political Organizations* (New York: Basic Books, 1973), chap. 16; and Kenneth Entin, "Interest Group Communication with a Congressional Committee," *Policy Studies Journal,* 3 (1974), 147–150.

13. Milbrath, *The Washington Lobbyists,* p. 352.

14. Problems in creating and maintaining strong, vigorous organizations are explored later in this chapter.

Maintaining size, as well as unity and motivation, is a particularly difficult task. The national Chamber of Commerce is, for example, a large
group, but in attaining this size it has to include businessmen from many
different fields with many different interests. As one former employee of
the Chamber has stated: "The Chamber's main problem is to get the
interest of businessmen—men whose interests are so diffuse. . . . The
Chamber has to compete with lots of single-interest groups who have just
one axe to grind and can grind it all the time."[15] And another former
employee succinctly said: "The whole thing about the Chamber is that its
very existence shows that there isn't any 'industry-wide viewpoint' on
anything important."[16] The smaller trade associations such as the Retail
Druggists Association and individual corporations are able to achieve
greater unity—but they lose in size. In short, large organizations are rarely
united and united organizations are rarely large. About the only effective
way a large organization can maintain its unity is to limit severely the
number of issues in which it becomes involved. It is reduced to selecting
the one or two issues on which its membership agrees and then working
on these; to add more issues would divide the group and result in a lack
of support for the group or even loss of membership.

In short, it is difficult for an interest group to possess all four or even three
of the potential interest group resources.

On the other hand, decision makers are rarely left stripped of all resources of their own. Often their institutional setting offers them protection. The geographic basis of representation in Congress almost assures
that each congressman will be vulnerable to influence from certain interest
groups—the United Auto Workers for a congressman from a working-class
district in Detroit, the NAACP for a congressman from an inner-city district, and the American Farm Bureau for a congressman from a rural Iowa
district—but it also assures that a majority of congressman will rarely
be vulnerable to influence from any one interest group. The interest
groups just listed have institutional inroads to only a minority of congressmen.

Sometimes, however, a coalition of interest groups comes together to
press for a particular policy, as when automobile clubs, highway contractors, cement manufacturers, gasoline retailers, and oil companies all
come together to press for additional highway construction. In such situations a coalition may have institutional inroads to a majority or near majority of congressmen. But for this to happen the coalition has to be broad
enough and its membership committed enough to possess both the necessary contacts and the willingness to exploit them. (An interest group is

15. Quoted in Donald R. Hall, *Cooperative Lobbying: The Power of Pressure* (Tuscon,
Arizona: University of Arizona Press, 1969), p. 224.
16. Quoted in Hall, *Cooperative Lobbying,* p. 224.

careful not to go to the same congressmen too often, and thus it carefully picks the issues it really pushes.)

Judges and bureaucrats are partially protected by their nonelective positions, and the President by his nationwide constituency in which no one group (or even coalition of groups) is likely to be dominant. This is not meant to suggest that decision makers' institutional settings never make a majority of them in an institution vulnerable to powerful group or coalition of groups. It does occur. But it is the exception, not the rule.

Countervailing groups are normally present—although frequently an imbalance is created by a group on one side of an issue being opposed by a much weaker group. At times, however, an extreme imbalance is created when the efforts of one interest group are not countered by those of any opposing group at all. The existence of a bias in the interest group structure —which accounts for most of the imbalances in countervailing groups— is explored in the next section of the chapter.

Probably the decision maker resource most frequently missing is public attentiveness. Many decisions with strong policy implications are made— especially in the bureaucracy, but also in the presidency and in Congress —with the public only barely aware they are being made. In fact, an absence of public attentiveness is more likely than not to be the case.

In summary, interest groups typically possess one to three resources and decision makers one or two resources, a situation likely to lead to significant, yet limited, interest group influence.

Interest Group Dominance   An interest group or a coalition of interest groups is most likely to gain a preponderance of power when they possess several resources and the decision makers have neither countervailing groups nor public attentiveness going for them. Although such situations are not the norm, some highly significant exceptions do exist. Most frequently they take the form of a three-way mutually supportive relationship among an interest group, certain congressmen in key positions (usually members of the committee that handles most of the legislation with which the group is concerned), and the bureaucratic agency responsible for carrying out the policies of concern to the group. When this occurs, the interest group and the bureaucracy are supportive of each other, with the bureaucracy making decisions favorable to the interest group and urging favorable congressional action, and the interest group defending the bureaucracy from attacks from Congress, the presidency, or the press. Key congressmen are also drawn into this mutually supportive relationship, with the interest group giving them electoral support and other favors, and the congressmen acceding to the interest group's requests and supporting the bureaucracy's actions favorable to the interest group.

Normally at the heart of this three-way supportive relationship lies the interest group-bureaucracy relationship (rather than the interest group-

Congress relationship). The basic cause of the ability of interest groups to attain more frequently a close working relationship with a bureaucratic agency than with Congress lies in the specialized, technical nature of the decisions made by the individual bureaucratic offices. The individual bureaucrat is therefore likely to be under fewer countervailing pressures than the individual congressman. Various interest groups may be trying to influence a congressman on a given issue, whereas the bureaucrat who deals with relatively narrow questions is not as likely to be the center of the attention of several conflicting groups. And certainly when comparing Congress as a whole with an individual bureaucratic office, Congress is subjected to many more conflicting group pressures than the bureaucratic office. Frequently the only interest group paying attention to a bureaucratic office is the group most directly affected by its decisions.

The specific, technical nature of bureaucratic decisions also tends to decrease public attentiveness to them. Thus a second resource is taken from the bureaucratic decision makers. The net result is that the bureaucrat is under few countervailing pressures and thus is free to go along with the interest group.

Once a close working relationship has been established between an interest group and a bureaucratic office, key congressmen are then drawn in to create the three-way relationship. They are usually institutionally vulnerable congressmen, representing constituencies in which the interest group and its allied groups are strong. The three-way, mutually supportive relationship is then complete. The interest group, with what are now its allies in the bureaucracy and Congress, turn public policies to its advantage.

Examples of this type of relationship are not difficult to find: the dairy interest, the Department of Agriculture, and key Representatives and Senators on the agriculture committee is one; the transportation industry, the Interstate Commerce Commission, and certain Representatives and Senators on the commerce and banking committees is another.

The Bias of the Interest Group Structure

Political scientist E. E. Schattschneider once observed that "The business or upper-class bias of the pressure system shows up everywhere."[17] It is hard to deny the truth of this observation. The bias of the interest group structure arises from the fact that the resources discussed earlier are not distributed in random fashion to all types of interest groups, but rather tend to be concentrated in certain types of groups. The strongest groups tend, as Schattschneider indicated, to be business or upper-class groups. There

17. E. E. Schattschneider, *The Semisovereign People* (New York: Holt, Rinehart and Winston, 1960), p. 31.

are some nonbusiness and nonupper-class groups, however, that are also strong—the major labor unions, for example—but they remain the exceptions. The interests of the disadvantaged segments of the population, such as the poor, minority group members, and migrant farm laborers, and of very broad diffuse groups, such as consumers, the aged, and women, are not represented by any group at all or by comparatively weak groups.

A partial explanation for this bias is fairly easy to understand. Disadvantaged individuals have neither money nor prestige, while the upper-class and business groups have both prestige and money. But a complete explanation is not this easy. Some working-class groups, such as labor unions, the Ku Klux Klan, and some veterans groups, have achieved strong organizations. And many of the disadvantaged groups have large potential memberships, and the broad, diffuse groups especially have a potential for significant financial strength.

To understand the varying resources of groups and the bias this variation creates, it is helpful to understand a distinction that has been made between selective and collective benefits that group members can receive.[18] *Selective benefits* are benefits gained by a group that go only to the members of that group, whereas *collective benefits* are benefits gained by a group that go to all members of a category or class of persons whether or not they are members of the organized group. An example of a selective benefit is the lower price of food that members of a consumers cooperative pay; an example of a collective benefit is the higher standards of food purity that a consumers group wins from the government for all consumers.

It is not difficult to understand that selective benefits are more effective than collective benefits in holding a group together and eliciting membership support for it. When selective benefits are at stake, only group members will receive whatever benefits are won by the group, and therefore it is rational, in terms of one's self-interest, to join and work for the group. On the other hand, when collective benefits are at stake, people will receive the same benefits whether they are members of the group or not. Thus it really is not rational, in terms of self-interest, for them to invest time or money in the group. The only exception to this is when a group is composed of a few powerful persons or organizations, so that one dropping out could significantly reduce the chances of the group obtaining benefits. If, for example, the Ford Motor Company were to drop out of an organization of auto manufacturers, its doing so would seriously affect the ability of that organization to achieve its goals. Thus it would not be rational for Ford to drop out, even though the benefits are collective (that is, would go to all auto manufacturers).

18. See Mancur Olson, Jr., *The Logic of Collective Action* (Cambridge, Mass.: Harvard University Press, 1965) and Robert H. Salisbury, "An Exchange Theory of Interest Groups," *Midwest Journal of Political Science,* 13 (1969), 1–32.

In addition to the selective or collective nature of the benefits a group provides its membership, the available time and money of a group's potential membership affects the likelihood of persons joining. As the time and money an individual has available increases, the likelihood that he or she will be willing to spend them on a group that offers fairly weak benefits also increases. A basic fact of interest group life is that the strong, active groups—for the most part upper-class, business groups—tend to give selective benefits to their members, while the weak, sporadic groups tend to give only collective benefits to their membership. In addition, the potential memberships of the weak groups tend to be persons with less money and time to invest. As a result business and upper-class groups are more stable, are composed of more active members, and have more financial resources.

All business concerns pursue selective benefits in the form of profits. They seek as large a return as possible on the investments of their owners or stockholders. Thus such businesses as General Motors and Standard Oil would constitute strong organizations even if they had no desire to influence political decisions. This means that when they seek to influence political decisions, they already have strong, on-going organizations. Interest group activity becomes a side effect or spinoff from other activities even more basic to the existence of the organization. Most strong interest group organizations are of this type: they exist primarily to provide selective benefits to their members—influencing the political system is not their primary purpose.[19] The bias in the interest group structure thereby results from the fact that certain types of groups—particularly business groups—tend naturally to have stronger motives for organizing apart from political concerns than do certain other types of groups—particularly consumer and other groups defending broad, diffuse interests.

The individual oil companies are already organized when they enter the political arena seeking tax concessions and removal of price controls, but the gasoline and fuel-oil consumers have no on-going organization, for they have no real motive for organizing apart from the purely collective benefits they would gain by opposing the oil companies. In addition, oil companies' industrywide organizations tend to be strong, even though pursuing largely collective benefits, because they are composed of a relatively few, powerful oil companies. Thus each oil company knows that its failure to work hard in the organization could spell its defeat. An individual oil consumer, on the other hand, knows his withdrawal from an oil consumer group will have no real effect on that group's chances of success.

The examples could be multiplied—whether it be organized physicians compared with unorganized patients, organized lumbering interests com-

19. This point is particularly well developed by Olson, *The Logic of Collective Action,* chap. 6.

pared with poorly organized conservationists, or organized small loan companies compared with unorganized low-income families.

This bias ought not to be overstated, however. Sometimes working-class groups are able to organize on the basis of some very emotional issue, as are the KKK and antibusing groups. Sometimes diffuse or working-class groups can organize successfully on the basis of certain selective benefits they can offer their membership, as labor unions have done through higher wages and better working conditions; the National Rifle Association on the basis of cheaper ammunition, shooting contests, and a very emotional issue (gun control); the Sierra Club on the basis of campgrounds and wilderness trails; and some senior citizen clubs on the basis of social centers and group insurance plans. Then while the group membership is maintained by the selective benefits, the group leadership can lobby the political system for certain collective benefits such as minimum-wage legislation, no gun controls, wilderness preservation, or higher social security payments.

Recent years have seen the rise of a number of fairly successful groups seeking to protect general, diffuse interests and offering their membership largely collective benefits. Environmental groups like the Friends of the Earth come to mind, as do Common Cause and Ralph Nader and his "raiders."[20] Their strength and stability over a period of time remain to be tested, but they have had some notable successes. Nevertheless, the existence of an upper-class, business bias in the interest group structure remains. It is far from a total bias, but it is a very real tendency.

Saying that a bias exists in the interest group structure is not, however, the same as saying that a tightly knit, elite structure controls the American political system, as some have claimed. The interest group structure is open in that the bias results not from legal strictures, imposed by the upper-class business groups, but from the very nature of group organization. And the groups strengthened by the bias hardly constitute a tight clique. They often clash with each other, and their failures in influencing political decisions are not infrequent.[21]

Interest Group Power and Interest Representation

The foregoing discussions of interest group power and of the bias in the interest group structure have many crucial implications for the performance of the interest representation function. Whenever interest groups are powerful enough to impose their will on the policy makers without

20. On Common Cause, a self-styled "citizens' lobby," see John W. Gardner, *In Common Cause* (New York: Norton, 1972).

21. See, for example, their failure to persuade Congress to proceed with the subsidization of a supersonic transport, Congressional Quarterly, *The Washington Lobby* (Washington, D.C.: Congressional Quarterly, 1971), pp. 108–112.

regard to other forces, they greatly weaken democracy, for the often narrow interests of particular groups are then enacted into policy irrespective of the demands coming from other segments of the population. Interest groups are then no longer merely representing or giving voice to interests in the political system—they themselves are in effect making the authoritative policies. But the normal situation, as seen earlier, is for interest groups to have a limited degree of influence. Although there are exceptions, some very significant ones, interest groups are usually reduced to persuading, pleading, and competing with a host of other forces. As a result, democracy is promoted because the interests represented in the political system by a variety of interest groups and other forces reflect the wide range of demands present in the general population.

The bias of the interest group structure means that interest groups do not give fair and equal representation to all significant interests present in American society. Some are more effectively represented than others. This does not mean, however, that interests poorly represented through interest groups are necessarily not represented at all in the political system (although they may not be). They may find themselves being represented by other means—parties who nominate candidates who speak to their concerns, for example, or congressmen or bureaucratic officials who address themselves to their concerns—but they are undeniably in a weaker position because of the bias in the interest group structure.

This bias may affect the success with which the interest group structure generates support and creates legitimacy for the political system. Persons who feel left out in terms of the interest group structure will suffer a loss of feelings of efficacy, concluding that the political system is impenetrable. "No one in government cares about the problems of folks like us." Unless other structures in the political system make up for the deficiencies of the interest group structure, a loss in support and legitimacy would seem to be the inevitable result.

Methods of Influence

All interest groups, as we have seen, can possess certain resources: members, financial strength, prestige, and unity and motivation. Yet having resources is not the same as having influence: resources must be translated into actual influence. The methods by which interest groups attempt to accomplish this transformation are explored in this section.

Basic Patterns

The Question of Shady Dealings   Professor Donald Matthews tells the story of a Washington lobbyist who once overheard a conversation between two women while he was in the Senate waiting room. One woman, evidently a Washingtonian, was showing a second woman, who appeared to be a tourist, through the capitol building.

"That's Senator _____," the Washingtonian whispered to her friend, "and that,"—indicating the man with whom the Senator was in deep conversation—"is _____, the lobbyist for what's-its-name."

"Oooh!" responded the tourist. "Is he bribing him now?"[22]

The notion of lobbyists and lobbying as somewhat shady is not limited to naïve tourists. To many persons, their methods of influence consist simply of buying the person to be influenced. But all the available evidence indicates that outright bribery is rare in national politics, if for no other reason than that the danger of being exposed is too great.

The extent to which interest groups use more subtle forms of bribery is difficult to determine, both because of problems in uncovering the facts and because of differences of opinion on what constitutes bribery. This indirect bribery—if it is to be considered bribery—comes in a variety of forms. Contributions by interest groups and individual members of interest groups to election campaigns are fully accepted as being legitimate, even though one can question whether or not influence is being bought in the process. But contributions to congressmen for their personal use are not considered proper. Former Senator Dodd of Connecticut was formally censured by the Senate in 1968 for spending campaign contributions for his personal use.

In addition, interest groups can attempt to create *conflicts of interest*— situations in which the decision maker has a personal stake in a decision he must make or in which he may feel indebted to an interest group that will be affected by his decisions. The 1972 revelations that International Telephone and Telegraph had offered the Republican Party $400,000 toward their convention expenses at the same time the Justice Department was reaching a favorable out of court settlement with it raised conflict-of-interest questions, as did the disclosure that three dairy cooperatives pledged $400,000 to the re-election campaign of Nixon at the same time the Nixon administration was reaching a decision to raise price supports paid to milk producers.[23] Corporation planes are often made available to congressmen. Conflict-of-interest problems are also raised by the fact that many of the 300 congressmen who are lawyers maintain holdings in law partnerships in their home towns. Thus, interest groups can indirectly bribe —if that is what it is—congressmen by giving their business to congressmen's law firms. "Some of the biggest corporate names in America are

22. Matthews, *United States Senators and Their World,* p. 176.
23. For more information on these controversies see *Congressional Quarterly Weekly Report,* 30 (March 11, 1972), 519–524, 564–567, and Congressional Quarterly, *Watergate: Chronology of a Crisis,* Vol. II (Washington, D.C.: Congressional Quarterly, 1974), pp. 179–259.

listed as clients of congressmen's law firms in such out-of-the-way places, say, as Nicholasville, Kentucky, and Pascagoula, Mississippi. . . . The Travelers Corporation, for one, has retained legal counsel in such unlikely places as Piqua and Findley, Ohio, where the company's political radar led them straight to the law firms of Representative William McCulloch and Jack Betts, respectively."[24]

In summary, outright, crass bribery is virtually nonexistent. Conflict-of-interest problems do exist, however, as gifts and favors are offered, the line between what is proper and what is not being hazy and in dispute. Ethically questionable attempts at influence will, no doubt, not be effective with persons opposed to a group's position. Such persons are likely to react very negatively to any indirect "bribery" attempts. Instead, ethically questionable attempts at influence are more likely to be used to reinforce the tendencies of persons already favorably disposed toward a group.

Influencing Personnel Selection   Probably the most effective means of influencing the decisions of the political system is to influence the selection of the individuals making the decisions. If a key decision maker is favorably predisposed toward a group's interests, all the group has to do is reinforce and channel these predispositions. If, on the other hand, the same decision maker is hostile to the group's interests, it will be nearly impossible to influence him or her. In fact, as will be seen shortly, the basic strategy of most interest groups is largely to work with and through those decision makers favorable to them. Thus, the success of a group mainly turns on the number of persons in decision-making positions who are favorably inclined toward it and its cause.

In the case of elective decision-making positions, interest groups may attempt to influence the selection of personnel by supporting candidates favorable to their cause. Exactly what form this support takes depends on the group and its characteristics. A large-membership group may concentrate on getting its own members to vote for a particular candidate and on providing volunteer canvassers and other campaign workers. A small but prestigious group may simply publicize its endorsement of a candidate. Or a financially powerful group may contribute campaign funds. By such means, interest groups can sometimes affect the outcome of elections, yet their actual impact ought not to be exaggerated. Usually, only a limited number of marginal votes are changed by interest group support.

Interest groups can sometimes also affect the nomination of candidates. This is especially true in areas where a large, powerful group has strong influence in one of the parties, as in some areas labor unions have in the Democratic party, and in other areas farm or business organizations have in the Republican party.

24. Drew Pearson and Jack Anderson, *The Case Against Congress* (New York: Simon and Schuster, 1968), p. 104.

In this case of appointive positions, as in the bureaucracy or judiciary, interest groups must influence the appointing official—either the President or an executive in the bureaucracy. In influencing such individuals, the standard means of lobbying (which are discussed later) are used. A variety of contacts and avenues are used to get through to the appointing official the suggestion that "these are able, deserving persons."

Interest groups seem to be the most effective in influencing the selection of persons to fill key positions in the bureaucracy. The absence of public attention works to their advantage here. Not many newspaper headlines are made by the appointment of someone to the Federal Power Commission or the Interstate Commerce Commission. Thus in making such appointments the President—or his underlings who normally make the actual choices—has little to worry about in terms of close press scrutiny and negative public reactions if they go along with the appointment of persons having close ties with the very interest they will be regulating. In addition, bureaucratic positions often require a certain amount of expertise in the field in which the person will be working. Often, therefore, persons are tapped who have had years of experience with—and thus probably a favorable attitude toward—the very interest he or she as a bureaucratic will be regulating. Top executives in the bureaucracy often come from backgrounds in the very interest they will be regulating and after serving in the bureaucracy go back to a job with that same interest. Table 6.1 shows the current occupations of the eleven commissioners leaving the Interstate Commerce Commission in the years before 1970. All were either retired or were employed by the very transportation industry the Interstate Commerce Commission regulates.

Influencing Public Opinions   Probably the least effective means of influencing decisions are the attempts to influence public opinions; yet, interest groups seem unable to resist the temptation to resort to this tactic. At times the goal is a short-range one: to alter the opinions of the public so that it will support a specific course of action desired by the interest group, in the hope that the decision makers will then follow these opinions. But it is doubtful whether groups can influence the public's opinions on specific issues to any appreciable degree, and even if they can, it is still doubtful whether decision makers would readily respond to the altered public opinions.

More realistic is the hope that public opinions can be neutralized. In this case the interest group attempts to create, through a continuing, long-range campaign, a generally favorable image of itself—or at least tries to eliminate strong negative images. Then, when other methods of influence are used, especially lobbying, the interest group is not handicapped by the decision makers' fears of negative reactions from opinion leaders if they go along with it. Recent attempts by some oil companies and other busi-

Table 6.1   Employment status of the last eleven commissioners to leave the Interstate Commerce Commission

Owen Clarke, left 1958
  Vice-President, C&O–B&O Railroad
Robert W. Minor, left 1958
  Senior Vice-President, Penn Central Co.
Anthony Arpaia, left 1960
  Vice-President, REA Express, now retired
John H. Winchell, left 1960
  Now retired, Washington, D.C.
Donald McPherson, left 1962
  ICC practitioner,[a] Washington, D.C.
Clyde E. Herring, left 1964
  ICC practitioner, Washington, D.C.
Abe M. Goff, left 1967
  Now retired, Moscow, Idaho
Everett Hutchinson, left 1965
  ICC practitioner, Washington, D.C.
Howard Freas, left 1966
  Assistant to the President, Southern Railway System
Charles Webb, left 1967
  President, National Association of Motor Bus Operators, Washington, D.C.
William H. Tucker, left 1967
  Vice-President, Penn Central Co.

[a] An ICC practitioner is someone who represents the interest of regulated industries before the administrative and judicial proceedings of the ICC.

Source: Robert C. Fellmeth, *The Interstate Commerce Omission: The Public Interest and the ICC* (New York: Grossman, 1970), pp. 20–21.

ness concerns to create images of themselves as being deeply concerned over the environment and actively at work preventing pollution is an example. The hope, no doubt, is to build public confidence in Texaco's or Gulf's or some other company's public-spirited concern with the quality of the environment. Then, when the company becomes embroiled in an environmental controversy, the public will more easily accept its claims. Public opinions will have been effectively neutralized. But even these attempts rest on the ability of an interest group to change public attitudes toward itself—a difficult task at best.

The methods used by interest groups to influence opinions range from overt means, such as newspaper advertising and billboards, to more subtle ones, such as planting articles in magazines and sponsoring public service television programs.

Lobbying

Once the individuals filling the decision-making positions have been determined and public opinions have crystallized, the context within which an interest group must work has been established. The givens are there, and the group must do the best it can within the bounds set. This is where lobbying enters in—that is, influencing the decisions made by the political system's decision makers. Lobbying methods vary somewhat from one institution of the political system to another. Therefore, the following section discusses some of the basic approaches to lobbying used in each of the four major institutions of the political system.

Congress   There are two public and two private means of influencing congressmen.[25] The public means are of doubtful effectiveness; the private can be very effective. One public means of influence is testifying at formal hearings conducted by a committee on pending legislation. A lobbyist himself may testify at these hearings, but, especially on important issues, he may go to great lengths to arrange for key, prestigeful officers of the interested group—or, at the other extreme, for ordinary, everyday members of the interest group—to give testimony before the committee.[26] The usual ineffectiveness of this approach results from the fact that most congressmen are committed ahead of time to one position or the other, as well as from the fact that the witnesses often do not give the congressmen the type of information they want or need. In fact, these hearings often give the appearance of a ritual that the committees' members go through because it is expected of them, rather than frank attempts to gain information to help them make up their minds. Often hearings are used more as attempts to influence public opinions than to influence congressmen—who probably have already heard everything the witnesses have to say.

A second public means of influence is the stimulated letter-writing campaign. Members of the interest group are urged to flood Congress with letters in the hope that Congress will listen. This strategy rests on giving the appearance to congressmen that their constituents are aroused and concerned that a certain action be taken (or not taken). But as soon as a congressman realizes that the flood of letters coming in is a result of a letter-writing campaign organized by some interest group, much of its force is lost. If a Senator receives 10,000 spontaneous letters in one week, urging a certain action by him, he probably will be impressed, assuming that this is an indication of a strong swing in sentiment back home. But if he receives 10,000 stimulated letters, he is likely to discount them, assuming that even a small interest group of 20,000 members might get at least

25. For more complete discussions of methods of influence used by interest groups in Congress, see Clapp, *The Congressman,* chap. 4; Matthews, *United States Senators and Their World,* chap. 8: Zeigler and Peak, *Interest Groups in American Society,* chap. 6; and Bauer et al., *American Business and Public Policy,* Part V.

26. This has a side advantage for the lobbyist in that he can impress the officers of the interest group—who have hired and pay him—with his contacts and effectiveness. A lobbyist's first job is to convince the interest group he is representing that he is earning his pay.

one half of its members to write. Thus those letters do not represent a widespread sentiment in his state and are not likely to be very influential.

But this leaves two private means of influence used by interest groups that, when pursued by the skillful lobbyist, can result in a significant amount of influence for the group. They normally form the core of lobbying efforts by the well-established, major interest groups. First, the skillful lobbyist attempts to build long-standing relationships of trust, respect, and perhaps even friendship between himself and certain congressmen. The congressmen with whom a lobbyist selects to build this type of relationship are those favorable toward the group's interests and in key positions in Congress, having, for example, membership on a committee to which most of the legislation with which the group is concerned goes. Because of the favorable attitude of these congressmen toward the group there is some hope of achieving a favorable relationship, and because of their key positions they are in a position to help the interest group. As one lobbyist expressed it: "I do not attempt to contact a large number of congressmen and senators. I concentrate on a few men, strategically placed on the Appropriations Committees. These men are economy minded and are generally in sympathy with our political outlook."[27]

To build a relationship of trust and respect the lobbyist must play a certain role that the informal rules of Congress have established for him.[28] The heart of these informal rules is to treat congressmen honestly and courteously and to be well informed. The quickest ways for a lobbyist to ruin his reputation and his influence is to give false information, not to know his field well, or to act condescendingly toward congressmen or to be discourteous in other ways. The essential thing the lobbyist must provide is information—information on the content of a bill, on its probable effect on a congressman's constituency, on its probable effect on a particular economic group, and so forth.

Over a period of years the careful, capable lobbyist can build up a favorable reputation with a number of congressmen, who will then be willing to listen to him and to consider in a favorable light what he has to say. Then, when a specific issue comes up, the lobbyist can go to the congressmen he knows well and lay his case before them. If he has laid the groundwork well, the chances are good that he will be successful in winning their support.

But even if he is able to persuade to his position these congressmen he knows well, that normally will not be enough go achieve his goal, since each lobbyist can know only a limited number of congressmen well. The second private means of influencing congressmen consists of at least three indirect methods of getting at congressmen with whom the lobbyist does not have a close working relationship: to have the congressmen whom the

27. Quoted in Matthews, *United States Senators and Their World,* p. 181.
28. Especially helpful on this point is Milbrath, *The Washington Lobbyists,* pp. 286–294.

lobbyist knows well and who agree with him on the issue approach their colleagues and attempt to persuade them; to work with sympathetic interest groups in order to have their lobbyists reach the congressmen they know well; and to work through persons in the bureaucracy favorable to the interests of the group in order to have them reach congressmen.

The degree of success a lobbyist achieves by pursuing these methods depends in part on the nature of the group he is representing. For the size, unity, and prestige of the group will help determine with how many and which congressmen he will be able to develop close working relationships. And these same group characteristics help determine how successful he is likely to be in winning the support of others needed to reach additional congressmen indirectly. A close union between a skillful lobbyist and a powerful interest group is normally needed if the group is to exert its full influence on Capitol Hill.

The Bureaucracy   The methods used by interest groups in influencing the bureaucracy are very similar to those used in influencing Congress.[29] Various formal means of influence are available that are similar to the hearings of congressional committees. Sometimes interest groups are even given representation on official advisory boards. On occasion interest groups may attempt to stimulate mail to a certain bureaucratic office in the hope of obtaining a favorable decision, but this is much more frequently done with Congress.

It is the careful cultivation of close, working relationships with appropriate bureaucrats that has done the most to give interest groups their influence in the bureaucracy—probably a greater influence than they have in any other branch of government. This tactic is pursued in the same manner as it is in Congress, but usually with more success. As seen earlier in the chapter, the basic reason for frequent interest group success in the bureaucracy is the specialized, technical nature of the decisions made by the individual bureaucratic offices, the fewer countervailing groups, and less public attentiveness that results.

As they do in Congress, lobbyists often use indirect means to influence bureaucrats they cannot influence directly. Congress, other bureaucrats, the President, and other lobbyists are possible indirect means.

The Presidency   Interest groups that wish to influence the presidency face a problem that is not as severe when they are attempting to influence Congress or the bureaucracy: access. With a little effort and persistence a lobbyist can normally obtain at least a hearing with a congressman or

29. For more complete discussions of methods of influence used by interest groups in the bureaucracy, see Marver H. Bernstein, *The Job of the Federal Executive* (Washington, D.C.: Brookings Institution, 1958), chap. 6; Truman, *The Governmental Process,* chaps. 13 and 14; and Louis M. Kohlmeier, *The Regulators* (New York: Harper & Row, 1969), chap. 6.

a bureaucrat. But the same lobbyist may face an impossible situation in trying to obtain a hearing with the President or even with one of his close advisers. This fact, plus the fact that the presidency is subjected to the widest possible variety of countervailing forces, makes the presidency the institution in which interest groups probably have the hardest time lobbying successfully. Actually, their best tactic is to influence the selection of the President.

Nevertheless, interest groups attempt to lobby the presidency and sometimes do so with success. Assuming they have not alienated him in the past, the leaders of the largest, most prestigeful groups can normally obtain an appointment directly with the President himself. Roy Wilkins of the NAACP and George Meany of the AFL-CIO are examples. For them access is not a major problem, but most groups must use indirect channels to reach the presidential ear, and even the largest groups must supplement their brief interviews with the President with indirect contacts. Some groups may be able to obtain a hearing with one of the top presidential aides and hope that he will plead their case before the President. An influential congressman, a cabinet member, or other high-ranking executive officials are also frequently used as indirect channels to the President. Thus the problem of the interest group is frequently reduced to winning the support of an influential person, who in turn may be able to influence the President. Hardly a procedure likely to result in high interest group influence with the President!

The Judiciary   Interest groups attempting to influence the judiciary also face the problem of access.[30] The political mores of the United States forbid lobbyists to approach judges directly. For a lobbyist to arrange a private meeting with a key senator or a top executive official is accepted as proper, but such a meeting with a Supreme Court justice or other judge is looked on as a breach of ethics. Stimulating a letter-writing campaign to judges considering a certain case is viewed as equally improper.

Yet interest groups wishing to influence the courts are not without recourse. The most common one is sponsoring a test case in the court system. An interest group that wants the courts to make a certain decision selects a case that raises the question it wants decided, being careful to select one that presents its side in the best light. The group then hires the lawyers, pays the court fees, and does anything else needed to take the case through the court system—an expensive and time-consuming process if the case is appealed up through several courts.

Another formal means of influencing the judiciary is by filing *amicus curiae* briefs in cases that a group is interested in. These briefs, which are

30. For more complete discussions of methods of influence used by interest groups in the judiciary, see Clement E. Vose, "Litigation as a Form of Pressure Group Activity," *The Annals of the American Academy of Political and Social Science,* 319 (1958), 20–31; and Zeigler and Peak, *Interest Groups in American Society,* chap. 8.

discussed in Chapter 10, give an interest group the formal opportunity to express its opinions and to give additional information to the judiciary.

In addition to these formal means of influencing the judiciary, a few indirect means of influence may be available to an interest group. One is to obtain favorable publicity for the group and its cause, hoping to create a climate of opinion that will make it easier for the courts to make a favorable decision. This tactic takes into account the courts' sensitivity to the general tenor of the times, which is discussed in Chapter 10. Another indirect tactic used occasionally is to persuade scholars to write articles in law journals that support the case of the group. This has a twofold purpose: the judges may read these articles and be influenced by them; moreover, the articles may be cited in briefs filed in future test cases in order to give greater weight. But the effectiveness of such indirect methods of influence remains very problematical—the test case is clearly the interest groups' strongest weapon in influencing the judiciary.

This chapter rejects the image of interest groups as all-powerful organizations that cow decision makers into submission. Although some interest groups in dealing with some policy makers attain this sort of power, most interest groups in dealing with most policy makers do not. Interest groups are usually forced into competing with other interest groups and a variety of other forces to influence the policy decisions. Sometimes they are successful, sometimes not. Although some interests are not adequately represented by interest groups—especially broad, diffuse interests and those of the lower social and economic groups—they do represent a wide range of interests, and as a result, on balance, they increase the public's impact on public policy making and at the same time help build support and legitimacy for the political system.

Some Exploratory Questions

1. What changes could be made in the bureaucracy to make it less vulnerable to interest group influence?

2. Does the chief blame for the bias in the interest group structure lie with the political system itself, with the general public and its often selfish concerns, or in the very nature of groups and group life?

3. To what extent can mass demonstrations and perhaps even civil disobedience serve as alternatives to interest group activity by minorities and other disadvantaged groups who are not organized into effective interest groups?

Bibliographical Essay

Two very helpful general works on American interest groups are L. Harmon Zeigler and G. Wayne Peak, *Interest Groups in American Society,* 2d ed. (Englewood

Cliffs, N.J.: Prentice-Hall, 1972) and David B. Truman, *The Governmental Process* (New York: Knopf, 1951). A briefer, paperback book also presents a helpful, general picture of interest groups: Abraham Holtzman, *Interest Groups and Lobbying* (New York: Macmillan, 1966). Two more theoretical considerations of interest groups are found in Mancur Olson, Jr., *The Logic of Collective Action* (Cambridge, Mass.: Harvard University Press, 1965) and James Q. Wilson, *Political Organizations* (New York: Basic Books, 1973).

Discussions of the place of interest groups in the American political system are found in E. E. Schattschneider, *The Semisovereign People* (New York: Holt, Rinehart and Winston, 1960); the Truman book cited earlier; and Arthur Bentley, *The Process of Government* (Chicago: University of Chicago Press, 1908).

An excellent picture of interest groups and their lobbying activities is presented by a study of the efforts of business groups to influence decisions concerning trade policies. See Raymond A. Bauer, Ithiel de Sola Pool, and Lewis Anthony Dexter, *American Business and Public Policy: The Politics of Foreign Trade* (New York: Atherton, 1963). Helpful in illuminating the activities and influence of lobbyists is the excellent study by Lester Milbrath, *The Washington Lobbyists* (Chicago: Rand McNally, 1963). On interest group influence in Congress, see Andrew M. Scott and Margaret A. Hunt, *Congress and Lobbies* (Chapel Hill, N.C.: University of North Carolina Press, 1966).

On the methods of lobbying used by interest groups in the various institutions of the political system, one should consult the Truman and the Zeigler and Peak works cited earlier, as well as the books cited in the bibliographical essays of the chapters dealing with the specific institutions.

For a survey of specific interest groups, see the section on interest groups in V. O. Key, *Politics, Parties and Pressure Groups,* 5th ed. (New York: Thomas Y. Crowell, 1964). There are not very many good studies devoted to specific interest groups. But see Seymour Martin Lipset, Martin Trow, and James S. Coleman, *Union Democracy* (New York: The Free Press, 1956); and John W. Gardner, *In Common Cause* (New York: Norton, 1972). Judith G. Smith, ed., *Political Brokers* (New York: Liveright, 1972) is a collection of individual articles describing a number of different interest groups. On the attempts of state and local governments to lobby the federal government, see Donald H. Haider, *When Governments Come to Washington* (New York: The Free Press, 1974).

There are several anthologies with many good selections on interest groups. See Sanford A. Lakoff, ed., *Private Government* (Glenview, Ill.: Scott, Foresman, 1973) and Robert H. Salisbury, ed., *Interest Group Politics in America* (New York: Harper & Row, 1970).

The Major Political Institutions

The Politics of Policy Making

Part Three

Introduction
to Part Three

The television technicians counted down the time in a detached, professional manner and then signaled to the tense, haggard man sitting behind a large oak desk that he was on the air. President—and soon-to-be former President—Richard Milhouse Nixon began: "Good evening. This is the thirty-seventh time I have spoken to you from this office. . . ." Thus the thirty-seventh President of the United States, elected less than two years earlier by one of the widest margins in history, became the first President ever to resign his office. His doing so had an obvious, immediate impact on the political system as the presidency was turned over to Gerald Ford and the persons he brought with him.

But the impact on the American political system of the sordid corruptions and abuses that were part of the Watergate scandal goes far beyond the simple replacement of Richard Nixon by Gerald Ford as President. The presidency, Congress, the bureaucracy, and the judiciary were all deeply affected by Watergate. They will never be the same. The balance of power among them—especially between Congress and the presidency—and the balances of power within them have been altered.

And the bottom line reads—to succumb to some of the White House jargon made familiar by Watergate—that the policy-making processes of American politics have been altered. The contributions made by the various decision-making structures of American politics and the internal processes by which the various structures determine what their contributions will be have been altered. Part Three explores the basic policy-making institutions and structures of American politics and in the process examines how they have been affected by the wrenching events of recent years.

To have the perspective needed to analyze and understand these policy-making structures we must recall that, as was stressed in Chapter 1, the policy-making process ought to be represented by a circle, not a straight line. For a straight line implies that in any particular policy area policy alternatives are considered, one is adopted, and policy making thereupon ends in that area. A circle, on the other hand, implies that policy making is a continuous process with neither beginning nor end and with each stage of the policy-making process being affected by what came before it and affecting what comes after it.

Part Two examined the basic means and mechanisms by which inputs are fed into the American political system. It thereby considered the source and nature of the numerous demands and pressures put on the system. As we saw in Chapter 1, it is these demands and pressures that the political system, by a series of conversion functions, transforms into policy outputs. The first of these conversion functions—*interest representation*—has already been explored in Part Two. We have seen how political parties and interest groups take the welter of opinions and predispositions present in society and channel them— sometimes ably and sometimes poorly—into the political system. But now the policy alternatives that are thereby put before the political system's decision-making structures must be shaped and molded into actual policy outputs. This transformation is done by the four political institutions or structures considered in Part Three: the presidency, Congress, the bureaucracies, and the judiciary. Within these institutions the policy alternatives channeled into the political system by the interest representation function considered in Part Two are converted into actual policy outputs through the three remaining conversion functions: *rule initiation, rule application,* and *rule interpretation.*

It is essential to consider two questions of particular importance if we are to grasp the nature of the processes by which the conversion functions transform inputs into actual policy outputs. The first question has two parts: Which political structures perform these conversion functions, and what is the nature of the processes by which they do so? And how have these processes been altered by the fallout from the traumatic Watergate scandal?

The second crucial question grows out of the elite nature of the political structures that perform the conversion functions. Relatively small groups of highly educated, well-paid, largely white males make the actual decisions by which the conversion functions are performed. Thus the question that begs for exploration is whether these elite groups of decision makers respond largely to their own private views, to those of parallel elites in business and industry, or to those dominant within the general population. Part Two, exploring the means by which demands flow to the political decision makers in a compelling manner, gave a partial answer to this question. Part Three completes the answer, as it considers the political structures that perform the three remaining conversion functions—rule initiation, rule application, and rule interpretation—and the sources of the demands to which the decision makers who perform these functions respond.

Chapter 7   **The**   The Politics of
               Presidency   Leadership

Of the seven Presidents who have held office in the past forty years two died in office (one by assassination), two left office in the midst of unpopular wars with their personal popularity at very low levels, and one was forced to resign in the midst of a scandal. Only Dwight Eisenhower left office in good health and with his public esteem intact. Thus we might easily agree with Woodrow Wilson, who once declared that the presidency "requires the constitution of an athlete, the patience of a mother, the endurance of an early Christian," or with Warren Harding, who once expressed a similar sentiment much more succintly: "God, what a job!"[1]

In fact the demands of the presidency are great: within the space of a single week the President may be called upon to decide whether or not to extend diplomatic recognition to a new foreign government, to send American troops into a troubled area of the world, to intervene in a threatened strike, and to use nationwide television to plead for support for a new attack on inflation. It is difficult to think of any area of national political life where the President's hand does not reach, whether it is a congressional committee's deliberations; the American embassy in Lagos, Nigeria; the Pentagon's procurement office; or his party's national committee. It is this office, the presidency, which reaches into all parts of the political system and struggles with questions of immeasurable importance, that we shall explore in this chapter, attempting to discover the essence of its nature and why it is as it is.

But first the meaning of several terms must be clarified. The President can be distinguished from the presidency in that the President is, of course, the single individual holding the office of President, whereas the presidency refers to all those persons who are directly involved in helping the President perform his functions. This chapter is concerned, as the title

1. Both quotations are from Arthur B. Tourtellot, *Presidents on the Presidency* (Garden City, N.Y.: Doubleday, 1964), pp. 363, 366.

indicates, with the *presidency,* or, as it can also be called, *the presidential subsystem.*

We should also note that the presidency is not the same as the executive branch of government. The presidency is included in the executive branch, but the executive branch also includes the general bureaucracy. To consider the President and a trial examiner of the National Labor Relations Board or a research analyst for the Department of Agriculture or others of millions of bureaucrats as part of the same subsystem is clearly not warranted. The functions they perform are so different that it makes much better analytic sense to treat them as members of different subsystems, even though on an organization chart (and legally) the President is the head of the bureaucracy. Thus this chapter is concerned only with the presidential subsystem—the presidency—not with the many subsystems that compose the bureaucracy. They are considered in Chapter 9.

The Functions of the Presidency

The President, as one observer has expressed it, "wears many hats." His job is, in fact, many jobs. His activities are as broad as government itself as he battles Congress, extends diplomatic recognition to a new foreign government, settles a petty partisan squabble, and lights the traditional White House Christmas tree. With the President involved in so many activities—with his, in effect, holding so many different jobs—it appears difficult to pick out any single basic function of the presidency.

Exerting Leadership

Yet, after some thought, what appeared difficult is really not difficult at all: The basic function that runs as a thread through the host of specific activities the President engages in is *exerting leadership*—giving direction and guidance in pursuit of certain self-conscious goals. The President is, above all else, a leader, a chief, a catalyst. He sets the goals that he feels the political system should attain—and then exhorts and prods the necessary individuals in order to achieve these goals. The presidency can be detected at virtually every stage of policy making. Most of Congress's time is spent in debating the program of legislation proposed and promoted by the presidency—and often it is the presidency that gets Congress off dead center. The Pentagon unperturbedly goes on its routine way; presidential intervention is necessary to change its course and presidential initiative is required to order its armed forces into action or to withdraw them from action. In times of crisis—whether it is 1941 and the attack on Pearl Harbor, or the late 1970s and severe energy shortages—the nation looks to the President for guidance; it expects him to take the lead in expressing the sentiments of the nation and in proposing courses of action. In short, the distinguishing, fundamental function of the presidency is the exercise of leadership.

Although presidential leadership reaches virtually all parts of the policy-making processes, seven areas in which the President exerts leadership are most frequently cited: (1) the Congress, where the President proposes new initiatives, prods for action, and threatens vetoes; (2) the bureaucracy, where the President exercises his constitutional mandate "to take care that the laws be faithfully executed"; (3) the armed forces, where the President is under the Constitution the commander-in-chief; (4) the judiciary, where the President appoints all federal judges; (5) American society more generally, where the President serves as the symbol of the government and calls the nation to greater efforts; (6) the President's own political party, of which he is the generally acknowledged head; and (7) the world beyond the United States, through his dominant role in the forming of American foreign policy.

The importance of this leadership function of the presidency lies in a tendency for other American political institutions—and especially Congress—to attempt to establish a harmony or a balance among contending forces.[2] Often the resolution of conflicts in such a way as to satisfy the greatest number of persons and interests is viewed as the highest good. This means compromise and accommodation. The net result is *incrementalism,* or incremental change; minor, marginal adjustments are made in current policies in the attempt to win the support of those advocating change while not alienating those opposed to it.

This politics of accommodation—which is explored more fully in Chapter 8—has certain positive advantages for the political system and society. The political system and the course it sets for society are not marked by wild fluctuations: stability is maintained. And most persons and interests are—to a greater or lesser degree—satisfied with the decisions of the political system: support is thereby maintained. But the politics of accommodation also means that the political system tends to react slowly to changing circumstances and new demands. And in a rapidly changing environment the political system must sometimes react rapidly. Injustices may remain for years as the political system slowly—in incremental fashion—addresses itself to them.

In the light of the nature—and especially the disadvantages—of the politics of accommodation, the leadership function of the presidency stands out. For the presidency is the chief political institution with the power, force, and drive necessary to overcome the incrementalism of the politics of accommodation and to effect major, rapid changes.

2. The following discussion is based largely upon James M. Burns, *Presidential Government: The Crucible of Leadership* (Boston: Houghton Mifflin, 1965), pp. 225–236.

For the Presidency is the only force in American society that can operate on such a wide scale, with such speed, and with such force and direction, as to have a significant, measurable and predictable effect on the balance of social forces. Only a President can move as swiftly as Truman did in the face of political deterioration in western Europe. Only a President can mobilize public power along a lengthy line of action, as did Kennedy and Johnson in the civil rights struggles of the 1960s. . . . Only the President, in short, can supply the powerful and sustained kind of collective leadership necessary to affect basic social forces.[3]

This is not to say that the President is so powerful that whenever he acts, he achieves his goals. As we shall see later in the chapter, the President's power is limited and he frequently fails to achieve his goals. The point is that presidential action and support is normally needed if major, rapid changes in policy are to be effected. Presidential support is a necessary, but not sufficient, condition to break the bonds of incrementalism.

Because the presidency's basic function is the exertion of leadership, it is not primarily involved in performing any one of the four conversion functions of the political system, as is true of the other subsystems. It is involved in all four. The presidency is involved in *interest representation* when it calls attention to and articulates major demands present in society. When the presidency prods and guides Congress, it is especially involved in *rule initiation*. When the presidency gives leadership to the bureaucracy, it is deeply engaged in *rule application*. When it influences the making and implementation of judicial decisions, it is engaged in *rule interpretation*. In short, the presidency, through its primary function of exerting leadership, is involved in performing all four of the political system's conversion functions. As a result the presidency is involved at almost every stage of policy making.

Presidential Leadership and System-maintenance Functions

Conflict Resolution. Conflict creates the opportunity for leadership. Where there is no conflict, there is usually no exertion of presidential leadership. Questions on which there is no conflict will normally not even come to the attention of the President. And if they do, for the President to help the unanimously supported side is a waste, and to oppose it futile. Thus it appears as though the presidency is irresistibly drawn into the vortex of every major political conflict. Congress is hopelessly divided on a new mass transportation bill; the President intervenes. The Supreme Court makes a decision that is bitterly opposed by large segments of the population; the President defends the need for compliance with the Court —or calls for legal actions aimed at reversing the Court's decision.

As Theodore Sorensen, special counsel and confidant of President John Kennedy, put it: "If I were to name one quality which characterizes most

3. Burns, *Presidential Government,* p. 235.

issues likely to be brought to the President, I would say it was conflict—conflict between departments, between the views of various advisers, between the Administration and Congress, between the United States and another nation, or between groups within the country: labor versus management, or race versus race, or state versus nation."[4]

In exerting leadership on issues in conflict, the President is resolving conflict. He does not necessarily do so by negotiating a compromise, but often by deciding to support one particular side in the dispute. He makes choices—choices concerning which groups, persons, or nations he is going to support—and then throws the weight of the presidency on that side of the issue. In the process he is resolving conflict.

Generating Support   The President is the most visible of all governmental officials. Many persons do not know the names of their Senators and Representatives. Everyone knows who the President is. The President is the first political figure young children perceive.[5] Almost everything the President does—even the trivial—is front-page news. Add to this the fact that he is perceived by most persons as being more than a successful politician: He is President of the United States of America, and as such symbolizes the American government and even the American people. Some of the aura of Washington, Jefferson, Lincoln, and Roosevelt rubs off onto even the most mediocre Presidents.

The result is a tremendous potential for the President to generate support for the political system and for specific policy decisions. The President speaks from a pinnacle of prestige and with the weight of tradition behind him. When he speaks, the nation—for the most part—listens. In particular the President's activities as leader of the political community can be used to generate support. His quiet concern over combat deaths on the occasion of giving out a Congressional Medal of Honor may help him gain support for the government's war policy. And a homey President munching a hot dog at a football game may serve to humanize the government in the eyes of the public and thereby gain support for it. But all this is potential—potential that the skillful President can exchange for increased support and the inept President—as Richard Nixon amply demonstrated—can squander.

Creating Legitimacy   The position of prestige and visibility occupied by the President can help him create legitimacy as well as generate support. A President can make his ordinary duty of signing a bill into law a solemn public occasion, useful in adding to the legitimacy given the new law. Or

4. Theodore C. Sorensen, *Decision-Making in the White House* (New York: Columbia University Press, 1963), pp. 14–15.
5. See R. D. Hess and D. Easton, "The Child's Changing Image of the President," *Public Opinion Quarterly,* 24 (1960), 632–644.

he may announce a certain crucial decision—as Presidents sometimes remind us—while sitting at the desk or in a room that Abraham Lincoln or some other admired President used while making a crucial decision during his administration. The hope no doubt is that some of the aura of the admired President will rub off onto the current President and his decision, thereby adding to its legitimacy in the eyes of the public.

In short, the prestige and traditions associated with the presidency can be used by a skillful President to create feelings of respect, and at times even of awe, toward governmental decisions. A greater legitimacy is thereby imparted to those decisions.

Recruitment to the Presidency

The path to the American presidency is long, rough, and tortuous, probably longer, rougher, and more tortuous than that to any other office, public or private. The competition is keen, the expectations are demanding, the hours are exhausting, the negotiating is endless—and the energy, money, and time are limited. And, one might add, the process is unending—as soon as one presidential election is over, the speculating and jockeying for the next begins.

In 190 years 37 men have been President of the United States. And despite the appealing log-cabin-to-White-House dream, very few Presidents have come up from poverty to be President. There were less than seven at last count. George Washington and Franklin D. Roosevelt are the rule; Abraham Lincoln and Richard Nixon the exceptions. And of these 37 Presidents, none has been a black, none a Jew, none a woman, only one a Catholic, and (by constitutional prohibition) none foreign-born. Not only has the constitutional prohibition against foreign-born Presidents been followed, but of the 37 Presidents, 31 have been of prerevolutionary British ancestry. And of the remaining six, five are of prerevolutionary Dutch or German ancestry. John Kennedy, a third-generation Irish immigrant, was the only President who could not trace his ancestry back to prerevolutionary times.

The Electoral College

But more important than these factors for an understanding of the presidency is the political-ideological background of the Presidents. And for an understanding of this we must examine the peculiar Electoral College method of electing the President and some of its little-realized results.

The formal operation of the Electoral College is quickly told: Each state is allotted as many electoral votes as it has Senators and Representatives; whichever presidential candidate receives a plurality of a state's popular vote receives all the electoral votes of that state, and a candidate receiving an absolute majority of the electoral votes is elected President. If no candidate receives an absolute majority of electoral votes, the House of Representatives, with each state delegation possessing one vote, then elects the President from among the three candidates having the greatest number of electoral votes.

There is almost universal agreement on two weaknesses in this Electoral College method of electing the President. The first arises from the fact that a state's electoral votes are not automatically cast for the candidate with a plurality of popular votes in that state. Instead, each party nominates a slate of electors—usually faithful party workers—and when the ordinary citizen votes for President he is, in fact, voting for a slate of electors pledged to vote for a particular candidate. The problem arises from the fact that occasionally one or more of these electors, even though pledged to vote for their party's candidate, ends up voting for someone else. In 1968 a disgruntled Republican elector in North Carolina voted for George Wallace instead of Richard Nixon, even though Nixon had defeated Wallace in North Carolina. Adding to the problem is the fact that unpledged electors are sometimes nominated by a party. In 1960 in Alabama the Democratic slate of electors consisted of five pledged to the national ticket of Kennedy-Johnson and six who were unpledged (they ended up voting for Senator Harry Byrd of Virginia). Fortunately, neither unpledged electors nor electors pledged to one candidate but voting for another person have affected the outcome of a presidential election in modern times. Yet the very real possibility of their doing so exists.

A second problem arises from the fact that the House of Representatives —with each state delegation possessing one vote—elects the President if no candidate has an absolute majority in the Electoral College. Fortunately, because of the strong two-party system, no election has gone to the House of Representatives for over 150 years (1825 and the election of John Quincy Adams was the last time). The possibility of throwing the election into the House has, however, served as an attraction to third-party candidates. The Dixiecrat Party in 1948 and George Wallace's American Independent Party in 1968 were based largely on the hope of accomplishing exactly this.

In short, the potential dangers present in the Electoral College method of electing the President have not, in modern times, constituted actual problems. Nevertheless, it is clear that as long as the present system is retained, the American people will be courting disaster every four years.

Reform Proposals

Proposals to reform the Electoral College have ranged from merely abolishing the office of elector and having each state's electoral vote cast automatically for the candidate winning a plurality in each state, to completely abolishing the Electoral College and having the President elected by simple, direct, popular vote, as is done now for governors and mayors on the state and municipal levels.[6] The latter proposal passed the House of Representatives as a constitutional amendment in 1969, but then stalled in the Senate.

Although there have been numerous reform proposals and although most persons agree that reform is long overdue, it appears likely that no changes will be made in the immediate future. For it seems next to impossible to obtain agreement on exactly which of the numerous reform proposals should be adopted. There is wide support for the proposition that reform is needed, but only narrow support for any one specific reform plan. As a result, the present system continues in existence by default.

The Effects of the Electoral College

Less frequently discussed and less well understood than the operation of the Electoral College and the problems it poses is the impact the Electoral College tends to have upon the political-ideological nature of the Presidents elected.[7] Under the Electoral College system, two key factors largely determine the importance of a state in a presidential election: the number of its electoral votes and the degree of partisan competition in the state. The importance of the number of electoral votes is obvious. The importance of the degree of partisan competition lies in the fact that if a state leans heavily toward one party, that party will take its electoral vote for granted, and the other party will write it off as a lost cause. Thus, that state is not vitally important to either. A state in which partisan competition is high, on the other hand, will be vigorously fought for by both parties.

A quick look at the facts shows us that these two factors tend to reinforce each other: Most populous, large-electoral-vote states are also states in which there is much partisan competition. According to the 1970 census, the 10 most populous states are California, New York, Pennsylvania, Texas, Illinois, Ohio, Michigan, New Jersey, Florida, and Massachusetts. These states tend to be highly competitive. In only two of these ten states were the two Senators and the governor all of the same party in 1975–76. And the two states in which they were all of the same party—California and Florida—are competitive by almost any other standard. These 10 states have a total of 239 electoral votes—only 31 short of the 270 needed

6. For an analysis of several of the more frequently discussed reform proposals, see Wallace S. Sayre and Judith H. Parris, *Voting for President* (Washington, D. C.: Brookings Institution, 1970), chaps. 4–7, and Alexander Bickel, *Reform and Continuity* (New York: Harper & Row, 1971), chap. 2.

7. For helpful analysis of the impact of the Electoral College's method of electing the President, see Joseph E. Kallenbach, "Our Electoral College Gerrymander," *Midwest Journal of Political Science,* 4 (1960), 162–191, and Sayre and Parris, *Voting for President,* pp. 44–48.

for election. Thus, if a presidential candidate carried all 10 of these states, he would be almost assured of being elected President—he would have to pick up only 31 more electoral votes from the remaining 40 states and the District of Columbia. The critical importance of these ten states emerges: Close to a majority of the electoral votes are here, and in any given election these states cannot be taken for granted by either party.

A much different situation would exist if there were no unit rule in the Electoral College (the rule that whichever candidate wins a plurality of votes in a state receives *all* its electoral votes). For, given the competitiveness of these states, no candidate is likely to win by a very large margin. Thus, if the states' electoral votes were divided in proportion to the popular votes, candidates would normally emerge from these states about evenly divided. A candidate could lose these states and yet not be far behind his opponent in electoral votes. Then the smaller states could still swing the election. But under the present system, it is essential for a candidate to carry at least a substantial number of these states in order to have any realistic hope of victory.

A close look at these critical states reveals much about the type of person who is likely to become President—because he must be appealing to the voters of these states. All these states (with the possible exceptions of Texas and Florida) are industrialized, urbanized states (and seven of the ten are located in the northeastern part of the United States). All six of the American cities with over a million in population are in them (New York, Chicago, Los Angeles, Philadelphia, Detroit, and Houston), as well as over half of all cities with over 100,000 population. It is within these states that one finds large concentrations of black voters, labor union members, and eastern and southern European nationality groups.

The fact that these states and their voters heavily influence the presidential recruitment process is readily seen in the fact that all but three of the nine Democratic presidential candidates from 1940 to 1972 were from these ten states, as were five of the eight Republican candidates and all but two of their vice-presidential candidates. Of the fourteen presidents who have held office in the twentieth century, all but three (Hoover, Truman, and Eisenhower) came from one of these ten states. And two of these three —Hoover and Eisenhower—were national figures very loosely tied to their home states at the time of their nomination and election.

The ideologies of the presidential candidates of both parties have also been of the type that appeal to the urbanized, populous states—a generally liberal or moderate, internationalist, and pro-civil-rights ideology. The one glaring exception is the Republican nomination of Goldwater in 1964—a nomination that proved to be disastrous for the fortunes of the Republicans.

In summary, because of the politics of the Electoral College we are almost assured of having Presidents in sympathy with the dominant aspirations and needs of the populous, urbanized, and, to a large extent, northeastern states. The demands arising from interests and individuals within these states are normally the ones most carefully considered by the President.

The Presidential Structure

The day is long past when the President was assisted by only a single aide and a stenographer or two, and went, as was the custom of President John Quincy Adams, for early morning swims in the Potomac River (reportedly occasionally in the nude). Today, the President is surrounded by a growing host of advisers, councils, and offices. Most of these councils and offices have been established in the past 35 years in an attempt to enable the President to maintain effective control of the vast bureaucracy and at the same time meet his other responsibilities. This structure of offices, councils, and personal aides constitutes the institutionalized presidency. But these offices and councils have become so numerous and unwieldy that some doubt arises as to whether the President can effectively control them. The never-ending need is to maintain a balance between machinery sufficient to enable the President to meet his duties and machinery that is not so large and complex that it dominates the President instead of his dominating it.

Each President must attempt to strike his own balance; each must develop his own pattern of decision making within the presidency's structure. Thus, the presidential decision-making process, and even to some degree the structure of the presidency, varies from one President to the next—the organization and lines of responsibility are not always the same. Even during the tenure of a single President, the decision-making process undergoes a process of evolution and change. One office may gain importance; another, lose. At one time, formal channels of communication may be largely relied on; later, informal channels may become more prominent. Yet we can make certain generalizations about the presidency as an institution and about the persons, offices, and patterns of authority that comprise it. First, we will consider the formal structure of the presidency and in the next section how Presidents use this structure in their decision making.

It is helpful to think of the structure of the presidency as consisting of ten concentric circles. The President is in the center, and the circles represent councils or groups of advisers. Beyond the "Inner Circle," each one is more distant from the President and less significant in the presidential decision-making process (see Figure 7.1).[8] It should be noted, how-

8. See Louis Koenig's description of the presidency as a series of concentric circles, on which this section is partly based: Louis W. Koenig, *The Invisible Presidency* (New York: Holt, Rinehart and Winston, Inc., 1960).

ever, that the particular circle in which each of the various offices and councils is placed is to some degree a matter of judgment. The relative importance is not something that is certain and fixed. Rather, it depends to a large extent on the personal decision-making style of a particular President, and thus it varies from one President to another. At any given point in time, the exact circle appropriate to a particular council or office may be in doubt. Nevertheless, Figure 7.1 indicates, in an approximate sense, the relative importance of the various offices and councils of the presidential structure. The first circle ("Inner Circle") will be skipped now and discussed later.

The White House Staff Each President has his own personal staff of aides. They are directly and personally responsible to him—they are appointed by him (without need of Senate approval) and serve completely at his pleasure. Often they are long-time associates of the President and

Figure 7.1   The structure of the presidency

have a fierce personal loyalty to him. Their chief function has been described as serving as the eyes and ears of the President and, one might add, the mouth and hand of the President. They expand the scope of presidential attention and influence by reporting events, making observations, and representing the President and his interests.

Normally, the White House staff numbers from 15 to 20 persons (excluding stenographers and other clerical workers). The division of labor among the staff members varies greatly from President to President. Usually, one of them is designated as press secretary and another as appointments secretary. Some Presidents designate one person as a chief of staff with responsibilities to coordinate the other staff members. The essence of the White House staff is its personal nature—it is the personal staff of the President, consisting of persons whom the President trusts and who, in turn, are strictly loyal to him. The President uses this personal staff in whatever way he sees fit—just so it accomplishes its key purpose of expanding the President's control and understanding of the situations at hand.

The Office of Management and Budget   The third circle away from the President is the Office of Management and Budget (OMB)—an office distinguishable from the White House staff by its more specialized functions and its more permanent, formal nature.[9] The OMB is formally provided for by law, and although its top administrators are presidential appointees, its rank-and-file members are permanent employees who may serve several Presidents during their careers. The OMB, prior to July 1, 1970, was known as the Bureau of the Budget. President Nixon changed its name and added to the functions it performs.

The chief function of the OMB is to prepare the yearly budget the President submits to Congress. This involves the monumental task of receiving budget request from all federal departments and agencies and then coordinating and shaping them to create a rational budget that conforms to the general policy objectives of the President. Since the allocation of money to the many federal agencies and programs involves policy decisions of the first magnitude, the OMB is a vital part of the presidency, and its director is normally a close adviser of the President.

The old Bureau of the Budget performed tasks other than preparation of the annual budget, but these other tasks have been expanded and reemphasized in the new Office of Management and Budget. Thus, the OMB is now intended to be the chief institutional means by which the President carries out his supervision of the bureaucracy (the general executive

9. On the Office of Management and Budget and some issues it is facing, see Hugh Heclo, "OMB and the Presidency—the Problem of 'Neutral Competence,' " *Public Interest,* no. 38 (1975), 80–98.

branch of government). It is also intended as a means to improve the efficiency of the bureaucracy. To accomplish these goals, the OMB has been given such responsibilities as evaluating program performance (evaluating whether and how efficiently programs in the executive branch are being carried out), coordinating bureaucratic agencies (coordinating the activities of various agencies that have overlapping jurisdictions), and clearing new legislative proposals (clearing proposals for new legislation coming from the bureaucracy before they are sent to Congress).

The Council of Economic Advisers A panel of three economists advises the President concerning the state of the economy, as well as current economic trends, and suggests measures that will help assure a stable, healthy economy. Their role is, of course, purely advisory, and the extent of their influence varies with the amount of confidence the President has in them. At times the President rejects their admittedly sound economic advice as being politically unfeasible. Under recent Presidents their significance has been growing.

The National Security Council The National Security Council is composed of the President, the Vice President, the Secretary of State, the Secretary of Defense, and the director of the Office of Emergency Planning (another of the agencies of the presidency). Other persons, for example, the chairman of the Joint Chiefs of Staff, the director of the Office of Management and Budget, and the director of the Central Intelligence Agency, frequently take part in council meetings. The council advises the President on the awesome questions and problems of national security. Its membership is drawn from a variety of departments, agencies, and offices, all of which conduct activities that touch on national security affairs. The National Security Council was first created in 1947 when it became apparent that twentieth-century national security is not purely a military problem, but consists of a complex interlacing of military, economic, diplomatic, and psychological factors.

The degree of reliance on the National Security Council varies with Presidents. Presidents Kennedy and Johnson relied on it in a limited way and met with it sporadically. Under Presidents Nixon and Ford the council has experienced something of a rebirth. Much depends on the President's personal style of decision making.

The Domestic Council At the same time that President Nixon created the Office of Management and Budget he also created the Domestic Council. The council plays a role in domestic affairs that parallels the role played by the National Security Council in foreign affairs. It is composed of the President, Vice President, and all the cabinet members except the

Secretaries of State and Defense. Other officials, such as the director of the Office of Management and Budget, may be added to the Domestic Council by the President.

The major purpose of the Domestic Council is to advise the President on domestic policy. While the Office of Management and Budget is primarily concerned with the effective carrying out of programs, the Domestic Council is primarily concerned with developing new policy alternatives. The Domestic Council faces some of the same problems that the cabinet does (to be discussed later). Much of the council's work appears to be accomplished not so much by the council itself, but by its fairly large staff of professional researchers and by temporary committees set up to explore particular policy areas.

The Vice-Presidency   The first Vice President, John Adams, once characterized the office as "the most insignificant . . . that ever invention of man contrived, or his imagination conceived." Since the days of John Adams, and especially in the past 30 years, the influence of the Vice President in the presidency's structure has grown to the extent that he is a significant part of the structure, but he still remains far from being second in power and influence.[10]

Two stubborn facts still stand as a barrier to the vice-presidency's evolving into a powerful office in its own right. First, although the Vice President is only the proverbial heartbeat away from the presidency, he has no real independent base of power: He makes no appointments, he signs no bills into laws, and he orders no troops into action. True, the President may delegate certain powers and responsibilities to the Vice President. Presidents normally assign Vice Presidents tasks such as going on overseas goodwill and fact-gathering tours and presiding at cabinet and National Security Council meetings in the President's absence. Presidents sometimes also use Vice Presidents to speak out on highly controversial topics and to engage in such highly partisan activities as campaigning and attending political dinners, thus enabling the President to remain above the din of bitter controversies and naked partisanship. Most of these duties that Presidents have given to Vice Presidents involve public relations or symbolic responsibilities—not real decision-making responsibilities. In addition, they are exercised by the Vice President at the sufferance of the President—they are not held by the Vice President as a right. Vice President Rockefeller once responded to the question of what he does with "Whatever he [Ford] wants me to do."[11]

A second basic fact is that most Presidents naturally and jealously guard their political power and thus are hesitant to delegate too much to their

---

10. On the vice-presidency see Paul T. David, "The Vice-Presidency: Its Institutional Evolution and Contemporary Status," *Journal of Politics,* 26 (1967), 721–748.

11. *The Grand Rapids Press,* January 26, 1975, p. 8-A.

Vice Presidents. As Rockefeller once tactfully said: "Politically it's very difficult for a President to give power to a vice president. . . . It's very delicate to create two power centers in the government."[12]

This natural reluctance of the President to give too free a rein to his Vice President is re-enforced by the tendency for Vice Presidents to be picked not for their loyalty and closeness to the President, but for their ability to broaden and strengthen the popular appeal of the presidential ticket. This ticket balancing at the national nominating conventions was seen in 1960 when John Kennedy, a northern liberal, chose Lyndon Johnson, a southern moderate, and in 1972 when George McGovern, a Protestant with rather weak ties to many of the regular party elements, chose first Thomas Eagleton and then Sargent Shriver, both Catholics with good ties to regular party elements. In 1974, even in the absence of an immediate election, the moderately conservative, midwestern Gerald Ford chose the moderately liberal, eastern Nelson Rockefeller as his Vice President. Ticket balancing may be a good way to broaden the popular appeal of the presidential–vice-presidential team; it is also a good way to assure that the President will not delegate very much power to the Vice President. For there will most likely be certain differences of outlook or temperament that tend to prevent the development of a close working relationship.

In short, the Vice President has recently gained in power and influence in the presidency—in an earlier age the vice-presidency could hardly have been conceived of as part of the presidency—yet the Vice President is still a relatively minor member of the presidency. Gerald Ford, while serving as Vice President, once expressed it well: "I've got all the perks. But power? Power is what I left up there on Capitol Hill."[13]

The Cabinet Although the cabinet is not provided for by the Constitution, ever since Washington the Presidents have had cabinets composed of the heads of the various administrative departments.[14] All Presidents have periodically held formal cabinet meetings to discuss and seek advice on questions and problems facing their administrations. Thus one might suppose the cabinet to be a vital part of the presidential structure and near to the heart of the decision-making process. But the facts indicate otherwise. The cabinet as a body is a relatively unimportant part of the presidency (and thus its position in the seventh ring out from the President). Under most Presidents cabinet meetings are not frank, open, and significant advice-giving and decision-making sessions. Instead, they are held largely because they are expected to be held, and they function more as

12. *The Grand Rapids Press,* January 26, 1975, p. 8-A.
13. Quoted in Jerald F. terHorst, *Gerald Ford and the Future of the Presidency* (New York: The Third Press, 1974), p. 171.
14. The most helpful book on the cabinet is Richard F. Fenno, Jr., *The President's Cabinet* (Cambridge, Mass.: Harvard University Press, 1959).

a device to increase the support and legitimacy of the presidency and its decisions than anything else. As George Reedy, special assistant to President Johnson, wrote of Johnson's use of his cabinet: "It is doubtful whether any president in our history made more of an effort to elevate the status of the institution, and the result was totally negative. Cabinet meetings were held with considerable regularity, with fully predetermined agendas and fully prewritten statements. . . . It was regarded by all participants except the president as a painful experience, somewhat akin to sitting with the preacher in the front parlor on Sunday."[15]

The specialization of its members appears to be largely the cause of the problem. Each member is the head of a particular specialized executive department, deeply immersed in the problems of his department. For him to give advice or make decisions in other departments would be to involve him in problem areas in which he has very little competence. To have the secretaries of Interior and Agriculture listen to the secretaries of State and Defense discussing nuclear disarmament strikes many as a waste of time.

What must be stressed, however, is that what we are talking about here is the cabinet as a body, not the individual members of the cabinet. According to Reedy, "The cabinet is one of those institutions in which the whole is less than the sum of the parts. As individual offices, the members bear heavy responsibilities in administering the affairs of the government. As a collective body, they are about as useful as the vermiform appendix —though far more honored."[16] Certain individuals in the cabinet will be of the utmost importance in the presidency and will be in the center of the decision-making process (at least in the case of decisions in their specialty). Some cabinet members will almost always be included in the crucial inner circle to be discussed shortly. Secretary of State Kissinger is certainly an influential member of the Ford presidency—but this is something different from saying that the cabinet as a whole is highly influential in the Ford presidency.

Miscellaneous Agencies   Included in the presidency are a number of agencies similar in their general nature and role to the National Security Council and the Council of Economic Advisers, but significantly less in influence and importance. Among these are the National Aeronautics and Space Council, Office of Emergency Preparedness, Office of Economic Opportunity, and Office of Science and Technology. Each of these agencies reports directly to the President and each is responsible for overseeing and coordinating action in a certain policy area.

15. George E. Reedy, *The Twilight of the Presidency* (New York: New American Library, 1970), p. 78.
16. Reedy, *The Twilight of the Presidency,* p. 77.

Presidential Commissions   Occasionally a President appoints a special-ized, ad hoc commission to study and report on a specific problem or issue.[17] In 1975 President Ford, for example, created a special commission headed by Vice President Rockefeller to study charges of CIA spying on American citizens.

These commissions are rarely significant factors affecting the policies of a President. In fact, they are frequently established not so much to obtain new information or new perspectives as to have an impact on public opinions and influential persons in and out of government or to cool off a flammable situation by giving the impression of presidential concern.

The Inner Circle   This leaves the inner circle—the circle closest to the President and the most influential in presidential decision making. The inner circle is composed of a number of close advisers and confidants of the President. These persons may be drawn from any of the nine circles discussed earlier, from outside the formal presidency, or even from outside the government altogether. Within the inner circle may be two or three members of the White House staff, a cabinet officer or two, the director of the Office of Management and Budget, an old associate of the President from Congress, a prominent Washington or New York lawyer, and an academician. Normally, however, the inner circle is largely drawn from the circles nearest the President—most notably his own White House staff.

The inner circle is, of course, purely an analytic concept—no one is officially designated as a member of the inner circle. Rather, someone gradually comes to be so depended upon and trusted by the President that he can be considered within the inner circle. The inner circle is constantly changing. A person may be a member of it one month, but then gradually recede in presidential favor and reliance until he can no longer belong. In the meantime someone else may be gradually gaining in favor. It is hard to exaggerate the importance of these persons—for it is on their advice that the President relies most heavily, and it is they who most readily obtain the presidential ear.

This, then, is the outline of the structure of the presidency—its members and their relative importance. But how a particular President makes use of them is up to him, and no two Presidents are exactly alike. We now turn to the decision-making process that goes on within the presidential struc-ture.

17. On presidential commissions, see George T. Sulzner, "The Policy Process and the Uses of National Governmental Study Commissions," *Western Political Quarterly*, 24 (1971), 438–448, and Frank Popper, *The President's Commissions* (New York: Twentieth Century Fund, 1970).

Presidential Decision Making

The persons, offices, and councils that make up the presidency do not determine the actual process of decision making. It is up to the particular President to mold and shape the presidential structure so that it reflects his concept of the presidency and his own role in it. There is no one pattern of authority and responsibility; each President brings to the presidential structure his own temperament, aspirations, and skills. It is he who breathes life into the formal structure.

Thus, the best approach to the study of the decision-making process is not to study some nonexistent "typical" presidential decision-making process or to examine decision making under only one President. Instead, we will examine presidential decision making under three recent Presidents: Kennedy, Nixon, and Ford. Kennedy and Nixon provide striking contrasts in their approach to presidential decision making. A comparison of their styles of leadership will provide a background against which we can examine the patterns in the Ford administration. Out of the similarities and contrasts that emerge we can gain a deeper understanding of the patterns and factors involved in presidential decision making.

Kennedy John Kennedy had a keen appreciation of what political power could accomplish and an insatiable appetite for detail.[18] He believed that to exercise power wisely he needed information—not predigested or summarized information. Thus he molded the presidential structure so as to maximize his own involvement in the decision-making process and his own access to firsthand information. He wished no subordinate official to make basic decisions, nor did he wish to make decisions on the basis of information that subordinate officials judged important. "Raw," often conflicting, inputs flowed directly to him.

His staff members and departmental secretaries therefore reported directly to him. He had what can be called a "hub and spokes" organization. The hub was the President, and the spokes were the direct ties with his aides and departmental secretaries.

In dealing with department secretaries and White House staff members Kennedy insisted upon direct relationships, unhampered by organization and hierarchy. He, for his part, remained highly accessible to a large circle of colleagues. "You've got one of the most accessible Presidents in history," one cabinet secretary said. "I must talk with him in person or on the phone twenty times a week," said another secretary. "I don't hesitate to call him if something important comes up—even at

18. The following analysis of decision making in the Kennedy presidency is based on the following sources: Louis W. Koenig, *The Chief Executive,* 3d ed. (New York: Harcourt, Brace, Jovanovich, 1975), pp. 196–200; Theodore C. Sorensen, *Kennedy* (New York: Harper & Row, 1965); Sorensen, *Decision-Making in the White House;* and Arthur M. Schlesinger, Jr., *A Thousand Days* (Boston: Houghton Mifflin, 1965).

night or on Sunday." "I can pick up the telephone and call him at any time," said still another. "I'll call up the White House and say, 'I want ten minutes tomorrow or the next day.' "[19]

Kennedy did not rely heavily on formal councils like the National Security Council and the cabinet for advice. Instead he relied on special small groups called together to discuss a specific problem. Thus in the Cuban missile crisis of 1962, he relied largely not on the National Security Council, but on a small group of advisers drawn from the National Security Council, his own staff, and elsewhere. For long-range problems, he used "task forces" that were composed of individuals drawn from within government and outside it (usually liberally sprinkled with academicians). These groups would research problems in depth, and their reports often formed the basis for new presidential programs.

All this is not to say that Kennedy was involved at every stage of every problem—that would be an impossible task for any one human being. The point is that Kennedy injected himself into the decision-making process at any time he had doubts about what was going on—to request more information, to stimulate action, to change the direction in which things were moving, or to reserve to himself the right to make the final decision.

Nixon   If Kennedy's organization of the White House was a "hub and spokes" configuration, Nixon's was a pyramid.[20] Nixon believed that if he were to become directly involved in a host of controversies and listened to a host of voices, he would get bogged down in relatively minor issues and be distracted from more important issues and problems. He believed that by freeing himself from the competing chorus of discordant voices that besets any President, he would have more time to reflect and would receive well-rounded information and advice. Instead of receiving any information that by luck or a fluke got through to him, he wanted information to be passed on to him by an orderly, rational process. Therefore Nixon shaped his White House in the form of a pyramid—himself at the apex, next a few selected aides with direct access to him, and other aides and counselors spreading out to form the base.

Information, advice, and views flowed to Nixon through three or four close aides. Cabinet officers, congressmen, and even the Vice President had a difficult time getting to see or talk with Nixon. Formal White House agencies and councils and their professional staffs—the National Security

19. Louis Koenig, *The Chief Executive* (New York: Harcourt, Brace, Jovanovich, 1964), p. 175.

20. The following analysis of decision making in the Nixon presidency is based on the following sources: Richard M. Nixon, *Six Crises* (New York: Doubleday, 1962); Rowland Evans and Robert D. Novak, *Nixon in the White House* (New York: Random House, 1971); Dan Rather and Gary P. Gates, *The Palace Guard* (New York: Harper & Row, 1974); and a number of newspaper and magazine accounts.

Council, the Office of Management and Budget, the Domestic Council, and the Council of Economic Advisers, among others—were deeply involved in exploring problems, sorting out information, delineating policy alternatives, and preparing relevant advice. Nixon's close advisers then presented this collection of information and advice for his consideration. Nixon took it, retired to a private office, and—usually all alone—carefully studied the assembled information, documents, and reports. He then emerged to announce his decision.

H. Robbins (Bob) Haldeman, who was the key person controlling access to Nixon, defended this form of organization on the basis of its ability to give Nixon well-rounded information and advice in an efficient manner:

We make a studious effort to present to him all sides of the problems he is dealing with. And because it is done in a somewhat organized fashion rather than haphazardly, he gets more. We try to eliminate demands and diversions that are not pertinent to what is particularly important at that time. This enables the President to devote attention to matters of particular concern and results in him being able to concentrate in depth on the things only the President can deal with and ignore or handle as speedily as possible matters of great importance but which do not require presidential action.[21]

On another occasion Haldeman made a similar defense of such organization:

Ehrlichman, Kissinger, and I do our best to make sure all points of view are placed before the President. We do act as a screen, because there is a real danger of some advocate rushing in to the President or some other decision maker . . . and actually managing to convince them in a burst of emotion or argument. We try to make sure that all arguments are presented calmly and fairly across the board.[22]

It is clear that this pattern of decision making fit Nixon's personality and needs. One commentator has noted: "And if there is one pattern in Nixon's checkered political career—and it is not easy to find a dominant one —it is his effort to impose some degree of order on what William James called the 'great, booming confusion of the world.' "[23] In addition, Nixon was very ill at ease with small groups of persons and unable to relate well in a one-to-one or one-to-two situation. Thus a pyramid organization fit his needs well: It enabled him to deal with only three or four trusted, intensely loyal aides, and it imposed a certain order and tidiness on the "great buzzing, booming confusion" that besets all Presidents.

But the price that Nixon had to pay was an isolation that no doubt played a major role in his downfall. When, as Haldeman says, the President's

21. Quoted in Eugene V. Richer, "Bob Haldeman to Blame If Nixon Isolated," *The Grand Rapids Press,* May 20, 1970, p. 5-E.
22. Quoted in Allen Drury, "Inside the White House: 1971," *Look,* October 19, 1971, p. 41.
23. James M. Burns, "The Nixon Tightrope," *Life,* 70 (April 12, 1971), 48D.

aides and advisory councils presented all sides of an issue to him and eliminated "demands and diversions that are not pertinent to what is particularly important," these aides are making judgments on what is pertinent and what is not, what is important and what is not, what are all sides of an issue and what are irrelevant aspects of it. Nixon ended up seeing the world through the eyes of his top aides and the information and views they judged pertinent. In the first year or two of his presidency, this was not such a problem because a number of people with rather diverse views had access to him. But when such persons as Daniel Moynihan, Robert Finch, and Arthur Burns left (or were forced out of) the inner circle of advisers, Nixon relied on a more and more homogeneous group of close advisers, who themselves had become isolated from much of the real world. One White House aide, Jeb Magruder, has written: "When Haldeman went on the 'Today' show and called our antiwar critics traitors, he was reflecting our frustrations, but also his own insularity. . . . If Haldeman had talked more to our critics, and seen that they weren't all radicals or revolutionaries, it might have made a difference. As it was, there was too little fresh air blowing through the White House, and we all tended to become caught up in the 'enemies' mentality."[24] The end result could be nothing but a President isolated from the real world, without the feel for it which any President needs to act and react.

In summary, as President, Nixon attempted to create an orderly, efficient approach to White House decision making. But Nixon's desire for efficiency led to the creation of a rigid hierarchy that, while maintaining the trappings of efficiency, gave way to the ultimate inefficiency of misinformation, false perspectives, and options never considered. The blame for Watergate lies more in the character of Nixon himself and the particular men with whom he surrounded himself, but his organization of the White House decision-making apparatus was such that it was unable to warn him of his deepening troubles.

Ford   After taking over the presidency from the thoroughly discredited Nixon, President Ford moved quickly to create a style and pattern of decision making that were his own.[25] In so doing he moved away from the Nixon hierarchical organization and toward the Kennedy "hub and

24. Jeb Stuart Magruder, *An American Life: One Man's Road to Watergate* (New York: Antheneum, 1974), p. 101.

25. The following analysis of decision making in the Ford presidency is based on the following sources: Jerald F. ter Horst, *Gerald Ford and the Future of the Presidency* (New York: The Third Press, 1974); Bud Vestal, *Jerry Ford Up Close* (New York: Coward, McCann, & Geoghegan, 1974); John Hersey, "The President," *New York Times Magazine,* April 20, 1975, pp. 30–121, and a number of newspaper and magazine accounts. It is difficult to analyze the decision-making style of a President while he is still in office, before memoirs are written and personal papers made public. Thus the analysis here must be taken as a tentative one.

spokes" organization. There are at least nine persons who have immediate, direct contact with Ford on a daily basis. No one person controls access to Ford as Haldeman did to Nixon. Thus in addition to the persons who report to Ford directly as a matter of course, there are a larger number of persons who also enjoy direct access to him. As Robert Hartman, one of Ford's top aides, put it early in the Ford presidency when his staff procedures were still evolving: "At present, nothing is fixed. My guess is that what will evolve eventually will not be a military general staff or a corporate pyramid. It will probably be more on the pattern of a congressional or senatorial staff operation, in which you have lines of responsibility going from the center out to various people and coming back the same way."[26] Ford seeks to broaden his outlook by meeting about every six or seven weeks for a give-and-take session with an informal group, largely old-time associates from his congressional days and from the business world.

But Ford does not use his "hub and spokes" organization to encourage the flow of a large stream of diverse, clashing views and ideas. Ford does not have the keen desire for political power, the appetite for detail, or the mind eager to grapple with novel or unconventional ideas that Kennedy did. Thus he does not use his organization to assure the stream of fresh ideas and raw inputs that Kennedy encouraged. Instead he moves in the Nixon direction both in preferring predigested, summary communications and in not building conflict and clash into his staff. John Marsh, another top Ford aide, has noted that Ford prefers oral presentations to written ones and prefers brief, summary statements, which list objectives and alternative courses of action, to larger, more discursive statements. Marsh has stated: "He's not given to long philosophical discussions with individuals. He likes things laid out very rapidly. Frequently it's best if you can carry on a short conversation with him and can do it succinctly and summarize. . . . If you put things on paper, he likes to have short summaries, precise and objective, laid out with the various courses of action. Really, though, he likes best the oral presentation where it's presented in an objective way."[27]

In staffing his White House, Ford has opted for team-player types—solid, competent persons noted more for their middle-of-the-road styles and outlooks than for excitement, innovation, and creativity. As a result there is less conflict, excitement, and clash of ideas in Ford's White House than in Kennedy's. Ford does, however, depart from the tidy Nixon White House in his frequent practice of giving the same assignment to two or more persons in order to see who comes up with the best idea or approach. This sort of untidyness was anathema in the Nixon White House.

26. From "How Ford Runs the White House," *U.S. News and World Report,* September 23, 1974, p. 30.
27. From "How Ford Runs the White House," p. 29.

The White House organization that Ford has developed fits his personality and style well. He is an open, honest person who enjoys people. Although he may not be the bland, not-too-bright person his distractors sometimes claim, he is more of a practical, down-to-earth, moderate person than an innovative, creative thinker and doer. He concentrates on immediate questions and issues, trying to solve the problems of the day in the most effective and least disruptive way possible. And he has organized the decision-making procedures of his White House to achieve these goals, relying on face-to-face contacts with a large number of persons and on solid, but rather unexciting, uncolorful persons molded into a closely knit team.

Summary   Out of this survey of decision making under three Presidents, there emerge two fundamental questions with which a President is faced in molding and shaping the presidential structure. One concerns whether the President shapes his staff and advisers in a hierarchical, pyramid form, as Nixon did, or whether he shapes them in a "hub and spokes" form, as Kennedy and Ford did. Some Presidents are more comfortable with the orderliness and organizational logic of the hierarchical form. Their days are more structured and information flows to them in a planned and—it is hoped—well-rounded, comprehensive fashion. Other Presidents, especially those who seem to enjoy meeting with people in the flesh, feel that such an approach runs the risk of their becoming isolated and receiving only those views and ideas some one else judges to be of merit. These Presidents prefer to involve themselves directly in issues and problems through a "hub and spokes" organization. They run the risk of being overwhelmed by trivia, and there is no guarantee that they will receive all the information they need. Much depends on the character and personality of the individual President, how he relates to other people, his intellectual curiosity, and how threatened he is by a lack of clear lines or organization and responsibility.[28]

A second basic question with which a President is faced in shaping the presidential structure is to what extent he wants a free-wheeling spirit to exist, with clashing ideas and a certain sense of excitement as persons of diverse views and backgrounds struggle with innovative approaches; and to what extent he prefers instead a spirit of quiet competence, managerial efficiency, and responsible team work. Kennedy clearly preferred the former—the clash of ideas and the excitement that goes with the search for innovative approaches. This fit his personality and his views of presidential leadership. Ford is more comfortable emphasizing teamwork and putting efficiency over innovation, preferences in keeping with his emphasis on

28. For an excellent discussion of how the background, character, and personality of individual Presidents affect their approach to the presidency, see James David Barber, *The Presidential Character* (Englewood Cliffs, N.J.: Prentice-Hall, 1972).

solid, middle-of-the-road values. Nixon started out his presidency giving some emphasis to innovation and clashing ideas, but his hierarchical approach to decision making quickly led him into the teamwork, efficiency-over-innovation approach.

Presidential Power

The presidency is an office of power—limited power.[29] The President stands astride the American political system, giving orders, appealing for action, and leading the public. But often his orders are side-tracked, his appeals forgotten, and his leadership ignored. To understand presidential power, we must understand both its strengths and its limitations—for the two combine to create an office of real significance and power, but also of real limitations and weaknesses.[30] The American President is neither an impotent figurehead nor an all-powerful dictator. This section, therefore, explores first three sources of presidential power and then four sources of limitations on presidential power. Finally, it considers a specific area—foreign policy making—where special circumstances work to increase the President's power.

However, before going into these sources of presidential power and the limitations on it, we must note that on accession to the Presidency no one inherits a neat bundle labeled *Presidential Powers.* The power a President has is not something that automatically devolves on the incumbent President. Instead, any person who takes the presidential oath receives certain resources that his own skill and the flow of events can turn into actual, living power. He receives potential power; it is up to him to turn that potential into actual power.

Sources of presidential power

Constitutional-Legal Grants of Power   A consideration of presidential power almost has to start with the grants of power formally given the President by the Constitution, laws passed by Congress, and the court's interpretations of them. Among the powers the President holds because he has been given them by law or by the Constitution, and because the courts have confirmed his right to exercise them, is, for example, the

---

29. *Power* is being used here in the sense of the ability to cause someone to do something he otherwise would not have done. It is being used synonymously with *influence,* although as already seen in Chapter 6, some theoreticians make a distinction between them. See Robert A. Dahl, *Modern Political Analysis,* 2d ed. (Englewood Cliffs, N.J.: Prentice-Hall, 1970), chap. 3.

30. Two of the most helpful works on presidential power, which stress both its strengths and weaknesses are Richard Neustadt, *Presidential Power* (New York: Wiley, 1960), and Emmet John Hughes, *The Living Presidency* (New York: Coward, McCann & Geoghegan, 1972).

power to appoint a large number of officials. The Constitution specifically gives him the power to appoint ambassadors, Supreme Court justices, and "all other officers of the United States . . . but Congress may by law vest the appointment of such inferior officers, as they think proper, in the President alone, in the courts of law, or in the heads of departments."[31] Thus by law the President appoints the members of independent regulatory commissions, such as the National Labor Relations Board and the Federal Communications Commission, lower court judges, and certain administrative officials.

The President's power to veto bills passed by Congress is, of course, a classic example of a constitutional grant of power. The Constitution also makes the President commander-in-chief of the armed forces and thus gives him the power to order troops into action or to withhold them. The Constitution gives the President the responsibility to "take care that the laws be faithfully executed" and vests him with "the executive power."[32] Because executing laws involves making decisions, this, too, gives power to the President.

Because of the formal, legal nature of these powers, we ought not to assume that they are certain and inflexible. Laws and the Constitution, as we shall see in Chapter 10, are anything but certain and inflexible—there is room for flexibility in interpretation. Thus some Presidents have interpreted their constitutional-legal powers broadly and have exercised them skillfully to their utmost limit (until slapped down by the courts, Congress, or other forces), whereas others have ineptly squandered them or have taken a more modest view of what they could do under their constitutional-legal powers. As a result, the power Presidents actually exercise under constitutional-legal grants of power varies greatly, from administration to administration.

Events also work to increase or decrease the actual power a President receives from constitutional-legal grants. In times of war the President's powers as commander-in-chief assume much greater significance—give him more actual power—than in peacetime. And today's world of international tensions, missiles, nuclear warheads, and one-million-man standing armies works to give Presidents more actual power than in the long-past day of isolation from world problems, slow communications, and skirmishes with the Indians.

Thus we see that even the formal, constitutional, and legal grants of power are very flexible in their application and use and can result in different degrees of actual power, depending on the person serving as President and on the flow of events.

The Use of Rewards and Sanctions   The great prestige attached to the President's office, the glare of publicity that surrounds him and everything

31. Art. II, sec. 2.
32. Art. II, secs. 3, 1.

he does, and the high popularity that he often enjoys, as well as his formal powers, can be used by the determined and skillful President to increase his power. All can be used as "carrots" or "sticks" with which to prod the reluctant individual into a desired course of action. Perhaps it is a bureaucrat who wishes a promotion the President can give, a freshman representative who would be flattered by an invitation to a White House party, a cabinet member who wants the President to give publicity to a pet project of his, or a veteran Senator up for re-election who would be helped if the popular President campaigned for him in his home state. In every case the President can promise to give the person something he wants (or, alternatively, threaten to withhold it), *if* that person will give the President something he wants (a vote on a key bill in Congress, support for his budget proposals, or backing in testimony before a congressional committee). Thus a bargaining situation exists: the President has something the person to be influenced wants, and the person to be influenced has something the President wants. The President has the publicity, the support, or the appointment the person to be influenced wants; the person to be influenced has the vote or the backing the President wants.

The bargains usually struck as a result of such a situation are not explicit, tit-for-tat arrangements—"You do this, and I'll do that." More often they involve informal or tacit understandings. The President intervenes to get a new post office in the district of a certain representative, for example, and in turn expects support in the future.

Theodore Sorensen, Special Counsel to President Kennedy, clearly illustrates President Kennedy's use of rewards and sanctions:

Although charged with employing high-pressure tactics and threats, the O'Brien team [Kennedy's Special Assistant for Congressional Affairs] pumped far more arms than they twisted and brandished far fewer sticks than carrots: advance notification of Federal contracts, special privileges for White House tours, detailed data on a bill's effect, material for speeches and releases, birthday notes from the President, campaign help from the National Committee, autographed pictures from the President, and whatever flexibility was possible on patronage, public works and other budget items.[33]

The clearest examples of the presidential use of rewards and sanctions come from the President's relations with Congress, as is illustrated by Sorensen's observations. But this does not mean that the use of rewards and sanctions is limited to presidential attempts to increase his power with Congress; it extends to the administrative branch of government and even outside the formal governmental structure. A career diplomat in the State Department may back the President on some project largely because he is hoping for a presidential appointment as an ambassador. Or the organizers of a major march on Washington may call off the march after a sudden shift in presidential policies. Or in the area of foreign affairs, a nation's

---

33. Sorensen, *Kennedy,* p. 357.

leaders may impose limitations on its exports of certain products to the United States, because the President has threatened certain trade retaliations if they do not do so. The examples could be multiplied, but the point is clear: the President is in a position to increase his power by making tacit —and on occasion explicit—bargains with individuals and groups of individuals.

The White House Enemies List drawn up in the Nixon Administration was a clumsy—and sometimes illegal—effort to punish with sanctions those who were in presidential disfavor.[34] Audits by the Internal Revenue Service and obtaining and then leaking information about the personal lives of individuals in disfavor were two of the attempted sanctions. These efforts were as ineffective as they were morally shady because they were aimed more at vindictive punishment than at the potentially more effective nudging of persons to take a desired course of action.

The actual power a President receives from the use of rewards and sanctions varies greatly from one President to the next. Some Presidents have had little desire to engage in bargaining and "deals." Others enter into this game with apparent zest—eager to match wits with the next person in an attempt to win his support.

Presidents also vary in the skill with which they play this game. It is important to know that one person is a soft touch for a little flattery, that another will respond only to heavy threats, that another will react negatively to the same threats. Each person must be approached in a way that takes into account his aspirations, personality, and values. The President must assess both the person to be influenced and his own resources and then use this knowledge to the fullest in achieving what he wants from the other person. This is no job for amateurs!

The Prestige of the Presidential Office Finally, presidential power flows from the tremendous prestige that inheres in the office—*if* the President uses this prestige to his advantage. It can be useful in building presidential power largely because it enables the President to obtain the attention of those whom he wishes to influence as well as to secure a careful consideration of his views.

The President can pre-empt any program in order to appear on nationwide television. And the next day the lead story in newspapers from coast to coast will be on the presidential address. Editorials will praise, condemn, or artfully avoid taking a stand on the President's views. He has obtained the attention of the nation—his views are taken seriously, considered, and debated. In other words, the President has the power (or at least the potential power) to influence the opinions of the public. Theodore Roosevelt once referred to the presidency as a "bully pulpit" from which the President can exhort the people, and three more modern observers, think-

34. On this "Enemies List," see Rather and Gates, *The Palace Guard,* pp. 296–299.

ing of the President's ability to use television, have referred to the President's "electronic throne."[35] Although the ability of the President to influence the general public is less than is often supposed, it is a factor that should not be ignored.

Virtually no leader, in or out of government, would refuse a request to come to the White House for a conference with the President—again largely because of the prestige of the presidency. These leaders normally consider and weigh what the President has to say. Labor disputes have been settled by the President's calling labor and management representatives to the White House, requesting them (with varying degrees of firmness) to bargain seriously, and perhaps even suggesting a fair settlement.

We should recognize that the prestige of the presidency as a source of presidential power is closely bound up with the other sources of presidential power. The prestige of the office, as we saw in the previous section, can in itself be used to create rewards or sanctions. And certainly persons who listen to and weigh the words of the President do so out of a realization of the power of the presidency, not purely because of the prestige of the office. Yet the prestige of the presidency is an independent factor with its own potential for power. Even a "weak" President—one who does not exercise his constitutional-legal powers vigorously and who bargains ineptly or not at all—will be listened to and shown a certain amount of respect simply because he is "Mr. President."

If we ended our consideration of presidential power at this point it would appear that the skillful and vigorous President could build up almost limitless power. His advantages appear overwhelming. But the picture so far presented is an unbalanced one. In addition to the sources of presidential power, there are very real and very severe limitations on presidential power, which must be considered.

Limitations on Presidential Power

Constitutional-Legal Limitations on Presidential Power Just as the Constitution and laws grant the President power, so also they withhold power. The Constitution gives the President the power to appoint ambassadors, Supreme Court justices, and other officials, *but* only "with the advice and consent of the Senate."[36] The President appoints the members of the independent regulatory commissions, other administrative officials, and lower-court judges; but again the Senate must confirm these appointments. That this need for Senate approval of presidential appointments is no idle threat is seen in the Senate's rejection of two of Nixon's Supreme Court

35. Newton Minow, John B. Martin, and Lee Mitchell, *Presidential Television* (New York: Basic Books, 1973).
36. Art. II, sec. 2.

nominees: Clement Haynsworth and G. Harold Carswell. The President may make treaties with other nations, but two thirds of the Senate must ratify a treaty before it goes into effect. The President proposes legislation to Congress, and, as we have already seen, he has some means of persuading Congress to act, but presidential failures in getting Congress to act seem, if anything, to outweigh presidential successes. The President, in short, exercises his power within certain specified, legal limits.

The constitutional power of the House of Representatives to impeach the President and of the Senate to convict him is a power that was given new life during the events of 1973–1974. In July of 1974 the House Judiciary Committee voted in favor of impeachment of then-President Nixon, and observers are almost unanimously agreed that had Nixon not resigned he would have been impeached by the full House of Representatives and convicted by the necessary two thirds majority of the Senate. These events may or may not make the threat of impeachment and removal from office more of a real limitation on presidential power than they were in the past, but they have already had the effect of encouraging a greater congressional independence from presidential direction.

Although the courts have tended to be generous in upholding presidential power, they have been willing on occasion to step in and declare that a President has passed the limits of legal permissibility. In July 1974, the Supreme Court unanimously ruled that Nixon was constitutionally required to surrender the taped White House conversations subpoenaed by the special Watergate prosecutor—a decision fought by Nixon and one that set in motion the final events leading to his resignation fifteen days later. In that decision the Court ruled that *executive privilege*—the doctrine that the President and other executive officials may on order of the President withhold information from Congress and the courts—"must yield to the demonstrated, specific need for evidence in a pending criminal trial."[37] Presidential power is definitely limited by legal and constitutional restraints and prohibitions.

Popular Accountability The President is an elected official—an official nominated by a party, elected by the voting public, and limited to a set term of office. These simple, obvious facts have far-ranging implications for presidential power, for they mean that the President is a politician in the fullest sense of the word, and any politician ignores the public at his own risk.

Franklin D. Roosevelt once wrote: "I cannot go any faster than the people will let me." This, no doubt, is a simplification of a complex relationship, yet in making his decisions, in deciding what he should and should not do, the President is certainly limited by popular reactions

37. *United States v. Nixon* 418 U.S. 683 (1974).

(actual and anticipated). Because of the high visibility of the President to the public, much of what Chapter 4 says about the influence of public opinions on elected officeholders is especially applicable to the President. Thus, a President may believe that a balanced budget is necessary to stave off inflation, but he decides not to recommend a tax increase for fear of negative public reactions. Or a President may delay asking for new funds for military aid to an ally until soon after a foreign affairs crisis, realizing that the public will be more ready to accept expenditures at that time.

The point is not that the President slavishly follows the latest public opinion polls or the latest editorials in the nation's leading newspapers, but rather that he must take such evidences of public reactions into account. At times he may decide that, despite public reactions, he must carry through with a certain decision because of its vital nature. At other times he may decide that the issue at stake is really not that vital and so completely reverse himself because of anticipated public reactions. More likely he will modify his decision or alter its timing in order to help head off strong negative public reactions. But whatever his final course may be, the point is this: He is taking probable public reactions into account and weighing his actions in the light of them. To this extent his power is being limited by the fact that he is a popularly accountable official.

Events Beyond the President's Control   To a large degree the President is acting and working in a world that is not of his own creation. He does not lay down the policies or make the commitments of his predecessor, he does not start the communist guerrilla activity in a Latin-American country, he does not precipitate the clash between two communist nations, like the Soviet Union and China, and he does not control the stock market. Yet these are all situations and conditions to which the American President must react. The President makes his decisions within the bounds set by a flow of events that he himself has had no hand in shaping. At times he may attempt to alter this flow and may even succeed to some degree, but he will always find himself unable to control or even influence many events that nonetheless have a direct and pervasive impact on his decision making.

A new leader may come to power in a foreign country and render obsolete the President's carefully laid policy toward that part of the world. Or a President may decide to put off requesting more stringent air pollution standards from Congress until the following year. He carefully lays his plans accordingly. Then unusual weather conditions create a dangerously high level of air pollution. Schools and factories are closed, several elderly people die, and the public is aroused. As a consequence, he may decide that he must make his proposals immediately.

Decisions made by a President's predecessor can create similar situations: They help set the limits within which the President must act. A new

President cannot suddenly renounce all the policies of the former President and start out with a clean slate. Emmet John Hughes has stated the situation clearly:

On the eve of his inauguration, a newly elected President is given to contemplating the legacy of the Presidential past as a matter of unmatched prestige; on the morning following, he is certain soon to be thinking of it in terms of unwanted precedents. For he quickly discovers that the hand of the past, in the White House, is not at all dead but all too alive. And it goes on writing an oppressive number of things: a law now impossible to erase, a subsidy politically impossible to slash, an agency too entrenched to eliminate, a welfare program too popular to reverse, a depressed stock market beyond quick revival, or a careless foreign alliance beyond instant renunciation. Such are a few of the shackling souvenirs likely to be left behind by any President's immediate predecessors.[38]

But what is true of the policies of the previous President is, in a certain sense, also true of a President's own policy decisions. Although a President has a large amount of control over his own decisions, once they are made and publicly implemented they have passed out of his control and comprise the given conditions within which he must operate. A President's policies must have a certain amount of consistency; thus, when he makes a decision, he is limiting his range of future choices. When President Ford in 1975 decided to ask Congress for a tax cut to stimulate the depressed economy and later decided to sign the tax bill Congress passed even though it cut taxes more than he had requested, certain forces were set in motion—among them a huge budget deficit, inflation, and economic recovery—which then became givens; they could no longer be changed, and he then had to work with them. And so it is with every presidential decision—it closes certain future options (as well as opening up others, of course) and thereby carries with it its own restrictions on presidential power.

In summary, presidential power is exercised within the limits set by a multitude of events—events that were created by the decisions of others and by those of the President himself and events over which he has no control. These events serve to restrict the possible decisions the President can make in a given situation. Presidential power is thereby limited.

Incomplete Control Within the Executive Branch   Richard Neustadt told how President Truman once sat at his desk toward the close of his administration and said of Eisenhower: "He'll sit here and he'll say, 'Do this! Do that!' *And nothing will happen.* Poor Ike—it won't be a bit like the army. He'll find it very frustrating."[39] Almost every President, or one of his aides, has echoed such sentiments of frustration. President Kennedy's aide Theodore Sorensen wrote:

38. Hughes, *The Living Presidency,* p. 181.
39. Neustadt, *Presidential Power,* p. 9.

Surprisingly enough, a President's decision in either domestic or foreign affairs may also depend upon its acceptance within the Executive branch itself—on the President's ability to gain acceptance for his point of view over dissent, inertia, incompetence, or impotence among his own appointees and policy officials as well as the permanent bureaucracy. . . . I can recall more than one occasion when it was necessary for the President to convince his own appointees before they could undertake to convince the Congress, the Soviets, or some other party.[40]

And Nixon aide Jeb Magruder once concluded an account of a conflict between the White House and the Bureau of Labor Statistics: "It was a small victory, one achieved only after a great deal of pushing, but it seemed to us outrageous that a bureau of the Labor Department should defy a reasonable request by the President."[41]

Many are surprised to learn of the difficulties a President has in getting his orders carried out by those responsible to him. They expect the President to have his difficulties with Congress and are not too surprised if the judiciary steps on a few presidential toes, but the executive branch—isn't the President the *chief* executive? They view the executive branch as though it were a neat pyramid, with the President at the top and lines of authority running from top to bottom. The President pushes a button and immediately people spring to action all down the line.

The reasons for the President's difficulty in controlling the executive branch are not hard to find. One is the sheer size of the executive branch and the resulting impossibility of the President's following through on all his orders to ensure that they are carried out as he intended. The bureaucracy is so large and its number of officials so great that it is simply physically impossible for the President—or even his staff—personally to make certain that all presidential orders are carried out. It is relatively easy for an executive official to drag his feet if he is not personally convinced of the wisdom of the presidential decision. Chances are—especially if one of the frequent crises that absorb the President's attention comes up—that this failure to act will not even be discovered for several months, and by then it may be too late to implement the original decision.

The President also has trouble controlling the executive branch because many key officials in it have high prestige as well as a personal following in their own right. Any attempt by the President to remove these officials or take other sanctions against them would result in howls of protest and possibly reactions adverse to the President. Especially if the individual has —as is often the case—a strong following in Congress or among certain segments of the public, the President may be loath to take action against him. Doing so may place key elements of his legislative program in jeopardy or damage his standing with the public.

40. Sorensen, Decision-Making in the White House, pp. 25–26.
41. Magruder, *An American Life,* p. 103.

In 1970 Nixon fired Walter Hickel, his Secretary of the Interior, for opposing a number of Nixon programs and publicly criticizing the President. But the President had to pay the price to rid himself of an insubordinate official—many conservationists, college youth, and antiwar groups had come to admire the outspoken Hickel and the President no doubt lost support among those groups because of his action. And later, when Nixon wished to be rid of George Romney, his Secretary of Housing and Urban Development, he did not dare fire him for fear of a renewed public furor.[42] Faced with situations such as this, Nixon was not the first—or the last—President willing to put up with a limited amount of insubordination from an appointee in order to avoid adverse public reactions.

In short, the President, in surveying the executive scene, sees a very large number of independent, strong-minded persons, many of whom have strong political followings in their own right. When we realize this, it is easy to understand why the President is so often reduced to persuading and bargaining instead of ordering. In the process presidential power is reduced—for the President must consider whether the decisions he wishes to make can be sold to his executive officials who will be responsible for carrying them out.

Summary   The President exercises very real power—but power with equally real limitations upon it. As a result, the presidency is able to exert leadership—but no more than leadership. If the powers of the presidency were greatly decreased, the President would no longer be exerting leadership but would be largely outside the policy-making process, hoping that somehow the other structures of the political system would decide to adopt his suggestions. If, on the other hand, the power of the presidency were greatly increased, the President would no longer be merely exercising leadership in the policy-making process—he would be able to control it. He would no longer be merely seeking to persuade other individuals and institutions to make the policies he desired, by initiating the rules he thought wise and then applying and interpreting them in the ways he believes proper. Instead he would be able, for all intents and purposes, to initiate the rules himself and then to apply and interpret them himself. Thus the leadership function of the presidency grows out of its possession of limited, yet real, power.

Presidential Power and Foreign-Policy Making

Before concluding the discussion of presidential power, one special area must be considered—an area to which some of the observations just made

42. For an account of the events surrounding the dismissal of Hickel and the problems that Romney was seen by the White House to be causing, see Rather and Gates, *The Palace Guard,* pp. 180–190.

do not apply without modification. For in the area of foreign-policy making, presidential power is considerably greater than in other areas of presidential decision making. In the area of foreign affairs, the presidency—at least until very recently—does not merely exert leadership, but is able both to initiate rules and to control their application and interpretation. Even with recent changes it is not very much of an exaggeration to say that the presidency is *the* foreign-policy maker.

Sources of Presidential Power in Foreign-Policy Making   The increase of power in the area of foreign-policy making is largely the result of two factors.

First, the Constitution and the laws of Congress give the President vast power to make foreign policies. The grants of power are more generous and the limitations less severe than in other areas of decision making. We have already observed the tremendous power given the President as commander-in-chief of the armed forces: military policy is for the most part an aspect of foreign policy. Thus, the President's power as commander-in-chief acts to increase immeasurably his foreign-policy-making power.

Other legally or constitutionally granted powers also contribute. The President appoints all ambassadors and has the power to extend or withhold diplomatic recognition of foreign countries. It was the presidency, not Congress or some other institution, that decided in 1949 to isolate the new communist government of China, and in 1971 it was the presidency that reversed the policy.

The President has the legal authority to conclude *executive agreements* with foreign powers. These have virtually the same force and effect as treaties, but do not require Senate confirmation as treaties do. The President makes executive agreements completely on his own initiative (and often secretly) on the basis of either his general constitutional powers or general authorization by Congress. In the early days of World War II, while the United States was still officially neutral, President Roosevelt gave hard-pressed Britain 50 old American destroyers in exchange for long-term leases of naval bases in British territories in the Caribbean. This significant step was taken by executive agreement, without Congress's approval or even full knowledge. The recent trend has been for the President to negotiate fewer treaties, which need Senate ratification, and more executive agreements, which need no Senate ratification.[43]

Also helping ensure presidential power in foreign affairs has been the courts' willingness to uphold sweeping legal and constitutional powers for the President. In a 1936 decision the Supreme Court intemperately declared that in foreign affairs "the President *alone* has the power to speak

43. Prior to 1939 the United States had entered into 800 treaties and 1,180 executive agreements, from 1945 to 1970 it entered into 368 treaties and 5,600 executive agreements. See Hughes, *The Living Presidency,* p. 230.

or listen as a representative of the nation." And it spoke of the "plenary and *exclusive* power of the President as the *sole organ* of the federal government in the field of international relations. . . ."[44] Probably we ought not to take this pronouncement completely literally, but no one can deny that the Supreme Court has been most generous in supporting the President's legal and constitutional powers in the field of foreign policy.

A second major factor, in addition to the legal-constitutional grants of power, working to increase the President's foreign policy-making powers is the tendency of Congress and the public to accord the President greater freedom and deference in foreign-policy making than in domestic-policy making. As we shall see this tendency has weakened in recent years, but it is still present.

One political scientist has found that "American public opinion is characterized by a *strong* and *stable* 'permissive mood' toward international involvements."[45] This permissiveness in foreign-policy formation is illustrated by opinions on the question of bombing North Vietnam. In May 1966, just before the bombing of Hanoi and Haiphong, only 50 percent of the public favored bombing; in July 1966, just after the Johnson administration had begun the bombing, 85 percent favored such bombing. Then in March 1968, just before President Johnson ordered a limited bombing halt, 51 percent of the public opposed a bombing halt; in April 1968, just after the bombing limitation, only 26 percent opposed it.[46] Another researcher has noted a "rally round-the-flag" tendency in public opinion.[47] That is, Americans tend to feel a sense of duty to support their government (the President) in the face of a foreign threat. To some degree, being a good, loyal American includes supporting foreign-policy decisions in the face of an outside threat; not to do so implies a certain disloyalty to our country.

No doubt largely because of the public tendency to defer to presidential judgment in foreign-policy making, Congress has tended to do the same. Congress is more concerned with and makes a more searching examination of domestic-policy proposals made by the President than it does of foreign-policy proposals.

Recent Trends in Presidential Foreign-Policy-Making Power   Under the battering of the blood and frustration of the Vietnam War, then Watergate,

44. *United States v. Curtiss Wright Export Corporation,* 299 U.S. 304 (1936). Italics added.

45. William R. Caspary, "The 'Mood Theory': A Study of Public Opinion and Foreign Policy," *American Political Science Review,* 64 (1970), 546.

46. See John E. Mueller, "Trends in Popular Support for the Wars in Korea and Vietnam," *American Political Science Review* 65 (1971), 369, 370.

47. See John E. Mueller, "Presidential Popularity from Truman to Johnson," *American Political Science Review,* 64 (1970), 18–34, and Mueller, "Trends in Popular Support for the Wars in Korea and Vietnam," p. 365.

which further discredited the presidency, and then the fall of South Vietnam and Cambodia to insurgent communist forces in 1975, public and congressional trust in the presidency's foreign-policy leadership has been shaken. As a result Congress has been showing a leadership and a willingness to challenge the presidency in foreign policy that have been unknown in Washington for decades. The role played by the President in foreign-policy making is currently undergoing rapid change.

It started in the late sixties with public demonstrations against American military involvement in Vietnam and mounting criticism of the war by Congress. Then in 1972 Congress by legislative action prohibited the use of American ground forces in Cambodia and Laos, and in 1973 Congress prohibited the use of American air power in Cambodia, Laos, and Vietnam. Also in 1973 Congress passed legislation limiting the President's war-making powers by requiring him to receive congressional approval within 60 days of sending American troops into action.[48] In 1975 Congress refused to vote the additional military aid requested by President Ford for Cambodia and South Vietnam.

Meanwhile Congress showed greater initiative in other areas of American foreign policy as well. Whether in American-Soviet detente, aid to Israel, force levels of NATO, military aid to Turkey, or protection from threatened oil embargoes, Congress in the mid-1970s was undergoing a renaissance of interest, ideas, and leadership in foreign-policy making.

As a result it is clear that the President's foreign-policy-making power has been reduced. He must move more cautiously, weigh his actions more carefully, and prepare the public and Congress for his decisions more thoroughly than was the case ten, or even five, years ago. Having granted this much, the fact remains that the President's foreign-policy-making power still far outstrips his power in domestic-policy making. The President's legal-constitutional powers in the foreign-policy field remain largely intact. The rally-round-the-flag phenomenon would no doubt operate in a major national emergency. The military aide with the black suitcase containing the codes with which to launch a nuclear attack still follows the President—not congressmen—around. And thus far it has been only in Southeast Asia that presidential wishes have actually been thwarted by Congress. In other areas of the world the President, under greater challenge, still has his way almost completely.

Thus we can say—even while acknowledging his weakened position—that the President is *the* foreign-policy maker. For the most part he has the power to initiate rules and dominate their application and interpretation—a power he does not have in the domestic field.

48. On the exact provisions and passage of this significant legislation, see *Congressional Quarterly Weekly Report* (July 28, 1973), pp. 2068–2069 and (November 10, 1973), pp. 2985–2986.

The basic function of the presidency is to exert leadership. It thus takes part in all four of the political system's conversion functions, and it provides much of the force and direction the American political system needs to embark on new courses of action. The President is able to exert leadership because he has the necessary power and is provided by the institutionalized structure with the necessary information, advice, and control. Except in foreign policy however, because of severe and clearly recognized limitations on his power, he is stopped short of being an all-dominant policy maker.

Some Exploratory Questions

1. How would the proposal to elect the President by direct popular vote of the people, if adopted, affect the type of person likely to be elected?

2. The decision-making pattern of which of the three Presidents discussed in this chapter is most likely to lead to the wisest decisions?

3. Is one of the basic lessons of the Watergate scandal of the Nixon administration that there are too few limitations on presidential power?

4. Is the recent trend toward less presidential power and more congressional initiatives in foreign-policy making likely to lead to wiser, more effective decisions?

Bibliographical Essay

Probably the three best general works on the presidency are Emmet John Hughes, *The Living Presidency* (New York: Coward, McCann & Geoghegan, 1972); Louis W. Koenig, *The Chief Executive,* 3d ed. (New York: Harcourt Brace Jovanovich, 1975); and James M. Burns, *Presidential Government* (Boston: Houghton Mifflin, 1965). A work rich in the historical development of the presidency is Edward S. Corwin, *The President: Office and Powers, 1787–1957,* 4th ed. (New York: New York University Press, 1957).

Recently, several helpful, brief paperback studies of the presidency have been published: Dale Vinyard, *The Presidency* (New York: Scribners, 1971); Grant McConnell, *The Modern Presidency* (New York: St. Martin's, 1967); and Dorothy B. James, *The Contemporary Presidency* (New York: Pegasus, 1969).

A number of studies concentrate on certain aspects of the presidency. Theodore Sorensen's very brief study of presidential decision making is illuminating: Theodore C. Sorensen, *Decision-Making in the White House* (New York: Columbia University Press, 1963). Another book that does a good job of considering presidential decision making is Erwin C. Hargrove, *Presidential Leadership* (New York: Macmillan, 1966). For an excellent discussion of how the background, character, and personality of individual Presidents affect their approach to the presidency, see James David Barber, *The Presidential Character* (Englewood Cliffs, N.J.: Prentice-Hall, 1972). On the nature and basis of presidential power, see Richard E. Neustadt, *Presidential Power* (New York: Wiley, 1960). For an able analysis of the presidency from the point of view of the President's relations with those with whom he must deal, see Robert J. Sickels, *Presidential Transactions* (Englewood Cliffs, N.J.: Prentice-Hall, 1974).

On problems Presidents face in relationship to the executive branch, see Richard P. Nathan, *The Plot That Failed* (New York: Wiley, 1975). The best book on the President's cabinet is Richard F. Fenno, Jr., *The President's Cabinet* (New York: Vintage Books, 1959). For a study that explores the background and nature of key White House aides of the Presidents from Roosevelt through Johnson, see Patrick Anderson, *The Presidents' Men* (New York: Doubleday, 1968). A book written by a former insider gives a number of valuable insights into the presidency (and reaches a number of pessimistic conclusions): George E. Reedy, *The Twilight of the Presidency* (New York: New American Library, 1970). On the electoral college method of electing the President and alternatives to it, see Wallace S. Sayre and Judith H. Parris, *Voting for President* (Washington, D.C.: Brookings Institution, 1970).

For critical analysis of the growth in presidential power in foreign-policy making in the past forty years, see Arthur M. Schlesinger, Jr., *The Imperial Presidency* (Boston: Houghton Mifflin, 1973). For a defense of the President's dominant role in foreign-policy making, see Horman Hill, *The New Democracy in Foreign Policy Making* (Lincoln: University of Nebraska Press, 1970). Sidney Warren, *The President as World Leader* (New York: McGraw-Hill, 1964), gives a good historical survey of the Presidents as foreign-policy makers, from Theodore Roosevelt to John Kennedy. Also helpful in understanding the President's foreign-policy role is John E. Mueller, *War, Presidents and Public Opinion* (New York: Wiley, 1973).

Probably the most comprehensive anthology on the presidency is Aaron Wildavsky, ed., *The Presidency* (Boston: Little, Brown, 1969). Other rich sources of information on the presidency—although often far from objective and usually lacking in theoretical development—are the personal memoirs of Presidents and their aides. See, for example, Arthur M. Schlesinger, Jr., *A Thousand Days* (Boston: Houghton Mifflin, 1965); Theodore C. Sorensen, *Kennedy* (New York: Harper & Row, 1965); Dwight David Eisenhower, *Mandate for Change* (New York: Doubleday, 1963); Harry S. Truman, *Memoirs,* 2 vols. (New York: Doubleday, 1955 and 1956); Lyndon B. Johnson, *The Vantage Point* (New York: Holt, Rinehart and Winston, 1971); and Jeb Stuart Magruder, *An American Life: One Man's Road to Watergate* (New York: Atheneum, 1974). While not a memoir, also rich in insights into some of the internal struggles in the Nixon White House is the book by two reporters, Dan Rather and Gary Paul Gates, *The Palace Guard* (New York: Harper & Row, 1974).

Chapter 8　　**Congress**　　The Politics of
　　　　　　　　　　　　　　Accommodation

January 16, 1975, is a date likely to live in the modern history of Congress.
On that day the Democratic caucus in the House of Representatives voted
to unseat two previously powerful committee chairmen—F. Edward Hebert of Armed Services and W. R. Poage of Agriculture—and to replace
them with men of less seniority. This action was significant in itself: there
was a shift in power in the House. But its significance was greater than the
immediate effect on the balance of power in the House. It was the culmi-
nation of a reform movement that had been developing in Congress for
several years, and it proved that those committed to change were in
control.

To understand the changes that resulted and their meaning not only for
Congress but also for public policy making, we must first understand
Congress—its nature, structures, and patterns of behavior. First we will
consider the functions that Congress performs for the political system.
Next the all-important institutional setting within which the legislative process takes place is considered. Then the inputs that influence the decision
making of the Senators and Representatives are examined; and finally, the
basic nature of the congressional decision-making process is explored.

Congressional Functions

Rule Initiation

Congress's primary function is *rule initiation,* one of the four conversion
functions of the political system. It is in Congress that new policies and
major changes in present policies are debated and accepted or rejected:
new tax programs are adopted and old ones abandoned; an all-volunteer
army is established; a national, governmentally sponsored health insurance
system is rejected. It is true that the original proposals for many policies
originate outside Congress—with the President, in an administrative
agency, or in an interest group—yet it is Congress that determines whether

or not such proposals are in fact established as governmental policies. Thus Congress's chief function concerns initiating basic rules—rules that are then molded and shaped into public policies through the two remaining conversion functions: rule application and rule interpretation.

An important secondary function of Congress grows out of its key characteristic: its representative nature. Each member is elected from the geographical area that he or she represents. And within the 435 House districts and within the 50 states, which form the senatorial districts, are all the diversity, conflict, and peculiarity that make up the United States. In some districts extreme segregationists are dominant, in others the population is mostly black; in some districts labor union members are the powerful group, in others dairy farmers are in control; in some districts irrigation and water resources are major concerns, in others the problems of mass transportation are overriding. In short, the tremendous variety of interests and concerns present in the United States are all represented in Congress.

As a result Congress plays an important role in *interest representation.* Almost all conceivable—and some not so conceivable—interests have their spokespersons in Congress. The demands and support of a welter of interests are thereby being channeled into the political system.

Congress also has an important secondary role to play in *rule application* through its power to oversee the bureaucracy. Through its control of appropriations and by other means, Congress often influences—with varying degrees of effectiveness—the decisions the bureaucracy makes in applying the generalized rules that Congress itself or some other subsystem has initiated.

In summary, the *primary* function of Congress is rule initiation; two important *secondary* functions are interest representation and rule application.

System-maintenance Functions

Conflict Resolution   Congress has an especially important part in *resolving conflicts.*[1] The diverse interests represented in Congress create problems in the form of conflicts, to which the diversity naturally leads. But their presence also gives Congress the opportunity to perform the vital function of reconciling these conflicting interests. By way of open debate and numerous opportunities for negotiation, agreements can be struck and coalitions built. Ideally, conflicting elements are forced into negotiation and coalition building in order to avoid deadlock and total paralysis. As

1. For good discussions of the system-maintenance functions performed by legislative systems, see Malcolm E. Jewell and Samuel C. Patterson, *The Legislative Process in the United States,* 2d ed. (New York: Random House, 1973), chap. 1; and John C. Walhke, Heinz Eulau, William Buchanan, and LeRoy C. Ferguson, *The Legislative System* (New York: Wiley, 1962), pp. 4–7, 24–28.

this is done, conflicts are resolved. Perhaps the cotton farmers are able to have a certain section of an act modified slightly, perhaps the textile manufacturers can have a section they object to deleted, and perhaps the unions, in exchange for their support, are able to obtain support for a bill they want. The point is that when many interests are able to obtain concessions, even though they may not be entirely happy with the final outcome, they are at least able to accept and "live with" it.

This is the ideal. And often Congress does, in practice, live up to this ideal. But often it does not. Some of the recent changes in Congress' internal structures hold promise that Congress will be able to do so more frequently in the future than it has in the recent past, as we shall see later.

Generating Support A second system-maintenance function is *generating support* for the political system. As we saw in Chapter 1, it is essential that every political system keep the support of the population. Whenever the demands of the public are met in an acceptable manner, public support grows. Thus, whenever Congress resolves a conflict in a manner acceptable to the conflicting interests, it has helped increase support for the political system. But when it fails to do so, support is weakened.

In addition, the bare fact that interests have their say—can feel as though they have had their day in court—helps increase support. When an interest fails to gain its goal or even a few concessions, it still feels it has been given a fair hearing, that it at least was given an opportunity to speak out and try to influence the final decision. The deliberations, hearings, and open debates of Congress can act as a safety valve. Thus, an interest is more likely to give support to the final decision—or at least to the political system that made the decision—than it would if it felt it has never been given a fair opportunity to try to influence the decision.

Creating Legitimacy Closely connected with the function of generating support is the function of *creating legitimacy*. Just as Congress' resolution of a conflict in a manner acceptable to the conflicting interests increases support, so it helps create the feeling that the decision is legitimate. It is unlikely that an interest would accept a decision of Congress as being acceptable and fairly reached while at the same time denying its legitimacy. By the same token, failures in conflict resolution can lead to a loss in legitimacy.

It is generally accepted today that Congress, because of its broad, representative nature, should make its basic policy decisions, that this is primary responsibility and right. Thus, when Congress makes an authoritative decision, this decision is normally accepted as legitimate. If some other institution—say, a department in the bureaucracy or the Supreme Court—had made the same decision, it might very well not have been accepted as legitimate. Contrast the general acceptance—even though often a begrudging acceptance—of the provisions of several civil rights acts passed by Congress in the latter half of the 1960s, acts that touched on some very sensitive areas such as black voting rights in the South and open housing, with the widespread rejection of the legitimacy and authority of numerous court decisions in the early 1970s requiring busing of school children in order to obtain racially integrated schools.[2]

The rest of this chapter explores how Congress, with varying degrees of success, performs these functions.

Congress as an Institution

Congress is an exceedingly complex institution, interlaced with innumerable rules of organization and procedure. But we could know in detail every one of its formal rules and still have no idea of the way Congress operates in practice. For interwoven with the formal rules of organization and procedure are a host of informal rules—or generally held expectations of how things are to be done—that play a crucial role in determining how Congress does in fact operate. This section of the chapter explores five structural features of Congress—concentrating on both their formal and informal aspects—in an attempt to construct a composite picture of actual congressional practice.[3]

Apportionment

Perhaps the most fundamental feature of the structure of Congress is the way in which the 535 seats—435 in the House and 100 in the Senate— are apportioned. The apportionment of the seats helps determine the strength of the interests represented in Congress and thus the way in which Congress performs its function of interest representation. Depending on the apportionment of the seats, states and regions may gain or lose representation. Some interests may obtain representation out of proportion to their numbers; other interests may have less representation than their

2. The different institutions that made the decisions of the 1960s and the decisions of the early 1970s may not, of course, have been the only factor causing the more ready acceptance of the earlier decisions. The fact that many of the congressional acts were largely aimed at forms of racial discrimination traditionally found in the South may have helped assure their acceptance in the rest of the nation. Nevertheless, it is difficult to deny that part of the explanation for the basic acceptance—even in the South—of the civil rights acts lies in the fact that Congress—the broadly representative institution—made them.

3. On congressional rules of procedure see Lewis A. Froman, Jr., *The Congressional Process* (Boston: Little, Brown, 1967). Also very helpful in giving an understanding or "feel" for both the formal and informal rules of procedure in Congress is a case study of the passage of a single piece of legislation. See Robert L. Peabody, Jeffrey M. Berry, William G. Frasure, and Jerry Goldman, *To Enact A Law* (New York: Praeger, 1972).

numbers warrant. To a large degree, the inputs flowing into the congressional subsystem are determined by the apportionment of its 535 seats. In addition, apportionment may make it either easier or more difficult for a party to capture control of certain seats.

The Senate   The story of apportionment in the Senate can be told quickly and simply. Each state is given two Senators by the Constitution; and according to Article V, no state can be deprived of equal representation without its approval.

Americans tend to take this situation for granted and lose sight of some of its results. It means that Alaska, with a population of 295,000 (according to the 1970 census), has as much representation in the Senate as California, with a population 67 times as large—19,700,000. Thus, Alaska has one Senator for every 148,000 persons; California, one for every 10 million. Or looking at it another way, the Senators from the twenty-six least populous states, with only 16 percent of the population of the United States, can outvote the Senators from the twenty-four most populous states, with 84 percent of the population.

The House of Representatives   In the House, because there are a fixed number of seats to be apportioned among a shifting and growing population, apportionment is a real problem. The number of seats is fixed by law —not by the Constitution—at 435, a number that has remained essentially unchanged since 1911. The apportioning of these 435 seats is done in two stages: first, they are apportioned among the states, each state receiving its share in proportion to its population; then district lines must be drawn for the seats each state has received.

The first stage is carried out automatically by the Bureau of the Census after each decennial census, with each state guaranteed at least one seat. Thus, after each census some states gain seats, others lose seats, and some keep the same number.

The second stage in apportionment is carried out by the state legislatures. A state may choose to have all its Representatives elected at large, but this is rarely done. Instead, the state legislature normally divides the state into districts, one for each seat it has been allotted. Federal law provides that if a state receives an additional seat following a census and does not create a new district, the new Representative will be elected at large. If a state loses representation and does not redraw its district lines to take this loss into account, *all* its Representatives will be elected at large.

Although the process of drawing district lines appears to be a rather dry, unexciting exercise, in fact it deeply affects the interests represented in the House and thus is the source of intense conflict and struggle. Every ten years, after the census, state legislatures are scenes of much political maneuvering because how the district lines are drawn will affect the partisan advantages of the political parties, the political prospects of individual Representatives and would-be Representatives, and the representation of certain racial, ethnic, and occupational groups. Results such as one party's gaining (or losing) seats, an incumbent Representative's losing his or her seat, and an additional black being elected often depend on how the lines are drawn. That much drama and struggle attend the drawing of district lines in such circumstances is understandable.   *gerrymandering*   ,

Informal Norms

Most college dormitories have certain formal rules about such matters as study hours or visiting in dormitory rooms by members of the opposite sex. But certain informal norms or unwritten rules are also bound to develop. "Do not report infractions of the formal rules" and "Be sociable, not too withdrawn or too studious" may be examples of unwritten norms in some dormitories. Often the sanctions taken against violators of the informal norms—perhaps social ostracism or some hazing in a dormitory situation —are more severe than the sanctions taken against violators of the formal rules.

What is the case in dormitories has been found to be the case in virtually all human institutions: In addition to formal, written rules, certain unwritten understandings develop that define what behavior is considered proper and what improper. And those who do not conform to the informal norms find certain sanctions being taken against them. Thus, it is not surprising to find the existence of unwritten norms for congressmen.[4] Although references are made to certain informal congressional rules throughout this section on Congress as an institution, certain informal norms that have a general application throughout Congress are separately considered here.[5]

Work Hard   One informal norm is that one should *work hard* at the job of being a legislator. Senator Carl Hayden of Arizona reported that when he was first elected to Congress many years ago, he was told: "There are two kinds of congressmen—show horses and work horses. If you want to gain the respect of your colleagues, keep quiet and be a work horse."[6] A Senator or a Representative loses respect among his colleagues if, instead of working unheralded on necessary congressional tasks, he is constantly attempting to get his name in the headlines or is constantly making trips to his home district. House members speak derisively of the "Tuesday

4. Throughout this chapter, "congressman" is used to refer to all members of Congress— the members of both the Senate and the House of Representatives.

5. For an excellent, although somewhat dated description of the informal norms in the Senate, see Donald L. Matthews, *United States Senators and Their World* (Chapel Hill: University of North Carolina Press, 1960), chap. 5.

6. Quoted in Matthews, *United States Senators,* p. 94.

to Thursday Club" to refer to Representatives who go to their home districts every weekend, leaving late Thursday or early Friday and not returning until late Monday or early Tuesday. One Senator stated simply: "There is no substitute for hard work whatever you do."[7]

Specialization   Complementing the norm of hard work is the norm that a member should *specialize* in a certain area of legislation, not try to be a jack-of-all-trades. One Representative reports: "The members who are most successful are those who pick a specialty or an area and become real experts in it. As a consequence, when they speak they are looked upon as authorities and are highly respected. Even though they may be an authority in only one field, their influence tends to spread into other areas.[8] A Senator tells of his own experience: "I belong to twelve or thirteen committees and subcommittees. It's physically impossible to give them all the attention I should. So I have picked out two or three subcommittes in which I am especially interested and have concentrated on them. I believe that this is the usual practice around here."[9]

Honesty   Another informal norm is simply to be truthful and *honest*. In Congress a man's word has to be his bond. A congressman could not lose his influence with and the respect of his colleagues more quickly than to agree to support a fellow member on a bill and then not do so, or to mislead a fellow member on the contents of a bill. One Republican Representative has expressed it this way: "Integrity is a very important quality, a priceless ingredient. We have to rely so much on specialists and people we believe in. . . . Integrity crosses party lines. You rely on some of your Democratic colleagues equally; those you know possess integrity."[10]

Courtesy   Some would argue that the most important informal norm is *courtesy*—to extend, at least outwardly, common courtesies and even compliments to one's colleagues and to refrain from personal attacks on them. The *Congressional Record* abounds with such phrases as "the distinguished Senator from . . ." and "the able and gracious gentleman. . . ." A fellow member is always "mistaken," never a liar. The congressman is expected not to attack the motives or private lives of his colleagues

7. Quoted in David W. Rohde, Norman J. Ornstein, and Robert L. Peabody, "Political Change and Legislative Norms in the United States Senate," paper given at the 1974 annual meeting of the American Political Science Association, p. 33.

8. Quoted in Charles L. Clapp, *The Congressman: His Work as He Sees It* (Washington, D.C.: Brookings Institution, 1963), p. 24. Recent research indicates that the norm of specialization, at least in the Senate, is not as rigidly held to as it once was. See Rohde et al., "Political Change and Legislative Norms," pp. 37–40.

9. Quoted in Matthews, *United States Senators,* p. 96.

10. Quoted in Clapp, *The Congressman,* p. 25.

—to engage in personalities. There are numerous small courtesies he is expected to pay his colleagues in the House or Senate. For example, so that the other congressman can be present to defend his bill, he is expected to inform a fellow congressman before he attacks it on the floor of Congress. This rule can perhaps be best summed up in the old saying that one should be able to disagree without being disagreeable. Often persons are surprised to discover that two Senators who violently disagree on certain policy issues and often attack each others' views are in reality very good friends and have a high respect for each other. The rule of courtesy makes this sort of respect and cooperation possible.

Reciprocity Another informal norm is *reciprocity*. A congressman is expected to help out his colleagues whenever possible. It may be a matter of voting for the pet bill of another member, or obtaining some information for him, or not objecting to his request to have a home town editorial printed in the *Congressional Record*. But the key to understanding this rule is realizing that the person who gives such favors expects them to be reciprocated: he expects members to vote for his pet bills, obtain the information he needs, and not object to his insertions in the *Congressional Record*. As the late Speaker Sam Rayburn is reported to have said, "To get along, go along."

Apprenticeship An informal norm, *apprenticeship,* is often mentioned but recent research indicates it is not nearly as important as it once was. This norm states that a new member is expected quietly to learn and observe, not try immediately to play a major role in the legislative process. Nevertheless, a recent study of the House found even among Representatives with six or more years of service that two thirds felt there was no norm of apprenticeship.[11] And a recent study of the Senate found that of 40 Senators interviewed only two felt there was an apprenticeship norm. The authors conclude that "the norm is simply gone."[12] They quote a junior Senator as saying: "all the communications suggest 'get involved, offer amendments, make speeches.' The Senate has changed, we're all equals, you should act accordingly."[13]

Sanctions The *sanctions* applied to those who violate these informal norms—and there are those who violate them—can be divided into two types. The first, and mildest, is social pressure. A respected, elder member may speak to the straying legislator. A senior Senator takes aside the

11. See Herbert B. Asher, "The Learning of Legislative Norms," *American Political Science Review,* 67 (1973), 511.
12. Rohde et al., "Political Change and Legislative Norms," p. 35.
13. Quoted in Rohde et al., "Political Change and Legislative Norms," p. 36.

freshman who is refusing to specialize and warns him that his varied activities are not being appreciated. Or the congressman who refuses to return favors done him may suddenly notice a certain coolness toward him on the part of his colleagues.

The second and more important sanction is a reduction in the influence of the nonconforming legislator in Congress. Through the comments of Senators and Representatives quoted above runs the theme that the person who follows the informal norms will build his reputation and standing in Congress and, therefore, his influence. But the converse is also true: The person who does not follow the informal norms will lose respect, standing, and also influence. His bills will not be passed and his requests will be ignored. One Senator did not mince words in discussing the influence of his nonconforming colleagues: "There are Senators who stand on the floor and offer an amendment, and you just vote against it when you find out the name of the Senator who offered the amendment."[14]

Functions of the Informal Norms   In Congress one finds persons with very strong and very different views: Republicans and Democrats, women's liberation advocates and male chauvinists, integrationists and segregationists. In addition, the stakes are high: A congressman may win or lose (or think he will win or lose) a coming election depending on whether or not a certain bill passes. Thus, there is a danger that antagonisms among congressmen will become so deep and bitterness so great that cooperation among them becomes impossible. Congress could soon be deadlocked with a majority of the members not even speaking to each other!

However, the norms of courtesy, honesty, and reciprocity clearly help prevent such a situation. Cooperation is promoted, bitterness is tempered, and antagonisms are softened. As a result, 535 strong-minded individuals, representing many different points of view and working with all their might to have their views prevail, are still able to work together. Thus, the informal norms make possible the negotiating, compromising, and coalition building so essential to rule initiation, conflict resolution, and the other functions of Congress.

The performance of congressional functions is helped in other ways by the informal norms. Much of the work of Congress is dull, routine, and unglamorous—but also very necessary. The rule of working hard makes possible the completion of such work. Moreover, much of the work of Congress is technical and complex. Here, because it encourages members to develop expertness in certain areas, the norm of specialization helps.

14. Quoted in Randall B. Ripley, *Power in the Senate* (New York: St. Martin's, 1969), p. 168. See pp. 164–170 of this work for a brief, but excellent discussion of the bases of either effectiveness or ineffectiveness in the Senate.

The informal norms also help create a "take it easy," "go slow"—some would say, conservative—mood in Congress. Several norms militate against the person who, full of enthusiasm, wishes to set right the many wrongs he sees. Reciprocity, specialization, courtesy, and the habit of working hard all have in common an element that discourages the zealous reformer and encourages the cautious, "non-boat-rocking" type.

Thus, the informal norms play a vital role in making it possible for Congress to fulfill its functions, but they also lead to a more conservative, cautious Congress.

The Party Organizations and Their Leaders

The 100 Senators and 435 Representatives do not exist as 535 autonomous individuals, without distinctions in position and rank and without organizational ties binding them into subgroups. Instead they are organized into groups and into hierarchies of position and rank based on two organizing principles. First, they are organized into committees, with each committee in turn possessing its own internal organization. (More about the committee system of Congress in the next section.) Second, Congress is organized into two party groups, and each party group has its own internal organization. This section considers the party organizations and their leaders in Congress.[15]

The House of Representatives There are five party leaders of special importance in the House. The first is the *Speaker of the House of Representatives.* The Speaker is both the presiding officer of the House and the leader of the majority party. As the presiding officer, his main responsibilities are to assign bills to committees, to preside over the House sessions, and to interpret House rules; as party leader, his main responsibilities are to serve as the spokesman of his party and to attempt to coalesce and hold together his party's forces.

In fulfilling his responsibilities the Speaker has certain powers, such as the right to recognize members during floor debates and a role in appointing new members of committees. However, most of his power rests on more nebulous factors, for example, the prestige of his position, a close relationship with the President when they are of the same party, his own experience in and understanding of the House, and his personal persuasiveness. On bases such as these the skillful Speaker—and it is unlikely anyone would be chosen Speaker if he were not skillful—can slowly build

15. For more information on the party organizations and their leaders, see Randall B. Ripley, *Party Leaders in the House of Representatives* (Washington, D.C.: Brookings Institution, 1967); Randall B. Ripley, *Majority Party Leadership in Congress* (Boston: Little, Brown, 1969); and Charles O. Jones, *The Minority Party in Congress* (Boston: Little, Brown, 1970).

up his influence so that normally he is the most powerful individual in the House.

Two other persons in the majority party organization occupy important leadership positions: the majority floor leader and the majority whip. The responsibilities of the *majority floor leader* are what the name implies— he is the leader and spokesman of the party during floor debates, and he serves as a general assistant to the Speaker as party leader. He is involved in such activities as scheduling floor debates on bills, conferring with other congressional leaders and the President on the party's program, and rounding up votes for key bills. The majority floor leader can build up some power by doing favors for other members and by playing a role in commit- tee assignments. But he is working in the shadow of the Speaker, and most of his power depends on the extent to which he has the confidence and support of the Speaker.

The *majority whip* is chiefly a liaison man between the majority party leadership (that is, the Speaker, the majority floor leader, and the chairmen of the most important committees) and the rank-and-file members of the majority party. Sometimes his function is thought to be merely that of rounding up votes for the party—hence the name "whip"—but today the position is more than that. He reports to the party leadership the opinions, feelings, and requests of the ordinary members. To the ordinary members he reports the views and wishes of the leadership, as well as answers and solutions to the requests and problems of the members. The whip can build up a following in his own right by winning the confidence and respect of his fellow members, but to a large degree his power depends on the amount of trust and reliance the other party leaders place in him.

Two leaders in the minority party organization are especially important: the *minority floor leader* and the *minority whip.* They perform the same functions for the minority party as their counterparts in the majority party do. The only significant difference is that the minority floor leader is the number-one person in the minority party and is its official spokesman and leader, whereas the majority floor leader works under the Speaker.

The Senate In the Senate, five party leadership positions correspond to the five in the House, although there are several differences, the chief being that the Senate has no position comparable to that of the speakership in the House. The Vice President is the presiding officer of the Senate, as the Speaker is of the House, but in other respects the Vice President does not resemble the Speaker. He is not a party leader and possesses much less power and prestige because officially he is not even a member of the Senate, does not take part in the Senate debates, and cannot vote except in the unlikely event of a tie.

The Senate elects a *president pro tempore,* who is the official head of the Senate and has the duty of presiding over the Senate in the absence of the Vice President. But neither is the president pro tem (as it is usually shortened) equivalent to the House Speaker. In fact, he fills a largely honorary position, which is usually given to the senior member of the majority party. Almost no power goes with it.

The most important party leaders are the *majority* and *minority floor leaders* and the *majority* and *minority whips.* The functions, duties, and powers of these leaders are roughly the same as they are for the corresponding leaders in the House. The majority floor leader is more powerful in the Senate than is his counterpart in the House because he is not acting under a Speaker. Thus, he is usually the most powerful person in the Senate.

Methods of Selection   How do these party leaders obtain their positions? Both the Speaker of the House and the president pro tem of the Senate are formally elected by the entire membership of the body over which they are to preside. But, in practice, the real decision is reached in the *majority party caucus* (sometimes called the *party conference*). At the start of each new Congress the members of the majority party in the Senate meet to elect one of their members as president pro tem, normally, the member of the majority party with the most seniority. Afterward in a full Senate session he is formally elected, but the result by then is a foregone conclusion because all the members of the majority party will vote for him.

In the House of Representatives the same procedure is followed by the majority party in electing the Speaker. The Speaker is not necessarily the person in the majority party with the most seniority—in fact, he usually is not—but he is always a person with many years of experience in the House. The key to being elected Speaker by one's colleagues is to build up over a period of years a great deal of respect by working hard, by demonstrating skill and ability, and by not being so extreme as to alienate certain important factions in one's party. In addition, there is a fairly strong —but not unbreakable—tradition that when the speakership is vacant, the majority floor leader will be elected to his position. This tradition was strengthened in 1971 when Carl Albert, the former majority floor leader, was elected Speaker to replace the retired John McCormack. At the start of each new Congress a Speaker is elected, but the former Speaker is virtually always re-elected (unless, of course, he has retired or was defeated for re-election, or his party has lost its majority).

The floor leaders and whips in both House and Senate are elected by their respective party caucuses. Often, these positions are closely contested, and although former holders of these positions are usually re-elected at the start of a new Congress, there is no guarantee that they will be.[16] In 1965, at the start of the Eighty-ninth Congress, Gerald Ford upset the former minority floor leader, Charles Halleck. Halleck had been minor-

16. For an excellent analysis of conditions that encourage revolts against existing leaders, see Robert L. Peabody, "Party Leadership Change in the United States House of Representatives," *American Political Science Review,* 61 (1967), 675–693.

ity (Republican) floor leader since 1959, but the Ford group argued that new blood, fresh ideas, and more vigorous leadership were needed. And in 1971, Robert Byrd was elected Democratic whip in the Senate, upsetting the incumbent whip, Edward Kennedy. As is the case with the speakership, seniority enters in only to the degree that a member must have been in Congress long enough to gain experience and to build a reputation for skill, fair-mindedness, and moderation. In 1969 Robert Griffin was elected Republican whip while serving his first term in the Senate and Howard Baker of Tennessee—another first-termer—made a strong bid to be elected the minority (Republican) floor leader, although in the end he lost out to Hugh Scott of Pennsylvania. Skill, reputation, and contacts count more than seniority.

The Committee System

The House sits, not for serious discussion, but to sanction the conclusions of its Committees as rapidly as possible. It legislates in its committee-rooms; not by the determinations of majorities, but by the resolutions of specially commissioned minorities; so that it is not far from the truth to say that Congress in session is Congress on public exhibition, whilst Congress in its committee-rooms is Congress at work.[17]

These are the words with which the young Woodrow Wilson described congressional committees in a book that has since become a classic in American political science. Today's Congress is not exactly thus; but few political scientists would deny that there is still much truth in Wilson's observations of 80 years ago.[18]

The 22 *standing* (that is, permanent) *committees* of the House and the 18 standing committees of the Senate exercise a great deal of power and maintain a great deal of independence. Both the power and the independence of the committees are considered here.

Committee Power   Almost all standing committees are responsible for certain subject areas of legislation: appropriations, banking and currency, foreign relations, agriculture, and so forth. A bill, after its introduction in Congress, is immediately sent to the appropriate committee for consideration. That committee can report out the bill (return the bill to the full body of the House or Senate) favorably, not report it out at all, or report it out

17. Woodrow Wilson, *Congressional Government* (New York: Meridian, 1956), p. 69.

18. On the congressional committee system see Richard F. Fenno, *Congressmen in Committees* (Boston: Little, Brown, 1973), and George Goodwin, Jr., *The Little Legislatures* (Amherst: University of Massachusetts Press, 1970). Giving excellent insights into the operation of congressional committees are John F. Manley, *The Politics of Finance* (Boston: Little, Brown, 1970), and Richard F. Fenno, *The Power of the Purse* (Boston: Little, Brown, 1966).

with certain (sometimes very drastic) changes. If the committee does not report out the bill, it is for all practical purposes dead. There is a procedure by which committees can be discharged from further consideration of a bill, but it is very rarely used.

The power of the committees is also demonstrated by the generally high level of success they have in getting legislation they have reported out approved by the full House or Senate. Although committees vary in the degree to which they are successful in winning passage of measures they report out, their success rates are usually high. From 1955 to 1966, for example, 59 percent of the bills reported out by the House Education and Labor Committee were approved by the full House, and 94 percent of the bills reported out by the House Ways and Means Committee were approved.[19] Success rates such as these can be explained largely by a tendency to give a great deal of weight to the views of the committee members who have considered the bill because of their expertise and experience in their particular area. This tendency is re-enforced by the informal norms of reciprocity, which encourages congressmen to support the recommendations of other committees in the expectation that the other congressmen will in turn support the recommendations of their committees, and specialization, which encourages congressmen to defer to their colleagues recognized as specialists in certain areas.

Committees also are the means through which Congress becomes to some degree involved in rule application: the committees, based on specialized subject areas, exercise a general oversight of the application of rules by the corresponding bureaucratic departments and agencies. For example, the agricultural committees oversee the Department of Agriculture's application of rules. The appropriation committees exercise a more general oversight of the bureaucracy, because appropriations for all the bureaucratic departments flow through them. To the extent that committees check on the bureaucracy's application of rules initiated by Congress and attempt (by way of public exposure, threatened reductions in appropriations, or other pressures) to influence the way in which rules are applied, they are engaged in rule application.[20] Most observers are agreed that the committees—and Congress as a whole—do this more in a sporadic, selective manner than in a continuing, pervasive way.

Committee Independence   Until very recently it was possible to speak with complete assurance of the congressional committees' independence

19. See Fenno, *Congressmen in Committees,* p. 235.

20. For more complete discussions of the committee's oversight of the bureaucracy see John F. Bibby, "Committee Characteristics and Legislative Oversight of Administration," *Midwest Journal of Political Science,* 10 (1966), 78–98, and Ira Sharkansky, "An Appropriations Subcommittee and Its Client Agencies: A Comparative Study of Supervision and Control," *American Political Science Review,* 59 (1965), 622–628.

from control by party leaders, blocs of legislators, or other forces such as the President. The seniority system assured that the committee members could not be removed from a committee and that the committee member of the majority party with the most seniority on that committee would be its chairman, no matter how much he might have defied party leaders or other powerful persons and groups.[21]

At the start of the Ninety-second Congress, in 1971, the first real cracks appeared when the House made some modifications in the seniority system. Then at the start of the Ninety-fourth Congress, in 1975, the seniority system—at least in the House—was split wide open when the Democratic caucus first unseated the two long-time committee chairmen mentioned earlier and then a third, and replaced them with new chairmen with less seniority.[22] Eighty-four year old Wright Patman, chairman of the Banking, Currency, and Housing Committee, was replaced by Henry Reuss, who ranked fourth in seniority on the committee; and W. R. Poage, chairman of the Agricultural Committee and F. Edward Hebert, chairman of the Armed Services Committee, were both replaced by the persons ranking second in seniority on their committees.

What this breaking of the seniority system in the House of Representatives will mean in terms of committee independence in Congress depends largely on two questions. First is the question of whether or not the Senate will follow the lead of the House, something it has not yet done. Second is the question of the extent to which the seniority system will remain as a basis for selecting committee chairmen. In succeeding Congresses the new precedents set in 1975 can be continued and strengthened, or they can be weakened and abandoned. At least for the present, House committee chairmen—and, because of their power, the committees as a whole—have to be more responsive to the demands and wishes of party leaders and other persons influential in the majority party's caucus. Congress is undergoing change in this area, and about the only certain thing at this time is that the shape of power in Congress has been altered. More on this in the last section of the chapter.

Committee Procedures   There are three especially significant characteristics of the workings of the committees: Much of the actual work is done through subcommittees; many final decisions are made in executive (that is, secret) session; and the chairman is in a strong—and often dominant—position. The *subcommittees* may be either permanent or temporary. The

21. On the seniority system, see Barbara Hinckley, *The Seniority System in Congress* (Bloomington: Indiana University Press, 1971).

22. For an account of these events, see *Congressional Quarterly Weekly Report,* 33 (January 18, 1975), 114–116 and (January 25, 1975), 210–215.

temporary ones are appointed by the committee chairman to consider one specific bill (or several bills dealing with the same issue) or to conduct a certain investigation. Once its specific task is completed, the subcommittee is disbanded. A permanent subcommittee (also appointed by the chairman) is assigned a specialized subject area within the full committee's jurisdiction and considers bills in its particular area, or it is merely designated by a number or letter and considers whatever bills the chairman assigns to it.

A bill usually receives its most intensive examination by a subcommittee. If the bill is a major one, this normally involves public hearings. Various witnesses—largely members of Congress, representatives of executive departments, and leaders of interest groups, all of whom are especially concerned with the bill for one reason or another—are called in to give their views, pro or con. After hearings, the subcommittee meets to mark up the bill, that is, to make whatever changes, additions, or deletions it thinks proper. Until recently meetings to mark up a bill were always executive sessions (that is, secret sessions). Since 1973, when changes were made in the House and Senate rules, a majority of House mark-up sessions and a minority of Senate mark-up sessions have been open meetings. After the mark up the resulting version of the bill is then reported back to the full committee.

After the full committee meets to take its turn in marking up the bill, the committee approves or rejects it. If there is strong opposition in the committee to a bill, and especially if the chairman is included in this opposition, it is unlikely ever to get beyond the public-hearing stage. In fact, it may not get to that stage.

The give and take that go on in the subcommittees and committees offer ample opportunity for the negotiating and bargaining that are vital for compromises to be struck and the legislative process to move ahead. More on this later.

The *committee chairman* normally has a great deal of power within his committee.[23] The chairman sets the agenda of the committee and thus can maneuver to prevent bills he opposes from coming before it. He appoints subcommittees and subcommittee chairmen and can thereby put committee members in his debt. He appoints and controls the committee's professional staff. The chairman has had vast experience on the committee and often devotes more time and energy to committee affairs than the regular members do (remember that all Senators and many Representatives must

23. For a description of the sources of the committee chairmen's power, see Matthews, *United States Senators,* pp. 159–162. Also very helpful is a study of one particularly influential committee chairman, Wilbur Mills of the House Ways and Means Committee. See John F. Manley, "Wilbur D. Mills: A Study in Congressional Influence," *American Political Science Review,* 63 (1969), 442–464.

divide their attention between two committees). All these factors are bases on which the skillful chairman—by means of bargaining, threatening, and persuading—can build up a considerable amount of power.

The extent to which the recent moves away from pure seniority as a means of determining committee chairmanships will reduce the chairmen's power remains to be seen. Chairmen will probably retain most of the power they had previously, but will not be able to exercise it as arbitrarily as some were able to do in the past. At least in the House, the possibility of losing one's chairmanship in the next Congress hangs over each chairman's head.

Committee Membership   The size of the congressional committees varies from 7 to 50, with the number of Democrats and Republicans on them roughly in proportion to the number of Democrats and Republicans in the House or the Senate. Senators normally serve on two committees and many Representatives also serve on two committees, although some are on only one.

At the start of each Congress a number of committee vacancies must be filled, vacancies created by defeated or retired congressmen and by some committee members moving to new committee assignments. A somewhat complicated procedure is followed in filling these committee vacancies. In the House, this task is carried out by the Republican and Democratic committees on committees. Each party's Committee on Committees is constituted differently, but their tasks are the same: to assign the party's members to committee vacancies.[24] Although these two committees follow somewhat different procedures, the end result is very similar: Senior members and the leadership of the parties are the most influential in making committee assignments. In the Senate, the party leadership (especially the majority and minority floor leaders) plays a larger role than it does in the House.

The Rules Committee   Three types of congressional committees perform certain specialized functions. The first of these, the House Rules Committee, is one of the standing committees of the House of Representatives, but it does not specialize in a certain subject area of legislation as do the other standing committiees. With 435 members in the House there must be some means of scheduling the full House's consideration of bills, limiting the length of debate on them, and limiting the amendments that can be proposed on the floor. Otherwise the House would soon be bogged down

24. For an excellent description of the assignment process in the House, see Nicholas A. Masters, "Committee Assignments," *American Political Science Review,* 55 (1961), 345–357. Also very helpful is David W. Rohde and Kenneth A. Shepsle, "Democratic Committee Assignments in the House of Representatives: Strategic Aspects of a Social Choice Process," *American Political Science Review,* 67 (1973) 889–905.

in a quagmire of endless bills, proposed amendments, and seemingly interminable debate. The Rules Committee—often called the "Traffic Cop" of the House—has been established to prevent this from occurring.

After a bill has been approved by a standing committee, it goes to the Rules Committee. Then it is up to the Rules Committee to determine in what order the bills it has received are to be taken up by the full House, how much time will be alloted to the debate on a bill, and what limitations (if any) will be put on the amendments that can be offered. Sometimes the Rules Committee stipulates that no amendments may be offered, or that only certain types of amendments may be offered, or that amendments may be offered only by members of the standing committee that considered the bill. Usually, however, the only stipulation is that a member who proposes an amendment has only five minutes to speak in behalf of it. When the Rules Committee has made its decision on a bill and reports it to the full House, the bill is said to have been *granted a rule*.

The Rules Committee has often been a source of great controversy. Even though its function appears to be a neutral, "housekeeping" one, in reality it has often been anything but neutral or routine. At times the committee grants a rule (or refuses to grant it) on the basis of its evaluation of the merits of a bill. Thus, if the committee opposes a bill, it may delay granting it a rule or even refuse it a rule altogether. Or it may grant a bill it favors a rule that will help assure its quick passage in undiluted form or it may grant a bill it opposes a rule that will delay its passage or help assure its being greatly altered. At times, the committee has been able to persuade the sponsors of a bill to accept certain amendments as the price for their giving it a rule. Adding to the controversy is the fact that in recent years the committee had a decidedly conservative cast. Frequently in the 1950s and 1960s southern Democrats with conservative views teamed up with Republican members of the committee to block, delay, or alter liberal legislation in such areas as civil rights and aid to education. Today, because of changes in its membership and its leadership, the Rules Committee is playing a less independent and less conservative role than it did in the past.

Select Committees   Another type of committee that differs from the standing committees is the *select,* or special, *committee.* These are temporary committees especially appointed to investigate a certain problem or question. They have little formal power because they do not receive bills for consideration as the standing committees do. But they frequently exert a considerable amount of influence because of the power and prestige some of their members may have or because of certain spectacular situations they may uncover.

The most recent select committee with great influence was the Select Committee on Presidential Campaign Activities, which was chaired by Senator Sam Ervin and investigated in 1973 charges of illegal campaign activities and coverups of these activities in the 1972 presidential campaign. Its nationally televised hearings did much to awaken the nation to the Watergate scandal and helped set in motion the forces that resulted in Richard Nixon's near impeachment and his resignation from the presidency.

The obstensible purpose of select committees and their investigations is to obtain information needed to legislate properly. However, they often serve other purposes as well: to build the prestige and popularity of the Representatives or Senators conducting the investigations or to embarrass one of the political parties or its leaders. It is often charged that the investigations conducted by select committees, instead of serving legitimate legislative purposes, degenerate into circuses timed for maximum publicity. Although the Ervin Committee's 1973 investigation generally received high marks for its care and thoughtfulness, other select committees in the past have not been evaluated so favorably.

Conference Committees   The third type of committee that differs from the regular standing committee is the *conference committee*. [25] These are joint committees, composed equally of Representatives and Senators, and their function is to iron out differences in House and Senate versions of the same bill. They are temporary committees—a new committee is appointed for each bill that passes the House and Senate in different forms. Their members are drawn from the House and Senate standing committees that originally considered the bill, normally either the chairman of the committee or the chairman of the subcommittee that considered the bill in committee, the ranking majority members (the person of the majority party second in seniority), and the ranking minority member. If additional or different individuals are appointed, the chairmen of the committees name them.

When a conference committee meets, it attempts to hammer out a compromise between the positions of the two houses. This compromise is then reported to the House and Senate, and they must either accept or reject it—no changes may be made. If both houses accept the compromise, that is the end of the matter, and the bill is sent to the President for his signature. If, however, either house rejects the compromise, the conference committee tries again. If it is able to come up with another compromise (or if one house just gives in to the other), the compromise goes to the houses again. If the committee cannot reach agreement or if one of the houses should reject the agreement a second time, the bill is, in most cases, dead.

25. For a comprehensive consideration of the nature and politics of conference committees, see David J. Vogler, *The Third House: Conference Committees in the United States Congress* (Evanston, Ill.: Northwestern University Press, 1971).

These conference committees can exert a great deal of influence at this final, crucial stage of the legislative process. Because the product of a conference committee must be either accepted or rejected in its entirety, the House or the Senate may be forced into voting certain provisions it really does not favor. And the conferees (as the members of the conference committee are called) can kill a bill by failing to reach a compromise or by agreeing to a version of the bill they know one or both houses will reject. Although conferees are not supposed to include provisions in the new version of the bill that were not in either the House or Senate version of the bill, this rule has been frequently violated.

The Filibuster

Because of the Senate's rules of procedure, a group of Senators strongly opposed to a bill that appears headed for passage has one last weapon— the *filibuster,* a means of preventing the passage of a bill by using long speeches and other parliamentary maneuvers to prevent it from coming to a vote. But the filibuster has been seriously weakened in the past fifteen years, and whether or not it is still a potent weapon is now in doubt.

Until 1975 it took a two-thirds vote to close off debate in the Senate. This meant that if a minority of Senators were strongly opposed to a particular piece of legislation, one of them could obtain the floor and speak for hours, then yield the floor to another one of the filibustering Senators, who would speak for hours and who in turn would yield to another, and so forth. Those filibustering would gladly yield the floor to anyone who wished to speak on the bill, offer amendments, or bring up other matters for Senate consideration. But as soon as there was an attempt to bring the bill to a vote, they would obtain the floor again and continue their speeches.

Senators fighting a filibuster had three options. First, they could give in, agreeing to drop the bill completely or striking a compromise by accepting certain changes in the bill in return for the end of the filibuster. Often the mere threat of a filibuster was enough for the opponents of a bill to obtain certain concessions.

The supporters of the bill could, as a second option, fight the filibuster and hope to wear out and outlast the others. This maneuver included keeping a quorum of Senators on hand in order to force those filibustering into nearly round-the-clock sessions. They could finally try to obtain a two-thirds majority in favor of shutting off debate after some specified time, that is, to *impose cloture* (also called *closure*). The difficulty Senators had in mustering the two thirds necessary to impose cloture is revealed by the fact that from 1917, when cloture was first provided for, to 1962 it was imposed only four times.

But since 1962 things have been changing. First, cloture became easier

to obtain. From 1962 to 1975 cloture was imposed 18 times (compared
to only four times in the previous 45 years).[26] In part, the effectiveness of
the filibuster rested on Senators who took pride in the Senate as "the
greatest deliberative body in the world" and as the one legislative body
with unlimited debate. Once that tradition started to fall, it apparently
became easier for Senators to vote for cloture. Then in 1975 the Senate
voted to allow three fifths of its members elected and serving to close off
debate. This means that 60 senators can now impose cloture.

It is too early to judge the full effect of the new cloture rule, but it is
bound to weaken further the ability of a minority of senators to block
legislation or to obtain concessions as the price for the end of their filibuster. Only time can tell how much the filibuster has been weakened, but
it clearly has lost much of the potential it once had.

Determinants of Congressional Behavior

A question that has intrigued political scientists, journalists, and casual
observers of Congress is what causes a member of Congress to act as he
does. When a Senator introduces a bill or votes "no" on a bill in a
committee session, what motivates him? His own convictions, his party's
position, his constituents' views? In other words, what sources of inputs
are especially important to congressmen?

With the many potential influences that surround legislators, it is unlikely
that any of their acts spring from only one motive. Usually, a Representative or a Senator acts in response to multifarious influences. Their significance varies, depending on the specific question at stake. At one time,
constituency influences may be especially strong; at another time, party
influences may be predominant. Table 8.1, based on interviews with Representatives about how they had decided several important issues on
which they had recently voted, shows the importance the Representatives

Table 8.1   Reported importance of influences by Representatives

Reported importance	Constituency	Fellow congressmen	Interest groups	Presidency	Reading	Staff	Party leadership
Determinative	7%	5%	1%	4%	0%	1%	0%
Major importance	31	42	25	14	17	8	5
Minor importance	51	28	40	21	32	26	32
Not important	12	25	35	61	52	66	63
Total %	101%	100%	101%	100%	101%	101%	100%
Total N	222	221	222	222	221	221	222

Source: John W. Kingdon, *Congressmen's Voting Decisions* (New York: Harper &
Row, 1973), p. 19.

26. For a listing of all the cloture votes held in the Senate from 1917 to 1975, see the
Congressional Quarterly Weekly Report, 33 (January 18, 1975), 119.

attached to several potential sources of influence. Their constituencies and their fellow congressmen ranked the highest in influence, interest groups were ranked near the center, while party leadership, the presidency, their staffs, and their own reading ranked relatively low. This section of the chapter seeks to sort out the basic influences that affect congressmen's decisions and to understand more fully why the sort of rankings found in Table 8.1 are as they are.

Constituencies

Campaign oratory is often liberally sprinkled with "I will fully represent the people of the great state of _____" or "My opponent has failed to protect the interests of the third district of _____." Appealing as such phrases are to an electorate conditioned to the clichés of campaigns, they are gross simplifications of a complex and not fully explored relationship: the legislator and his constituents.

The Problem   It is obvious that no legislator can represent *all* people or *all* interests within his constituency.[27] In every constituency there are people who have conflicting desires that result in conflicting demands being made on a congressman. To represent (to speak for, to work for) one interest is not to represent another. Thus, every Representative and Senator must choose (though perhaps unconsciously) the points of view in the constituency to which he is going to give priority and the points of view he will relegate to secondary positions. On this basis a congressman's legal constituency (the entire population of the state or district that elects him) can be distinguished from his actual constituency (those groups and persons whose interests he is especially active in promoting). Normally, his actual constituency consists of those groups and persons who are especially important to him electorally. Thus, if most of a Representative's votes come from organized labor, blacks, and certain ethnic groups, it is very likely that these will also make up his actual constituency and that business and professional groups will receive much less, if any, of his attention.

Compounding the complexity and adding to the uncertainty is the problem of the congressman's knowing what his constitutents—legal or actual—are thinking. Often we picture the constituent-legislator relationship as being one of the constituent actively putting pressure on the congressman, forcing him to move in one direction or another. But as we saw in Chapter 4, most constituents know very little about their congressman, care little what he does on most issues, and rarely if ever communicate their views

27. For a development of this point, see Lewis Anthony Dexter, *The Sociology and Politics of Congress* (Chicago: Rand McNally, 1969), chap. 8.

to him.[28] As a result, the congressman often has to guess what his constituents' opinions on a given issue are.

Degree of Influence   The foregoing discussion helps us understand why the clarity of the positions taken by constituencies, and therefore the amount of their influence, vary with the type of issue and type of constituency. They vary with the type of constituency because some are so homogeneous in interests or are so dominated by one interest that any congressman has to include that interest or interests within his actual constituency in order to be elected. It is difficult to conceive of a Senator being elected from Iowa who does not include the corn and hog farming interests within his actual constituency, or of a Representative being elected from a working-class area of Detroit who ignores organized labor. One representative from a tobacco-growing area put it this way: "I've got many, many families in my district who make a living on tobacco. Now, I never argued that cigarettes are good for your health. . . . If you could show me some way my people are going to eat if I vote against cigarettes, I'll do it. [Interviewer: So you start with this constituency factor.] It starts there and it ends there. That's all there is to it. If you don't, you aren't going to be around here very long. Not on something like this, where their livelihood is involved."[29]

On the other hand, a congressman representing a heterogeneous constituency faces so many diverse groups and interests that on any given issue his constituency is likely to speak with many conflicting voices. As a result, he can pick and choose the interests and groups to which he will appeal for votes. A Senator representing a very diversified state, like New York or Ohio, or a Representative from a partly working-class, partly middle-class district has a considerable amount of latitude in determining to which interests and groups he will appeal.

However, even the most homogeneous constituency is divided or apathetic about many issues. On these the congressman is fairly free to determine his position. The Iowa Senator may face a united and aroused constituency on an issue affecting corn and hog farming, but a divided and apathetic constituency on a foreign-policy issue. And even in the most heterogeneous constituency there are at least one or two issues on which the constituency is in so much agreement and with such intensity that its congressman almost has to take the constituency's side. One Representative explained his vote for an amendment at the time of many college disruptions, even though he personally did not favor it, on the basis of an aroused, intense constituency:

28. See pp. 66–77. Also very helpful in this regard is Warren E. Miller and Donald E. Stokes, "Constituency Influence in Congress," *American Political Science Review,* 67 (1963), 45–56.

29. John W. Kingdon, *Congressmen's Voting Decisions* (New York: Harper & Row, 1973), p. 36.

People are terribly upset about the colleges, and Congress has been getting a lot of complaint. "What are you characters doing down in Washington, anyway?" That's a potentially dangerous situation for the country, when people feel this way about their representatives. This was one way to show them that we have noticed what's going on. It was a bit of demagoguery, if you will, but I think that has its place. It lets people know that Congress cares. I wouldn't do it if it would really do some damage. But it wasn't going to do any damage. It was pretty innocuous. So my conscience is clear on this.[30]

In short, constituency influence seems to be determined by an interplay between the congressman's own views and other influences on the one hand, and the nature of his constituency and the intensity and unity of its feelings on any particular issue on the other hand.[31]

Fellow Congressmen

A second important source of influence on congressional behavior is the congressmen's colleagues in the House and Senate. We have seen earlier in the chapter that Congress, through its committee structure and through its informal norm of specialization, operates to a large degree on the principle of a division of labor. Instead of everyone attempting to be expert in all areas, members specialize. The corallary of this division of labor is influence of one congressman by another. It is no gain to have a division of labor if those specializing in one area have no influence over the nonspecialists in that area.

Several additional reasons why a congressman is likely to be influenced by his fellow congressmen have been pointed out by John Kingdon: "He is a professional politician, and will give advice appropriately tailored to the congressman's political needs. His past performance as a cue-giver, including his judgment, his knowledge of facts, and his trustworthiness, is known to the congressman. He is readily available at the time of voting, a consideration of paramount importance. He is also of equal status with his fellows, so that a colleague feels comfortable about discussing legislation with him."[32]

Of course one is not likely to be influenced to the same degree by all one's colleagues. Influence seems to be greatest among congressmen who are in basic agreement on political philosophy and general approach to policy issues and who are perceived as having some specialized expertise in a particular area. Influence also seems to vary with the type of issue under consideration, with influence being the greatest on relatively minor issues. As one Representative put it: "A lot of votes come up that you know absolutely nothing about. On major issues, you will think about it before-

30. Kingdon, *Congressmen's Voting Decisions,* p. 39.
31. On this point, see Miller and Stokes, "Constituency Influence in Congress," and Kingdon, *Congressmen's Voting Decision,* pp. 29–65.
32. Kingdon, *Congressmen's Voting Decisions,* p. 70.

hand. But on other things—scores of votes, really—many members rush on to the floor, seek out someone on the committee they know, have a 3- or 4-minute talk, and make up their mind on the spot."[33]

Interest Groups

Another factor in the world of forces acting upon congressmen is interest groups. Literally hundreds of groups spend hundreds of thousands of dollars every year attempting to influence congressmen. As we saw in Chapter 6, however, the influence possessed by interest groups and lobbyists on Capitol Hill is usually limited.

The most significant role of interest groups in Congress—given the problems inherent in winning overwhelming influence—is not that of an independent factor swaying congressmen, but that of a reinforcing factor, strenthening constituency influences and personal beliefs. When a former tobacco farmer, now a tobacco-state Senator, works hard for tobacco price supports, or a black Representative from Detroit's inner city votes for an affirmative action program in government hiring practices, are they responding to constituent pressures, to their own beliefs, or to organized group demands? The probable answer is that they are responding to all three. The American Tobacco Institute is likely to have as little impact on the black Detroit Representative as is the NAACP on the tobacco-state Senator. In these examples, as in others, interest groups are reinforcing factors—calling attention to needs with which the congressman is already sympathetic—and not independent factors changing the position of congressmen whose own beliefs and constituencies are negative toward the group.[34]

Political Parties

"[B]y any measure party remains the single most important factor in roll-call voting. No other measurable dichotomy better predicts voting behavior in the House of Representatives. Most votes on most issues produce significant, meaningful, and consistent partisan dichotomies."[35] This conclusion—based on a careful, thorough study of congressional roll-call voting—comes as something of a surprise to those who are used to thinking of the two parties as hopelessly split and without a dime's worth of differ-

33. Kingdon, *Congressmen's Voting Decisions,* pp. 94–95.

34. This leaves the situation in which a congressman's constituents are apathetic and he himself has no clear beliefs. In such situations—especially when interest groups have some of the resources mentioned in Chapter 6—interest groups act as an independent force.

35. Julius Turner, *Party and Constituency: Pressures on Congress,* rev. ed. by Edward V. Schneier (Baltimore: Johns Hopkins Press, 1970), p. 239. Also see David B. Truman, *The Congressional Party* (New York: Wiley, 1959).

ence between them. And it seems to contradict Table 8.1, which shows party leadership ranking lowest in the amount of influence attributed to it by Representatives.

In trying to understand these apparent conflicts, we should first recognize that each party has its share of mavericks. There are Senators, like Clifford Case of New Jersey, who in 1974 voted against a majority of his Republican colleagues and with a majority of the opposition Democrats on 79 percent of the roll-call votes in which the majorities of the two parties were opposing each other. There are Representatives like David Satterfield of Virginia, who in 1974 voted against a majority of his fellow Democrats and with a majority of the opposition Republicans on 88 percent of the roll-call votes in which the majorities of the two parties were opposing each other. For such individuals, inputs arising from their parties are clearly of little importance.

Such persons are the exception, however, not the rule. Over the past several years only 10 to 13 percent of the House members have voted with the opposition party more often than with their own.[36]

Voting along party lines becomes even more sharply defined when certain areas of legislation are considered separately. Figure 8.1 shows the voting of the two parties in 1974 on several issues that the Americans for Democratic Action (a strongly liberal organization) thought crucial. The Democrats in both the House and Senate were much more liberal than the Republicans. This pattern also held true when comparing southern Democrats with southern Republicans.

But this leaves the puzzle of why there is a significant amount of voting along party lines at the same time that congressmen have indicated they are not greatly influenced by party leaders. The answer lies in the false assumption that party voting can only be a result of the influence of party leaders. Much of the relationship between party affiliation and voting can be explained on bases other than that of a party exerting influence or pressure on congressmen. Members of a party tend to have similar personal views and to come from similar constituencies—both factors that tend by themselves to result in voting similarities. Also of great importance are the subtle ways in which a person's sense of identification with his party is reinforced by the customs and organization of Congress. One freshman Senator reported seeing how party spirit develops.

The Republicans and Democrats sit on the floor of the Senate in separate groups, the Republicans on the right, the Democrats on the left. Most members eat their lunch in a small dining room "For Senators Only," and there the Republicans and Democrats eat separately. Republicans and Democrats even have separate lounges so that the contacts a freshman senator makes are largely with members of his own

36. See Turner, *Party and Constituency,* p. 36.

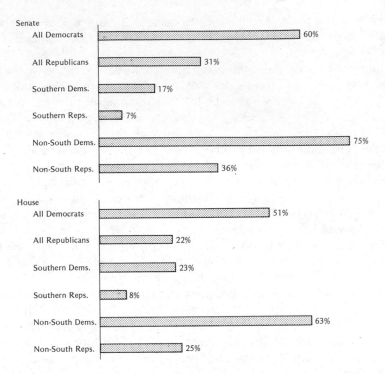

aThe figures are the average of the percentage of liberal votes cast on 21 issues in the Senate and 23 issues in the House, selected by Americans for Democratic Action as key votes in 1974.

Source: Compiled from *Congressional Quarterly Weekly Report,* 33(February 22,1975), pp.389–391.

Figure 8.1   Liberal votes on key issues, 1974a

party. He loafs, he even takes a nap in this lounge, but it is a Republican—or Democratic—nap.[37]

In the House of Representatives the members of each party from a state or an area often meet together informally to share ideas, plot strategy, and incidentally reinforce each other's sense of party identification. Thus, if a member bolts his party on too many votes, he may be shunned or made to feel unwelcome by his colleagues. As one member of the House expressed It: "If you don't go along [with the party's positions], you are made to feel like an illegitimate child at a family dinner."[38] Professor Matthews summed it up well: "Party 'discipline' may be weak, but party 'identification' is strong."[39]

37. D. P. Griswold, "A Freshman Senator Makes a Report," *New York Times Magazine* (March 8, 1953), p. 53. Quoted in Matthews, *United States Senators,* p. 121.

38. Quoted in Ripley, *Party Leaders in the House of Representatives,* p. 153.

39. Matthews, *United States Senators,* p. 123.

Nevertheless, party leaders can exert some influence by offering favors on the basis of their ability to influence committee assignments, assignment of bills to committees, recognition of speakers during floor debates, and so forth. Thus, strong party leaders can do something to help create party unity by persuading, bargaining, and threatening.

The President

As we saw in Chapter 7, the President's influence over Congress is far from complete. Nevertheless one of the central phenomena of the American political system in the twentieth century has been the tremendous growth of this influence—an influence that waned as a result of Watergate and the greater congressional independence that followed it, but still remains formidable. The President plays—and is expected to play—a major role in identifying the issues and problems Congress is to consider and then in working for adoption of the solutions he favors. To a large degree, Congress takes the proposals of the President and accepts, rejects, or modifies them; it rarely takes the initiative in proposing major new programs. A committee chairman gave an excellent illustration of this situation when he told an administration witness at a committee hearing: "Don't expect us to start from scratch on what you people want. That's not the way we do things here—*you* draft the bills and *we* work them over."[40] This is in sharp contrast to the day—seen as recently as the 1920s in the Coolidge and Harding administrations—when the President to a large degree sat back, waited for Congress to act, and then either signed or vetoed the bills passed by Congress.

Presidential influence results from the need for some centralizing, coalescing force in the face of Congress's splintered authority. As is detailed more fully in the last section of this chapter, decision making in Congress is marked by bargaining and negotiating among many conflicting individuals and interests. The power of one checks the power of another. This leads to either deadlock and inaction or slow, incremental change. The presidency is the one institution with the drive and power necessary to move Congress off dead center and in new directions. Not that the President usually obtains exactly what he wants from Congress, but by the skillful use of his powers (outlined in Chapter 7) he is often able to persuade it to initiate policies that are basic departures from old ones.

The President's influence in Congress, great as it is, is not all-powerful, and it varies considerably with changing circumstances. It is usually at its greatest immediately after his election to the presidency, a period often referred to as his "honeymoon with Congress." This harmony probably

40. Quoted in Richard E. Neustadt, "Presidency and Legislation: Planning the President's Program," *American Political Science Review*, 69 (1955), 1015.

results from the freshness of the new President, the absence of old animosities, and the patronage that a new President is able to dispense. As the President uses up his patronage, for a variety of reasons alienates certain congressmen, and loses the magic glow of success, criticism in Congress mounts and his legislative proposals face tougher and tougher going. The "honeymoon" is over.

The President's influence also varies from one subject area to another. Normally, as was stressed in Chapter 7, his influence is significantly greater in the area of foreign affairs—an area in which the President is better informed and traditionally has had greater power—than in domestic affairs.

Personal Beliefs

Thus far a variety of influences on congressmen have been considered, but all of them are influences acting on—not arising from within—the congressmen. What impact do the Senators' and Representatives' own ideas of right or wrong, of what is needed or not needed, have on their actions? Clearly, a congressman is not some automaton completely controlled by a complex of outside influences. He is not a balloon floating in the air, drifting with the prevailing winds. To make such a claim is to deny the "humanness" of legislators. All persons are guided to some extent by their own beliefs, attitudes, and perceptions. And, given the ambiguities and conflicts often present in the external influences, opportunities to exert one's own convictions and beliefs are certainly present.

That such is the case has frequently been attested to by congressmen in interviews with political scientists. One study found that, of 87 Representatives interviewed, 28 percent said they follow their own judgments entirely, and an additional 46 percent said they partly follow their own judgments and partly follow their constituents' views. Only 23 percent reported following their constituents' views to the exclusion of their own judgments.[41]

Another researcher, who had engaged in extensive interviewing of members of the House of Representatives, commented in this way:

When a congressman says, as several did, "I usually vote my political philosophy," it is not an idle statement. . . . Examples of the importance of policy attitudes on votes abound at every hand in the interviews. On defense matters, one congressman will cite as an influence on his ABM vote his belief in a "strong national defense"; another expresses his willingness to "take some risks for peace" and adds, "it's a value judgment, not a question of fact.". . . On education matters, one congressman told me, "I've always been for aid to education. It's the liberal

41. Roger H. Davidson, *The Role of the Congressman* (New York: Pegasus, 1969), pp. 116–117.

position, you know''; while another explains, ''I'm conservative by inclination and I don't believe in massive federal aid to schools''; while yet another notes, ''I think education is the best investment we can make.''[42]

Studies that have analyzed the roll-call voting of congressmen also indicate that the influence of personal beliefs is present and measurable. One study concluded that the ''evidence of our research indicates that members of the House do in fact vote both their own policy views and their perceptions of their constituents' views, at least on issues of social welfare, foreign involvement, and civil rights.''[43]

In short, both the congressmen's own perceptions of the basis for their decisions and their actual roll-call voting indicate that their convictions and beliefs do affect their actions as legislators.

The foregoing discussion of congressional behavior indicates that congressmen are not under clearly perceived, rigid mandates. They are not slaves to any particular set of inputs—whether it comes from their party, the President, their constituents, their personal beliefs, or interest groups. Rather, congressmen receive inputs from a profusion of sources, none of which holds predominate power over them. The net result is, first, that in their interest representation function, congressmen have a considerable amount of latitude in determining which interests they are going to represent. This is particularly important because it creates a potential for Congress to overcome much of the bias in interest representation caused by the bias in the interest group structure noted in Chapter 6. The extent to which Congress in reality does so, however, is questionable. It is undeniable that most of the groups underrepresented in the interest group structure —such as migrant farm workers, consumers, and the poor—do have at least a few strong spokesmen in Congress, but it is equally undeniable that these spokesmen usually seem to be outnumbered and lack enough power to have a significant impact on legislative decisions.

A second result of the diverse inputs flowing into Congress is that it is able to maintain a large degree of flexibility in its rule initiation. The rules initiated by Congress are not the predictable outcomes of one or two overwhelming forces. Rather, they are the outcomes of a large number of inputs, whose impact constantly shifts from one issue to another and from one congressman to another.

The third result of the welter of inputs to which congressmen must react is that the largely white, male, high social class, highly educated congressional decision makers cannot be a law unto themselves. There are numerous inputs to which they must react. Although this does not mean Congress is a mirror, reflecting the public's exact wishes—we have seen that constituency is only one of the inputs and that there are reasons why congress-

42. Kingdon, *Congressmen's Voting Decisions,* pp. 245–246.
43. Miller and Stokes, ''Constituency Influence in Congress,'' p. 51.

men do not fully reflect their constituencies' views—it does mean it can not be a closed elite, merely pursuing its members' private interests.

Decision Making in Congress: Implications

Congress and the decision-making process that goes on within it are such that its performance of its functions is both helped and hindered, but clearly helped more than hindered. In this final section of the chapter the decision-making process is analyzed in order to determine how it affects the functions of Congress and its role in policy making. The crucial point that must be stressed is that Congress is so constituted that bargaining among the many interests represented in Congress is both necessary and possible.

The Need for Bargaining

From one point of view, all congressmen are equal: All have one vote, all have the right to introduce bills and to take part in floor debates. But, in fact, the power and influence of congressmen vary greatly. This in part results from the members' observance or nonobservance of the informal, unwritten rules and the resulting gain or loss in influence. It also results from their committee assignments and their occupation of formal leadership positions. The prestige and power of congressional committees vary; thus the prestige and power of their individual members also vary. A member of the House Appropriations Committee has a more effective base on which to develop his influence than has a member of the District of Columbia Committee, simply because the Appropriations Committee's decisions have a greater impact than have the District of Columbia Committee's decisions. And the chairman of a committee—or of a subcommittee—obviously has a stronger base of power than the regular members of his committee. The same, of course, holds true for the floor leaders and other party leaders in relation to the regular members of the House or Senate.

But this does not mean that there is a unified elite power structure in Congress. For power is distributed widely among a number of key individuals and groups—individuals and groups who are often in conflict with each other. In addition, most congressmen are not equally powerful (or equally powerless) in all subject areas. A representative who is known as an expert on agricultural affairs and is the chairman of a subcommittee of the Agriculture Committee is probably very influential on issues within his subject area, but not especially influential on, say, foreign-policy issues.

In summary, there is an *uneven distribution* of power in Congress with the result that, on any given issue, there are key individuals and groups who are in a position to wield a great deal of influence.

This uneven distribution of power helps create a situation that forces the sponsors of legislation to enter into negotiations with the other congressmen and makes it highly unlikely that any single interest is able to get legislation passed by itself. Key, powerful individuals and groups are often in a position where they can block, or seriously delay, legislation. The committees in the House and Senate to which a bill is referred and their chairmen, the Rules Committee in the House, and blocs of Representatives or Senators strongly opposed to a piece of legislation and willing to use their power to stop it are all examples of individuals or groups often able to block or delay legislation. Therefore, in order to succeed in getting legislation passed, its sponsors must bargain with these key individuals or groups in order to win their support, or at least their acquiescence. In the process, a coalition containing different interests, groups, and individuals is formed. Most legislation that passes Congress does so not because one side has overwhelmed its opposition and won a clear-cut victory, but because one side has bargained with its opposition and won its support or acquiescence. This is the *politics of accommodation*.

The Nature of Bargaining

There are two types of bargaining that congressmen resort to in building coalitions.[44]

Compromise   A situation in which two or more conflicting individuals or groups reach agreement by finding a middle ground between their positions that all are willing to accept is a *compromise*. This type of bargaining is illustrated by an appropriations bill whose supporters want to appropriate, say, $100 million to a certain program; its opponents want a $50 million appropriation. A compromise is struck, and some figure between $100 million and $50 million is settled on. Whether it is closer to $100 or $50 million depends on the relative power of the two forces. Compromises work equally well in nonappropriation areas: certain modifications can be made in any bill—perhaps certain exemptions are included in it, or perhaps its enforcement procedure is altered.

Logrolling   Coalitions can also be built by a process called logrolling. In *logrolling* the sponsors of the legislation win the support of those opposed to it by giving them something they want. The "something" in this case may be either support for the adoption of a policy desired by the opposing forces or support for a nonpolicy goal of theirs. An example of the former is the famous *"pork barrel" legislation,* legislation that includes a large

44. This section draws heavily from Froman, *The Congressional Process,* pp. 22–27. For another helpful and sophisticated discussion of coalition building, see William H. Riker, *The Theory of Political Coalitions* (New Haven, Conn.: Yale University Press, 1962).

number of public works—new post-office buildings, dams, flood control projects, and so forth. A winning coalition is built up by including projects in the constituencies of enough congressmen. Another form of logrolling occurs when those opposed to the legislation agree to support it in exchange for the support of the legislation's sponsors for some other piece of legislation that the opponents are urging.

A Representative once gave an excellent example of logrolling in response to an interviewer's questions concerning a bill that would prohibit the banning of cigarette advertising by regulatory agencies: "This will be sort of a buddy vote. I know cigarettes are harmful and I wouldn't touch them myself. But a lot of my friends are concerned about this, because tobacco means a lot to the economy of their areas. They do things for me when I need it, and I'll do this for them. Frankly, it's just a matter of helping out your friends."[45]

Often logrolling is more implicit than explicit. A Congressman goes along on a bill assuming in a general way that its sponsors owe him their support at some future time. The informal norm of reciprocity is a direct encouragement of logrolling.

The Facilitation of Bargaining

The rules of organization and procedure help create an atmosphere in which bargaining and coalition building are made likely. The informal norms—reciprocity, courtesy, honesty, and specialization—are particularly helpful in encouraging compromises and logrolling. As we have seen, they make possible the cooperation and the negotiation among the members of Congress on which the reaching of agreements depends. The rule of reciprocity is especially important. Members are expected to "go along," to cooperate and support each other's projects as much as possible.

The fact that most of Congress's work is done by committees also promotes negotiation. It is easier for a committee of 25 persons to negotiate and bargain than it is for an assembly of 100 or 435. Bargaining is also facilitated by the existence of many informal contacts among congressmen. No doubt many bargains are struck over tables in the Senate and House restaurants, over the telephone, and in the lounges off the Senate and House floors. And as was seen in the preceding section, congressmen are normally not under any rigid mandate or strict pressure from their party, constituents, or other forces. The inputs flowing into Congress do not rigidly bind its members. Thus, on most issues, they have room to maneuver—they have sufficient flexibility to engage in compromising and logrolling.

45. Kingdon, *Congressmen's Voting Decisions,* p. 97.

In summary, for every proposed piece of legislation there will usually be a number of individuals and groups with sufficient power to block or seriously delay it. As a result, the sponsors of the legislation must enter into negotiations with these individuals and groups in order to win their support. Both the formal and informal natures of Congress, its members, and its procedures make possible the negotiating and bargaining that are at the heart of this process.

This process leads to a time-consuming, cumbersome process of decision making that sometimes fails to work at all, as was clearly seen in 1975 when Congress—after bright promises of new congressional initiatives—floundered throughout 1975 seeking effective new policies to deal with the energy shortage. This was an issue that was so divisive that the reaching of agreement by the processes of compromise and logrolling proved to be impossible. The fact that President Ford pushed for an approach different from the one the leaders of Congress were pushing added to the difficulty of reaching agreement. With each of 535 strong-willed individuals pressing his own point of view, the wonder is less that congressional decision making is cumbersome and sometimes breaks down than that it usually is able to muddle through to agreements on basic questions of public policy.

Bargaining and Conflict Resolution   The significance of bargaining and coalition building lies in the fact that this is the process by which Congress performs the vital system-maintenance function of conflict resolution. Coalition building is, in fact, almost synonymous with conflict resolution. When a winning coalition (one with sufficient strength to pass the legislation) has been assembled, it means that a large number of diverse interests have come together and agreed on the desirability of a piece of legislation. This would not necessarily be true if a bare majority in Congress could ram through its policies. But the fact is that more than a majority is needed—a large number of powerful individuals and groups, occupying key positions, must be satisfied. Moreover these individuals and groups represent certain interests and points of view. Thus, every time one of these individuals or groups has been satisfied, another interest has been satisfied. In line with the two basic types of bargaining, this satisfaction arises either from concessions that were granted in the legislation itself or from other policy or nonpolicy advantages that were gained. But in either case the interest has been satisfied—or at least it feels it can "live with" the legislation. In short, conflicts are being resolved in a manner acceptable to the interested parties.

In addition, as we saw in the first section of this chapter, to the extent that Congress is able to resolve conflicts successfully, it is helping to generate support and to create a feeling of legitimacy. Thus, more than just conflict resolution is involved.

This is, of course, the ideal. Sometimes Congress is unable to satisfy all interests involved and no successful coalition emerges. Then deadlock sets in, no action is taken, and the status quo is preserved. Or despite strong demands for a bold, new policy, only minor alterations are made in existing policies. To the extent that this happens (and in fact it happens frequently), the conflicts remain and Congress is not successfully performing its conflict-resolution function. This occurs most often when a very controversial and divisive issue is at stake, a situation that prevailed in 1975 in the area of the energy shortage. As explained earlier, one of the key reasons why this does not occur more often is that the President is often able to affect the flow of events in Congress. By throwing the weight of his office behind one side in a struggle, he assures the victory for it and the initiation of a new policy. Presidents also, of course, often fail in such attempts—or, knowing that the attempt is doomed to failure anyway, do not try.

The Question of Bias

One question remains: Do the congressional rules of procedure and the importance they give to key, strategically placed groups and individuals result in Congress as a whole being more favorable toward some interests and less favorable toward others? Until very recently the answer to this question was clearly yes, but today the correct answer is less certain. Until the 1970s all the cards seemed to be stacked in favor of conservative, rural, and southern-oriented interests and points of view. The filibuster was defended by the conservatives and southerners and was seen as an important protection for them; a conservative coalition of southern Democrats and Republicans dominated many roll-call votes—and, some would say, dominated Congress—and the seniority system put conservative southern Democrats in the chairmanships of almost all the important committees. In addition, the informal norms of Congress tend to create a conservative, "go slow" atmosphere. The end result was a Congress much more responsive to the demands arising from a conservative, rural, southern point of view than from a liberal, urban point of view.

But we must return to the recurring observation of this chapter: Congress is undergoing rapid change. Congress in 1976 is different from the Congress of 1966—and even 1971. Earlier we saw that the filibuster is only a vestige of the once-powerful weapon of a determined minority.

Table 8.2 shows what has happened to the southern dominance of the key committee chairmanships from 1971 to 1975. Southern Democrats chair only one of the six most important House committees, whereas only four years ago they chaired five of the six. The Senate has changed much less—especially its most important committees—but even in the Senate

Table 8.2   Geographic distribution of committee chairmanships, 1971 and 1975

	Senate		House	
	1971	1975	1971	1975
Number of Committees	17	18	21	22
Percentage of southern Chairmen[a]	52.9%	33.3%	18.1%	40.9%
Percentage of southern chairmen of six most important committees[b]	100.0%	83.3%	83.3%	16.7%

[a] The South is here considered to be the eleven states of the old Confederacy: Virginia, North Carolina, South Carolina, Georgia, Florida, Alabama, Mississippi, Tennessee, Louisiana, Texas, and Arkansas.

[b] The six Senate committees considered most important are Appropriations, Armed Services, Finance, Foreign Relations, Judiciary, and Banking, Housing, and Urban Affairs. The six House committees are Appropriations, Armed Services, Judiciary, Rules, Ways and Means, and Banking, Currency, and Housing.

Source: Compiled from *Congressional Quarterly Weekly Report*, 29 (Feb. 5, 1971), 341–343 and (Feb. 12, 1971), 368–372, and 33 (Feb. 8, 1975), 295–301.

Table 8.3   The conservative coalition: Frequency and successes in roll call votes, 1968–1974

Year	Percentage present[a]	Percentage successful[b]		
		Total	Senate	House
1968	24%	73%	80%	63%
1969	27	68	67	71
1970	22	66	64	70
1971	30	83	86	79
1972	27	69	63	79
1973	23	61	54	67
1974	24	59	54	67

[a] A roll call vote on which the conservative coalition is present: one in which a majority of the southern Democrats and a majority of the Republicans are voting together against a majority of the nonsouthern Democrats.

[b] Roll call votes on which the conservative coalition was successful.

Source: *Congressional Quarterly Weekly Report*, 33 (January 25, 1975), p. 190.

there has been a shift away from southern dominance of committee chairmanships.

Table 8.3 shows the strength of the conservative coalition from 1968 to 1974. Over the years, the number of roll-call votes on which a majority of the southern Democrats and a majority of the Republicans voted together against a majority of the nonsouthern Democrats has gone up and down, as has the number of coalition victories. If anything the success rate has been in decline in recent years. Although the conservative coalition is still a potent factor to be reckoned with in Congress, its strength may be waning.

All this means that an earlier bias in the rules and structures of Congress that gave great advantages to conservative, rural, southern interests now seems on the way to being dismantled. In the years ahead, the varied points of view and interests of the American populace will, it seems, compete more fairly and evenly when they attempt to have their impact on the legislative process than they have been able to do in the recent past. In its interest representation and rule initiation functions, Congress, while it sometimes unfairly gives the advantage to one interest and then to another, is well on its way to eliminating the systematic bias in favor of a single set of interests and one point of view.

In the process, Congress should also become better equipped to perform its system-maintenance functions. When interests are evenly balanced, they are forced into negotiation and coalition building and the compromise and logrolling inherent in coalition building. This, in turn, results in an adjustment of differences in such a way that most can at least live with the results. In the process, support is generated and legitimacy created. When congressional rules—and especially the filibuster and seniority system—gave dominance to conservative, southern interests, those interests could simply block a bill altogether and thus have no need to bargain and to build coalitions by compromise and logrolling. Then conflicts went unresolved, which in turn hindered the generation of support and the creation of legitimacy. Many are convinced that much of the unrest and alienation of the 1960s can be traced to the bias then existing in Congress and to its resulting inability to respond adequately to the needs of a changing society.

After examining the most involved institution of the American political system—Congress—we find that no single dimension, no single explanation, can adequately reveal this institution and explain the behavior of the people who make it up. Instead, we must understand the blend of formal and informal rules and the complex of influences working on each congressman in order to understand the legislative struggle that results in the representation of interests and the initiation and to some extent the application of rules, a struggle in which—sometimes poorly but sometimes very well—conflicts are resolved, support is generated, and legitimacy is created.

Some Exploratory Questions

1. Perhaps the most frequently criticized aspect of Congress has been its use of seniority to choose committee chairmen. What are the likely results, both negative and positive, of Congress's move away from seniority as the only criterion?

2. Which of the six sources of influence on congressional behavior should play the stronger roles and which more modest roles in influencing congressmen?

3. Is there any way in which congressional decision making could be streamlined and made more efficient without weakening Congress's ability to represent a wide diversity of interests and resolve conflicts successfully?

Bibliographical Essay

Recent years have seen a surge in the publication of books on Congress, many of them excellent. But one of the more insightful—and one that has influenced many later books—was published several years ago: Donald Matthews, *United States Senators and Their World* (Chapel Hill: University of North Carolina Press, 1960). Also helpful are two more recent studies of Congress by Randall B. Ripley, *Power in the Senate* (New York: St. Martin's, 1969), and *Congress: Process and Policy* (New York: Norton, 1975).

Textbooks that can be especially helpful as reference works are Malcolm E. Jewell and Samuel C. Patterson, *The Legislative Process in the United States,* 2d ed. (New York: Random House, 1973). William J. Keefe and Morris S. Ogul, *The American Legislative Process,* 3d ed. (Englewood Cliffs, N.J.: Prentice-Hall. 1973), and Leroy N. Rieselbach, *Congressional Politics* (New York: McGraw-Hill, 1973). Two collections of readings that are especially worthwhile are Robert L. Peabody and Nelson W. Polsby, eds., *New Perspectives on the House of Representatives,* 2d ed. (Chicago: Rand McNally, 1969), and Nelson W. Polsby, ed., *Congressional Behavior* (New York: Random House, 1971). For an in-depth case study of the passage of a single act, see Robert L. Peabody, Jeffrey M. Berry, William G. Frasure, and Jerry Goldman, *To Enact a Law* (New York: Praeger, 1972). For a good sense of the nature of Congress there are the eassays found in Sven Groennings and Jonathan P. Hawley, eds., *The Promise and the Power* (Washington, D.C.: Acropolis, 1973).

Many works concentrate on certain aspects of Congress. For a consideration of the rules of procedure and their impact on the decision-making process, see Lewis A. Froman, Jr., *The Congressional Process* (Boston: Little, Brown, 1967). For discussions of the role of the parties and the party leaders, see David B. Truman, *The Congressional Party* (New York: Wiley, 1959); Randall B. Ripley, *Party Leaders in the House of Representatives* (Washington, D.C.: Brookings Institution, 1967); Randall B. Ripley, *Majority Party Leadership in Congress* (Boston: Little, Brown, 1969); and Charles O. Jones, *Minority Party Leadership in Congress* (Boston: Little, Brown, 1970).

Probably the best book on congressional committees is Richard F. Fenno, *Congressmen in Committees* (Boston: Little, Brown, 1973). Also helpful are George Goodwin, Jr., *The Little Legislatures* (Amherst, Mass.: University of Massachusetts Press, 1970), and John F. Manley, *The Politics of Finance: The House Committee on Ways and Means* (Boston: Little, Brown, 1970). For a thorough study of the seniority system, see Barbara Hinckley, *The Seniority System in Congress* (Bloomington: Indiana University Press, 1971).

Julius Turner, *Party and Constituency: Pressures on Congress,* rev. ed., by Edward V. Schneier (Baltimore: Johns Hopkins Press, 1970), is a standard work that has been recently updated. It considers the relative impact of party and constituencies on congressional voting. Also very helpful is the excellent study of the chief influences on Representatives' voting choices by John W. Kingdon, *Congressmen's Voting Decisions* (New York: Harper & Row, 1973). On congressmen's decision making, see also Aage R. Clausen, *How Congressmen Decide* (New York: St. Martin's, 1973).

Richard F. Fenno, in *The Power of the Purse* (Boston: Little, Brown, 1966), explores Congress' role in the appropriations process and thereby does an excellent job of illuminating many aspects of Congress. Congress' control of the bureaucracy is considered by Joseph P. Harris, *Congressional Control of Administration* (Washington, D.C.: Brookings Institution, 1964). For a book that both analyzes and evaluates the internal processes of Congress, see Gary Orfield, *Congressional Power: Congress and Social Change* (New York: Harcourt, Brace, Jovanovich, 1975).

Finally, the Congressional Quarterly Service should be mentioned. This private corporation publishes the *Congressional Quarterly Weekly Report* and the annual *Congressional Quarterly Almanac,* both extremely valuable sources of information on congressmen, roll-call votes, and current issues before Congress.

Chapter 9

The Bureau-cracies The Politics of Administration

Americans are in more direct and frequent contact with the bureaucracy than with any other branch of the political system. The person who never writes his congressman nevertheless sends in his income tax form to the bureaucracy every year. The person who has never received a court subpoena receives a monthly social security check from the bureaucracy. The person who has never gone to Washington, D.C., frequently goes to her local post office to buy stamps and send off her mail through the bureaucracy.

But the ironic fact is that, in spite of this direct and frequent contact between bureaucracy and citizen, the bureaucracy—the myriad of departments, commissions, offices, and agencies that make up the executive branch of government—is probably the least understood of all the branches of the political system. The person who has a rudimentary knowledge of the structure of Congress is likely to have no idea how the State Department is organized. The person who has a basic grasp of the concept of representation will probably have no knowledge of the concepts underlying the bureaucracy. This chapter explores this "dark" area of American politics: the nature and functions of the bureaucratic subsystems.

Bureaucracy: Ideal or Otherwise

To many Americans the word "bureaucracy" suggests the vast federal government complex of some two and one-half million individuals, or perhaps the state and local government complexes of over six million individuals. Yet governmental bureaucracies are not unique—they are a particular type within a larger, more general category. Industrial corporations, labor unions, and universities possess bureaucracies that are much the same as governmental bureaucracies. Thus, our consideration of bureaucracy starts with the more general category and then proceeds to the more particular category of governmental bureaucracies.

Weber's Ideal Bureaucracy

A German sociologist of the early twentieth century, Max Weber, perceived with great insight the essential nature of bureaucracy, and his ideas have profoundly affected subsequent theories about it. The six basic characteristics that Weber claimed to be the attributes of the model bureaucracy are clearly summarized by Peter M. Blau.[1] Weber did not claim, nor has practice indicated, that actual bureaucracies conform exactly to the model bureaucracy described below. Weber's purpose was to illuminate the nature of bureaucracy by conceptualizing an ideal, or model, bureaucracy. Later we will see in which ways actual bureaucracies tend to differ from Weber's model.

The first characteristic (according to Weber) that marks bureaucracies is *a clear-cut division of labor,* resulting in specialization. The task of a bureaucracy is divided into its component parts, with each part being performed by specialized experts. The second mark of a bureaucracy is *hierarchy*—its divisions or units are organized into ranks, with its lower ones subordinate to the higher ones. The third characteristic is the existence of *formal rules and regulations* that govern procedures. Thus, bureaucratic procedures follow clearly formulated, uniform rules.

The fourth characteristic of bureaucratic structures is that the bureaucratic officials act in *a detached, rational manner* and not in an emotional or sentimental manner. Thus, they make their decisions and conduct themselves according to formal rules and the factual situation, not according to personal feelings and wishes. The fifth characteristic concerns the basis of employment. Persons are hired and promoted on the basis of their *skill and ability.* Competence and expertness count; appearance and "connections" do not. The final characteristic is *efficiency*—achieving the greatest output for the resources expended. Efficiency is the net result of the other five characteristics. Specialization helps ensure that individuals will bring essential skills and knowledge to their tasks; and hierarchy, that coordination will be achieved. Formal rules and regulations, along with impersonal, nonsentimental relationships, help ensure that actions will be reasonable, unbiased, and effective. And merit employment helps ensure capable personnel of high quality.

The key factor underlying all six of these characteristics is rationality— a bureaucracy is so organized that it can most efficiently accomplish its

---

1. See Peter M. Blau, *Bureaucracy in Modern Society* (New York: Random House, 1956), pp. 28–32. The basic writings of Max Weber, in which he develops his ideas on bureaucracy, are Max Weber, *The Theory of Social and Economic Organization,* trans. by A. M. Henderson and Talcott Parsons (New York: Oxford, 1947), and Max Weber, *From Max Weber: Essays in Sociology,* trans. by H. H. Gerth and C. Wright Mills (New York: Oxford, 1946). Also helpful in explaining the concept of bureaucracy and surveying the historical development of governmental bureaucracies is Reinhard Bendix, "Bureaucracy," in David L. Sills, ed., *International Encyclopedia of the Social Sciences* (New York: Macmillan and Free Press, 1968), vol. 2, pp. 206–217.

purpose, whether that purpose is making cars, collecting taxes, or fighting a war. Sentiment, family and friendship loyalties, and personal feelings are all subservient to this goal. Thus, a *bureaucracy* can be defined as a large organization that employs a division of labor, a hierarchical structure, formal rules and regulations, impersonal, rational relationships, and competence as a basis of employment in order to achieve the greatest possible efficiency.

A bureaucracy such as General Motors can build more and better cars than all its employees could do working independently. And it can build more and better cars than it could if all its employees did what their personal feelings led them to do or if its organization provided for no bosses, or if persons were hired and promoted on the basis of family background instead of ability. The same principle holds true when it comes to the political world. The Bureau of Internal Revenue can collect taxes more efficiently than could all its employees operating independently. The Internal Revenue Service, an organization of only 70,000 persons, can process each year 111 million tax returns, audit over 1.5 million returns, and give individual information and help to 35 million taxpayers.[2] Only an organization based on bureaucratic principles could achieve a degree of efficiency as great as this.

In addition, bureaucratic structures can help ensure impartiality. Everyone is assured of being treated on the basis of formal, set rules, not on the basis of some official's whim or fancy. A person does not fail to receive a social security check because some official does not like his looks, his race, or his religion. Instead, a person receives or does not receive a social security check on the basis of predetermined, known rules and regulations that apply to everyone else in the same way they apply to him. In fact, the formal, known rules can sometimes even allow greater creativity and more nonconformity in a bureaucratic organization than would be present in a nonbureaucratic organization. A person working for a large corporation and hired, paid, promoted, and fired on the basis of known, formal rules and regulations can often engage in more nonconformist behavior and can experiment in more innovative approaches—as long as he or she stays within the known rules—than can the person who is hired, paid, promoted, and fired on the basis of the personal whim of the boss. A person working in today's Ford Motor Company—and subject to the rules and regulations of the United Auto Workers union and the Ford Company— may more easily be able to criticize his superiors or wear his hair long or join the Black Muslims than could an employee hired by Henry Ford 70 years ago to help him in his backyard shop.

2. See Commissioner of Internal Revenue, *1971 Annual Report* (Washington, D.C.: GPO, 1972).

Two Problems

All this is not to say that bureaucracies are without problems and weaknesses. They are not. Two problems are especially prevalent. One is the problem of inefficiency. Bureaucracies—as we just saw—are intended for efficiency. That is their reason for being. But almost everyone can cite personal experiences with inefficient bureaucracies: social security checks lost, mail unbelievably slow, and credit card accounts totally confused. Bureaucratic inefficiencies can usually be traced to one of two causes. First, the formal rules, procedures, and structures may be overly cumbersome and not well suited to achieving the bureaucracy's goals. There is a constant danger that the rules and structures of a bureaucracy will be designed more to protect individuals from criticism and blame or to safeguard their jobs than to promote efficiency.

Second, all bureaucracies are marked by the emergence of informal rules and relationships that rival the formal rules and relationships. Friendships develop among employees, informal norms emerge (as Chapter 8 shows is the case in Congress), and informal channels of communication appear. These informal relationships and norms often lead to violations of the formal rules and patterns of authority. These violations can add to the efficiency of a bureaucracy—as when two officials quickly confer on a matter and reach a general understanding instead of going through the formal, time-consuming channels—but they can also lead to inefficiency —as when an incompetent person is promoted because of friendship, or rules are broken in order to delay a difficult decision.

A second major problem that frequently plagues bureaucracies, and especially governmental bureaucracies, revolves around a natural conflict between serving the broad public interest and serving the interests of supportive client groups.[3] To whom shall a bureaucrat be responsive? Governmental bureaucrats are often called public servants. But if they are servants, who is their master? The general public or the people is the obvious answer. This is what society expects. Yet this is only part of the picture. Bureaucracies considered in and by themselves are incomplete. One must also consider specific individuals, groups, and organizations that surround them as satellites. The American Farm Bureau Federation is a satellite of the Department of Agriculture; the drug companies are satellites of the Food and Drug Administration. Satellite or clientele forces such as these are of crucial importance to the bureaucrat. A particular bureaucrat or a division in a bureaucracy may be stronger or weaker than we might

3. For an excellent discussion of the importance of client or satellite groups to bureaucracies, see Lester M. Salamon and Gary L. Wamsley, "The Federal Bureaucracy—Responsive to Whom?" (paper given at the 1975 annual convention of the Midwest Political Science Association).

deduce from looking at the formal rules and structures because of the support or opposition of satellite forces.

Thus a certain tension develops for the bureaucrat: he or she is expected to serve the broad public interest or some other general cause; yet important satellite individuals and groups that can greatly help or hinder his bureau and his career are promoting narrow special interests. The rules and society's expectations say he should defend the public interest, political realities say he should protect himself and his bureau by defending special interests who can in turn defend and strengthen him. More on this problem later in this chapter.

Bureaucratic Functions

Rule Application

We have already seen that the political parties and the interest groups have the primary function of interest representation, the presidency has the primary function of exerting leadership, and Congress the primary function of rule initiation. The rules that Congress initiates do not, however, flow directly into society as outputs of the political system. Instead, the generalized rules must be applied to specific situations. Congress, in passing a law, establishes certain categories and says that all persons or situations falling into those categories must do such and such. The point is that the rule, or law, is general—it speaks to certain classes or categories, not to Mr. George Parsons of Celeryville, Ohio. The task of applying the general rule to specific persons and situations must still be done. Often—and seemingly increasingly—Congress delegates to the bureaucratic agencies broad discretion about application. It sets up certain basic goals and guidelines, but leaves virtually all the specifics to the bureaucracy. Thus, rule application is the primary function of the bureaucracy.

This is not meant to imply that the bureaucracy has a routine, mechanical function to perform. Nothing could be further from the truth. For, as the rest of this chapter documents, the bureaucratic process of rule application is a political process in the fullest sense. Rule application means making discretionary decisions and making decisions that allocate very real advantages and disadvantages. Thus, bureaucrats are subjected to many, often conflicting pressures and must make real choices. And in doing so, they are helping make policies. Thus, the bureaucracies are as much a part of the total policy-making process as are the other structures of the political system.

Rule Initiation and Interpretation

As was true of the other subsystems, the bureaucracy does not perform one function to the total exclusion of all others. Although rule application is the *primary* function of the bureaucracy, rule initiation, rule interpretation, and interest representation are also performed to some degree. Of these subsidiary functions, rule initiation is the most important one. A bureaucracy is involved in rule initiation when it recommends certain policies to Congress and the presidency—a bureaucratic activity that has taken on increased importance in recent years because of the complexity of many modern issues and because the technical expertise of the specialized bureaucrats. As a result, congressmen and persons in the presidency often rely on bureaucrats' advice and information pertaining to new legislation. It is estimated that over half the legislation considered by Congress originates in the executive branch. Thus, the bureaucracies are a source of inputs for both the presidency and Congress. In the process it engages in rule initiation. The bureaucracies also engage in rule initiation when they are delegated the power by Congress to establish generalized rules within certain circumscribed areas.

Rule interpretation occurs when certain bureaucratic agencies are allowed to try cases to determine whether or not laws and regulations have been violated. Interest representation occurs when certain bureaucratic offices become, in effect, spokesmen for particular interests, which (as we saw in Chapter 6) sometimes occurs.[4] But the *primary* function of the bureaucracy remains rule application.

The title of this chapter refers to bureaucra*cies,* not to a single bureaucracy. The bureaucracies cannot be considered a united, integrated institution or subsystem as Congress, the presidency, and the judiciary are. The different sectors of the bureaucracies all apply rules, but they apply different rules—each has its own area of responsibility and its own structure of organization and rules. Thus it is better to think of the executive branch of government as consisting of numerous bureaucracies instead of a single bureaucracy.

System-maintenance Functions

Generating Support   Probably the most important system-maintenance function the bureaucratic subsystems perform is generating support. This is a result of the direct and frequent contact between bureaucracy and citizen already noted. For in applying general rules to specific situations, bureaucracies comes into direct contact with the "man in the street." Thus, the citizens' attitudes toward the political system (including their level of support) are significantly influenced by their perceptions of the bureaucrats with whom they come in contact. Whether they view them as honest, fair, and efficient or dishonest, prejudiced, and wasteful will go

4. On the representation of interests by bureaucratic agencies see Harold Seidman, *Politics, Position, and Power,* 2d ed., (New York: Oxford University Press, 1975), pp. 150–157.

a long way toward determining support for the political system. Citizens of nations with low levels of support for their political systems typically possess negative, distrustful attitudes toward their bureaucracies.[5]

Conflict Resolution Because the bureaucracies are not performing a mechanical function but are makers of very real decisions that allocate very real advantages and disadvantages, there is bound to be conflict over the proper application of rules. Does or does not a certain section of a statute mean that plant X must provide safety device Y for its employees? Is city A or city B going to be selected for a certain pilot project in urban renewal? Merely posing the types of questions that frequently arise in the process of rule application reveals the virtual certainty of conflict. And it is a bureaucracy that must resolve such conflicts. Ideally, and usually in practice as well, that bureaucracy so resolves conflicts that the parties involved willingly accept the decision. If, however, one or more do not accept the bureaucracy's decision, they can turn to the courts—or possibly to Congress or to the presidency—in the hope of an overturn of the bureaucracy's decision. But in the meantime the bureaucracy's decision is authoritative: it has sanctions at its disposal to enforce its resolution of the conflict.

Creating Legitimacy The bureaucracies play a minor role in creating legitimacy. The legitimacy of the bureaucracies' actions largely derives from congressional authorizations, court decisions, and presidential support—not, first of all, from the bureaucracies' own nature and activities. However, to the extent that the bureaucracies successfully generate support and resolve conflicts, they help create legitimacy. When a decision is viewed as being fairly, reasonably, and efficiently reached, it is more likely to be accepted as legitimate than when its fairness, reasonableness, and efficiency are under question.

The Bureaucratic Structures

The 1974–1975 edition of the *United States Government Organization Manual* takes 524 pages to describe all the departments, agencies, and commissions that make up the federal bureaucracies.[6] For our purposes,

5. Italy is a case in point. See Gabriel A. Almond and Sidney Verba, *The Civic Culture* (Princeton, N.J.: Princeton University Press, 1963), pp. 106–114.
6. *United States Government Organization Manual, 1974–1975* (Washington, D.C.: General Services Administration, 1974). This manual, which is published annually, gives many details concerning the formal organization and legal authority of the various bureaucratic organizations.

there is, happily, no need to reproduce all the data, descriptions, and organization charts crammed into those 524 pages. We should, however, note the four basic types of bureaucratic organizations and some of their distinguishing features.[7]

The Executive Departments

There are 11 *executive departments:* the Department of State; the Department of the Treasury; the Department of Defense; the Department of Justice; the Department of the Interior; the Department of Agriculture; the Department of Commerce; the Department of Labor; the Department of Health, Education, and Welfare; the Department of Housing and Urban Affairs; and the Department of Transportation. By almost every standard these 11 departments are the most significant bureaucratic structures. They employ more people, spend more money, have a broader scope of authority, and are responsible for applying more laws than all other bureaucratic structures put together. They are the agencies responsible for providing most of the services (from medical research to national defense) and enforcing most of the regulations (from civil rights to taxes) of the political system.

The formal structures of these 11 departments in all their details are very complex and vary from one department to the next. But, their basic formal structures are relatively simple and do not vary greatly.[8] Each department is headed by a secretary who is appointed by and is responsible to the President. Collectively, the secretaries constitute the President's cabinet. Under each secretary are a number of offices, boards, services, divisions, desks, or bureaus, each responsible for a particular specialized area. They, in turn are broken up into additional subdivisions. These various sections of the departments can, in a rough way, be divided into line and staff divisions. The line divisions are those directly involved in carrying out the programs with which the department is entrusted, whereas the staff divisions help the secretary and the line divisions by coordinating, planning, and advising. Thus, in the typical department, several staff divisions are directly attached to the secretary's office. They are involved in such matters as budget, personnel, physical facilities, and over-all planning and analysis. After them are the line divisions, also directly attached to the secretary's office, but in practice often enjoying somewhat greater independence than the staff divisions do. They are responsible to the secretary directly, but often the secretary supervises them largely through the staff divisions.

7. For an excellent description of the various types of federal bureaucratic organizations, see Seidman, *Politics, Position, and Power,* pp. 221–263.

8. For organization charts of each of these departments, see *United States Organization Manual,* pp. 94–407.

Independent Regulatory Commissions

The second most significant type of bureaucratic structure is the *independent regulatory commission,* of which there are nine: the Interstate Commerce Commission; the Federal Trade Commission; the Federal Power Commission; the Securities and Exchange Commission; the Federal Communications Commission; the National Labor Relations Board; the Civil Aeronautics Board; the Federal Reserve Board; and the Federal Maritime Commission.[9]

These independent regulatory commissions are distinguishable from the basic executive departments in two ways. First, their structure differs from that of the executive departments. They are headed by boards or commissions and not by a single individual; more important, the members of these commissions are appointed by the President for set terms. Each commission has five or seven members, except the Interstate Commerce Commission, which has eleven members. The commissions head large bureaucratic structures of several thousands of employees, organized into staff and line subdivisions much as the executive departments are.[10] The President appoints commissioners for fairly long terms (five or seven years for most of the commissions) and may not remove them during their terms. of office. In additon, commissioners serve staggered terms so that a new President can only gradually place his appointees on the commissions. The end result is that a President has little direct control over the commissioners—thus, the name *independent* regulatory commissions.

The second way in which the independent regulatory commissions differ from the executive departments is that their rule-initiation and rule-interpretation functions are more important than the executive departments' (although their primary function is still rule application). Thus, the independent regulatory commissions engage in more legislative-like and judicial-like activities than the executive departments do. The rule-initiation function has been given the independent regulatory commissions because all of them regulate complex economic activities—transportation, utilities, labor-management relations, and so forth—that require a great deal of strict, continuous regulation. Thus, Congress has given them considerable leeway in establishing standards and guidelines. But it should be noted that although, over-all, the rule-initiation function of the independent regulatory commissions is greater than that of the executive departments, certain subdivisions within the executive departments do fully as much rule initiation as the independent regulatory commissions do.

9. For good analyses of the independent regulatory commissions, see Charles E. Jacob, *Policy and Bureaucracy* (Princeton, N.J.: Van Nostrand, 1966), chap. 4, and Louis Kohlmeier, *The Regulators* (New York: Harper & Row, 1969).

10. For organization charts of some of the independent regulatory commissions, see *United States Government Organization Manual,* pp. 408–605.

The independent regulatory commissions also have a rule-interpretation function. When a dispute breaks out over the application of a rule and one party claims that the facts indicate that it was not in violation of the rule as the rule was intended to be applied, the independent regulatory commission must decide who is in the right. In doing so, the commission acts much like a court of law, holding a hearing to determine the facts in the case and the guilt or innocence of the accused party. If the accused party is found to be in violation of the law, the commission can order remedial action and take sanctions against it. These rule-interpreting decisions of the independent regulatory commissions can be appealed into the regular federal court structure.

The basic rationale for establishing independent regulatory commissions, instead of lodging their functions in the regular executive departments, rests on the assumption that they operate in complex economic areas that need technical, not political, expertness. Thus, it was thought that their functions could be better placed outside political control, in the hands of nonpolitical technical experts. But this rationale founders on the fact that the independent regulatory commissions must settle many political questions—questions that involve the allocation of advantages and disadvantages that cannot be settled purely on the basis of technical factors. Thus, some persons have argued that the commissions are questionable in a democratic political system: crucial policy decisions are being made by persons who are not directly responsible to the President, the Congress, or the general voting public. As discussed later in this chapter, this autonomous character has resulted in the independent regulatory commissions often being dominated by certain special-interest groups. Nevertheless, the independent regulatory commissions have come to be accepted, and no doubt are a permanent feature of the American political scene.

Independent Agencies

A number of agencies are not in any of the 11 executive departments and thus are called *independent agencies.* In form and function they are more like the executive departments than the independent regulatory commissions. Most of the more important ones are headed by a single individual who is appointed by and is responsible to the President, as is true in the executive departments. The National Aeronautics and Space Administration, the Veterans Administration, the United States Information Agency, the Selective Service System, and the General Services Administration are the five most important. A few important independent agencies and a number of less important ones are headed by commissions; the Atomic Energy Commission, the Civil Service Commission, the Tariff Commission, and the Historical Monuments Commission are examples. The newest and no doubt one of the most important of the independent agencies headed by a commission is the United States Postal Service. Until recently the postal system was organized as an executive department. But in 1971 the Post Office Department was reorganized into the United States Postal Service, an independent agency headed by an 11-person board, most of whom are appointed by the President. The independent agencies headed by commissions can be distinguished from the independent regulatory commissions in that they are not primarily engaged in the regulation of economic activities; thus, their functions and authority resemble those of the executive departments more closely than those of the independent regulatory commissions.

Governmental Corporations

A final type of bureaucratic structure is the *governmental corporation,* a governmentally created organization that administers a certain economic enterprise. The Tennessee Valley Authority, the Federal Deposit Insurance Corporation, and Amtrak are three examples. They are controlled by boards and commissions and have a considerable amount of autonomy, unlike the rest of the political system. In organization and activity the governmental corporations resemble private corporations. They have been created in order to assure freedom of action and flexibility in what are, it is hoped, largely self-financing business enterprises.

Recruitment to the Bureaucracy

Just as a study of the skeletal structure of an individual tells us little about personality and temperament, so the preceding discussion of the bureaucratic structure tells us little about the actual nature of bureaucratic rule application. To understand this, we must add to the skeletal structure the men and women who constitute the bureaucracy and the decision-making process in which they take part. This section explores the process by which the members of the bureaucracy are recruited; the next section explores the bureaucratic decision-making process.

Almost all jobs in the bureaucracy fall into one of two categories, determined by the way the job is obtained: career positions and appointive positions.

Career Positions

In a professional career bureaucracy, persons get their positions by way of competitive examinations and merit ratings. Persons get their original appointments by scoring high on a competitive examination, are promoted on the basis of merit ratings by their superiors and possibly additional competitive examinations, and are protected from arbitrary dismissal. They are not, of course, protected from all dismissal—they may be dismissed for demonstrated ineffectiveness or as the result of a cutback in programs or budget. Such a system results in permanent bureaucrats, who serve as career professionals. Various terms are used to refer to career positions: merit positions, classified positions, and civil service positions. But all refer to positions gained and held by means that attempt to measure ability objectively, not by winning the favor of an appointing official.

The vast majority of the bureaucrats in the American political system are now professional career bureaucrats. This was not always the case. Until 1883 there was no provision for a career bureaucracy. Instead, each new presidential administration brought with it a large turnover in the bureaucracy, as appointees of the old administration were released and deserving supporters of the new administration were rewarded with jobs. This was called the spoils system—"to the victor belong the spoils."

Then, in 1883, the Civil Service System was created, and a professional career bureaucracy began. During its early years, only about 10 percent of the bureaucrats were included in the system, but additional positions were gradually added until today over 90 percent of the positions in the bureaucracies are either under it or under some other independent merit system—such as the Tennessee Valley Authority's, the FBI's, or the Foreign Service's. Thus, almost all bureaucratic positions are now career positions.

One group of positions in the general category of career positions should be noted. There are about 5,000 positions in what is sometimes referred to as the *supergrades.* These are the top career positions, and the people who hold them are the elite of the career bureaucrats. Their salaries range from $34,000 to $46,000, they are highly trained and skilled in their fields, and "they play a significant role in formulating governmental policies, for they provide the long experience, the intimate knowledge, and often the essential insight on which politically appointed executives must rely in order to discharge effectively their policymaking and overseeing responsibilities."[11]

Appointive Positions

Appointive positions are obtained by winning the favor of the appointing official rather than by demonstrating one's skill and ability through presumably objective measures. But this does not mean that appointed officials are less competent than career officials. The skill and ability of prospective appointees are factors normally weighed by appointing officials. There are

11. John J. Corson and R. Shale Paul, *Men Near the Top* (Baltimore: Johns Hopkins Press, 1966), p. 6.

two types of significant appointive positions: the political positions and the independent regulatory commissioners.

The Political Positions   Legally and formally, the President is the head of the bureaucracy. To help ensure that what is true in form is also true in fact, a little over 500 of the top positions within the executive departments and some of the independent agencies are filled by presidential appointees who serve at the will of the President. In addition, some 700 positions are in turn filled by persons named by the presidential appointees. All 1,200 of these positions are exempt from the Civil Service System. They are the political positions and include the department heads, undersecretaries, assistant secretaries, and various other highly placed officials in the executive departments and some of the independent agencies.[12]

Thus, the political positions include the most significant policy-making positions, as well as those positions superior to and therefore supposedly in control of the career positions. As we will see in the next section on bureaucratic decision making, the career bureaucrats have a great deal of discretion and independence; yet the general guidelines are set by the political appointees, who have the authority to intervene in the affairs of the career bureaucrats if they feel the need to do so.

The rationale for the existence of the political positions is that because the persons filling these positions are appointed by the President (or his appointees) and can be removed by him, they will share his general philosophy and aims. This is important both for coordination within the bureaucracy and for public influence on the bureaucracy. The latter point is based on the presumption that the President reflects the dominant public desires; thus, it follows that the top policy-making bureaucrats will also reflect the dominant public desires. To the extent that the President loses control of his political appointees in the bureaucracy (which happens to some degree, as we saw in Chapter 7), and to the extent that the political appointees lose control of the career bureaucrats (which also happens to some degree, as we will soon see), this causal chain breaks down. Yet it is not without significance. The chain may be weak—and often breaks— but it is still a factor that must be taken into account. And certainly the contribution that the political executives make to coordination among and within bureaucratic structures is significant. Coordination may not be complete, but imagine what it would be like if the secretary of Health, Education, and Welfare believed strongly in public welfare programs and one of his assistant secretaries just as strongly opposed public welfare programs.

12. For a very good analysis of the recruitment process and background characteristics of the political appointees, see Dean E. Mann, "The Selection of Federal Political Executives," *American Political Science Review,* 58 (1964), 81–99.

The Independent Regulatory Commissioners   The members of the independent regulatory commissions are similar to the political appointees in that they are appointed by the President. But the commissioners can be distinguished by the fact that they serve set terms of office—they cannot be removed by a President until their terms expire. Thus the President, once he has named a commissioner, loses much of his influence over the person, who may frequently oppose his wishes. Presidents attempt to name persons who are in general agreement with them, but the set terms of office assure that the commissioners have greater independence from presidential control than the political executives have.

Bureaucratic Decision Making

The Nature of Bureaucratic Decision Making

Bureaucrats are decision makers, and the rule-application process is a decision-making process in which literally every bureaucrat takes part. There is no neat division, with the top-level bureaucrats making the decisions and the lower-level bureaucrats carrying them out. Instead, bureaucrats on all levels are decision makers. Even a lower-level official in a district office of the Internal Revenue Service may have to decide whether to allow a certain deduction in one taxpayer's tax return or whether to audit another.

Sometimes it is suggested that top-level bureaucrats make important decisions and lower-level bureaucrats unimportant or trivial ones. But even this can be questioned; it depends on what is meant by "important." A decision by a relatively minor bureaucrat in the Small Business Administration to grant or not to grant a loan to a particular business may be of life-and-death importance to that business. Without the loan it will fail. The point is that many lower-level decisions may be of crucial importance to the individuals and groups affected by them. A better distinction is based on the scope of a decision (the number of individuals and interests directly or indirectly affected). The scope of the decisions made by the higher-level officials tends to be considerably greater than the scope of those made by lower-level officials. More are affected—the scope is greater—but the extent to which persons are affected is not necessarily greater.

Bureaucratic decisions are also discretionary decisions. Bureaucrats are in positions in which they can exercise a significant degree of autonomy. This is true, first of all, because the rules that bureaucrats apply leave room for choice in their application. There is no one obvious way in which they are to be applied. In addition and for a variety of reasons, to be discussed, the inputs flowing into the bureaucracies are less than all-pervasive and all-compelling in their influence. Because they are not all-pervasive, there are many occasions when the bureaucrat can establish his own policy; because they are not all-compelling, the bureaucrat can frequently resist their pressure.

Rationality in Bureaucratic Decision Making The intended rationality and impartiality characteristic of bureaucracies have led many observers to urge and to assume the possibility of bureaucrats following strictly rational decision-making procedures.[13] It is assumed that legislators and other elected politicians must—because of past obligations and voter pressure—make decisions on bases other than strictly rational ones. But bureaucrats are supposedly not under such constraints and thus can make their decisions in an independent, fully rational manner.

Under the concept of rational decision making a bureaucrat would, in making his decisions, go through several distinct steps, such as these:

1. Identify the problem;
2. clarify the goals, and then rank them as to their importance;
3. list all possible means—or policies—for achieving each of the goals;
4. assess all the costs of and the benefits that would seem to follow from each of the alternative policies; and
5. select the package of goals and associated policies that will bring the greatest relative benefits and the least relative disadvantages.[14]

Appealing as such a conception of rational decision making is, bureaucrats are simply unable to come near this sort of rational, antiseptic process. Decision makers—including bureaucrats—lack the full information the conception demands, and they are under a host of compelling pressures that often cause them to deviate from it. The lack of all the necessary information is clear: some of their information is of uncertain reliability, the consequences of possible alternatives obscure, and some alternatives perhaps not even recognized.

Less frequently understood are the many pressures that comprise the day-to-day world of the bureaucrat. Inputs flow in from a number of sources, and he must consider all these demands and expectations. If he does not do so—even while following rational decision making procedures to his utmost ability—he may find his directives being ignored, his budget cut, and his programs given to others. The wise bureaucrat must be a good politician: he must know the art of the possible as well as the goal of perfection, the balancing of conflicting demands as well as the single-minded pursuit of the ideal.

13. For an excellent discussion of the concept of rational decision making, the reasons bureaucrats cannot live up to it, and the bases on which they do in fact make decisions, see Ira Sharkansky, *Public Administration,* 2d ed. (Chicago: Markham, 1972), pp. 41–79.
14. Sharkansky, *Public Administration,* p. 43.

Thus to understand bureaucratic decision making one must understand the environment in which the decision maker operates. Part of that environment consists of the decision maker's own roles and values; part of it consists of the influential persons and groups that feed inputs into the bureaucratic structures. The rest of this section is concerned with these factors.

Bureaucratic Roles and Values

Within the bureaucracy there no doubt exist individuals of almost every personality type holding to almost every imaginable value and possessing widely varying role expectations.[15] In this area political scientists have so far done only limited research; hence, our knowledge is less than satisfactory. But on the basis of the admittedly scattered, sometimes impressionistic evidence that is available, three central tendencies can be noted.

One tendency—and probably the most important—is that most bureaucrats seem to maintain a rather fine balance between submission to authority and exertion of autonomy. The bureaucrat must balance two contradictory role expectations.[16] On the one hand, he feels he should submit to those in authority over him. After all, he is part of a hierarchy, and endless confusion would result if each member, ignoring everyone else, were to do what he thinks is best. On the other hand, he feels he should exert leadership and creativity, take action on his own initiative, and not be a mere cog in a machine. The conflicting expectations are seen in the American people's expectations of bureaucrats. We call bureaucrats public *servants* and expect them to be submissive and to follow regulations, but at the same time we charge them with a lack of initiative, being too impersonal, and slavishly following set procedures.

A majority of bureaucrats appear to respond to these conflicting expectations by maintaining a balance between the two. They exhibit a limited autonomy—they show independence and initiative, but only within a circumscribed area. This conclusion is supported by W. Lloyd Warner and his associates, who, after their intensive study of upper-level bureaucrats, concluded:

On the whole, [the bureaucrat] views authority in a positive way. Authority figures are looked up to as persons of eminence and high status. They support, direct, and

15. For a good analysis of several different types of bureaucrats in terms of their motivations and role expectations, see Anthony Downs, *Inside Bureaucracy* (Boston: Little, Brown, 1967), chap. 9. And for a helpful survey of the personal and attitudinal characteristics of the bureaucrats, see Sharkansky, *Public Administration,* pp. 142–159.

16. See W. Lloyd Warner, Paul P. Van Riper, Norman H. Martin, and Orvis F. Collins, *The American Federal Executive* (New Haven, Conn.: Yale University Press, 1963), pp. 243–250.

set goals. He cooperates with authority, and a good relationship is maintained. This is a dominant theme among most federal executives. . . .

This is not to say that he is an automaton. He is actively intelligent; in responding to the demands of authority he seeks to behave rationally and sometimes with independence. . . . There can be no question that the issue of autonomy or emotional independence is crucial. Even though he accepts structure and needs it, he seeks independence, seeks to "go it on his own."[17]

A second tendency is that most bureaucrats—in reaction to the natural conflict (mentioned earlier) between loyalty to the broad public interest and loyalty to the interest of certain supportive client groups—tend to strike a balance between these two obligations. Thus an official in the Department of Agriculture feels certain obligations both to the general public and to the farmers; an official in the Atomic Energy Commission feels obligations both to the general public and to the power companies using atomic energy to generate electricity.

One study quoted upper-level bureaucrats as making such comments about their jobs that reveal concern for the broad public interest:

I have a feeling of participation in something important and worthwhile.
These are significant days, I have a feeling of participating in them—of working on world problems.
I don't feel I would be doing something of importance if I were to work for industry. They are not interested in the public welfare.
I like hard work; the habits of business amaze me.
Who could possibly be interested in selling soap?[18]

Although there is no reason to believe that people making such statements as these are insincere, it is also true that when bureaucrats' commitments to the general public interest clash with their commitments to the special interests of certain client groups, the special interests often win out or at least modify the bureaucrats' commitments to the public interest. The reason for this appears to be twofold: bureaucrats, after many years of working together, often develop sympathetic leanings toward the clientele groups they serve or regulate; and bureaucrats are usually confronted with direct attempts at influence by the clientele groups, but not by representatives of the broader public.

A third tendency frequently found among bureaucrats is a strong commitment to their particular unit within the bureaucracy and to its traditions and history. Harold Seidman has written of bureaucratic agencies with "deeply ingrained cultures and sub-cultures reflecting institutional history, ideology, values, symbols, folklore, professional biases, behavior patterns, heroes, and enemies."[19] This strong sense of institutional loyalty some-

17. Warner et al., *The American Federal Executive,* pp. 193–194.
18. Warner et al., *The American Federal Executive,* pp. 223–224.
19. Seidman, *Politics, Position, and Power,* pp. 121–122.

times leads bureaucrats to challenge their superiors or parallel bureaucratic agencies, if they perceive them as threatening the integrity of their agency or its programs.

These are a few of the more important characteristics of the bureaucrats' roles and values—characteristics that condition how the bureaucrats react to the decision-making situations with which they are faced.

Their Fellow Bureaucrats

One of the four sources of inputs that influence bureaucratic decision makers consists of their fellow bureaucrats, those who make up the context within which they work. It is generally recognized that a bureaucrat's superiors in the bureaucratic hierarchy are an influential source of inputs for him, but it is less widely recognized that his peers and subordinates are also influential. All three are sources of inputs; all three have a significant influence on him.

Superiors   A bureaucrat's superiors help set the bounds within which he makes his decisions—they review his decisions and sometimes overrule them, and they establish guidelines for him to follow.[20] What probably needs explaining is not why a bureaucrat's superiors influence his decisions, but why their influence is less than complete—why a bureaucrat is not completely submissive to those above him in the hierarchy.

There are four basic reasons for this situation. The first is the role expectations of the bureaucrats. To some degree the bureaucrat conceives of his job as exerting initiative and not merely following orders. He has a greater feeling of satisfaction and accomplishment when he has been able to use his own initiative. The superior gives orders, but the bureaucrat under him seeks, to a *limited* degree, to exert independence from that superior.

Second, because of the division of labor and specialization characteristic of bureaucracies, a bureaucrat often has greater knowledge within a particular area than does his superior, who by the nature of his position has a broader, more general area of concern. Thus, the higher-level bureaucrat must often depend on those on lower levels for information and recommendations. Often, when a lower-level bureaucrat tells his superior that he cannot carry out a certain order because it is technically impractical to do so, the superior does not have the expertness in that area to challenge the lower-level bureaucrat effectively.

Third, a bureaucrat is given a certain amount of freedom and discretion because his superiors do not have the time and physical capacity to check on every decision he makes. Much, of necessity, goes unnoticed and unobserved by his superiors.

20. For a good consideration of the relationship of bureaucrats to their superiors, see Corson and Paul, *Men Near the Top,* pp. 25–30, 62–64, 86–88.

Finally, as the rest of this section shows, a bureaucrat may be able to gain a certain amount of independence from his superiors by playing off a particular force against them. Perhaps a division head has close friends in Congress and is able to use them to withstand the department head successfully. Or perhaps the fact of having certain interest groups in his corner enables him to ignore a directive of his superiors. Some individuals may in form be subordinate, but in actual power equal or even superior to their formal superiors.

Peers   A bureaucrat is also bound to be influenced by inputs coming from other bureaucrats on approximately his own level in the bureaucratic hierarchy.[21] Most commonly, these bureaucrats are individuals occupying positions corresponding to his own, but in other departments, agencies, or offices. Thus, the secretaries and agency heads influence each other as they work out policies of mutual concern to their organizations. The Undersecretary of State for African Affairs persuades the Undersecretary of State for Inter-American Affairs to modify a certain decision of his. Or, on a lower level, a trial examiner for the National Labor Relations Board negotiates an agreement with an official in the Department of Labor. This interaction between peers rests largely on the need to cooperate if common goals are to be achieved, and on the concept of reciprocity: "You help me now and later I'll help you."

Subordinates   Perhaps most surprising is the fact that often a bureaucrat's subordinates are able to influence his decisions to a great extent.[22] It can be explained on the basis of the inputs—advice, recommendations, and information—flowing from those lower to those higher in the bureaucracy. A modern student of bureaucratic behavior has written a book whose central thesis is that there is a "growing imbalance between ability and authority."[23] Those bureaucrats on the higher levels have the authority, the right, to make the basic decisions, but because of specialization and the highly technical fields with which they deal, they do not have the knowledge or the expertness to carry out or even make the appropriate decisions. Thus, the higher-level bureaucrat is, to a degree, dependent on the lower-level bureaucrats for information and advice.

In addition, a bureaucrat may defer to his subordinates—possibly even against his own judgment—out of a fear that disregarding his subordinates' recommendations would be bad for morale or out of a sense of loyalty to his "team."

21. For a brief but helpful discussion of this point, see Corson and Paul, pp. 35–37.
22. For a discussion of the bureaucrat's relationship with his subordinates, see Corson and Paul, pp. 30–35, 64–65, 88–91.
23. Victor A. Thompson, *Modern Organization* (New York: Knopf, 1961), p. 6.

The Presidency

For the upper-level bureaucrats, inputs flowing from the presidency are a very real force that frequently must be reckoned with in making decisions.[24] Certain of their decisions touch on presidential policies and thus are decisions in which the President is vitally interested.

There are several means the presidency can use to enforce its demands on bureaucrats. For example, the Office of Management and Budget, which is part of the presidency, has a general supervising and coordinating responsibility for the bureaucracy. Finding their budgets cut or losing a desired program are two possibilities that can help keep bureaucratic officials eager to please the President and certain persons and agencies in the presidency. The presidency can also influence bureaucrats because of its powers over the organization of the executive branch. The possibility that his agency or subdivision may be split in two or combined with another is always on the bureaucrat's mind. Obviously, it is to his advantage to maintain good relations with the presidency. In addition, political executives are especially susceptible to presidential influence because they owe their positions to the President. By means of the President's skillful use of rewards and sanctions and his great prestige, presidential influence can also often reach the career officials and bureaucrats serving set terms.

On the other hand, bureaucrats are often in a position to resist the demands of the presidency. Whether and how bureaucrats respond to presidential directives often of necessity goes unnoticed by the President and his aides because of their limited time and the sheer size of the bureaucracies. Months may pass before the White House learns that a directive has not been carried out. Bureaucrats are also frequently able to avoid following presidential wishes if—as is often the case—they have strong supporters in Congress or in outside client groups.

Both the sources of and the limitations on presidential power (discussed in detail in Chapter 7) are applicable to the President's relationship with bureaucrats. In short, the situation is one in which the President has influence, but limited influence, over the bureaucrats he wishes to influence.

Richard Nixon found intolerable this situation in which bureaucrats possessed an independence that allowed them to ignore or circumvent his authority. Thus at the start of his second term he devised a scheme whereby, through a system of presidential assistants and counsellors, the bureaucracies would be brought under the President's control.[25]   One

24. For a discussion of the impact of the presidency on the bureaucracy, see Marver H. Bernstein, *The Job of the Federal Executive* (Washington: D.C.: Brookings Institution, 1958), chap. 4, and Seidman, *Politics, Position, and Power,* chap. 3.

25. On this attempt by Nixon, see Seidman, *Politics, Position, and Power,* chap. 4, and Richard P. Nathan, *The Plot That Failed: Nixon and the Administrative Presidency* (New York: Wiley, 1975).

result of Watergate and the downfall of Nixon was the end of a scheme that, if successful, would have changed the relationship between the President and the bureaucracies and in the process the basic nature of the Washington bureaucracies.

Congress

Although the President is constitutionally proclaimed the "chief executive," inputs coming from Congress also have a significant influence on the decisions of bureaucrats.[26] Before making a decision, bureaucrats must frequently ask themselves what the reactions of certain congressmen are likely to be. There are three reasons for this.

The first reason is Congress's "power of the purse." Each year almost all the bureaucratic agencies and departments must submit a budgetary request for the coming fiscal year—a request that may or may not be approved by Congress. Thus, the wise bureaucrat, in making his decisions, is careful not to offend powerful congressmen (especially those on the appropriations committees).[27] Several studies have shown, however, that Congress's control of appropriations does not lead to thorough, all-pervasive oversight of the bureaucracy.[28] This is largely the result of the huge budget, which contains innumerable requests for funds, and the often superior technical expertness possessed by the bureaucracy. Nevertheless, the unwary bureaucrat may suddenly find his funds being cut if he has forgotten to cultivate a favorable relationship with certain congressmen and has spurned too many congressional demands.

Much the same can be said concerning Congress's more general legislative power of program authorization and amendment. New programs receive their legal life from Congress; often major changes in and additions to existing programs must receive congressional authorization. Thus, once again, the wise bureaucrat attempts to maintain good relations with Congress: tomorrow he may be coming to Congress with a request for authorization of a new program for his agency; or tomorrow an interest opposed to his agency's program may attempt to persuade Congress to cripple that program or even to do away with it.

A third factor increasing the influence of congressmen is the long tenure of the most powerful among them. The still-existing seniority system means

26. On the influence of Congress on the bureaucracy, see Bernstein, *The Job of the Federal Executive,* chap. 5, and Seidman, *Politics, Position, and Power,* chap. 2.

27. For a good account of how bureaucrats attempt to guard their interests from congressional attack during the appropriations process, see Aaron B. Wildavsky, *The Politics of the Budgetary Process* (Boston: Little, Brown, 1964).

28. See John F. Bibby, "Committee Characteristics and Legislative Oversight of Administration," *Midwest Journal of Political Science,* 10 (1966), 78–98, and Ira Sharkansky, "An Appropriations Subcommittee and Its Client Agencies: A Comparative Study of Supervision and Control," *American Political Science Review,* 59 (1965), 622–628.

that the committee chairmen and other important committee members are those who have been in Congress for some time and are likely to be there for some time to come. Thus, the bureaucrat knows that if he offends a powerful congressman, that congressman will probably still be in a powerful position five, ten, or perhaps even twenty years later. This is in contrast to the President and his political appointees, who will be there at most for eight years and possibly for a considerably shorter period of time. Thus, if a politically astute career bureaucrat has to choose between going against the demands of a powerful Senator or going against the President or one of his appointees (who is legally the bureaucrat's superior), he may well choose to keep peace with the Senator and go against the President or his appointee.

Interest Groups

Almost every bureaucratic subdivision has what can be considered its clientele: the individuals and organizations with whom the office is dealing. The Department of Agriculture and the farmers, the Department of Commerce and business, the Civil Aeronautics Board and the airlines, the Social Security Administration and persons receiving social security benefits are all examples. Often, but not always, these clienteles are organized into formal groups.

In considering the influence of the inputs arising from these interest groups, it is helpful to note that the relationship of a bureaucratic subdivision to an interest group may take one of two forms: The bureaucracy may either be providing the interest group with certain services or be regulating the interest group. Examples of the first are the detailed statistics prepared by the Department of Commerce concerning the economy and population for the use of businessmen, and the soil conservation and disease control research done by the Department of Agriculture for farmers. In such cases the role of the interest group is usually one of encouraging the bureaucracy, giving any help it can, and forming a united front with the bureaucracy whenever the program is threatened by budget cuts or other curtailment. The bureaucratic agency in turn seeks to provide effective services to the client group so that it can be sure of its support in any conflicts with Congress or the President.

The situation is more complex when the bureaucratic organization's primary task is not to service but to regulate the interest. Examples are the National Labor Relations Board and management interests, and the Securities and Exchange Commission and investors and brokers. One would expect such a relationship to be marked by antagonisms and struggles by the interest group to have the bureaucratic organization limited or even abolished. The surprising fact is that this rarely happens—the relationship is usually cordial and even friendly. The explanation is quite simple: the regulated interest is often able to capture control of the agency regulating it.

Several writers have noted that regulatory agencies tend to go through a definite life cycle, which begins when the agency and its authority are created by an act of Congress, an action bitterly opposed by the interest to be regulated.[29] During its first few years of life the agency is in an era of development and expansion. It is staffed by young, zealous individuals who enforce the law stringently and take a generally anti-interest stance. But then, as public (and congressional) attention shifts to other areas and as the young, zealous reformers grow older or move on to other jobs, the regulated interest is able to work out a *modus vivendi* with the bureaucracy. It is able to place men more favorable to its position in the agency or to persuade those already in the agency, after years of working together, to see things in a light sympathetic to the interest. The bureaucrats, who have become more concerned with convenience and security than with zealous, controversial actions, are comfortable going along with the interest. Eventually the agency actually protects the interest by limiting competition and fixing rates at a high level. The life cycle is complete.

All regulatory agencies may not go through such an orderly and predictable life cycle; yet there is overwhelming evidence that regulated interests and regulating agencies frequently develop very comfortable, supportive relationships. Samuel Huntington wrote: "The attitude of the railroads toward the Commission [Interstate Commerce Commission] since 1935 can only be described as one of satisfaction, approbation, and confidence. At times the railroads have been almost effusive in their praise of the Commission."[30] And Walton Hamilton, a professional economist, concluded after surveying the Civil Aeronautics Board and its regulation of the airlines: "Here an agency of government has proved itself a willing instrument of vested carriers seeking to maintain a closed industry."[31] Thus, in a mutually advantageous arrangement, the regulatory agency often ends up serving the interests of the regulated group and slighting the interests of the general public, and the regulated group supports and protects the regulatory agency from any attacks from Congress, the White House, or press.

The methods used by interest groups in creating situations such as these

29. See Walton Hamilton, *The Politics of Industry* (New York: Knopf, 1957); Downs, *Inside Bureaucracy,* chap. 2; Marver H. Bernstein, *Regulating Business by Independent Commission* (Princeton, N.J.: Princeton University Press, 1955); and Kohlmeier, *The Regulator,* chap. 6.

30. Samuel P. Huntington, "The Marasmus of the I.C.C.," in Francis E. Rouke, ed., *Bureaucratic Power in National Politics* (Boston: Little, Brown, 1965), p. 77. This article gives a good example of a regulatory agency's life cycle.

31. Hamilton, *The Politics of Industry,* p. 62.

have been discussed more fully in Chapter 6. Briefly, they result largely from lack of public awareness and the absence of competing interests (most regulatory agencies regulate only one type of interest, not several). Usually the passive—if not active—support of key congressmen is part of the total picture. Interest groups are thereby frequently able both to influence the appointment of personnel and to exert influence on the existing personnel.

Decision Making: Conclusions

A student of bureaucracy once wrote an article entitled "Survival in the Bureaucratic Jungle," in which he stressed that the able bureaucrat must possess "the ability to manage and the talent to build political support for what is managed."[32] In many ways the title of this article is apt and its thesis valid. The preceding discussion of the sources of influences that affect bureaucratic decision making ought not to create the impression that bureaucrats are largely passive, that they are acted upon by several forces and then merely respond to them. The nature of these forces is such that bureaucrats are often able to use and manipulate them to their own advantage.

The politically astute bureaucrat, out to protect his agency's programs or to acquire new powers, may play off one force against another. A favorite tactic is to assure that there are active, organized clientele or satellite groups willing and able to support one's program and agency. This can be done by responding favorably to whatever powerful, organized groups may be interested in one's agency, even at the expense of less powerful, less well-organized clientele groups. The Department of Agriculture, for example, largely responds to the demands and wishes of the large agribusiness interest represented by the American Farm Bureau Federation, not to the demands and wishes of small, marginal farmers or farm laborers. If there is no organized client group, the bureaucratic agency may even take a hand in helping to create a satellite client group. This was done in 1967 by the new Department of Housing and Urban Affairs Development, when it helped form the Urban Alliance, a broad coalition that lobbies for urban programs.[33]

Thus bureaucratic decision making becomes a matter of individual bureaucrats balancing interests and demands that arise from a number of sources so as to maintain a degree of autonomy and to achieve the political support they need to protect themselves and their programs—all within certain values and commitments to which they hold.

32. Harlan Cleveland, "Survival in the Bureaucratic Jungle," *The Reporter,* 14 (April 5, 1956), 29.
33. See Salamon and Wamsley, "The Federal Bureaucracy," p. 10.

Bureaucracy and Democracy

Bureaucracies, as noted in the opening section of this chapter, were created for the purpose of efficiency. Their existence rests on the belief that division of labor, objective standards, and rational procedures contribute to efficiency. But this leaves in doubt whether bureaucracies contribute to, or are even compatible with, democracy. In other words, do demands flow from the public to the bureaucrats and in the process have a significant impact on them? Weber's model bureaucracy does not take into account or make provision for the impact of popular demands on bureaucrats. His bureaucracy rests on rationality and efficiency, not popular control. The question of democratic control of the bureaucracy is becoming more urgent because of Congress' increasing tendency to delegate broad discretion to bureaucratic agencies in implementing legislative acts.

On the surface, the bureaucracy does not exhibit the characteristics we generally associate with democratic institutions. No bureaucrats stand for election, and most bureaucrats are removed from the public eye and do not face an organized opposition. Consequently, questions of whether or not and how bureaucrats are responsive to public demands have arisen.

Two Traditional Responses   Traditionally, two responses have been made to the question of the responsiveness of bureaucracies to the public. The first rests on an assumed sharp division between making policies and executing them.[34] According to this view, the "political" (elected) branches of government make policies, and the bureaucracy merely carries them out. Thus, the fact that the populace has no direct influence on bureaucrats does not really matter because they make no policies anyway. But this view has been thoroughly discredited. Bureaucrats are policy makers. The supposed policy-making versus policy carrying-out distinction has proved an illusion. This has been a basic contention throughout this chapter.

The second response that has traditionally been made to the problem of the place of bureaucracy in a democratic political system stresses the fact that the elected officials and their appointees, who are directly responsible to them, control the bureaucrats. Thus a three- or four-link chain of causality is established that runs from the general public to the bureaucracy by way of the president and Congress and the top political executives. In this way the people have indirect control over the bureaucracy.

But to the extent that any one link in the chain is broken, this interpretation fails. And, as we have seen, there are some weak links in the chain. The President's and Congress' control over both the political executives

34. This view is most closely associated with Frank J. Goodnow, who wrote at the turn of the twentieth century. See Frank J. Goodnow, *Politics and Administration* (New York: Macmillan, 1900).

and lower-level bureaucrats is less than complete. This is certainly true of the President's control of independent regulatory commissions. Congress relinquishes much of its control when it passes laws that delegate very broad discretion to the bureaucracy. And the higher-level bureaucrats' control over their subordinates is also less than complete. Thus, this response is not a complete answer to the question of popular impact on the bureaucracy, although it is a partial one. To a *limited* degree the bureaucracy is democratized by the influence that politically responsible individuals have over it. But two additional factors also work to create a bureaucracy that is in fact relatively responsive to public demands.

Bureaucratic Roles and Values   An earlier section of this chapter stresses the fact that the public expects bureaucrats to act as public servants, and the bureaucrats themselves feel they should. The situation would be quite different if every bureaucrat defined his job as ignoring demands and needs as much as possible while gaining as many advantages for himself as possible. To a limited degree we can speak of most bureaucrats as having a self-imposed sensitivity to public needs and demands (as, of course, perceived by them). The point is that such people help create a bureaucracy more responsive to public demands, a more democratic bureaucracy. This tendency, however, is qualified by many bureaucrats' felt need to respond to certain supportive client groups, which may lead them to act contrary to the broader public wishes.

Interest Groups   The role played by interest groups in democratizing the bureaucracy must be mentioned. As we saw more fully in Chapter 6, interest groups are subsections of the population; thus, when an interest group has an impact on the bureaucracy, a subsection of the population has an impact on the bureaucracy. And when we consider the large number and great variety of interest groups present in American society, it becomes clear that large segments of the society have an impact on the bureaucracy by way of interest groups. It is equally clear (as was also stressed in Chapter 6) that some interests, such as those of the consumer and the disadvantaged sectors of the population, are not well represented by interest groups, and their impact on the bureaucracy is thereby limited. Also when a certain interest group has a dominate influence on a bureaucratic agency, that group can virtually exclude the consideration of broader public interests that in a democratic scheme certainly should be considered. Thus interest groups can help democratize bureaucracies, but they have their own deficiencies and problems.

Shared Attitudes   Finally, attitudes and values shared by the bureaucrats and the general public can also lead to bureaucratic decisions in keeping with popular wishes. A recent study found that in fact the attitudes of high-level bureaucrats tend to coincide with those of the general population.[35] Thus, even when bureaucrats pursue their own private desires, they are not necessarily acting contrary to popular wishes. In fact, they sometimes are acting in keeping with them.

Conclusions   The net result of the various forces working on the bureaucrats is a situation in which, to a limited yet significant degree, a wide range of public demands flow into bureaucratic offices. In addition, each bureaucratic agency labors under the constant possibility that public attention and condemnation will suddenly center on it. As the result of a congressional investigation, revelations by an enterprising reporter, or other cause, it may be subjected to strong, insistent demands.

Swift to censure and slow to praise, the public exerts its pressures upon the federal executive in no uncertain terms. . . . The public, in making its demands known, makes use of (and is used by) a whole arsenal of weapons. There is the irate congressman making the headlines by defending the interests of the people back home. There is the syndicated columnist, the new press phenomenon with his outlets in hundreds of cities and towns. There is the Executive Mansion, dissociating itself in order to leave responsibility with the executive only. There is the rival executive in another department moving at the tactically correct moment to expand his own domain at the expense of a colleague held up to public censure.[36]

Thus, bureaucrats, feeling somewhat insecure and constantly vulnerable, try to act so as to minimize the chances of public controversy and condemnation by attempting to maintain good relations with the public. This means, to a large degree, responding to public demands. In other words, we arrive at the key characteristic of a democratic institution: an institution that reacts positively to public demands.

Some Exploratory Questions

1. Do personal security and initiative tend to be aided by bureaucracies with their known, uniform procedures, or do bureaucracies lead to a rigidity that ignores the human element and special circumstances?

2. Is the tendency of bureaucratic agencies to respond to the needs and desires of certain supportive clientele or satellite groups an evil to be combated or a proper and necessary result of the nature of bureaucratic decision making?

35. See Kenneth J. Meier and Lloyd G. Nigro, "Public Opinion, Public Policy, and Administrative Responsibility: A Belief Sharing Model" (paper given at the 1975 annual convention of the Midwest Political Science Association), pp. 10–16.

36. Warner et al., *The American Federal Executive,* p. 241. On this point also, see Bernstein, *The Job of the Federal Executive,* pp. 208–213.

3. What if any steps could be taken to make bureaucratic offices more responsive to popular demands?

Bibliographical Essay

For good discussions of the basic nature of bureaucracies, see Peter M. Blau, *Bureaucracy in Modern Society* (New York: Random House, 1956); Anthony Downs, *Inside Bureaucracy* (Boston: Little, Brown, 1967); and Martin Albrow, *Bureaucracy* (New York: Praeger, 1970).

General, brief discussions of the American bureaucracy are found in four books: James W. Davis, Jr., *The National Executive Branch* (New York: Free Press, 1970); Louis C. Gawthrop, *Administrative Politics and Social Change* (New York: St. Martin's, 1971); Lewis C. Mainzer, *Political Bureaucracy* (Glenview, Ill.: Scott, Foresman, 1973); and John Rehfuss, *Public Administration as Political Process* (New York: Scribner's, 1973).

Also fairly brief, but particularly well-written and insightful is Harold Seidman, *Politics, Position, and Power: The Dynamics of Federal Organization,* 2d ed. (New York: Oxford University Press, 1975). More comprehensive discussions of the bureaucracy are found in a number of public administration textbooks, which are especially helpful as reference works. One of the better ones is Ira Sharkansky, *Public Administration,* 2d ed. (Chicago: Markham, 1972).

An exploration of policy making by bureaucratic agencies in several policy areas is found in Don Allensworth, *Public Administration: The Execution of Public Policy* (Philadelphia: Lippincott, 1973). Three anthologies with a number of good selections are Dean L. Yarwood, ed., *The National Administrative System* (New York: Wiley, 1971); Michael D. Reagon, *The Administration of Public Policy* (Glenview, Ill.: Scott, Foresman, 1969); Francis E. Rourke, *Bureaucratic Power in National Politics,* 2d ed. (Boston: Little, Brown, 1972).

Many books concentrate on certain aspects of the bureaucracy. Four very enlightening volumes that examine bureaucracy from the point of view of the bureaucrats themselves and the nature of their work are: W. Lloyd Warner, Paul P. Van Riper, Norman H. Martin, and Orvis F. Collins, *The American Federal Executive* (New Haven, Conn.: Yale University Press, 1963); John J. Corson and R. Shale Paul, *Men Near the Top* (Baltimore: Johns Hopkins Press, 1966); Marver Bernstein, *The Job of the Federal Executive* (Washington, D.C.: Brookings Institution, 1958); and David T. Stanley, *Men Who Govern* (Washington, D.C.: Brookings Institution, 1967). A number of good insights are found in a study of the Department of Justice under Attorney General Robert Kennedy; see Victor S. Navasky, *Kennedy Justice* (New York: Atheneum, 1971). How bureaucratic departments and agencies protect themselves in the struggle for appropriations is analyzed by Aaron Wildavsky, *The Politics of the Budgetary Process* (Boston: Little, Brown, 1964). Samuel Krislov, *Representative Bureaucracy* (Englewood Cliffs, N.J.: Prentice-Hall, 1974), considers the extent to which bureaucrats are representative of the larger population.

The relationship between the independent regulatory commissions and business interest groups is discussed by Marver Bernstein in *Regulating Business by Inde-*

pendent Commission (Princeton, N.J.: Princeton University Press, 1955). Another perceptive analysis of the activities of the regulatory agencies is Louis M. Kohlmeier, Jr., *The Regulators* (New York: Harper & Row, 1969). For highly critical analyses, see Robert C. Fellmeth, *The Interstate Commerce Omission: The Public Interest and the ICC* (New York: Grossman, 1970), and James Turner, *The Chemical Feast* (New York: Grossman, 1970).

The question of the role of bureaucracy in a democratic society is explored by Charles S. Hyneman, *Bureaucracy in a Democracy* (New York: Harper & Row, 1950); Norman J. Powell, *Responsible Public Bureaucracy in the United States* (Boston: Allyn and Bacon, 1967); and Emmette S. Redford, *Democracy in the Administrative State* (New York: Oxford University Press, 1969).

Chapter 10

The Judiciary   The Politics of Law

Benjamin Cardozo, one of the more able justices ever to have served on the Supreme Court, once wrote:

> I was much troubled in spirit, in my first years upon the bench, to find how trackless was the ocean on which I had embarked. I sought for certainty. I was oppressed and disheartened when I found that the quest for it was futile. I was trying to reach land, the solid land of fixed and settled rules. . . . As the years have gone by, and as I have reflected more and more upon the nature of the judicial process, I have become reconciled to the uncertainty, because I have grown to see it as inevitable. I have grown to see that the process in its highest reaches is not discovery, but creation.[1]

Justice Cardozo's experience is shared by many: we search for certainty in law, but find uncertainty; we expect predictability, but find unpredictability.

Our expectations of certainty and predictability go back to the venerable concept of law as an almost mystical entity that rules the affairs of men. This concept looks on law as something that is certain and impartial. Thus "a government of laws and not of men," a fair, objective, impartial government, is extolled. The function then assigned to the judiciary is that of announcing the clear, obvious meaning of the laws. Judges merely make certain that the clear dictates of law are followed—they exercise no discretion. Thus we have "a rule of laws and not of men." Judges do not count. They are hardly human.

But Justice Cardozo and many others have made the disquieting discovery that law as a certain, objective entity does not exist. We have no choice between a rule of law *or* a rule of men; a rule of law *is* a rule of men. It is human beings who make, apply, and interpret laws. In the process, certainty, objectivity, and predictability vanish like mirages. This

---

[1]. Benjamin N. Cardozo, *The Nature of the Judicial Process* (New Haven, Conn.: Yale University Press, 1921), p. 166.

chapter considers the men and the forces that determine the nature of the judical subsystem and the politics of law that characterizes it.

Judicial Functions

Rule Interpretation

If judges are not the automatic dispensers of certain justice, exactly what function do they perform? Perhaps we can best begin to answer by first asking another question: Exactly what distinguishes judicial decision making from legislative or executive decision making? We must recall that the first of the conversion functions by which authoritative decisions are made for an entire society—interest representation—is largely performed by the political parties and interest groups and to a lesser degree by Congress. Through them, interests (concerns and points of view) are given expression throughout the political system. In the climate set by interest representation the other three conversion functions are performed.[2] Congress initiates rules: It makes decisions in the form of generalized rules that govern society. These generalized rules must then be applied in ongoing, concrete situations; this rule application is largely done by the bureaucracies found in the executive branch of government. Usually, the decisions of the bureaucracies go directly into society as outputs of the political system— and then the feedback process is set in motion. But sometimes a dispute arises over the proper application of a rule. The issue becomes "Has the bureaucuracy applied the rule as it should be applied?" Then the additional conversion function of rule interpretation—determining the intent of a rule in order to settle a conflict about its meaning—must be performed. And rule interpretation is what judicial decision making entails. Most of the decisions made by the judiciary are interpretations of generalized rules that must be made because of some conflict that has arisen about their proper application.[3] In practice, as we shall see, the rules interpreted by the judiciary are normally either statutes passed by Congress or provisions of the Constitution.

In 1974, for example, a dispute arose between the special prosecutor in the Watergate scandal, Leon Jaworski, and then President Nixon. Jaworski wanted as evidence the tapes of certain White House conversations that had been secretly recorded by Nixon, and Nixon held that under the constitutionally implied concept of executive privilege he did not have to surrender the tapes. The question was one of constitutional interpretation:

2. See Figure 1.2 p. 13.
3. In Chapter 1, pp. 4–22, the important distinction between rule application and rule interpretation, as the terms are used in this book, was explained more fully.

Does the Constitution protect a President from having to surrender evidence requested for a criminal trial if he believes that doing so would violate his need to keep certain information secret? As we saw in Chapter 7, the Supreme Court ruled that under the Constitution executive privilege "must yield to the demonstrated, specific need for evidence in a pending criminal trial." In making this decision the Supreme Court was declaring exactly what the meaning of the Constitution is in order to settled a dispute that had arisen. This is rule interpretation.

The performance of the rule interpretation function does not, however, distinguish the judiciary in an absolute sense: the judiciary performs additional functions, and other institutions also engage in rule interpretation to some degree. Nevertheless, the *primary* function of the judicial system is rule interpretation; the *primary* functions of the other institutions differ.

The lower courts perform a fact-finding function as well as an interpretation function. Often they must determine whether A committed a murder or whether B failed to pay his income taxes, as well as whether A's actions fall under the legally defined category of murder and whether B's claimed exemption from income taxes is within the law. But even in lower courts the fact-finding function is often secondary to the interpretation function; in the higher courts, questions of fact rarely enter in.

Powers of Interpretation   The judicial subsystem is able to perform the function of rule interpretation because it has a wide range of powers at its disposal—powers so vast that they make the American judiciary unique among judiciaries in liberal-democratic countries. In short, the federal judiciary—capped by the Supreme Court—has the power to interpret the Constitution and all federal statutes to determine whether actions of governmental officials (federal, state, and local) or private individuals are in conformity with them.

In the case of the Constitution, the courts have the sweeping authority to declare laws passed by Congress, actions of the President, decisions of the bureaucracies, or any state or local action to be in violation of the Constitution. This is the famous *power of judicial review*—the power to declare actions of other branches or levels of government unconstitutional and therefore null and void. This power was not explicitly given the Supreme Court by the Constitution but was first asserted by Chief Justice John Marshall in 1803 in the now famous case of *Marbury v. Madison,* the first case in which a federal law was declared unconstitutional. Marshall argued in this case that because the Constitution is the supreme law of the land, any "act of the legislature, repugnant to the constitution is void." Although this was a much-debated position at the time, it is now fully accepted and is an integral part of the political system. The power of the Supreme Court to hold executive actions and actions of state and local officials unconstitutional is fully accepted and well established. The key fact to recognize in all these cases is that what the courts are doing is interpreting the Constitution—they are clarifying the meaning of the Constitution in order to settle disputes that have arisen over its proper meaning.[4]

The power of the Supreme Court to judge unconstitutional the laws passed by Congress has been stressed so much that it is easy to overemphasize its significance. In recent years—in fact, throughout almost all of the Supreme Court's history—this power has been exercised very sparingly. From 1940 to 1972 the Supreme Court declared unconstitutional a total of only 32 federal laws. And almost all of these were relatively minor pieces of legislation.[5] In contrast, many recent decisions of the Supreme Court holding certain actions of state or local officials unconstitutional have been of first-rate importance. The 1954 school desegregation decision,[6] a series of decisions forcing apportionment of congressional and state legislative districts on a strict population basis,[7] the Miranda decision of 1966 restricting police officers' questioning of suspects,[8] and the 1973 decision holding state laws restricting abortions unconstitutional[9] are four prime examples. All are of fundamental and far-reaching significance; all declared that certain state or local actions were in violation of the Constitution.

In reviewing the rule interpretation powers of the courts, constitutional interpretation should not be stressed so much that statutory interpretation is lost sight of. Constitutional questions usually raise fundamental, far-reaching issues and thus receive more publicity in the news media, but the power of the courts to interpret laws and statutes passed by Congress is also of great importance. Courts, by way of interpretation, can either broaden or restrict the impact of a law.[10]

Significance of Interpretation   If the old concept of law as a certain, unwavering entity were accurate, the judges' function of rule interpretation

4. I am speaking here, of course, only about cases that arise concerning the federal Constitution. Federal courts have no authority to interpret state constitutions. The only time federal courts concern themselves with state constitutions is when it is claimed that a state constitution violates the federal Constitution. Even then, the federal courts are not interpreting the state constitution. The only question they consider is whether the provisions of the federal Constitution are such that the state constitution is contrary to them. Thus, it is the meaning of the federal—not the state—Constitution that is in dispute and that the federal courts are settling.

5. Glendon Schubert, *Judicial Policy Making,* 2d ed. (Glenview, Ill.: Scott, Foresman, 1974), p. 75.

6. *Brown v. Board of Education,* 347 U.S. 483 (1954).

7. *Baker v. Carr,* 369 U.S. 186 (1962); *Wesbury v. Sanders,* 376 U.S. 1 (1964); and *Reynolds v. Sims,* 377 U.S. 533 (1964).

8. *Miranda v. Arizona,* 384 U.S. 436 (1966).

9. *Roe v. Wade,* 410 U.S. 113 (1973) and *Doe v. Bolton,* 410 U.S. 179 (1973).

10. It must be stressed again that the federal courts interpret only federal laws, not state laws. The same point made in footnote 4 concerning constitutional interpretation is also true of statutory interpretation.

would be reduced to a mechanical routine. Laws would be clear to all rational, reasonable persons. Only the foolish or perverse would misconstrue a law, and only then would the judiciary step in to set things right, announcing the clear intent of the law. But law, by its very nature, is ambiguous and therefore subject to varying interpretations. Thus, equally rational and equally reasonable persons are often in disagreement about the meaning of the law.

As we saw in Chapter 3, the Constitution is marked by extreme ambiguity. Because of this fact the Constitution is far from self-explanatory, and the intent of many of its provisions far from self-evident. Thus, different individuals and interests are bound to read different meanings into the Constitution. And the courts are left with the task of deciding which of a number of conflicting interpretations is to be declared the proper one. As Chief Justice Charles Evans Hughes once said, ''The Constitution is what the judges say it is.''

The same situation exists with regard to statute law—laws passed by Congress. Although laws vary greatly in their degree of ambiguity—some are very explicit and tightly drawn, whereas others are very general and loosely drawn—the extent to which courts are brought into the interpretation process is surprising to most persons. It almost seems as though no statute can be made sufficiently explicit and detailed that there will not be some borderline cases in which it is unclear whether and how the statute applies. If one drafts an income-tax law and defines income very exactly, situations will still arise that were not anticipated and for which the law has made no clear provision.

Thus, we come to the same conclusion we came to concerning constitutional interpretation—time and again the courts have a large number of possibilities to choose from in making their interpretations. The net result is to turn the courts—and especially the Supreme Court—into policy-making bodies of the first magnitude. The contribution of the courts to the policy-making process is crucial, far-reaching, and pervasive in impact.

System-maintenance Functions

Creating Legitmacy The most significant system-maintenance function performed by the judiciary is creating legitimacy. When a court decides that a law passed by Congress or a decision of the bureaucracy is constitutional, it puts the stamp of legitimacy on that law or decision. The courts—including the Supreme Court, with all its dignity and prestige—have stated that a certain action of the government is legal, proper, and ought to be obeyed as the law of the land. The judiciary is thus acting as the means by which the great honor and prestige of the Constitution is placed in support of the law or action under question. Or in the case of statutory interpretation, the centuries-old tradition of respect for law is brought to bear on a particular law. Even when the judiciary holds a law or action unconstitutional, it is still creating legitimacy—this time by legitimatizing the position held by those opposed to the law or action. And when two parties are in conflict over the meaning of a law, the judiciary puts the stamp of legitimacy on one of the positions.

In creating legitimacy the courts must of necessity be viewed by the public as being themselves legitimate. The courts are only able to create legitimacy because some of the respect and even awe in which they are held carries over to the interpretations they make. Thus the courts, more than the other branches of government, must be sensitive to tradition, symbols, and public reactions in order to assure that they can fill their function of legitimizing the actions of the other political institutions. The black robes of the judges, the respect shown even mediocre judges ("Your honor, I . . ."), and the solemn, formalized courtroom proceedings carried out in usually ornate, often even cathedral-like courtrooms all contribute to maintaining a sense of respect and perhaps awe for the courts. In the process the courts' ability to create legitimacy for the political system and its institutions and policies is enhanced. At various points in the chapter we shall note actions of the courts that help them to maintain the respect of the public needed to create legitimacy effectively.

Conflict Resolution   Central in the courts' function of rule interpretation is the resolution of conflicts. For the courts are brought into the picture only when there is a dispute (conflict) over the meaning of the Constitution or a law (or often in the lower courts over the facts in a situation). Thus, as the courts interpret rules and determine facts, they resolve conflicts.

Generating Support   When two parties involved in a conflict (and the interested public generally) accept a court decision as a legitimate, acceptable resolution of the conflict, support is being generated for the political system. They are accepting and obeying the political system's authoritative decision—a basic way of showing support. Thus, in creating legitimacy and resolving conflicts, the judicial system is generating support for the political system. The courts can also generate support for themselves and their decisions—and thus for the political system as a whole—by making decisions that appear to the American people and to leaders in the other political structures to be reasonable, just decisions. In addition, the use of symbols and rituals—the judicial robes and the solemn proceedings of the courtroom, for example—help teach a respect for (gain support for) the judiciary.

There is a considerable amount of evidence that the Supreme Court, because of a large number of controversial decisions made during the 1950s and 1960s, has lost much of the support and respect it once had.[11]

11. For a good summary of much of this evidence see Sheldon Goldman and Thomas P. Jahnige, *The Federal Courts as a Political System* (New York: Harper & Row, 1971), pp. 131–148.

The Court may regain much of this lost support—it has been considerably changed by the philosophical position of Nixon's four appointees—but until this occurs the Court will be handicapped in its generation of support because it is itself suspect in the eyes of a large segment of the population.

Throughout the rest of this chapter the means by which the judiciary performs the function of rule interpretation and the three system-maintenance functions are explored in some detail.

The Courts

The Court Structure

The basic structure of the federal court system is simple. Yet when all the intricacies are added, a complex structure appears. The basic structure consists of three types of courts: 89 district courts, 11 federal courts of appeals, and one Supreme Court. (See Figure 10.1 for a diagram of the court structure.)

District Courts   The vast majority of cases originate in one of the *district courts.* These are the *general courts of original jurisdiction,* the trial courts, where juries sit (at least in many cases), where witnesses are called, and where judgments are made. The entire United States is divided into 89 districts, with one court for each district. Each court, however, has from one to 24 judges, and because each judge normally conducts court separately, the larger district courts can handle a large volume of business.

Federal Courts of Appeals   Most appeals (requests for a review of the decision of a lower court) go to one of the 11 federal *courts of appeals,* although a few cases (such as any case in which the United States is a party and in which it has been decided an act of Congress is unconstitutional) can be appealed directly to the Supreme Court. The entire United States is divided into eleven circuits, and appeals go to the federal court of appeals of the circuit in which the district court that previously heard the case is located. There are from three to nine judges on each federal court of appeals, where normally cases are decided by panels of three judges.

The Supreme Court   At the top of the appeal route is the *United States Supreme Court,* which can hear appeals from the federal courts of appeals, the highest state courts of appeals, and other sources. It is composed of one *chief justice* and eight *associate justices.* Cases are always heard and decided by the full court.

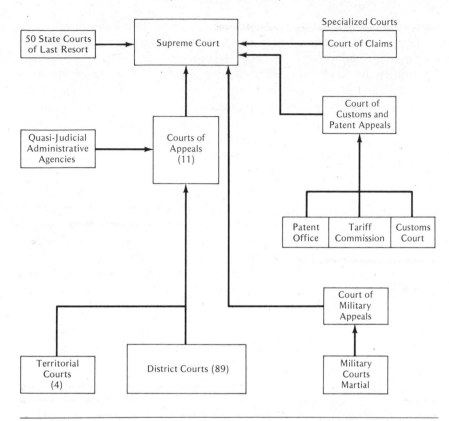

Figure 10.1   The federal court structure (with arrows indicating the routes of appeals)

These three types of courts constitute the heart of the federal judicial system, but additional courts and routes of appeal must be noted in order to complete the picture.

Territorial District Courts   In addition to the 89 regular district courts, there are four territorial district courts for the four territories of Puerto Rico, Virgin Islands, Panama Canal Zone, and Guam. These are similar to the regular district courts although their legal status is somewhat different and (except in Puerto Rico) they also hear cases that ordinarily would be heard in state courts. Cases can be appealed from the territorial district courts to the federal courts of appeals, as is done with cases from the regular district courts.

Administrative Agencies   Many administrative agencies and offices—for example, the National Labor Relations Board, the Interstate Commerce Commission, and the Food and Drug Administration—have certain quasijudicial rule interpretation functions in addition to their more normal administrative duties. Decisions made by these administrative agencies in their quasijudicial role may be appealed into the federal courts of appeals. Thus, when the NLRB, after holding hearings and taking evidence, decides that management in a certain plant has been engaging in unfair labor practices in violation of the law and must reinstate several fired employees with back pay, that decision may be appealed to the proper federal court of appeals. The federal court of appeals for the District of Columbia handles most of these appeals from administrative agencies.

Specialized Courts   Finally, Congress has established three courts with specialized jurisdictions. Cases from all three may be appealed to the Supreme Court. These specialized courts are the *court of claims,* which handles claims by individuals against the federal government; the *court of customs and patent appeals,* which hears appeals from the Patent Office, the Tariff Commission, and the customs court; and the *court of military appeals,* which is composed of three civilian judges who hear appeals from military courts-martial.

Recruitment to the Judiciary

Formal Methods of Selection   The formal method of selecting federal judges can be quickly and simply described: All are appointed by the President with the concurrence of the Senate. And all are appointed for life, except the judges serving on the territorial district courts and the court of military appeals, who are appointed for long terms.

Saying merely this hides more than it reveals: Behind this formal process lie many intricate factors that determine which individuals out of thousands of potential judges do, in fact, become federal judges. We will concentrate on the judges of the district courts, the federal courts of appeals, and the Supreme Court because these form the heart of the federal judicial system.

District Court Judges   In selecting district court judges, the President finds his freedom of choice sharply circumscribed, for tradition has accorded Senators and local party leaders a large voice in their selection.[12] If there is a Senator of the President's party in office from the state in which the district court judge will serve, the officials in the Justice Department, to whom the President usually delegates the task of obtaining names, screening possible appointees, and making recommendations, confer closely

12. For more information on the selection of federal judges, see Harold W. Chase, *Federal Judges: The Appointing Process* (Minneapolis: University of Minnesota Press, 1972).

with that Senator. Frequently the President does appoint the person suggested by the Senator (or Senators, if both are of the President's party). If there is no Senator of the President's party from the state in question, state leaders of the President's party may play a similar—but somewhat less influential—role of advising and submitting names.

The explanation for this appointing process is the President's need to build support for himself and his legislative program in the Senate. Presidents hesitate to risk alienating influential Senators by going against their wishes. They keep in mind the effects that accepting or rejecting senatorial recommendations can have on their legislative proposals (which are normally considered to be of greater importance than district court appointments).

In addition, there is the unwritten Senate rule of senatorial courtesy.

In our day, senatorial courtesy has come to mean that senators will give serious consideration to and be favorably disposed to support an individual senator of the president's party who opposes a nominee to an office in his state. But, as the chief clerk of the Senate Judiciary Committee has put it, "He just can't incant a few magic words like 'personally obnoxious' and get away with it. He must be prepared to fight, giving his reasons for opposing the nominee." If his reasons are not persuasive to other senators or if he is not a respected member of the Senate, he stands a chance of losing his fight.[13]

Facing the prospect of a Senator invoking senatorial courtesy, few Presidents are willing to wage an all-out Senate fight over a district court appointment. They typically find it easier—and more expedient—to defer to senatorial wishes.

One effect of this senatorial impact on district court appointments is that district court judges tend to reflect local and regional concerns and values, which sometimes are at odds with national judicial decisions. In the 1960s federal district court judges in the South frequently took prosegregationist stances even though the Supreme Court had adopted a prointegrationist position.

Federal Courts of Appeals Judges   Senators and party leaders also have some influence over presidential appointments to the 11 federal courts of appeals, but significantly less influence than they have over district court appointments. This is true largely because the jurisdiction of the federal courts of appeals takes in more than one state, and thus there is no one Senator or state party organization with a special, personal stake in the appointment. As a result, the President—although he must still give attention to the suggestions of key Senators and party officials—has considerably more freedom of choice than he does in appointing district court judges.

13. Chase, *Federal Judges,* p. 7.

The Supreme Court Judges   Most important of all judicial appointments, of course, are the President's appointments to the Supreme Court. These appointees will be passing judgment on the decisions of the lower courts, either approving or reversing their decisions, and thereby establishing precedents for the rest of the judicial system to follow. The type of persons a President appoints to the Supreme Court—given the policy-making role of the Supreme Court—has important and long-lasting effects; these appointments are among the most significant of all presidential actions.

One crucial fact emerges from any consideration of Supreme Court appointments: Presidents appoint persons with a political philosophy or outlook similar to their own. This is indicated by the simple fact that from 1789 to 1972, of some 100 persons appointed to the Supreme Court, only 13 had a party affiliation different from that of the appointing President. Presidents have almost always selected members of their own party.

But—and this is even more significant—whether a President appoints someone from his own or the opposite party, there is abundant evidence to indicate that he is careful to select someone whose political outlook is similar to his own. President Nixon once stated that in selecting his appointees to the Supreme Court he sought "individuals who shared my judicial philosophy which is basically a conservative philosophy."[14] And Robert Kennedy, while serving as the Attorney General in President John Kennedy's cabinet, said about the qualities desired in Supreme Court appointees: "You wanted someone who generally agreed with you on what role government should play in American life, what role the individual in society should have. You didn't think about how he would vote in a reapportionment case or a criminal case. You wanted someone who, in the long run, you could believe would be doing what you thought was best. You wanted someone who agreed generally with your views of the country."[15]

References to the political views of potential justices may appear improper to a public used to thinking of judges as purely legal technicians. Yet, if we can assume that the President is in tune with the dominant forces of the day, his appointing persons in agreement with his beliefs helps ensure that the Supreme Court and its decisions will also be in tune. And this has importance in assuring support and legitimacy for the Court—and in democratizing the Court. (The significance of this latter point is discussed more fully in the last section of this chapter.)

Presidents do, of course, sometimes misjudge their choice and discover to their sorrow that a recent appointee in actuality makes decisions on the Court totally contrary to what the Presidents expected and desired. President Wilson appointed James Clark McReynolds, "who proved to be the

14. *The New York Times* (October 22, 1971), p. 24.

15. Quoted by James E. Clayton, *The Making of Justice: The Supreme Court in Action* (New York: Dutton, 1964), p. 52.

total antithesis of everything Wilson stood for and became the most fanatic and hard-bitten conservative ever to grace the Court."[16] Whereas the arch conservative, President Coolidge, appointed Harlan Stone, who turned out to be one of the great liberal members of the Court, and was, ironically, frequently in conflict with Wilson's McReynolds. The politically moderate Eisenhower appointed Earl Warren as chief justice, only to have Warren lead the Court in a whole series of very liberal decisions in the area of individual rights. These are the exceptions—usually, Presidents have been successful in predicting the behavior of their appointees.[17]

Finally, there is some evidence that Presidents attempt to keep a geographic, religious, and ethnic balance on the Court. President Taft clearly took geographical area into account, wishing to have all the major sections of the nation represented on the Court.[18] President Nixon clearly indicated his desire to appoint a southerner to the Court—and succeeded in doing so on his third attempt, with the appointment of Lewis F. Powell, Jr., in 1971. From the time of Wilson's appointment of Brandeis until Fortas' resignation in 1969, there was at least one member of the Jewish faith on the Court. One or two Catholics are usually on the Court also. And President Johnson, with his appointment of Justice Thurgood Marshall in 1967, may have established the practice of having at least one black on the Supreme Court. President Ford is reported to want to appoint the first woman to the Court.

Maintaining a balanced Court may help establish legitimacy and support for the Court's decisions. If the Court were composed, for example, completely of white Protestants drawn from the northeastern seaboard states, it would certainly have a much more difficult time establishing legitimacy and support for its decisions than if it were composed of a more heterogeneous membership. A Court based on a very narrow, exclusive base would tend to alienate the groups and sections left out and cause them to feel that having had no say in the making of the decisions, they have no obligation to obey them.

Although the Senate must approve all Supreme Court nominations, it does not have a large voice in the appointment process. Presidential consultation with Senators prior to making appointments has been sporadic, and the Senate normally approves presidential appointees (it has failed to confirm only 4 of 50 presidential nominations in the twentieth century). The influence of the Senate on presidential appointments to the Supreme Court is reduced by the fact that the Supreme Court's jurisdiction

---

16. John P. Frank, *Marble Palace* (New York: Knopf, 1958), p. 45.

17. One political scientist has estimated that approximately one justice out of four has deviated significantly from presidential expectations and hopes. See Robert Scigliano, *The Supreme Court and the Presidency* (New York: Free Press, 1971), pp. 124–148.

18. See Daiel S. McHargue, "President Taft's Appointments to the Supreme Court," *Journal of Politics,* 12 (1950), 478–510.

is the entire United States, a fact that eliminates any special state or regional claim a Senator or group of Senators might have to name a justice; the Senate's influence is also modified by the high significance of the office, which tends to make Presidents unwilling to bargain away their power of selection. One study has shown that the Senate is more likely to reject a presidential nomination when a President is in the last year of his term or when the Senate is controlled by the party other than that of the President.[19] Three recent Senate rejections of presidential Supreme Court nominations can be explained on these bases. The Senate's failure to approve President Johnson's promotion of Abe Fortas from associate justice to chief justice occurred in Johnson's last year in office (1968), and the Senate's rejection of President Nixon's nominations of Clement Haynsworth and Harrold Carswell occurred in a Senate controlled by the opposition Democratic party. Nevertheless, the rejection of three Supreme Court nominations within four years (after none had been rejected in the previous 38 years) may indicate a trend in the Senate to look more critically at presidential nominations and thus take a more influential part in the selection process.

Judicial Decision Making[20]

To Accept or Not to Accept

The first decision—and in many ways the most important decision—the Supreme Court must make concerning each case is whether or not to hear the case at all. Each year the Supreme Court is asked to review some 1,500 to 2,000 cases, and of these only about 200 to 250 are accepted for review by the Court.

Virtually all cases accepted by the Supreme Court come before it by one of two paths: by a petition for a writ of *certiorari* or by a statement as to jurisdiction. The majority of cases come by way of *petitions for writs of certiorari*. These petitions (filed by one of the parties involved in the case) include the formal court records of a case and a statement of why the Supreme Court should review it. If four of the justices—sometimes called the *rule of four*—agree that the case should be reviewed, a writ of *certiorari* is issued. Technically this is an order to the lower court to send up the records of the case. Then, usually, the case is put on the Supreme Court's docket. Occasionally, however, the Court makes a decision on the

19. Scigliano, *The Supreme Court,* pp. 96–100.

20. Because of the limitations of space, I have concentrated on Supreme Court decision making and have not separately considered decision making in the district courts and courts of appeals. Although there are certain differences in procedure, the basic patterns and characteristics described in this section hold true for the lower courts as well as for the Supreme Court.

case at this time without any further proceedings. It issues what is called a *per curiam opinion,* an opinion that usually states the decision of the Court but does not give any elaborate explanations. This procedure is followed when the Court feels the issues in the case are relatively clear-cut and do not require lengthy study. The Court has complete discretion to accept or not to accept cases coming by way of *certiorari,* and it usually accepts less than 15 percent of the petitions.

The second path to the Supreme Court is taken by any case that falls into one of the categories of cases that the Supreme Court (supposedly) must review. Such a case comes before the Court on appeal—in distinction from coming before it by *certiorari.* A case is brought on appeal when (1) a state court has held a federal law unconstitutional, (2) a federal court has held a state or a federal law unconstitutional, or (3) a state court has held a challenged state law constitutional.[21] However, this does not mean that the Supreme Court accepts all cases that come on appeal. Using the rule of four again, about one half are rejected "for want of a substantial federal question" or "for want of jurisdiction." Thus, the two legally different paths are, in practice, not very different at all—in both instances the Supreme Court itself has control over which cases it will review and which ones it will not.

The Politics of Acceptance   Why is one case accepted by the Supreme Court and given a full and complete review while another case is quickly dismissed? In other words, what criteria are used by the Supreme Court in accepting and rejecting cases?

The basic theoretical criterion—and, normally, in practice the most significant one—is the degree to which the case raises issues that are fundamental and extend far beyond the immediate case. Chief Justice Vinson explained this clearly: "If we took every case in which an interesting legal question is raised, or our *prima facie* impression is that the decision below is erroneous, we could not fulfill the Constitutional and statutory responsibilities placed upon the Court. To remain effective, the Supreme Court must continue to decide only those cases which present questions whose resolution will have immediate importance far beyond the particular facts and parties involved."[22]

The second avowed criterion can lead the Court to accept relatively insignificant cases: A case will be accepted if different courts of appeals have made conflicting decisions on the question at issue. Such cases, however, are often immediately decided in *per curiam* decisions.

21. In all three of the following instances, it is of course the federal (not a state) Constitution that is involved. The Supreme Court does not interpret state constitutions.

22. From an address to the Assembly of the American Bar Association, Sept. 9, 1944. Quoted in Glendon Schubert, *Constitutional Politics* (New York: Holt, Rinehart and Winston, 1960). p. 92.

After reviewing the criteria openly avowed by the Supreme Court, we are still left with the feeling that all has not been told. There is persuasive evidence that the Supreme Court frequently refuses to hear a case if it feels that the issue it raises is so controversial or so inflammatory that a Supreme Court decision at that time would evoke strong criticism or widespread disobedience. Few cases on civil liberties managed to reach the Supreme Court during the Joseph McCarthy era of the early 1950s, when disregard of the civil liberties of individuals was widespread in many quarters. It was not until 1957—when the most flamboyant and questionable congressional investigations were over—that the Supreme Court put tighter restrictions on the investigative power of Congress.[23] During the 1960s and early 1970s the Court refused to hear all cases challenging the constitutionality of American involvement in the war in Vietnam.

A good example of judicial procrastination until a more propitious time is provided by John P. Roche:

The case of *Duncan v. Kahanamoku,* contesting the validity of military trials of civilians in Hawaii during the war, is a good instance of the judicial stall: Duncan was locked up in August, 1942, and only succeeded in bringing *habeas corpus* action in the District Court in April, 1944. In November, 1944, the Ninth Circuit affirmed the denial of the writ, and Duncan immediately applied to the Supreme Court for certiorari—which was granted in February, 1945. The Supreme Court studied the case carefully while the war ended, and then in February, 1946, determined that Duncan had been improperly convicted.[24]

Thus, the Supreme Court could have its cake and eat it too: It was able both to uphold civil liberties and to avoid the outcry that would have arisen if the Court had limited the military during wartime.

We may criticize the Court for timidity in situations like this, but, on the other hand, it is one way in which the Court can maintain its legitimacy. Every time the court is heavily criticized by the press and public leaders, and every time a Court decision is fully or partially ignored, both the Court and its prestige—and thereby the legitimacy it can impart to the rest of the political system—are damaged. Therefore, although the Supreme Court justices may seem timid, certainly they are not guilty of political naivete. Further implications of this type of judicial behavior are considered in the section on inputs later in this chapter.

The Decision-making Process

Written Briefs   After a particular case has been accepted by the Supreme Court and scheduled for full consideration, four steps precede the final

23. The case is *Watkins v. Unites States,* 345 U.S. 178 (1957). It is interesting to note that, after a barrage of criticism following the Watkins case, the Supreme Court drew back two years later and again widened the investigatory powers of Congress by narrowly construing the Watkins precedent. See *Barensblatt v. United States,* 360 U.S. 109 (1959).

24. John P. Roche, "Judicial Self-Restraint," *American Political Science Review,* 49 (1955), 767.

decision. The first step is the submission of written briefs by the two parties involved in the specific case, each arguing as cogently as possible why the case should be decided in its favor.

In addition to the briefs filed by the two parties actually involved, additional briefs may be filed by individuals or organizations who—although not one of the parties in the case—have some interest in its outcome. They are called *amicus curiae* ("friend of the court") *briefs*. For an organization to file an *amicus curiae* brief, it must have the consent either of both parties in the case or one of the parties and the Court. Because most Supreme Court decisions establish broad policies that affect many persons and groups other than those immediately involved in a specific case, *amicus curiae* briefs can be effective in acquainting the Court with all the implications and repercussions of the policy alternatives presented by the case. *Amicus curiae* briefs are one of the chief means by which interest groups can attempt to influence judicial decision making. Well-known interest groups—the NAACP, the Americal Civil Liberties Union, the AFL-CIO, and the American Legion for example—frequently file such briefs.

Oral Argument   For four hours a day, three days a week, during the nine months a year that the Supreme Court is in session, dignified lawyers, young observant students, and awed tourists are ushered into the imposing Supreme Court chamber to witness one of the more interesting public displays Washington has to offer: oral argument before the Supreme Court. Each party in a case submits a written brief and is given the opportunity (or, as some Supreme Court lawyers would say, is forced) to present its case orally before the entire Court. Usually, a half hour is given to each side, but more time may be allotted, depending on the importance of the case and the complexity of the issues. Oral argument is not a matter of a lawyer reading a prepared speech to nine half-dozing justices. It is a lively —and sometimes sharp—interchange between lawyer and Court. Any justice can interrupt the lawyer at any point in his remarks to ask questions or to probe for additional information. This right is frequently exercised.

On occasion, oral argument almost evolves into a sharp debate among justices as one asks searching, probing questions of the lawyer and another springs to the aid of the hard-pressed lawyer, asking leading questions: "Do you agree that . . .?"

Conference   On the Fridays following a week of oral argument the nine justices meet in conference. These conferences are secret. No one else is present (not even a stenographer), no official record is kept, and justices are very reticent to divulge what goes on. This secrecy is aimed at keeping differences of opinion and antagonisms among the justices from the public eye, thereby helping to preserve the prestige of the Court. The support and legitimacy accorded the final decision may be increased if the public does not know of the waverings and doubts that preceded it. In addition, discussion is no doubt freer and more candid because of the absence of publicity.

In spite of this secrecy, we know the formal procedures that are followed at the conferences and a little about the typical interaction among justices. The chief justice presides over the conference and starts the discussion of each case by summarizing it and stating his views and opinions on it. Next the associate justices give their views of the case, in order of their seniority on the Court. The chief justice then summarizes the major points of view that have been expressed and calls for any further comments (after giving his own first). When the chief justice feels sufficient discussion has taken place (or after a predetermined period of time), he calls for the vote—called the *conference vote*—which starts with the newest member of the Court and works up to the most senior and finally to the chief justice. Majority rules: Whichever side musters a majority wins the case.

The procedure puts the chief justice in a position in which, if he has the requisite skills and wishes to use them, he can exert a strong influence.[25] By his initial summary of the case he can set the tone for the discussion and delineate the issues around which the case will be discussed. And if he combines rapport with his colleagues and wide knowledge, he can gain a considerable amount of respect for his views from the other justices and thus exert significant influence on the Court.

The two qualities of chief justices most likely to enable them to develop strong influence in the Court are (1) sheer legal ability and thorough knowledge, and (2) tactfulness and skill at interpersonal relations. Chief Justice Charles Evans Hughes (1930–1941) is generally acknowledged to have been one of the most influential chief justices. His influence seemed to rest largely on his legal ability and thorough knowledge. As one of his clerks says:

In preparing for a discussion of argued cases, the Chief followed the practice he used in considering petitions for certiorari and jurisdictional statement: exhaustive study, many bookmarks and notes dictated for the purpose of assisting him in stating the case to the conference. Again his preparation was so thorough as to discourage challenge without equal preparation by the challenger, and his very thoroughness resulted in his views being given great weight.[26]

Chief Justice Earl Warren (1954–1968) is generally acknowledged to have been another influential chief justice. His influence appears to have

25. For an excellent study of the influence of the chief justice over the decision-making process of the Supreme Court, see David J. Danelski, "The Influence of the Chief Justice in the Decisional Process," in Walter F. Murphy and C. Herman Pritchett, eds. *Courts, Judges and Politics,* (New York: Random House, 1961), pp. 497–508.

26. Edwin McElwain, "The Business of the Supreme Court Under Chief Justice Hughes," in Robert Scigliano, ed., *The Courts* (Boston: Little, Brown, 1962), p. 295. Originally published in *Harvard Law Review,* 63 (1949), 5–26.

sprung largely from his tactfulness and skill at working with his fellow justices.[27]

One should be careful, however, not to exaggerate the power of the chief justice in the Supreme Court's decision-making process. Much depends on the man and his abilities and inclinations. While it is generally agreed that Hughes and Warren were influential chief justices, it is also generally agreed that Harlan F. Stone (1941–1946) and Fred M. Vinson (1946–1953) were weak chief justices. There is some developing evidence that the current chief justice, Warren E. Burger, is not as influential as his predecessor, Earl Warren, because he lacks Warren's skill in interpersonal relationships with the other justices.

Writing Opinions   After a case has been decided in conference, the next step is taken: writing the opinion of the Court. Except for its *per curiam* decisions, the Supreme Court does not merely state its decision and leave the public and lower courts to guess why it decided as it did. Instead, an official opinion of the Court, written by one of the justices, states the basic facts in the case and explains why the majority of the Court decided the case as it did. This opinion is helpful to lower courts and lawyers when they must determine the scope and intention of the decision. A decision can be made on very narrow grounds, with the result that only a few persons and situations are affected, or on very broad grounds, with the result that many persons and situations are affected.

Other justices may write a *concurring opinion.* This is an opinion written by one or more justices who agree with the decision but disagree with some of the reasoning contained in the official opinion of the Court. Thus, he (or they) sets down how his (their) basis for deciding the case differs from that of the Court. This type of opinion is not legally binding, but may influence future decisions of the Court and may lessen the impact of the majority's opinion.

A dissenting opinion is also frequently written by one or more justices who are in the minority. Such an opinion states how and why they would have decided the case. This opinion, which has no legal force, may influence future deliberations of the Court and may weaken the impact of the majority opinion. Concurring and, especially, dissenting opinions tend to lower the prestige of the Court and destroy the myth of law as a certain, unfailing force. Support and legitimacy are decreased. Compliance with a Court decision is often more difficult to obtain when the losing interests can point to a dessenting opinion. This latter situation is especially a problem when the Court is closely divided (5 to 4, or 6 to 3) and less a problem as the Court approaches unaminity. Thus, the majority justices

27. For a case study that reveals Warren's skill at interpersonal relations with the other justices, see S. Sidney Ulmer, "Earl Warren and the Brown Decision," *Journal of Politics,* (33) (1971), 689–702.

frequently work hard to win additional support for their side and often will modify the opinion of the Court in order to win over wavering justices. Chief Justice Warren's ability to obtain a unanimous decision in the famous, and exceedingly controversial, 1954 school desegregation decision was a feat of judicial persuasion and tact.[28]

The drafts of these various types of opinions are circulated among the justices, and frequently votes are picked up or lost as justices react to the opinions. The conference vote is only tentative. On occasion a strongly written dissent has been known to pick up enough votes to become the majority opinion of the Court.

The chief justice assigns the writing of opinions, unless he is himself in the minority, in which case the senior justice in the majority makes the assignment. By assigning the writing of the Court's opinion, the chief justice can affect the decision-making process, for he can assign the opinion to someone in the majority whom he knows is extreme on the issue and thereby obtain a clear-cut, extreme opinion (which probably will evoke strong dissenting opinions and, in controversial cases, strong public criticism of the Court). Or he can assign the writing to one of the moderate members of the majority and thereby obtain a more middle-of-the-road opinion (which may head off strong dissents and even pick up one or two additional justices, and help tone down possible adverse public reactions). But the more moderately written opinion may also cloud the issues and create uncertainty in the lower courts and the legal community. In any case, the choice is up to the chief justice.

The factors that may influence the chief justice's assignment of writing opinions are well illustrated in a letter written by Justice Robert H. Jackson to Chief Justice Harlan Stone.

I hope you will forgive me for intruding into the matter of assignments, the difficulties of which I feel you generally resolve with wisdom and always with fairness, but I wonder if you have not overlooked some of the ugly factors in our national life which go to the wisdom of having Mr. Justice Frankfurter act as the voice of the Court in the matter of *Smith v. Allwright*. It is a delicate matter. We must reverse a recent, well-considered, and unanimous decision. We deny the entire South the right to a white primary, which is one of its most cherished rights. It seems to me very important that the strength which an all but unanimous decision would have may be greatly weakened if the voice that utters it is one that may grate on Southern sensibilities. Mr. Justice Frankfurter unites in a rare degree factors which unhappily excite prejudice. In the first place, he is a Jew. In the second place, he is from New England, the seat of the abolition movement. In the third place, he has not been thought of as a person particularly sympathetic with the Democratic party in the past. I know that every one of these things is a consideration that to you is distasteful and they are things which I mention only with the

28. See the case study of this event cited earlier. Ulmer, "Earl Warren and the Brown Decision."

greatest reluctance and frank fear of being misunderstood. I have told Mr. Justice Frankfurter that in my opinion it is best for this Court and for him that he should not be its spokesman in this matter and that I intend to bring my view of it to your attention. With all humility I suggest that the Court's decision, bound to arouse bitter resentment, will be much less apt to stir ugly reactions if the news that the white primary is dead is broken to it, if possible, by a Southerner who has been a Democrat and is not a member of one of the minorities which stir prejudices kindred to those against the Negro.

I have talked with some of them [other members of the Court] who are still in the building, and they feel as I do.

I rely on the good understanding which I have always felt existed between us and upon our mutual anxiety for the welfare and prestige of the Court to excuse my intrusion in a matter which, having spoken my piece, is solely for your judgment.[29]

Chief Justice Stone followed the tactfully phrased advice of this letter and assigned the writing of the Court's opinion to Justice Stanley F. Reed, a Kentuckian, Democrat, and Protestant. Again one can hardly charge the Court with political naivete.

In summary, many features of the decision-making process operate so as to increase the support and legitimacy of the Supreme Court's decision. The ritual of oral arguments in the ornate, temple-like Supreme Court building, the secret deliberations, the carefully written opinions of the Court, and the unanimous and nearly unanimous positions usually taken by the Court work to increase the support and legitimacy accorded its final decisions. A closely divided Court and bitter dissenting opinions, which are far from rare, work in the opposite direction—decreasing the support and legitimacy given the Court and its decisions.

Principles of Interpretation: The Elastic Yardsticks

In both making and justifying their decisions, the Supreme Court justices rely on certain explicit, legal principles of interpretation. The justices are not supposed to make decisions simply on the basis of the wisdom or advantages that they believe inhere in the decisions. If the Supreme Court is to maintain the legitimacy of its decisions, it must be able to justify them on generally accepted legal grounds. The Supreme Court can thus claim that a certain decision was not the result of the justices' personal preferences, but the result of applying certain generally accepted principles of interpretation to an equally accepted Constitution or statute. In its extreme form, this theory would reduce the justices to mere ciphers mechanically appling set principles of interpretation and thereby arriving at predetermined results. But this does not occur. The principles of interpretation

---

29. Quoted in Alpheus T. Mason, *Harlan Fiske Stone: Pillar of the Law* (New York: Viking, 1956), p. 615. Reprinted by permission of William E. Jackson.

followed by the Court are, in practice, flexible enough to allow the justices to maintain their freedom of choice. The principles of interpretation truly are elastic yardsticks.

The Literal Meaning of the Words One accepted principle of interpretation is to handle the section of the Constitution or the law in question according to obvious, strict, literal meaning of the words. As Justice William Rufus Day has written in an official opinion of the Court: "Where the language [under question] is plain and admits of no more than one meaning the duty of interpretation does not arise and the rules which are to aid doubtful meanings need no discussion. . . . Statutory words are uniformly presumed, unless the contrary appears, to be used in their ordinary and usual sense, and with the meaning commonly attributed to them."[30]

At times the Supreme Court has pretended that this is the only principle of interpretation it ever has to invoke to come to its decisions. Justice Owen Roberts, speaking for the Court majority, once said: "When an act of Congress is appropriately challenged in the courts as not conforming to the constitutional mandate the judicial branch of the Government has only one duty,—to lay the article of the Constitution which is invoked beside the statute which is challenged and to decide whether the latter squares with the former."[31] It appears so simple—all one has to do is read the Constitution or the law and apply whatever it says.

Yet, in fact, this principle of interpretation is far from a magic formula that produces quick, predetermined decisions. This is true for three reasons: at times the Supreme Court simply ignores this principle altogether and reads more into the Constitution or statute than is, strictly speaking, there;[32] often, as Justice Day himself admitted in the quotation above and as we saw earlier, the meaning of the section under question is far from clear; and at times to give a section its strict, literal meaning would lead to wholly unreasonable or impractical results (and this is something the justices are cognizant of, as will be seen shortly).

The Intention of the Authors Another principle of interpretation frequently invoked is that the section under question means what it is assumed that those who wrote the Constitution or the statute intended it to mean. Thus, reports of the Constitutional Convention and writings of the participants of the convention, in cases of constitutional interpretation, and congressional debates and reports of committee hearings, in cases of statutory interpretation, are frequently examined intensively in order to

30. *Caminetti v. United States,* 242 U.S. 470 (1917).
31. *United States v. Butler,* 297 U.S. 1 (1936).
32. A classic, but far from isolated, example is Justice Brandeis's able dissenting opinion in *Olmstead v. United States, 277 U.S. 438 (1928).*

discover what the authors wanted to accomplish by the section under question.

But this also is a slippery rock for the Supreme Court to stand on, and it hardly leads to certain, predetermined results. Often the intention on the authors is very fuzzy.[33] In *Everson v. Board of Education,*[34] dealing with state support of parochial schools, both Justice Hugo Black (writing for the majority) and Justice Wiley B. Rutledge (writing in dissent) used the intention of the authors to justify their opposite conclusions! In addition, there is debate over how literally the intention of the authors is to be applied. Does the principle mean that a provision should be applied only to situations consciously in the minds of the authors, or may one take the very general intention or purpose of the authors and apply it to situations the authors may never have dreamed of? In other words, is the strict, literal intention to be followed, or the more generalized spirit behind the specific intentions of the authors? In short, this principle also turns out to be an elastic yardstick—the Court can apply or not apply it, expand it or contract it as the Court sees fit.

Stare Decisis "Let the decision stand" (*stare decisis*) is a principle as old as English law and is still used as a basis for the Supreme Court's interpretations. This is the principle of following precedents, or deciding a current case as similar cases were decided in the past.

The Supreme Court constantly refers to its earlier decisions to justify the decisions it makes. The difficulty with this rule is that there is usually some question whether the current case is similar enough to an earlier case to invoke *stare decisis,* for no two cases are exactly alike. Thus, the justices must decide if the essential elements of an earlier case are the same as the essential elements of the current case, and endless debate over essential elements can result. Adding to the confusion is the fact that, in most cases, both sides can find precedents to back their claims. The Supreme Court is then put in a position of having to select between two conflicting precedents.

Finally, we should note that the Supreme Court, if it so wishes, can and ocassionally does overrule a precedent and simply state that it will no longer follow that precedent. Thus the principle of *stare decisis,* like the other two principles discussed, hardly leads to definite, certain results.

Need Often the Supreme Court is guided by the likely consequences of a decision, not just in the particular case it is hearing, but in other cases,

---

33. For a good analysis of problems involved in deciphering the intention of the authors of the Constitution, see William Anderson, "The Intention of the Framers: A Note on Constitutional Interpretation," *American Political Science Review,* 59 (1955), 340–352.

34. *Everson v. Board of Education,* 330 U.S. 1 (1947).

trying to make a decision that will satisfy certain public needs or, negatively, will avoid creating an intolerable or unworkable situation. Although this principle of need is generally not explicitly stated as a justification for a decision and thus cannot be considered a legal principle of interpretation in the same class as the first three, it is frequently referred to indirectly.

Chief Justice John Marshall stated in 1819: "We must never forget, that it is *a constitution* we are expounding . . . a constitution, intended to endure for ages to come, and consequently, to be adapted to the various *crises* of human affairs.[35] Clearly, John Marshall was calling for the court to interpret the Constitution so as to meet the crises—the needs—of the American nation.

In perhaps the most extreme example of its willingness to follow this principle of need, the Supreme Court held in 1944 that the incarceration of American citizens in detention centers for an indefinite period of time, without trial or even without charges being brought against them, was constitutional. This case arose out of World War II, when, after Pearl Harbor, an attack on the West Coast by the Japanese was feared by certain military officials. In the event of such an attack, it was thought that some Americans of Japanese ancestry living on the West Coast might be disloyal to the United States and give aid to the enemy. Thus, in one of the saddest invasions of individual rights in our history, thousands of Americans of Japanese ancestry were forcibly moved inland to large detention camps. The Supreme Court held these actions constitutional in the light of the pressing military need:

Compulsory exclusion of large groups of citizens from their homes, except under circumstances of direct emergency and peril, is inconsistent with our basic governmental institutions. But when under conditions of modern warfare our shores are threatened by hostile forces, the power to protect must be commensurate with the threatened danger. . . . There was evidence of disloyalty on the part of some, the military authorities considered that the need for action was great, and time was short.[36]

It is hardly necessary to stress that the principle of need is an expandable and contractible principle.

Thus, the Supreme Court justifies its intepretations of the Constitution and statutes on the basis of certain legally sanctioned principles of interpretation—principles that in fact are so flexible and so subject to variation in application that they put few restrictions on the court. Yet they are vital in helping the court successfully perform the system-maintenance functions. The appearance of following the law is preserved, and support and legitimacy for its decisions are thus increased—certainty a formidable

---

35. *McCulloch v. Maryland,* 4 Wheaton 316 (1819). Italics in original.
36. *Korematsu v. United States,* 323 U.S. 214 (1945).

accomplishment and one vital to maintaining the stability and viability of the political system.

And with this, the circle of judicial decision-making power is complete: The judiciary has wide authority to interpret the Constitution and statutes; because of the ambiguity of the Constitution and many statutes, the judiciary must interpret a host of key constitutional and statutory provisions; and in making these interpretations the judiciary relies on very flexible principles of interpretation. As a result, the judiciary is a policy maker of the first importance.

Ideological Groups and Supreme Court Decision Making

It almost seems irreverent to speak of groups or cliques of justices on the Supreme Court, each committed to a certain ideological position, and each attempting to win decisions favoring its position. Yet, if we accept the obvious fact that a Supreme Court justice is human and that, as Justice Frankfurther once asserted, he "brings his whole experience, his training, his outlook, his social, intellectual, and moral environment with him when he takes a seat on the supreme bench,"[37] then one must also expect different justices to have certain ideological commitments that they will attempt to enact into policy.

What logical indicates, evidence confirms. Table 10.1 reveals the existence of certain ideological groups on the court. It shows, in matrix form, the percentage of times during the 1972 term that each justice agreed with

Table 10.1   Interagreement in split decisions, 1972 term

Percentage of times justices voted in the majority:	Douglas 33	Brennan 54	Marshall 55	Stewart 64	Powell 86	White 82	Burger 81	Blackmun 87	Rehnquist 67
Douglas		70[a]	70	51	30	27	25	28	13
Brennan	70		85	55	44	48	36	47	26
Marshall	70	85		54	49	48	41	47	30
Stewart	51	55	54		64	50	57	60	53
Powell	30	44	49	64		73	79	68	72
White	27	48	48	50	73		74	79	74
Burger	25	36	41	57	79	74		87	80
Blackmun	28	47	47	60	68	79	87		70
Rehnquist	13	26	30	53	72	74	80	70	

[a] The numbers are the percentage of times the two justices agreed on decisions on which the Court was divided. Total number of cases: 106.

Source: Compiled by the author from *United States Reports*, vols. 409–413 (Washington, D.C.: GPO, 1974, 1975).

37. Felix Frankfurter, "The Judicial Process and the Supreme Court," in Murphy and C. Herman Pritchett, eds., *Courts, Judges, and Politics,* p. 31.

every other justice on decisions in which the Court was not unanimous.[38] Two groups or blocs of justices appeared: Douglas, Brennan, and Marshall formed one highly cohesive bloc; Powell, White, Burger, Blackmun, and Rehnquist formed another highly cohesive bloc. The members of each group showed high rates of agreement among themselves and low rates of agreement with members of the other group. Stewart was a firm member of neither group. The fact that he had about equal rates of agreement with the members of both groups indicates he sided with each group about equally.

In 1972 the Powell, White, Burger, Blackmun, Rehnquist bloc constituted a majority of five on the Court and in fact its success rate—with its members being in the majority in 67 to 87 percent of the cases—was much higher than that of the Doublas, Brennan, Marshall bloc. The most likely way the latter bloc could win was by obtaining the support of Stewart and then persuading one of the majority bloc to defect to them.

Although the formal Friday conferences and the more informal contacts among the justices are hidden from public view, enough information has come out over the years (mostly from the papers released by justices no longer on the bench) for us to know that in such situations many sharp exchanges and much maneuvering can go on among the justices and blocs of justices.[39] A case is up for decision. Douglas, Brennan, and Marshall take one side. Powell, White, Burger, Blackmun, and Rehnquist take the opposite side. Attention shifts to Stewart. If he sides with Douglas, Brennan, and Marshall there is still hope they can persuade one of the majority justices and turn their minority of four into a majority of five. Can they pick up their needed extra vote by including or excluding certain points in the decision? Or by deciding the case on a slightly different basis?

Many attempts have been made to label these groups. "Liberal" and "conservative" are two favorites of the newspapers as well as of some serious students of the Court. The term *liberal* is applied to justices who take a libertarian stand on civil liberties and approve a wide range of governmental activities in economic and social spheres. *Conservative* is applied to those justices who take a less libertarian stand and restrict governmental activities in economic and social spheres. Thus, in Table 10.1, Douglas, Brennan, and Marshall would be the liberal bloc, and Powell, White, Burger, Blacknum, and Rehnquist the conservative bloc.

38. For other attempts to measure voting groups on the Supreme Court and discussions of these attempts, see Glendon A. Schubert, *Quantitative Analysis of Judicial Behavior* (East Lansing, Mich.: Social Science Research Bureau, Michigan State University, 1959); Joel B. Grossman, "Dissenting Blocs on the Warren Court: A Study in Judicial Role Behavior," *Journal of Politics*, 30 (1968), 1068–1090; and Harold J. Spaeth, *An Introduction to Supreme Court Decision Making,* rev. ed. (San Francisco: Chandler, 1972).

39. For an excellent consideration of the use of strategy on the Supreme Court, see Walter F. Murphy, *Elements of Judicial Strategy* (Chicago: University of Chicago Press, 1964).

Often, however, it is difficult to classify individual justices or groups of justices as one or the other.

Perhaps of more help in classifying differences in legal philosophies is the distinction between justices favoring judicial activism and those favoring judicial self-restraint. Activists believe the Court should be willing to grapple boldly with major problems and issues and to make clear-cut, definite decisions that go to the heart of the issue. Judicial self-restrainers, on the other hand, believe the Court should take a more modest position and avoid major problems unless these are what it narrowly defines as justiciable questions. They favor making decisions on narrow grounds and tend to avoid broad, sweeping decisions.

Chief Justice Warren Burger once made a clear statement in support of the judicial self-restraint position:

In my conception of it, the primary role of the Court is to decide cases. From the decision of cases, of course, some changes develop, but to try to create or substantially change civil or criminal procedure, for example, by judicial decision is the worst possible way to do it. The Supreme Court is simply not equipped to do that job properly. . . .

[Changing the world by litigation in the courts] is not the route by which basic changes in the country like ours should be made. That is a legislative and policy process, part of the political process. And there is a very limited role for the courts in this respect.[40]

A judicial activist has no such inhibitions, but sees the courts as a fully legitimate means of righting perceived wrongs and thereby bringing about fundamental change.

In recent years judicial activism has, for the most part, coincided with judicial liberalism, and self-restraint with conservatism.[41] Thus, the group in Table 10.1 identified as liberal or libertarian is for the most part also the activist group. In the 1960s, the activist-liberal group was able to win a series of victories; reapportionment was forced on the state legislatures, restrictions were placed on police forces and courts in the arrest and trial of individuals, religious exercises were banned from the public schools, and desegregation was supported.

In his 1968 campaign for the presidency, Richard Nixon in part campaigned against the Supreme Court and promised to move the Court away from its liberal tendencies. Through the four appointments he was able to make during his first three years in the White House Nixon was able to effect some basic change in the directions being taken by the Supreme

40. From an interview with Chief Justice Burger on the first anniversary of his becoming chief justice, *The New York Times* (July 4, 1971), p. 20.

41. This is not necessarily the case. In the 1930s during the struggle over the constitutionality of many New Deal pieces of legislation, the conservatives were the activists, reaching out time and again to strike down laws passed by Congress and supported by the President.

Court. Four of the five members of the conservative bloc shown in Table 10.1—Powell, Burger, Blackmun, and Rehnquist—are the Nixon appointees. With White—a Kennedy appointee—joining them, they have been able to pull the Court back from some of the liberal positions taken by the Court in the 1960s. This is especially true in the area of the rights of persons accused of crimes. It has permitted the conviction of persons by less than unanimous juries in noncapital cases; ruled that a person, unless already indicted, is not entitled to legal counsel when placed in a police line-up; and sanctioned the granting of only limited immunity from prosecution to a witness being forced to testify. In all three cases the four Nixon appointees provided the margin of victory for the nonlibertarian side.

Demands and the Supreme Court

Today one of the justices sitting on the Supreme Court—Justice William O. Douglas—makes policy decisions for a society over half of whose members have been born since he was appointed to the Court. He was appointed 37 years ago by a President who has been dead for 30 years —Franklin D. Roosevelt. In view of this and in view of the fact that all the Supreme Court justices are appointed, and appointed for life, can one consider the Supreme Court a democratic institution? If democracy means that the people are able to influence the governmental decision makers, how can one claim that an institution this far removed from the people is democratic?

Such questions assume that if demands arising from the public are to have an impact on decision makers, these decision makers must be either directly elected or directly under the control of elected officials. This is not necessarily true. The evidence is overwhelming that the Supreme Court— in spite of the absence of formal control by the general public—does react positively to the general demands put on the political system. This is not to say that the Supreme Court reacts to every shift in the opinions of the public, but the Supreme Court does keep in line with the more general mood or spirit of the times. It reacts to the general trend of demands, not to specific day-to-day demands.[42]

Countless examples could be given; two will have to suffice. During the first quarter of the twentieth century, laissez faire (the theory that government should not interfere in business) was the attitude of the dominant political forces in the country. And the Supreme Court went along, holding unconstitutional a whole series of laws aimed at regulating the economy

42. On this point, see the very enlightening article by Robert A. Dahl," Decision-Making in a Democracy: The Supreme Court as a National Policy-Maker," *Journal of Public Law*, 6 (1958), 279–295.

or working conditions.[43] With the coming of the New Deal and the abandonment of the laissez-faire philosophy, there was a bitter struggle on the court, which for a time fought the newly dominant political forces. But this lasted only a few years, and by the 1940s the court was interpreting the Constitution so as to uphold almost any governmental economic or labor program.[44]

During both World War I and World War II, dislike—even intense hatred—for the enemy and any one who opposed the war effort was high. Feelings were strong, and no opposition was tolerated. Under such conditions the Supreme Court approved the conviction of a pacifist who had merely written against the draft,[45] approved (as we saw earlier) the incarceration without trial of thousands of Americans whose loyalty was suspect,[46] delayed until after the war a condemnation of martial law in Hawaii (as also seen earlier),[47] and refused to intervene in the death sentence of a Japanese general tried under the most questionable circumstances.[48] The nation was at war, and the Supreme Court was no guarantor that one's rights would be respected if they were thought to interfere with the war effort. But whom do we blame (or, conceivably, praise) for such actions by the Supreme Court—the court or the prejudice and blindness of the American people and their leaders? Whichever position we take, the fact remains that the Supreme Court, for good or bad, was reacting to the mood or spirit of the people—exactly as a democratic institution is supposed to react.

The Appointment Process   Three factors help explain this reaction of the court to public demands. The first is the appointment process. We have already seen how careful Presidents are to select justices who reflect their own political views and outlook. Because we can assume that the President normally reflects the dominant political forces of the day, we can conclude that new appointees will also reflect them. Table 10.2 shows that Presidents normally do not have to wait too long in making appointments to the Supreme Court. All the Presidents from Hoover through Nixon had to wait only an average of 1.7 years between appointments. Given the fact that the court is often closely divided on key questions, only one or two appointments by the President are frequently enough to bring the court

43. For example, *Hammer v. Dagenhart,* 247 U.S. 251 (1918); *Baily v. Drexel Furniture Company,* 259 U.S. 20 (1922); *Wolff Packing Company v. Court of Industrial Relations,* 262 U.S. 522 (1923); and *Adkins v. Children's Hospital,* 261 U.S. 525 (1923).

44. For example, *United States v. Darby,* 312 U.S. 100 (1941); *Wickard v. Filburn,* 317 U.S. 111 (1942); and *West Coast Hotel v. Parrish,* 300 U.S. 379 (1937).

45. *Schenck v. United States,* 249 U.S. 47 (1919).

46. *Korematsu v. United States,* 323 U.S. 214 (1944).

47. *Duncan v. Kahanamoku,* 327 U.S. 324 (1946).

48. *In re Yamashita,* 327 U.S. 1 (1946).

Table 10.2 Frequency of presidential appointments to the Supreme Court

	Years to first appointment	Years to second appointment	Average years between appointments[a]
Hoover	1	0[b]	1.3
Roosevelt	4	1	1.6
Truman	0[c]	1	1.8
Eisenhower	0[c]	2	1.6
Kennedy	1	0[b]	1.5
Johnson	2	2	2.5
Nixon	0[c]	1	1.4

[a] Found by dividing the number of years a president was in office by the number of Supreme Court appointments he made.

[b] Appointment made during the same year as the first one.

[c] Appointment made during the first year in office.

Note: There may be some slight inaccuracies because the table is based on the year, not the month, of appointment.

Source: Compiled from Robert Scigliano, *The Supreme Court and the Presidency* (New York: Free Press, 1971), pp. 214–215.

into line with his—and presumably the country's—views. In fact, the whole struggle of the court in connection with Roosevelt's New Deal can be explained by the simple fact that Roosevelt had unusually bad luck in being unable to appoint a single justice throughout his first term. Normally, he would have been able to make at least two appointments during his first term, which probably would have been enough to tip the balance on the court in favor of his program.

The operation of this factor of the frequency of appointments was recently illustrated. Numerous surveys have shown that many decisions of the liberal-activist court majority in the 1960s—especially decisions relating to the protection of persons accused of crimes—were opposed by a majority of the public.[49] Nixon's victories in 1968 and 1972 can be seen as part of a more general opinion shift toward greater reliance on middle-class values and greater emphasis on strict law enforcement. As seen earlier, Nixon's apppointees to the court are now bringing about just such a shift on the court.

The Justices' Own Reaction to the Times   A second factor helps explain the court's reaction to public demands: The justices are part of the times and the society for which they are making decisions. Thus, the events and experiences that affect and help determine the mood and spirit of the country also affect the justices. They too read *The New York Times* and *Newsweek,* and they too listen to Walter Cronkite and to the NBC Evening

49. See Goldman and Jahnige, *The Federal Courts as a Political System,* pp. 138–146.

News. They share with the rest of the country—and more specifically with the political leaders in other branches of government—many of the same feelings and reactions—about the Japanese attack on Pearl Harbor, Hitler's slaughter of Jews, racial riots in large cities, or crass voting discrimination. Often, no doubt, the coincidence of the mood and spirit of the Supreme Court and of the nation can be explained as the natural result of persons from the same cultural background, and with the same loyalties and values, reacting in the same way to the same events.

A Concern for Support and Legitimacy A final factor explaining the Supreme Court's reaction to demands is its concern for the support and legitimacy given it. The justices realize, as practical men, that court decisions generally thought bad and unjust will probably be widely ignored, lower the prestige of the court, and thereby decrease its ability to spread the blanket of its legitimacy over the decisions and institutions of the political system. When in the early 1970s several lower courts ordered the busing of school children to achieve racially integrated schools, a storm of public criticism was loosed. State legislatures, Congress, the President, and presidential candidates seemed to compete with each other to see who could be the first with the strongest condemnations of the court decisions. Controversies such as this can only work to lower the support and legitimacy given the courts. Thus the justices apparently are sometimes willing to alter or moderate their decisions in order to avoid endangering the prestige of the courts. In other words, making decisions in keeping with the fundamental demands of American society is a means by which the Supreme Court generates support and creates legitimacy for itself and for the rest of the political system.

Justice Robert Jackson once wrote:

It is not idle speculation to inquire which comes first, either in time or in importance, an independent and enlightened judiciary or a free and tolerant society. Must we first maintain a system of free political government to assure a free judiciary, or can we rely on an aggressive, activist judiciary to guarantee free government? While each undoubtedly is a support for the other, and the two are frequently found together, it is my belief that the attitude of a society and of its organized political forces, rather than its legal machinery, is the controlling force in the character of free institutions.[50]

Much of the material contained in this chapter supports Justice Jackson's conclusion. Just as water does not rise above its source, it is extremely difficult for the judiciary to rise above—or to sink below—the standards and values of the society and the political system of which it is a part. It

---

50. Robert H. Jackson, *The Supreme Court in the American System of Government* (Cambridge, Mass.: Harvard University Press, 1955), p. 81.

is first not the Constitution and the courts that protect individual liberties and place restrictions on the government—and this is either frightening or reassuring, depending on one's faith in the American people and their leaders—it is ultimately the commitment of the country and the demands and expectations of the society that either uphold or destroy liberty and limited government.

Some Exploratory Questions

1. Is a more effective judicial system likely to result from Presidents' taking into consideration potential appointees' beliefs and views, or from only taking into consideration their technical ability in the field of law?

2. Should the Supreme Court adopt a self-restraint or an activist position?

3. Should Supreme Court justices serve long, set terms of about 10 years instead of being appointed for life?

4. How would you answer Justice Robert Jackson's question: "Must we first maintain a system of free political government to assure a free judiciary, or can we rely on an aggressive, activist judiciary to guarantee free government?"

Bibliographical Essay

Few books have been written on federal courts other than the Supreme Court; hence, almost all the books mentioned here deal primarily or exclusively with the Supreme Court. They may be divided into two categories: those primarily concerned with the content of the court's decisions (usually interpretations of the Constitution) and those primarily concerned with the process by which the court reaches its decisions. In the first category, the clearest, most comprehensive book is C. Herman Pritchett, *The American Constitution,* 2d ed. (New York: McGraw-Hill, 1968). For a book of readings which combines Supreme Court decisions with the points of view of commentators in several areas of recent controversy, see Charles Sheldon, *The Supreme Court: Politicians in Robes* (Beverly Hills, Calif.: Glencoe, 1970). There are numerous books available that reprint Supreme Court opinions, which often make informative, even fascinating, reading. Choose one, such as Robert Cushman, *Cases in Constitutional Law* 4th ed. (Englewood Cliffs, N.J.: Prentice-Hall, 1974), that reprints, in addition to the official opinions of the court, many of the concurring and dissenting opinions that often suggest the struggles that preceded the official opinion. *The Supreme Court Review* (Chicago: University of Chicago Press) is a volume published annually that comments on the leading decisions of that year's term.

Of the books primarily concerned with the process by which decisions are made, Walter F. Murphy, *Elements of Judicial Strategy* (Chicago: University of Chicago Press, 1964), which considers ways in which justices may seek to have their policy preferences approved, is especially interesting and helpful. Also helpful are five fairly brief, but comprehensive paperback books: Harold J. Spaeth, *An*

Introduction to Supreme Court Decision Making, rev. ed. (San Francisco: Chandler, 1972); Glendon Schubert, *Judicial Policy-Making* rev. ed. (Chicago: Scott, Foresman, 1974); and Sheldon Goldman and Thomas P. Jahnige, *The Federal Courts as a Political System* (New York: Harper & Row, 1971). The last-named book gives a considerable amount of information about the lower federal courts as well as the Supreme Court. For a perceptive study of the Supreme Court's decision making processes in the area of personal freedoms, see Samuel Krislov, *The Supreme Court and Political Freedoms* (New York: Free Press, 1968).

Three anthologies that contain many good selections are Walter F. Murphy and C. Herman Pritchett, eds., *Courts, Judges, and Politics* (New York: Random House, 1961); Robert Scigliano, ed., *The Courts* (Boston: Little, Brown, 1962); and Thomas P. Jahnige and Sheldon Goldman, eds., *The Federal Judicial System* (New York: Holt, Rinehart and Winston, 1968).

On the appointment of federal judges, see Harold W. Chase, *Federal Judges: The Appointing Process* (Minneapolis: University of Minnesota Press, 1972). On the appointment of Supreme Court Justices see Henry J. Abraham, *Justices and Presidents* (New York: Oxford University Press, 1974), and David J. Danielski, *A Supreme Court Justice is Appointed* (New York: Random House, 1964). Also helpful is a book that considers President-Supreme Court relationships more broadly: Robert Scigliano, *The Supreme Court and the Presidency* (New York: Free Press, 1971). On the implementation of Supreme Court decisions and public and political reactions to them, see Stephen L. Wasby, *The Impact of the United States Supreme Court* (Homewood, Ill.: Dorsey, 1970).

Biographies of individual justices can sometimes be helpful in illuminating the nature and processes of the Supreme Court. One of the best is Alpheus T. Mason, *Harlan Fiske Stone: Pillar of the Law* (New York: Viking, 1956).

Two books, both written by Supreme Court justices, that discuss on a theoretical level the nature and role of judicial decision making are Benjamin N. Cardozo, *The Nature of the Judicial Process* (New Haven, Conn.: Yale University Press, 1921); and Robert H. Jackson, *The Supreme Court in the American System of Government* (Cambridge, Mass.: Harvard University Press, 1955). Also giving helpful insights into the role of the Supreme Court in the policy making process is Sam J. Ervin and Ramsey Clark, *Role of the Supreme Court: Policymaker or Adjudicator?* (Washington, D.C.: American Enterprise Institute for Public Policy Research, 1970).

Public Policy Making

Processes and Outputs

Part Four

Introduction
to Part Four

The forest ranger frowns as he patiently reads over the new set of regulations received in that day's mail, the labor lobbyist calls his head office to get its reactions to a new bill, the freshman congresswoman quickly reads through a press release her staff has prepared, an appeals court judge decides to disqualify himself from hearing a pending case, and the President reaches for the phone to call the Secretary of State on a detail concerning an upcoming visit by the Saudi Arabian foreign minister. All these persons have one thing in common: They are helping to make public policy for the American political system. We have met all these people—the bureaucrat, the lobbyist, the congressman, the judge, and the President—in the preceding chapters. The functions they perform, the institutional structures within which they work, and the influences affecting their decisions have been discussed and analyzed.

What remains to be accomplished is to see exactly how public policies emerge from the innumerable acts and decisions of the some five to six million persons active in the political system's policy-making processes.[1] Why the authoritative outputs—the public policies—of the political system are as they are, how the total system functions, and how its parts contribute to the making of public policies are the questions Part Four attempts to answer.

Thus far our focus has been on the institutions and structures of American politics and the policy-making processes going on within them. This last part shifts the focus to the actual making of public policies and views the institutions of American politics and their internal processes as they relate to public policy making.

---

1. There are approximately three million civilians and two million military persons employed by the federal government. Add to this about another half million or so lobbyists, party officials, and other people who, while not on the government payroll, are sufficiently involved in the functions of the political system to be considered part of the policy-making processes.

Two basic characteristics of public policy making mentioned briefly earlier need to be re-emphasized here. One is that policy making is a continual process in which in any given policy area policies are constantly undergoing examination and modification. The demand-conversion-output-feedback circle discussed in Chapter 1 is basic to policy making. Thus whenever we look at a specific aspect of policy making we are cutting into a continuous never-ending circle of action and reaction.

A second fact to keep in mind is that there is no one policy making process. There are many. Depending on the policy area one is considering, somewhat different patterns are present. Thus Part Four takes the basic approach of dividing policy making into separate, meaningful categories and then examining both the similarities and the differences in the policy making processes in the various categories. A basic division is made between domestic (Chapter 11) and foreign (Chapter 12) policies, which possess clearly different processes. And both domestic and foreign policies are further subdivided in order to explain more clearly the nature of policy making in the American political system and how it differs from one policy area to another.

Chapter 11 **Domestic Policy Making** Patterns and Processes

The range of domestic policies pursued by the political system is extremely wide—from chemical research done for the small farmer to excess profits taxes levied on huge oil companies. Although the processes by which such diverse policies as these are developed and implemented vary significantly, they also have certain characteristics in common. This chapter analyzes both the similarities and the differences in the making of domestic policies. Most of the basic facts and information we will need have been presented in the earlier chapters; what we need to do now is put the pieces together to form an integrated picture of public policy making in the American political arena.

Most of the similarities among the policy-making processes arise from the fact that they are all characterized by the continuous input to conversion to output to feedback policy-making circle and by the conversion process consisting of interest representation, rule initiation, rule application, and rule interpretation. Although all policy-making processes are marked by the same continuous circle and by the same four conversion functions, they vary in having differing patterns of interest representation, rule initiation, rule application, and rule interpretation. Thus this chapter first explores a three-fold division of domestic public policies and then considers how the four conversion functions are performed in each of these three policy areas.

Regulatory, Distributive, and Redistributive Policies

Political scientist Theodore Lowi has suggested that domestic policies can be divided into regulatory, distributive, and redistributive policies, each possessing distinctive patterns of policy making.[1] This section of the chapter considers this three-fold division of domestic policies.

Regulatory Policies

Regulatory policies are those which state what a person—a person defined broadly to include groups of persons and businesses—may or may not do. Regulatory policies require automobile manufacturers to meet certain standards of auto emission purity, drug companies not to market new drugs until they have been approved by the Federal Food and Drug Administration, individuals not to discriminate against others because of their color or race in the rental of housing, and television stations not to show X-rated movies. In all these cases the political system is governing what persons do—requiring or forbidding certain actions.

In the process, advantages and disadvantages are being allocated under conditions in which there are clearly those who lose and those who gain. Stricter automobile emission standards are perceived by the automobile industry to be to its disadvantage, drug companies can gain or lose great profits depending on whether or not the Food and Drug Administration permits a new drug to be marketed, racist landlords may perceive the curtailment of their freedom to refuse to rent to minority group members a serious loss while minority group members may find the right to rent where they wish a significant enlargement of their freedom, and television stations may lose money by having to pass up X-rated movies. In short, regulatory policies allocate advantages and disadvantages in a fairly direct, concrete manner to fairly specific, identifiable persons and groups.

Distributive

Distributive policies are those which grant benefits or advantages to persons or groups under conditions in which they are not in direct competition with others for the benefits. Distributive policies often take the form of subsidies of one type or another: airports for the airlines and air travelers, guaranteed loans for floundering corporations, agricultural research for farmers, freeways for commuters, the dredging of harbors and rivers for shipping companies and the cities involved. The list is almost endless. All are stamped by a situation in which benefits are "dispensed unit by unit,

1. See Theodore J. Lowi, "Distribution, Regulation, Redistribution: The Functions of Government," in Randall B. Ripley, ed., *Public Policies and Their Politics* (New York: Norton, 1966), pp. 27–40. It should be noted that Lowi did not claim nor does this chapter assume that every public policy clearly falls into one and only one of the three categories. The dividing lines between the three are sufficiently imprecise and reality sufficiently complex for some policies to share characteristics of two or even all three of the categories.

each unit more or less in isolation from other units and from any general rule."[2]

Because of this isolation, it appears as though there are no losers, only winners. The Houston channel is dredged, the Kansas farmer receives help with his wheat rust problems, and the University of Michigan wins a large research grant. Yet there are, of course, losers. Disadvantages—especially in the form of taxes to the citizenry generally—are also being allocated. But because of the specific, narrow, concrete, and usually direct nature of the benefits and the broad, diffuse nature of the losses, distributive policies take on the coloration of grants, subsidies, and aids unencumbered by payment or loss.

Redistributive Policies

Redistributive policies are those which allocate benefits or advantages to one large, identifiable class or group at the expense of allocating costs or disadvantages to some other large, identifiable class or group. A graduated income tax—if it is genuinely graduated, with higher-income persons paying significantly more than lower income persons—is a redistributive policy. Money is gathered from one class or group—higher-income persons—and given in the form of government services to another class or group —lower-income persons. Various social welfare programs that give benefits to the poor and get their financing from the middle and wealthy classes are also redistributive policies. Policies that are thought to be highly redistributive are sometimes not nearly so redistributive as they are supposed to be, but as long as they are perceived to be so, they probably should be classified as being redistributive. Which policy making pattern a policy fits into is determined as much by how it is perceived as by the realities themselves.

These three types of policies have particular patterns of action and decision making associated with them. All three types of policies are made by a flow of interest representation, rule initiation, rule application, and rule interpretation; but exactly how and within what structures these conversion functions are performed varies from one type of policy to another. The following sections of the chapter consider how the performance of the four conversion functions differs among the three types of policies.

The Regulatory Policy-Making Process

Basic Patterns

When regulatory policies are being developed, each of the four conversion functions that constitute the policy-making process has certain distinctive

2. Lowi, "Distribution, Regulation, Redistribution," p. 27.

Table 11.1   Domestic-policy-making processes and the conversion functions

Policy-making processes	Conversion Functions			
	Interest representation	Rule initiation	Rule application	Rule interpretation
Regulatory	By fairly specific, narrow groups which usually clash with other groups	By Congress, usually incremental changes in general terms, making rule application important	By bureaucratic agencies. Very consequential decisions made at this stage	By some regulatory agencies but usually by courts. Frequent disputes and thus is very important
Distributive	By very specific, narrow groups & other spokesmen, do not clash with other groups or spokesmen	By Congress through log rolling & coalitions. Tend to be very detailed	By bureaucracy. Tend to be routine, without controversy, quickly carried out, little discretion	Rarely needed, rule application is non-controversial, thus few appeals
Redistributive	By broad, inclusive groups. Often by political parties. Elections may play a role	By Congress, is affected by outside forces. President often a major role. Major shifts in policy likely, non-incremental	By bureaucracy, often marked by controversy & conflict. President may be involved. Less discretion than in regulatory area	By the courts. Frequently needed. At times constitutionality at stake

tendencies.[3] Table 11.1 summarizes the most important of these tendencies, as well as those of distributive and redistributive policy-making processes.

At the interest representation stage of making regulatory policies, there typically are fragmented, competitive interests demanding—through organized interest groups—that mutually exclusive policies be adopted. This occurs because fairly specific, narrow advantages and disadvantages are typically allocated by regulatory policies. Thus one interest is cast into a competitive—not a cooperative—relationship with other interests. And because the advantages and disadvantages are usually specific and narrow, the interests that compete in pressing conflicting demands on the political system are fairly specific and narrow. Whether or not to grant airline Q or airline Y a lucrative route between two cities sets two very specific interests in competition with each other. And the determination of exactly what requirements for land restoration after strip mining should be throws coal companies into competition with environmentalists. Sometimes, as in the second example, a narrow, specific interest is confronted by a broader interest concerned with the needs of the general population or the public interest.

When, in a situation of competing interests, one is well organized and active in expressing its demands and the other is unorganized or poorly

3. For more complete discussions of the policy-making implications of regulatory policies, see Lowi, "Distribution, Regulation, Redistribution," pp. 31–34, and Robert H. Salisbury, "The Analysis of Public Policy: A Search for Theories and Roles," in Austin Ranney, ed., *Political Science and Public Policy* (Chicago: Markham, 1968), pp. 163–174.

organized and thus not expressing its demands, the competitiveness usually associated with regulatory policy making is lost. Then the policy-making process, for most intents and purposes, tends to take on the characteristics of the distributive policy-making process, as we shall see when we consider the distributive policy-making process.

At the rule initiation stage of regulatory policy making, Congress plays the dominate role. Congress sets down the basic regulatory rules—it creates the National Labor Relations Board and prescribes its duties and powers in regulating labor-management relations; it creates the Environmental Protection Agency and sets certain auto emission standards to be enforced by the Agency; it passes open housing laws and gives the Department of Justice the power to enforce them. In doing so the competing interests, through the interest representation process, make their demands known. Often Congress passes a compromise piece of legislation (as described in Chapter 8) that strikes a balance among the contending forces. As a result, the regulatory rules that Congress initiates are typically marked by incremental changes in existing rules rather than being sharp, major departures from existing rules. Because of the complexity and controversy of the regulatory area, Congress's regulatory rules tend to be cast in very general terms, leaving the working out of the specifics to the rule application stage.

Although Congress plays the dominant role in initiating regulatory rules, paradoxically Congress is usually less important to the competing interests than is the bureaucracy. Although Congress is normally dominant in rule initiation (more often than in the other types of policies), it is rule application—in which the bureaucracy is dominant—where the decisions most crucial to the regulated interests are made. Because regulatory rules are usually stated in very general terms by Congress, the rule application function is especially important in the regulatory policy-making process. The basic bureaucratic structures of the political system, which have been given the task of applying regulatory rules to specific interests in specific situations, do much to determine the actual content of the regulatory policies initiated by Congress as general rules. It may be the Department of Justice and civil rights laws, the National Labor Relations Board and labor-management relations, the Food and Drug Administration and the safety of food and drugs, the Interstate Commerce Commission and interstate transportation, the Federal Power Commission and the utilities, and on and on. Sometimes (as was mentioned earlier and as will be discussed more fully in the next section) these regulatory agencies take on more of the characteristics of distributive agencies. But their intended purpose is regulatory, and as long as public awareness and competing interests remain they keep their regulatory nature.

Rule interpretation—the final conversion function—is very important in the making of regulatory policies. Because regulatory decisions tend to be controversial decisions that give advantages and disadvantages to specific, identifiable persons or groups, and because many important regulatory decisions are made in the bureaucratic agencies that apply provisions of statutes initiated by Congress, conditions exist that are likely to lead to challenges of the interpretations of congressional acts. Thus the rule interpretation function is often called into play in order to make the final determinations of the meaning of the general rules. Sometimes rule interpretation is done in the regulatory agencies themselves, but more often it is done by the courts. The *United States Reports,* which records the decisions of the Supreme Court, is filled with cases in which the Court is determining the proper meaning of a regulatory rule. Thus the content and effect of the final public policy is often not certain until after the courts have made their authoritative interpretations.

Auto Emissions: A Case Study of Regulatory Policy Making

Congress on December 18, 1970, passed and President Nixon on December 31, 1970, signed into law the Clean Air Act Amendments of 1970.[4] A milestone was thereby reached in the struggle over the air-purity standards that the nation was to insist on by law. But this milestone initiation of a basic new rule by Congress was a single point in time in an on-going policy-making struggle. Many events had preceded it, and many events were to follow it. The chief protagonists in the struggle over the sections of the law dealing with auto emissions—the chief interests involved—were the auto companies on the one hand and a variety of environmental groups on the other. At various points fuel additive companies and manufacturers of emission control devices also entered the fray. As is typical in making regulatory policies the interests involved were fairly narrow, specific interests.

Particularly important in the 1970 act were provisions in the law which required the 1975-model cars to emit 90 percent less carbon monoxide and 90 percent fewer hydrocarbons than the 1970 cars, and the 1976 cars to emit 90 percent fewer nitrogen oxides than 1971 cars. Such specificity in regulatory legislation passed by Congress is fairly rare, and in fact the auto companies and President Nixon worked strenuously to have the act provide that the Environmental Protection Agency (EPA)—the bureaucratic agency charged with administering the law—be given a free hand in setting deadlines for the auto makers. Other sections of the law gave the

4. For more information on the auto emissions controversy, see *Congressional Quarterly Almanac, 1970* (Washington, D.C.: Congressional Quarterly Service, 1971), pp. 472–488; *Congressional Quarterly Almanac, 1973* (Washington, D.C.: Congressional Quarterly Service, 1974), pp. 653–656; *Congressional Quarterly Weekly Report, 32* (June 29, 1974), 1691–1693; *Congressional Quarterly Weekly Report, 33* (June 7, 1975), 1169–1175; and Arthur J. Magida, "EPA Study May Bring Reprive for Catalytic Converter," *The National Journal Reports, 7* (April 12, 1975), 552–558.

bureaucracy a greater, and more typical, flexibility: the EPA could postpone the deadlines for one year; if it did so, it could set interim standards; and it could regulate fuel additives and fuel composition.

The passage of this act was generally considered a victory for the environmentalists and a defeat—or at least a setback—for the auto industry. Subsequent events, however, have demonstrated the importance of the administrative process. The auto companies have been able to recover much of what they lost by the 1970 act.

This part of the story starts in early 1972 when the auto companies started to build up pressure for the EPA to put off the emission-standards deadline for one year—from 1975 to 1976—as the administrator of the EPA was empowered by the act to do. The auto companies claimed they could not meet the standards by 1975 and requiring them to do so would force them to close their plants. First, William Ruckelshaus, the administrator of the EPA, announced that he would not grant a one year delay to the auto companies, but less than a year later he granted it. Presidential influence may have played a part here although whether or not it did is unknown. Ruckelshaus cited "potential societal disruptions," which the auto makers had predicted would result from insistance on meeting the standards in 1975. Using the flexibility that regulatory rules typically give the bureaucracy, he imposed 1975 interim standards that were tougher than the auto makers had wanted. As a result nobody was happy. GM issued a statement saying it was "disappointed and dismayed" by the action, and Ralph Nader called the decision "capitulation to the domestic auto industry."

Then in the fall of 1973 the Arab oil embargo and the resulting shortages in fuel brought additional pressure to bear for the further relaxation and postponement of auto emission standards, because most of the emission control devices being developed by Detroit tended to result in lower gas mileage. The explicit deadlines Congress had written into the 1970 act made it necessary for the interests involved to go to Congress for the relaxation they wanted. After a long struggle they were able to do so. In June 1974, Congress delayed until September 1977 the final standards for carbon monoxide and hydrocarbons and until September 1978 for nitrogen oxides. A further one-year delay for carbon monoxide and hydrocarbons was also permitted.

At the same time a struggle was going on over an order by the EPA to reduce lead in gasoline over a four-year period, because lead in gasoline is a significant source of harmful auto emissions. Here the auto makers were not directly involved but the Ethyl and duPont corporations, both makers of lead additives, were. When they lost before the EPA, they took their case to the courts, filing suit on the grounds that the Clean Air Act required the EPA to consider "all relevant medical and scientific evidence available" before acting and that the EPA had not done so. An environmental group—the National Resources Defense Council—charged that the EPA time table for the reduction of lead in gasoline was not sufficiently stringent and also filed suit against the EPA. Both groups were unhappy with the interpretations being given the law by the EPA in its rule application function. Thus they challenged its action in court, and rule interpretation was brought into play. Given the highly controversial nature of regulatory decisions, this is a frequent occurance.

In March of 1975, Russell Train, who had replaced Ruckelshaus as administrator of the EPA, granted the auto makers the additional one-year delay, from September 1977 to September 1978 for meeting the carbon monoxide and hydrocarbons standards. Both President Ford and Train asked Congress to authorize a further delay until 1982. In doing so they cited first the need to improve fuel economy and second the health hazard posed by the emission of sulfuric acid pollution caused by the use of catalytic converters, the major emission control devise being used by the auto makers.

Environmental groups denounced this proposal with the aid of a new ally: the manufacturers of catalytic converters. Those opposed to the delay argued that the sulfuric acid problem would be solved if the EPA simply exercised the authority it possessed to require the sharp reduction in sulfur in gasoline—a step the oil companies opposed and the EPA refused to take.

There the issue stood in late 1975. Most industry groups would like Congress to give more discretion to the bureaucracy, allowing the EPA to take into account such factors as fuel economy and the productive capacity of the nation as well as clean air standards and public health. Environmental and public interest groups insist that fairly strict standards be followed and that public health is the primary factor.

Several characteristics typical of the regulatory policy-making process are present in this study of the struggle to control auto emissions. First is the specific, narrow nature of the conflicting groups that became involved in interest representation along with some more broadly based groups concerned with the wider public interest. The individual auto companies, the lead-additive companies, the makers of catalytic converters, the gasoline companies, a number of more broadly based environmental groups, and Ralph Nader's organization all became involved in interest representation at the points at which thier interests and concerns were involved: the auto companies and environmental groups throughout, the lead-additive companies in regard to the lead-additive issue, the oil companies in regard to removing sulfur from gasoline, and the makers of catalytic converters in regard to charges of their negative side effects.

Second, Congress' role in rule initiation is apparent. Congress passed the basic 1970 act, which gave the EPA its basic authority and duties. Often in regulatory policy making, Congress has virtually no involvement once the basic rule has been initiated. In this case, however, Congress continued to play a role because of the high public interest in this policy area and because of the exact standards written into the original 1970 law, which forced the bureaucracy and interests to come back to Congress for desired modifications. But in weighing the importance to the affected interests of Congress and the importance of the bureaucracy, we see that the bureaucracy was probably more important. The one-year delays given twice were given by the bureaucracy, the decision to require reduced lead in gasoline and not to require reduced sulfur were bureaucratic decisions, and the determination—when delays were granted—of the interim standards were bureaucratic decisions. This importance of the bureaucracy is typical of regulatory policy making.

Because of the controversial nature of regulatory policy making, rule interpretation is frequently required—as it was here in regard to lead additives. Finally the continuous circle of policy making is abundantly clear in the case study. The 1970 act was not the end but the beginning—and every subsequent decision was the same. Each decision resolved some issues at the time but, through the feedback process, led to other demands, other strains, and the need for other decisions. Ten, twenty years from now the political system's auto emissions policy will no doubt still be evolving.

The Distributive Policy-making Process

Basic Patterns

Distributive policies give benefits or advantages to persons and groups under conditions in which they are not in direct competition with others for the benefits or advantages.[5] Because of this very basic characteristic of distributive policies, the process by which they develop differs greatly from the process by which regulatory policies develop. (See Table 11.1.)

The demands channeled into the political system through interest representation tend to be nonconflicting, highly specific demands. Because the demands are fragmented and isolated in the sense that meeting or not meeting one demand does not affect the meeting or not meeting of other demands, coalitions among interests are encouraged. Dissimilar interests come together in order to plead jointly for governmental help or subsidies. Because their interests are separate, they are not in competition with each other, a situation that opens the way for cooperation and coalition. Thus communities subject to periodic flooding and communities in arid areas in need of irrigation sometimes come together to demand public works aimed at alleviating their dissimilar problems. Or highway contractors, cement companies, engineers, construction unions, trucking firms, bus

5. For more complete discussions of the policy-making implications of distributive policies, see Lowi, "Distribution, Regulation, Redistribution," pp. 29–31, and Salisbury, "The Analysis of Public Policy," pp. 163–174.

companies, and auto clubs all band together to press for additional highway construction. Often implicit coalitions exist: one specific interest receives aid without objections from other interests, on the assumption that it will not object to their requests for aid.

Congress typically takes an important part in the initiation of distributive policies. The famous "pork barrel" legislation is the clearest example of distributive rule initiation. Here large numbers of dissimilar subsidies—"pork"—are included in one bill—"barrel"—in order to assure its passage. Through the log rolling process, each additional project or subsidy—a new post office here, a flood control project there, a harbor improvement someplace else—brings in several additional congressmen. Add enough projects or subsidies and one has the votes needed to pass the entire package. The basic reason such coalitions are able to hold together is that the various subsidies are not perceived as competing with each other or with other interests. Thus one interest and one congressman desirous of promoting that interest can cooperate with other interests and other congressmen without fear of hurting anyone's cause.

Once a distributive rule has been initiated by Congress, its application by the bureaucracy is normally marked by a relative lack of controversy. In fact, the rule application process is often little more than a search for the way to carry out the initiated rule as efficiently and as expeditiously as possible. This lack of controversy is the result of the absence of competing interests challenging the decisions of the bureaucracy, the eagerness of bureaucratic agencies to please the clientele groups for whom the projects were enacted, and the large degree of specificity found in congressional authorizations for distributive projects. Thus when the Department of Agriculture is appropriated funds to further a program of research into a particular plant disease, it normally has neither discretion about going into a program or the type of program to go into nor strong opposition from interests attempting to block its efforts. And normally the Department of Agriculture itself is eager to please the farmers on whose support they depend and for whom the research program was created. For the same reasons, rule interpretation is rarely a part of the distributive policy-making process. Rule interpretation requires that someone has challenged the application of a rule. But with no competing interests such a challenge is rarely raised.

Earlier it was pointed out that a regulatory policy can sometimes take on most of the characteristics of a distributive policy. This occurs when, in a regulatory situation, the competing interests are not equally organized and powerful (as we saw in Chapter 5). If one interest is well organized and active in pressing its demands and opposing interest is organized very poorly or not at all, and if regulatory policies are at stake, the process takes on the coloration of the distributive policy-making process. The political system, in the form of congressional committees and bureaucratic agencies charged with regulating that interest, transforms its regulatory policies into distributive policies by rules and regulations that protect the regulated interest from outside competition, allow large profits, and make it hard for consumers, environmentalists, or other potentially critical groups to force it to change its ways. In such situations the policy-making process takes on the characteristics of the distributive—not the regulatory—policy-making process.

Two Cases of Pork: Distributive Policy Making

Distributive policies, which grant subsidies to particular individuals and groups who in the situation do not seem to be in competition with other individuals and groups, are found throughout the spectrum of public policies. Two instances of distributive policy making are considered here: a classic example of pork barrel legislation and the subsidization of a specific industry.

Reclamation: Thirteen Spells Success   In 1974 Congress passed a little-noticed bill authorizing almost 200 million dollars for 13 public works projects in 10 western states.[6] This exercise in distributive rule initiation by Congress sparked so little controversy that it passed by a 320 to 8 vote in the House and by a voice vote without even a roll call being taken in the Senate. The only controversy arose when the Jacarilla Indians claimed one of the projects would divert water that belongs to them, but after a compromise amendment was adopted in the Senate, the project remained in the bill.

The approved projects were specific in their description and their benefits: work on the Nueces River project to furnish drinking water for the Texas coastal region including Corpus Christi; a project to provide more water for Frederick, Oklahoma; improvements on a South Dakota dam; an irrigation drainage system in Utah; and construction of a fish passage facility on an Oregon river, for example.

The fact that a number of widely scattered, very specific projects were included in the same bill was, of course, no accident. Because they did not compete either among themselves or with other projects, putting them together in one "pork barrel" attracted a coalition of supporters (the Senators and Representatives whose states would benefit) without sparking opposition from other interests (because building a dam in Texas was not viewed as having any effect on Maine, Michigan, or any other state).

Because of its routine, noncontroversial nature, published information on the carrying out of such an initiated rule and others like it is difficult to find. Apparently the typical pattern held true: the responsible bureaucratic

6. For more information on this bill and its passage, see *Congressional Quarterly Weekly Report,* 32 (October 26, 1974), 3002–3003.

agency—in this case, the Bureau of Reclamation of the Department of the Interior—hastened to carry out the rule initiated by Congress. The ability of the Bureau of Reclamation (which sometimes has clashes with the Army Corps of Engineers because of overlapping jurisdictions and resulting competition for the authority to handle the same projects) to protect itself and its interests depends on its providing communities and their congressmen with efficient service. Thus it is in its own interest to provide the services and subsidies authorized and funded by Congress as expeditiously as possible. In such cases, rule application is likely to result in little conflict or controversy, and rule interpretation is not likely to be needed at all.

Shipping Subsidies   Since 1847, when Congress first approved ocean mail contracts, subsidizing the American merchant marine industry has been a part of public policy.[7] In 1969 President Nixon requested and in 1970 Congress passed legislation that significantly increased direct government subsidies for this industry. There were benefits in the bill for almost everyone connected with the shipping industry: the shipbuilders and shipbuilding unions gained from the provision of direct subsidies for the construction of 300 new merchant ships over the next 10 years; shipbuilders further gained by the removal of a 10 percent lid on profits in an earlier law; the shipping companies and maritime unions gained by the provision for direct subsidy of operating expenses; and the Great Lakes shippers were helped (on the insistance of the Senators from Michigan, Ohio, and Indiana) by including them in the subsidies. As is typical in distributive policy making, the only interests bothering to express their demands were the interests who were to gain benefits.

Loaded with all these goodies and without clashing interest groups, the bill swept in triumph through the House on a 307 to 1 vote and through the Senate on a 68 to 1 vote. A major distributive rule had been initiated. The 10-year price tag was five billion dollars.

The Department of Commerce moved quickly and with little conflict to implement the new act. It "generated the biggest shipbuilding boom in peacetime history. Old shipyards were expanded and new yards opened."[8] But a major problem arose because of a basic decision made in the rule application process. It was decided that the bulk of the subsidies for new construction were to go for the construction of oil tankers. Some one billion dollars in subsidy contracts were awarded. And then the oil-exporting nations, whose oil the ships were built to carry, quadrupled the price of oil, and the government embarked on a policy of cutting down

---

7. For more information on the events discussed below, see *Congressional Quarterly Almanac, 1970* (Washington, D.C.: Congressional Quarterly Service, 1971), and Louis M. Kohlmeier, "Shipping Subsidies Deny Trend," *National Journal Reports,* 7 (May 31, 1974), 826.

8. Kohlmeier, "Shipping Subsidies," p. 826.

on the importation of oil. As a result, by 1975 there was a surplus of oil tankers around the world. In mid-1975 there were 31 idle United States tankers. Construction of additional tankers came to a halt, which put the shipbuilding industry in economic difficulties—difficulties out of which the government sought to rescue it.

In 1975 both the House and Senate authorized without opposition 600 million dollars in shipbuilding subsidies. And the Commerce department moved quickly to guarantee a 40-million-dollar loan to the Seatrain Company so it could complete work on two additional supertankers—at the same time President Ford was taking action to cut down on oil imports!

Summary   In both of these instances—water and reclamation projects for the western states and subsidies to the shipping industry—the interests benefiting were narrow, specific interests, helped by narrow, specific subsidies. But as is typical of distributive policy making, their very narrowness and specificity helped them, because they were thereby perceived as "free" subsidies. These interests could be helped without hurting other interests. Thus the bills initiating policy changes were adopted by overwhelming margins in Congress, and at the rule application stage they were implemented with a minimum of controversy. Because the interpretations by the bureaucracy in the application process were never challenged, the rule interpretation function was never needed at all.

The Redistributive Policy-Making Process

Basic Patterns

The distinguishing mark of redistributive policies is the shift of benefits or advantages from one identifiable, recognized group or class to another identifiable, recognized group or class. Because the benefits and the losses are both real and recognized and perceived for what they are, the redistributive policy-making process is marked by fierce struggles of opposing forces.[9] (See Table 11.1.) The groups or classes who may gain or lose are large, and they see themselves and their interests directly involved . Therefore, all have strong motivation to organize and expend much effort to achieve their goals. In addition, major opposing groupings in society— liberals and conservatives, for example, the rich and the poor, business and labor—tend to disagree and clash over redistributive policies. Thus, when a major change in a redistributive policy or the introduction of a new redistributive policy is under consideration, two large, often powerful coalitions tend to form, working either for or against the proposal.

9. For more complete discussions of the policy-making implications of redistributive policies, see Lowi, "Distribution, Regulation, Redistribution," pp. 34–40, and Salisbury, "The Analysis of Public Policy," pp. 163–174.

As a result, interest representation in the redistributive policy-making process tends to consist of demands made by a broadly based interest group composed of many smaller interest groups—such as the United States Chamber of Commerce or the AFL-CIO. When political parties become involved in interest representation—articulating demands and voicing the concerns of broad groups in society—they usually do so in the redistributive policy-making process. Debates over these policies are between the haves versus the have-nots or, more accurately, the have-mores versus the have-lesses. In a rough sense the two major parties tend to divide philosophically on such issues, the Republicans favoring the have-mores and the Democrats the have-lesses. Redistributive policy debates often become partisan debates.

Struggles over the social security program in the 1930s, medicare and medicaide in the 1950s and 1960s, the War on Poverty program in the 1960s, and the periodic battles over closing tax loopholes to shift the tax burden to the rich all possess these characteristics. Large associations like the Chamber of Commerce, the National Association of Manufacturers, the AFL-CIO, and the other labor organizations take opposite stands on all these issues.

Congress plays a key role in rule initiation. Because of the direct and recognized importance of redistributive debates to large segments of the public, and the resulting public attention, the President and other forces outside Congress are likely to become more deeply involved in initiating redistributive rules than either distributive or regulatory rules. The press, electoral consequences, the political parties, bureaucratic agencies, and large interest groups and associations of interest groups all play an influential role. Thus it can be argued that, although Congress finally initiates new redistributive rules, it can exercise less discretion and must weigh and react to more outside forces in this policy area than in the other two policy areas. More often than is the case with the other types of policies, Congress initiates redistributive rules that are major innovations rather than small, incremental changes.

Typically the bureaucracies have less discretion in the application of redistributive rules than in the application of regulatory rules, but somewhat more discretion than in the application of distributive rules. Because of public attention and through the debates that typify the rule initiation stage, redistributive rules tend to be more tightly drawn and their details more carefully spelled out than in the more ambiguous regulatory area. Although many details of redistributive policies are filled in by the rule application process, with an effect on the exact content of the policies, the general outlines of redistributive policies are usually set at the initiation stage. Often the struggles between major, broad interests characteristic of the rule initiation stage are continued in the bureaucracies in the rule application stage. Thus the rule application process often becomes very controversial and marked by sharp conflicts. These controversies and conflicts often draw the presidency directly into the rule application process.

The rule interpretation stage is frequently reached in the process of making redistributive policies. The losers in the major struggles are likely to appeal the decisions against them. The courts are, of course, the place where such cases of challenged interpretations of the law are made. Sometimes a case is a challenge of the constitutionality of the whole policy, but more often it is a challenge to a bureaucratic application of the law, made in an effort to mitigate the law's redistributive effects.

The War on Poverty: A Case of Redistributive Policy Making

Redistributive policy-making struggles tend to divide individuals and groups along the fundamental lines that characterize American society and politics. Such divisions as labor versus business, liberal versus conservative, Democrat versus Republican, poor versus rich emerge in redistributive policy disputes, and monumental struggles result. These basic tendencies and their consequences are amply illustrated by the struggles over the Office for Economic Opportunity (OEO) and the War on Poverty declared by President Johnson in 1964.[10]

The story starts with President Johnson's call in his 1964 State of the Union address for a total War on Poverty. The war was to consist of several separate programs, all of which had been under discussion for some time in the Kennedy and Johnson White Houses. They were aimed at using the financial resources and initiatives of the federal government to stimulate education and training, create employment opportunities, and improve health care—largely by local efforts—so that the poor would possess the tools needed to work their own way out of poverty. Advantages were to be redistributed to the poor. The local orientation of the programs was re-enforced by the encouragement (or requirement) of participation by the poor themselves in the planning and running of the programs.

Just the list of individuals and groups who appeared for and against the proposal in congressional hearings reveals the extent to which a major redistributive proposal stimulates broad, major interests to become involved in interest representation, with divisions along predictable lines. Testifying for the proposal were representatives of the AFL-CIO, United Automobile Workers, the Urban League, the NAACP, and the National Farmers Union; testifying against it were the United States Chamber of Commerce, the National Association of Manufacturers, and the American

10. Much has been written on the War on Poverty and the struggles surrounding it. Every volume of the *Congressional Quarterly Almanac* from 1964 to 1974 contains lengthy analyses of the year-by-year events. Also very helpful is Sar A. Levitan, *The Great Society's Poor Law: A New Approach to Poverty* (Baltimore: Johns Hopkins Press, 1969), and Daniel Patrick Moynihan, *Maximum Feasible Misunderstanding* (New York: Free Press, 1969).

Farm Bureau Federation. The proposal became both a partisan and a campaign issue. Most of the congressional votes in committee and on the floor were party-line votes, with a majority of the Democrats voting in favor of the proposal and against attempts to weaken it, and a majority of the Republicans voting against it or to weaken it. The 1964 presidential candidates split over the proposal; Johnson, of course, favored it and Barry Goldwater, the Republican nominee, opposed it.

The basic components of the War on Poverty—including a new agency, the Office of Economic Opportunity (OEO), to administer it—were approved by Congress in a major rule initiation step in August of 1964. It passed in the Senate by 61 to 34 and in the House by 226 to 185. But the subsequent history of the implementation and modification of the War on Poverty was as stormy and as controversial as was the initial passage of the programs.

The OEO, through its rule application decisions, managed, perhaps unavoidably, to produce more critics of the programs with each passing year. Major business groups and traditionally conservative groups had been against the programs from the start because of their basic concept. But difficulties and problems—and to some extent successes—encountered by the program added to the critics. Some felt too much money was being funneled into urban areas rather than rural areas, many of the poor felt they were not being given the developmental role that the original act had envisaged, others complained of overly high salaries for persons in administrative positions or attacked waste and inefficiency—especially in the job corps program—and, in part because of success, local officials attacked efforts to organize the poor politically.[11] Fighting back, the director of the OEO, among other tactics, created five advisory groups to serve as bridges between clientele groups and the OEO.

Partisanship and the conservative-liberal split over the programs continued to plague OEO efforts to develop and stabilize its programs. The programs remained a constant source of conflict and struggle; there were frequent attacks in the press and continual struggles in Congress for funds and authorizations.

With the advent of the Nixon administration the White House changed from a supporter of the program to an opponent. By 1973 the Nixon administration had embarked on a concerted effort to dismantle the OEO, killing some of its programs and scattering others among existing departments and agencies. Its new director, Howard J. Phillips, sought to do just that.[12] But the interests trying to keep the OEO alive challenged in the

11. For a discussion of such complaints as these that developed early in the implementation of the programs and continued throughout their existence, see *Congressional Quarterly Almanac, 1965* (Washington, D.C.: Congressional Quarterly Service, 1966), pp. 498–509.

12. On these events, see *Congressional Quarterly Almanac, 1973,* (Washington, D.C.: Congressional Quarterly Service, 1974), pp. 585–586.

courts the administrative decisions being made by Phillips and won. The courts ruled that Phillips had failed to comply with legally binding procedures and, because he had never been confirmed by the Senate, could no longer serve as director. The defenders of the OEO thereby gained a victory through the rule interpretation process. Later in 1973 some programs were removed from OEO, but it was left with three significant programs.

Then in 1974 Congress again acted. It provided that OEO was to go out of existence on October 1, 1975, its programs to be taken over by the independent Community Services Administration, unless President Ford submitted a different reorganization plan not disallowed by Congress. To the end there was a liberal-conservative split, with conservatives arguing that antipoverty efforts should be left to the states and localities. Ford acted in January 1975, and created the new Community Services Agency ahead of the congressional schedule. OEO thereby went out of existence.

Four features typical of the redistributive policy-making process stand out in this brief overview of the birth and death of OEO. First is the existence of a basic struggle that pitted very broad, inclusive interests against each other—labor versus management, liberal versus conservative, and so forth. Interest representation was marked by the clash of national groups, not the narrow, specialized groups one tends to find involved in the regulatory and especially the distributive policy-making processes.

Second, the struggle over OEO was to a large degree a partisan struggle. Democrats and Republicans clashed, with Democratic Johnson and Republican Nixon taking opposite positions and with many of the congressional votes marked by the majorities of the two parties on opposite sides of the issues.

Third, because of the fundamental questions raised by the OEO programs there was presidential involvement at almost every stage of the continuing struggles. The ideas for the War on Poverty originated in the White House, they were guided through Congress by the President, and Johnson, Nixon, and to a lesser degree Ford were deeply involved in the issues surrounding the application of the basic programs.

Fourth, there was clash and conflict all through the interest representation, rule initiation, rule application, and rule interpretation stages of policy making. There were no unanimous votes, no quick acceptances of the status quo. The struggle and the controversy—and the evolution of the policy—were continuous.

Domestic-policy making varies greatly from one policy area to another. Regulative, distributive, and redistributive policy making—each calls forth a different complex of demands and demand-makers. From these differing complexes flow sharply differing patterns of initiating and implementing public policies. Thus to understand the flow and movement of domestic policy making, we must start with a recognition of the various policy areas and an awareness of how the patterns of interest representation, rule initiation, rule application, and rule interpretation vary from one area to another.

Some Exploratory Questions

1. What conditions would have to change in order to transform redistributive policy making into distributive policy making?

2. Which of the three policy-making areas comes closest to the ideal conditions you believe should be present in policy making?

3. The patterns of interest representation found in all three policy making areas rest on persons who are in the main pursuing their own self-interest. Is this the case because persons are selfish by nature, or because the American political and economic systems are such that they encourage this selfishness?

Bibliographical Essay

Books analyzing domestic policy-making processes can be roughly divided into two categories. In the first category are books that generally analyze the basic nature of the policy-making processes. One of the best brief analyses is found in Charles E. Lindblom, *The Policy-Making Process* (Englewood Cliffs, N.J.: Prentice-Hall, 1968). Three books containing selections by different authors that analyze the nature of public-policy making and the ways to study it are Randall B. Ripley, ed., *Public Policies and Their Politics* (New York: Norton, 1966); Austin Ranney, ed., *Political Science and Public Policy* (Chicago: Markham, 1968); and Frank P. Scioli, Jr., and Thomas J. Cook, eds., *Methodologies for Analyzing Public Policies* (Lexington, Mass.: Heath, 1975). Along the same lines is Ira Sharkansky, ed., *Policy Analysis in Political Science* (Chicago: Markham, 1970).

For a helpful analysis of policy making, which compares political and economic patterns, see Robert A. Dahl and Charles E. Lindblom, *Politics, Economics, and Welfare* (New York: Harper & Row, 1953). A book that stresses how policy-making tends to fall into patterns and remain unchanged unless disturbed by new forces is Ira Sharkansky, *The Routines of Politics* (New York: Random House, 1964).

In the second category are books that analyze policy-making processes from the point of view of specific public policies and the patterns that exist in their formation. For a book that considers a number of policy areas, see Thomas R. Dye, *Understanding Public Policy, 2d ed.* (Englewood Cliffs, N.J.: Prentice-Hall, 1975). For an analysis of American public policies from the point of view of policy development and change, see Ira Sharkansky, *The United States: A Study of a Developing Country* (New York: McKay, 1975). A book with good case studies of policy making in various political institutions and contexts is Allan P. Sindler, ed., *Policy and Politics in America* (Boston: Little, Brown, 1973). For a landmark in the area of the analysis of state public policies, see Thomas R. Dye, *Politics, Economics, and the Public: Policy Outcomes in the American States* (Chicago: Rand McNally, 1966).

There are, of course, innumerable books that describe the process by which particular policies have been developed. See, for example, on the War on Poverty of the Johnson administration, Daniel P. Moynihan, *Maximum Feasible Misunderstanding* (New York: Free Press, 1969); on federal housing policies, Lawrence M. Friedman, *Government and Slum Housing* (Chicago: Rand McNally, 1968); on programs to feed the hungry, Nick Kotz, *Let Them Eat Promises* (Garden City, N.Y.: Doubleday, 1969); and on environmental policies, Gerald Garvey, *Energy, Ecology, Economy* (New York: Norton, 1972).

Chapter 12   **Foreign**   Patterns and
              Policy   Processes
              Making

In a Latin American country an American diplomat is kidnapped and held for ransom, in an Asian country an angry mob marches on the American embassy and sets fire to the United States Information Service library, and in a European country the American Ambassador is unable to finish his speech because he is shouted down by university students protesting American policies. Fractured glimpses of violence and disruption like these indicate the tensions and turmoil that attend the conduct of American foreign policy.

The world of international politics is a big, troubled world, filled with violence and the threat of violence—as well as such gentler forms of persuasion as trade sanctions and monetary policies. And nowhere are the stakes higher. National independence, personal freedoms, economic stability, and the very survival of the human race all hang in the balance.

In this climate the American political system must act and react in the process of formulating those policies which define American action in the arena of world politics. One of the consistent themes of this book is that policy making is a never-ending process: It consists of a series of stages that are formed into a continuous circle, each stage affecting the subsequent stages and being influenced by the previous stages. This sequence is as true of foreign-policy making as it is of domestic-policy making. Both involve interest representation, rule initiation, rule application, rule interpretation, feedback, then interest representation again, and on and on. This is not to say that there are no differences between the foreign- and the domestic-policy-making processes. There are. Nor is it to say that there are no differences within the foreign-policy-making area. Again, there are.

The most significant factor that distinguishes different types of foreign policy making relates to whether the policies are being made in crisis or noncrisis situations.[1] A crisis situation is one in which new factors of great

1. The distinction I am making here roughly parallels one made by John Spanier and Eric Uslaner between rational actor and bureaucratic decision-making models. See John Spanier and Eric M. Uslaner, *How American Foreign Policy Is Made* (New York: Praeger, 1974), chap. 4.

342

significance to existing American policy suddenly arise in such a way that a very quick response is required. Situations like the Cuban missile crisis of 1962, when the Soviet Union began to install offensive nuclear missiles in Cuba, or the Soviet Union's 1968 invasion of Czechoslovakia, or Cambodia's 1975 seizure of the United States merchant vessel Mayaquez are all examples of crisis situations. All arose suddenly, all posed crucial questions for American policy, and all by their very nature required a quick response.

The process of making policies in crisis situations is different from the process in the more normal noncrisis situations, where the problem does not arise so suddenly and the response is not demanded so quickly. This chapter first explores the noncrisis policy-making process and then the crisis policy-making process. The similarities and differences are analyzed by examining interest representation, rule initiation, rule application, and rule interpretation under each of the processes. (See Table 12.1 for a summary of the two processes.)

The Noncrisis Policy-Making Process

Basic Patterns

Interest Representation   Interest representation in noncrisis situations is marked by the wide number and variety of interests that can make their demands and wishes known. In such situations time is available for a wide variety of interests to mobilize their forces and try to influence the decision-making process. In addition, noncrisis situations (as we shall see) are characterized by the large number of persons and institutions taking part in the decision-making process. Thus there are a fairly large number of points of access for the interests seeking to exert influence. As a result demands arise from a wide variety of sources. Six are especially important.

Table 12.1   Foreign-policy-making processes and the conversion functions

Policy-making processes	Conversion Functions			
	Interest representation	Rule initiation	Rule application	Rule interpretation
Noncrisis situations	By a wide variety of interests and groups	By President & his advisers and, secondarily, by Congress. Tend to be broad & general	By large number of persons & institutions, especially Departments of State and Defense and CIA. Very important	By the lowest common superior of persons in dispute. Frequently needed
Crisis situations	Who is involved decided by President. Usually persons from his inner circle and top officials in relevant agencies	Almost totally by President. Specific in nature, often no new rules initiated	Under presidential control. Often response to a crisis is the careful application of existing rules	Tends not to arise, or is immediately resolved by President

First, Foreign governments and foreign-based private interests—usually business concerns—are active in pressing their demands on the American political system. Turkey pushing for the resumption of military aid, the Soviet Union urging an expanded cultural exchange program, and a Japanese textile firm working for lower tariffs on textile imports are all examples. Sometimes these demands are made by the foreign originator through an American public relations firm hired by the foreign government or private interest. But more commonly they are made through public statements and speeches by foreign public officials or through the normal diplomatic channels.

Second, the State Department, represented either by the Secretary of State or by the numerous specialists in the department's bureaucracy, is also deeply involved in interest representation. It is both a channel by which the demands of foreign governments and foreign private interests are passed on to American officials and an independent source of demands. American ambassadors and other embassy officials are in daily contact with officials of the governments and leaders of the major interests in the countries in which they are stationed. Through these contacts they receive a host of requests—some minor, some major—which they then pass on to the department in Washington, and which the department in turn passes on to the appropriate officials in the American government. Foreign diplomats to this country normally deliver their messages through the Secretary of State; and abroad ambassadors usually relay information they have gathered through channels within the Department of State.

The State Department does not serve as a mere channel for the communication of demands, however. In the process of communicating demands it is active in molding and shaping them and sometimes initiating demands of its own. The many competing and conflicting demands that flow into the State Department from innumerable sources are not just passed on to the President and others involved in initiating or implementing foreign-policy decisions in the same form as they were received by the State Department. They are combined, refined, and sifted into a manageable number of demands, out of which basic policy decisions are initiated and implemented. In either case, State Department officials—with their values, biases, and insights—are deeply involved in representing interests in the foreign-policy-making process.

Congress is a third source of demands in the noncrisis foreign-policy-making process. Because foreign-policy decisions often have a direct domestic impact—decisions relating to tariffs that affect the relative competitive position of American industries, for example, or decisions about the levels of military armaments that affect businesses supplying arms to the government—congressional blocs often form in support of or opposition to specific policy proposals in order to defend the interests of their constituencies.

In addition, certain ideological blocs also form in Congress. These blocs are composed of congressmen who are committed to a certain foreign policy or a general approach to foreign-policy issues and who then speak and work in support of their views. Blocs of congressmen have at different times worked for a more militarist-interventionist foreign policy or, conversely, for one that stresses negotiation and detente. Some have urged greater participation and reliance on the United Nations; others have cast doubts on the value of American reliance on the United Nations. Acting on the basis of these ideological commitments, Senators and Representatives frequently give expression to certain policy alternatives and work for their adoption.

A fourth important source of demands that affects interest representation is the Department of Defense. Because foreign policy rests, ultimately, on the ability of a country to back its foreign-policy decisions with force, assessments of the relative strength of other countries and of American ability to give military backing to its policies is a crucial factor. Within the Department of Defense, interservice rivalry between the branches of the armed services often leads to conflicting demands for different foreign policies—each of the services arguing for policies that will put its particular skills in demand, thus strengthening its request for increased budgetary allocations. The civilian Secretary of Defense, the Joint Chiefs of Staff, as well as the various offices and agencies that make up the Defense Department, all have a hand in voicing demands and concerns.

The intelligence agencies—particularly the Central Intelligence Agency and the National Security Agency—are the fifth source deeply involved in interest representation. These agencies are active in gathering and interpreting factual information about the activities, strengths and weaknesses, plans, and potential policies of foreign countries—especially countries considered unfriendly to the United States. As these agencies gather information, interpret it, and reach conclusions concerning how the information should affect United States foreign policy, they are engaged in interest representation.

The sixth important source of demands is found in the many domestic interest groups that seek to influence American foreign policy. These interest groups can be divided into three basic types. First are those with a direct economic interest in the conduct of foreign policy. The American Beet Growers Association, for example, is concerned with the quotas established for the importation of sugar cane. The AFL-CIO has an interest in American immigration policies that might affect the supply of labor. Because military expenditures have become an important part of the American economy, a host of business interests involved in military contracting have joined with the Defense Department—both formally and informally—in representing the interests of the so-called military-industrial complex.

Second are groups specifically organized to influence certain foreign-policy decisions. Examples are the Women's International League for Peace and Freedom, the Committee for a Sane Nuclear Policy, the Liberty Lobby, and the United World Federalists. Lester Milbrath, who has studied such groups, concludes that they have little if any impact on American foreign policy: "Such groups are usually concerned with decisions where the President is the dominant or sole decision-maker. They concentrate mainly on the opinions of elites whom the President might consult. Their chances for getting clear channels through to the President or his closest advisers are relatively poor. Their chances for influencing broad general public opinion are also relatively poor. One would have to conclude that their impact on foreign policy is slight at best."[2]

The third type is made up of ethnic groups interested in foreign policies involving nations of particular concern to them. The Jewish community—particularly in areas like New York where it is densely concentrated—has effectively organized to influence American foreign policy in the Near East. The black community, through the emergence of the "Black Caucus" in the Congress, is seeking to influence policies toward South Africa. Immigrants from central and eastern Europe have since the late 1940s sponsored an annual "Captive Nations Week" to commemorate those living in the communist states of Europe.

About interest representation and these six sources of demands we must remember that it is the time available and the large number of persons and institutions involved in noncrisis decision making that enable them to formulate a position and then to mobilize political strength for their purposes. These are factors not present in a crisis situation.

Rule Initiation Rule initiation in the foreign-policy area—as in the domestic-policy area—consists in the establishment of certain basic guidelines or principles that must then be applied to specific, ongoing situations. When, for example, President Nixon in 1971 made the basic decision to seek a rapprochement with China, he was engaged in rule initiation. It is important to note that foreign-policy rules initiated in noncrisis situations tend to be very broad and general, leaving much to be determined in the implementation process.

The chief difference between the rules initiated in the area of domestic policy and the rules initiated in the area of foreign policy—apart from their obvious difference in content—is that basic domestic rules are usually embodied in written, legally enacted documents such as statutes passed by Congress and in guidelines established by regulatory agencies, while basic foreign-policy rules are more often found in the form of unwritten,

2. Lester W. Milbrath, "Interest Groups and Foreign Policy," in James N. Rosenau, ed., *Domestic Sources of Foreign Policy* (New York: Free Press, 1967), p. 248.

not formally promulgated decisions. The decision of the Nixon administration about a rapprochement with China was never drawn up in a formal proposal legally passed or enacted by one of the political institutions. Rather, the decision was made by Nixon in consultation with his advisers. This is true of most foreign-policy rules. Often, it is some time after a decision has been reached before it can be determined that a basic new foreign-policy decision has in fact been made. Occasionally, a new foreign-policy rule is embodied in a formally enacted, written form, as when a treaty is initiated by the President and approved by the Senate, or when Congress initiates a basic policy change through its legislative powers, as it did in 1973 when it forbade the use of American armed forces "in or over or from off the shores of North Vietnam, South Vietnam, Laos or Cambodia."

Foreign-policy rules in noncrisis situations are usually initiated by the presidency with Congress occupying an important secondary position. As we saw in Chapter 7, it is the President who has the power to initiate treaties and to enter into executive agreements, to appoint ambassadors, and to extend or withhold diplomatic recognition of other countries. And the President's powers as commander-in-chief of the armed forces substantially increase his role in foreign-policy making.

In addition, the President's power in foreign policy making rests—as we also saw in Chapter 7—on an unusual willingness of the public and Congress to defer to presidential judgments in this area. Such factors as the complexity and unfamiliarity of foreign-policy issues, the absence of an obvious, direct impact of most foreign-policy issues on the average citizen, the frequent need for secret decisions, and the "rally round the flag" tendency all help encourage a spirit of deference to presidential initiatives in the area of foreign policy not present in domestic policy. This deference tends to be even greater in crisis than in noncrisis situations, but it is still a very real factor increasing the President's power to make fundamental policy changes.

Thus it is within the presidency that basic foreign-policy guidelines and principles are established. It was the presidency that decided, after the victory of the communists in China in 1949, to adopt a policy of supporting the Chiang Kai-shek regime on Taiwan and of isolating the mainland Chinese regime—and it was the presidency that, 22 years later, altered this policy by seeking a rapprochement with mainland China. It was the presidency that decided to lean toward supporting Israel rather than the Arabs in the explosive Arab-Israeli conflict. We could multiply the examples, but the point is clear: The president—along with his top advisers—makes most of the basic foreign-policy decisions that are subsequently applied in specific situations.

But all this does not mean that the President has a free hand in initiating basic foreign-policy decisions. He is severely limited by a host of "givens," which go to make up the context within which he must initiate basic foreign-policy rules. Events, such as *coups d'état,* civil wars, and fluctuating international economic conditions, create the world in which the President must act and react. To say the President is a prisoner of events is to overstate the case; yet there is a real element of truth in that assertion. In addition to events, the President must act within the framework of his assessment of public and congressional reactions to his policies; he cannot go against strongly held beliefs (at least not without paying a high price in public and congressional support). He must also consider the reactions of the officials who will be charged with carrying out the decisions; to go against their strongly held opinions could result in resignations, lack of cooperation, and low morale. Thus, the President is not free to make any foreign-policy decision he pleases; nonetheless, within the political system, it is the President who sets most basic foreign-policy rules. As is true of all decision-making institutions, he makes these decisions within the limitations set by the context within which he operates.

Although the presidency is the pre-eminent force in noncrisis foreign-policy rule initiation, Congress has an important part as well. The clearest case of congressional rule initiation in the area of foreign affairs occurs when the Senate's approval of a treaty negotiated by the President is required. When the Senate approved the treaty establishing NATO in 1949, the Nuclear Test Ban treaty in 1963, and the Nuclear Non-Proliferation treaty in 1969, it was engaged in rule initiation. For it was—jointly with the presidency—adopting basic documents that established new directions in American foreign policy.

Congress also sometimes plays a role in foreign-policy rule initiation by way of its legislative powers. An example of this is the "Hickenlooper Amendment," which was adopted in 1962 and requires that the President cut off any assistance (economic or military) to any nation that expropriates American-owned properties without adequate compensation. In 1970 Congress adopted an amendment that forbade the use of funds for Americann ground forces and advisers in Cambodia. In 1973 Congress, as we just saw, forbade the use of American armed forces throughout much of Southeast Asia. And in 1973 Congress also legislated, over Nixon's veto, the requirement that the President receive congressional authorization within 60 days of ordering American troops into action; without it he must withdraw the troops. In recent years the trend has been for Congress to exert its potential powers in noncrisis foreign-policy areas more vigorously. But we must be careful not to exaggerate the importance of Congress in foreign-policy rule initiation. The presidency clearly has the upper hand. Even in cases in which the presidency legally needs the support and approval of Congress, he is usually able to obtain it. Nevertheless, Congress still plays a significant role.

Rule Application   A basic foreign-policy decision is no more self-imple-menting than is a basic law passed by Congress. In both cases, the general decision must be applied in specific, concrete situations. In doing so the number of persons and institutions able to have an impact on the nature and content of the foreign policy pursued by the United States in any particular area is widened. As with interest representation, the time avail-able in noncrisis policy making enables a large number of persons and institutions to develop and exert their influence on the implementation of a policy. One observer has commented on the influence of officials in the bureaucratic agencies dealing with foreign-policy implementation in this way:

While elected officials may have grand designs in international politics, it is the determination and skill of the bureaucratic apparatus which frequently determine whether these objectives will be realized. In many situations the policy alternatives open to these officials are confined to the courses of action their organizational machinery has the will and the means to carry out. Bureaucratic resistance or incapacity may spell the doom of even the most modest policy proposals.[3]

The point is that although the White House and Congress take the basic foreign-policy initiatives, they do not have the time or the expertise relating to foreign cultures and technical matters (as, for example, missile capabili-ties) to oversee and control the details of policy execution. And these details provide much of the actual content of foreign policies. It is to the persons and institutions most frequently involved in carrying out basic foreign-policy decisions—that is, involved in foreign-policy rule applica-tion—that we now turn.

   Earlier we saw how the Department of State is vital in interest represen-tation—transmitting, shaping, and initiating demands for certain policy decisions. Once basic decisions have been made in response to these and other demands, the State Department has another vital role to play: rule application. The Department of State—including its personnel located both in Washington and in its embassies and consulates scattered through-out the world—is deeply involved in carrying out basic foreign-policy decisions. This involvement takes the form of many different and specific activities: for example, ambassadors conferring with officials of foreign governments, American officials changing the regulations governing the shipment of surplus food abroad, American negotiators rejecting a pro-posal of the Soviet Union at an arms limitation conference.

   There are three other important governmental agencies under the broad supervision of the Secretary of State, although organized independently from the State Department itself. All three are important to the implemen-

3. Francis E. Rouke, *Bureaucracy and Foreign Policy* (Baltimore: Johns Hopkins University Press, 1972), p. 41.

tation of basic foreign-policy decisions. The Agency for International Development (AID) is responsible for administering economic and technical assistance programs. The United States Arms Control and Disarmament Agency (ACDA) is responsible for coordinating such disarmament negotiations as the Strategic Arms Limitation Talks (SALT) between the United States and the Soviet Union. The United States Information Agency (USIA) is the propaganda organ of the American government, managing the Voice of America, operating American lending libraries abroad, and distributing films and literature depicting life in the United States.

It is clear that military policy is in reality an aspect of foreign policy. Thus, the Department of Defense is deeply involved in the application of basic decisions whenever military force or the threat of military force plays a part in American foreign policy. More specifically, the military becomes involved in the implementation of foreign policy in three ways.

First, and most obviously, the military becomes deeply involved whenever actual fighting breaks out and the United States resorts to implementing its policy goals by military force. Use of American military forces in Southeast Asia is a recent example. In such situations, the military is given the leeway to make a great many implementing decisions with regard to military strategy, tactics, and timing. The basic decision to resort to military force and the basic guidelines within which that military force is to be used (for example, no bombing beyond such and such a point) are part of the initiation process, but within these limits the military makes a host of decisions in the process of implementing the initial basic decision.

Second, the military is involved in the implementation of basic foreign-policy decisions when the threat of force becomes a factor in foreign policy. Maintaining troops in Europe, keeping the Sixth Fleet in the Mediterranean, and maintaining Minuteman missiles ready in silos are all implementations of basic foreign-policy decisions. Again, the basic decisions are initiated elsewhere, but it is the Department of Defense that carries them out and, in the process, makes numerous decisions that relate to questions of deployment, location, timing, and means.

Third, the military is involved in foreign-policy implementation through its role in equipping and training military forces of foreign nations. One aspect of American foreign policy has been to provide arms and training for nations considered friendly to American interests. The Department of Defense clearly has a major role in implementing these basic decisions— sending advisers, training missions, and arms abroad, and bringing foreign military officers to the United states for training.

The primary purpose of the Central Intelligence Agency (CIA) is to gather information relevant to the basic foreign-policy decisions that must be made, and when it does so, it is engaged in interest representation. But the CIA is sometimes used to implement foreign-policy decisions, and then it is engaged in rule application. In the 1960s and early 1970s the CIA was active in recruiting and training forces to fight in Southeast Asia against insurgent communist forces. The policy implementation role of the CIA received renewed attention in 1975 when it was revealed that during the 1960s the CIA—presumably at the direction of higher officials—plotted and perhaps even had carried out the assassination of some foreign leaders considered hostile to American interests. Thus the CIA in practice plays a dual role: gathering information and carrying out basic policy decisions. (The highly secret nature of the CIA and its operations have periodically raised questions of how much control elected officials—Congress and even the President—exercise over it.)

In addition to the State Department, the Department of Defense, and the CIA, several other executive departments frequently become active in foreign-policy rule application. The Department of Commerce, through its involvement in questions of trade; the Department of the Treasury, through its involvement in questions of international finance; and the Department of Agriculture, through its involvement in the overseas distribution of American farm products, are three frequently active in implementing basic foreign-policy decisions.

Earlier we noted the crucial role that the presidency plays in rule initiation. But the presidency also has a part in rule application, although normally in noncrisis situations a fairly limited one. Usually it is not the President himself who actively oversees the carrying out of decisions; responsibility is assigned to staff members of the National Security Council or the staff of the President's adviser on foreign-policy issues. The presidency thereby sometimes becomes active in following through on the President's directives to see whether and how they are being carried out.

Rule Interpretation   Sometimes disputes occur over the proper application of a basic guideline or rule. For example, the President may initiate the decision to cut off all further military aid to a particular country whose government has been drifting increasingly into an antidemocratic, repressive mold. In applying or implementing this decision, a dispute may break out between the Department of State and the Department of Defense. State, hoping to gain favorable reactions from nearby nations by stopping aid to an antidemocratic government, interprets the decision to mean that all forms of military aid should be immediately and totally stopped; Defense may interpret it to mean that no new aid should be given the country, but that spare parts for military equipment already given or sold may be supplied. In such a situation, there must be some means by which a resolution of the dispute can be reached—the basic rule laid down in the original decision must be interpreted.

As a general rule, foreign-policy decisions are interpreted by the lowest common superior of the parties in dispute. Thus, if the dispute is between two country directors in one of the regional bureaus of the State Department, the Assistant Secretary of State for that regional bureau settles the dispute—he performs the rule interpretation function. If the dispute involves two of the regional bureaus, then the secretary of State is the lowest common superior of the disputing bureaus and settles the dispute. But if the dispute is between two executive departments, as in the example of Defense and State, rule interpretation must be made by the President or at least some authoritative figure in the presidency.

Also determining who settles disputes over the application of a foreign-policy decision is the importance and sensitivity of the issue at stake. The more important and sensitive the issue, the more likely that it will be settled on a higher level.

Thus, rule interpretation is performed by division heads, department and agency heads, presidential officials, and the President himself—the level being determined by the importance and sensitivity of the issue at stake and the departments and divisions in which the dispute takes place.

The ABM: A Case of Noncrisis Policy Making

In the late 1950s and early 1960s the technology needed to create missiles capable of destroying incoming nuclear missiles was being developed.[4] The political system was thereby faced with the question of whether or not to develop and deploy an antiballistic missile (ABM) system. Both the Johnson and Nixon administrations faced and sought to respond to this question. How they went about doing so illustrates many of the characteristics typical of noncrisis policy making.

In 1967 President Johnson was nearing the point where he would have to decide what his position on the development and deployment of an ABM system was to be. The major interests lining up in support of an ABM system were the Joint Chiefs of Staff, the Department of Defense bureaucracy—especially the Office of Defense Research and the Office of Engineering and Systems Analysis—defense contractors standing to gain from the contracts that would be necessitated by the ABM system, and key persons on the armed services committees in Congress. Congressional support for an ABM system is revealed by the 170 million dollars already appropriated in 1966, money Johnson had refused to spend.

Opposing an ABM system was Secretary of Defense Robert McNamara, joined by the Office of International Security Affairs within the Defense Department, and Secretary of State Dean Rusk. Thus the Departments of Defense and State, defense contractors, and Congress were all involved

4. For more information on the ABM controversy and how it developed, see Spanier and Uslaner, *How American Foreign Policy Is Made*, pp. 115–130; *Congressional Quarterly Almanac, 1969* (Washington, D.C.: Congressional Quarterly Service, 1970), pp. 1090–1096, and *Congressional Quarterly Almanac, 1972* (Washington, D.C.: Congressional Quarterly Service, 1973), pp. 589–593.

in interest representation at this stage of the issue. The CIA and the National Security Agency were also indirectly involved since many of the arguments being made were based on their estimates of the Soviet Union's and China's missile and nuclear capabilities.

In the fall of 1967 the Johnson administration made its move. It announced its decision to deploy a "thin" ABM system—called the Sentinel system—designed to protect American cities against a limited Chinese nuclear attack, not a "thick" system designed to protect against an all-out Russian attack. For the present, funding would go only for the procurement of certain ABM parts that required a long lead time, not for actual deployment of a functioning system. Thus Johnson made a compromise decision. He moved far enough in the direction of developing an ABM system to satisfy those interests pushing for a full system, yet made a commitment sufficiently limited so that those opposed to ABM could still hope it never would become operational.

Congress, in 1968, authorized and appropriated the necessary money for Sentinel. The key vote was the 34–52 defeat of a move to remove Sentinel from the defense budget. A major foreign-policy decision—to develop a limited ABM system designed to protect American population centers—had been established, with far-reaching implications for defense spending, the arms race with the Soviet Union, and the conditions of nuclear war.

But when the Defense Department sought to move into rule application, strong opposition to Sentinel quickly developed, especially from the local areas where land was purchased for Sentinel sites. The prospect of having nuclear missiles in the backyard proved unpalitable to many Americans. The United Automobile Workers, the United Mine Workers, and the National Committee for a Sane Nuclear Policy also voiced their objections. Therefore, before implementation of the Johnson policy could advance very far, a new President and a new administration decided early in 1969 to drop the Sentinel ABM program and develop the renamed Safeguard ABM system. Safeguard was designed to protect not population centers but a number of nuclear missile sites in an attempt to assure that they could withstand a nuclear attack and still be able to retaliate. With a new Secretary of Defense and a new Secretary of State and with the proposed ABM sites now to be located far away from population centers, most of the opposition to Nixon's plan came from Congress and a broad coalition of anti-ABM interest groups. Thus the issue was back to the rule initiation stage, with the whole nature and thrust of the program being debated and in doubt.

Supporting Safeguard were the Administration, the military, the defense contractors, scientists at Rand and at the Hudson Institute, and the bloc on the Senate Armed Services Committee that had pushed so hard for an ABM under Johnson (Stennis was now chairman, following the death of Russell). Most of the opposition to the ABM was found in Congress itself. Senate Majority Leader Mansfield, Majority Whip Edward M. Kennedy (D. Mass.), and Foreign Relations Committee Chairman Fulbright led the opposition forces. Media criticism of the system was also widespread.[5]

A Gallup poll showed that almost 70 percent of the population had heard or read something about the ABM, a surprisingly high figure, indicative of the attention being paid the issue by the public and the media.[6] Thus a wide-ranging number of persons and groups were drawn into the controversy and were making their demands felt.

In August 1969 the Senate, by a spare two-vote margin, provided funds for Nixon's Safeguard ABM system, and later the House approved it by a wide margin. Thus once again the political system had initiated a major ABM decision—this time for an ABM system thinner than before and aimed at defending the nation's nuclear retaliatory capacity rather than its cities.

But Safeguard was to face as much controversy and opposition in subsequent attempts to actually develop and deploy it as it faced in its original fight for approval. The anti-ABM interests and groups continued to try to limit or kill the Safeguard system. Each year's appropriations process turned into a fierce struggle.

In 1972 the Nixon administration negotiated and the Senate ratified a treaty with the Soviet Union that limited each country to only two ABM sites—one to protect the national capital, and one other site. The anti-ABM forces were able to block in Congress the building of an ABM site around Washington, D.C. Thus it was in late 1974—seven years after Johnson's original proposal—that one forlorn ABM site, near Grand Forks, North Dakota, designed to protect Minutemen missiles in their underground silos, went into operation. One observer remarked accurately: "The system has prospered by cancellations, the number of sites having been cut from the 17 originally envisaged to 12, to two and now one."[7]

This whole ABM struggle was marked by the involvement of many different interests and groups, in and out of government. The presidency and Congress shared decision making, and frequently the struggle took the form of a classic President versus Congress confrontation (or at least a President versus a near-majority bloc in Congress confrontation). The technical experts in the Defense and State Departments—experts in missile technology and diplomatic negotiations—played their role. In the course of implementing the original 1967–1968 Sentinel system, so many changes were made in the size, mission, and location of the system that the 1974

5. Spanier and Uslaner, *How American Foreign Policy Is Made* p. 129. Also see *Congressional Quarterly Almanac, 1969*, pp. 1092–1096, for a listing of pro- and anti-ABM groups.
6. See Spanier and Uslaner, *How American Foreign Policy Is Made*, p. 129–130.
7. Nicholas Wade, "Safeguard: Disputed Weapon Nears Readiness on Plains of North Dakota," *Science*, 185 (1974), 1138.

Safeguard system is barely recognizable as the ABM system first proposed by Johnson and approved by Congress. In short, as is typical in a noncrisis situation, there was a wide-open struggle, marked by a significant degree of decentralized decision making.

The Crisis Policy-making Process

It is October 16, 1962, and word reaches President Kennedy that the Russians are placing offensive nuclear missiles in Cuba. Or it is August 20, 1968, and the Russian ambassador requests a meeting with President Johnson to announce that the Soviet Union has just invaded Czechoslovakia. Or it is May 12, 1975, and the news that the Cambodians have seized the United States merchant ship Mayaquez reaches President Ford. All three of these events threw the United States' political system into a policy-making crisis. What all these crisis situations—and periodically others of a similar nature—have in common is that new factors of great import for existing policy suddenly arise in such a way that a very quick response is required.

Crisis situations thereby possesses three distinguishing characteristics: they arise suddenly, they must be responded to quickly, and they possess great significance. In noncrisis situations, policy can be debated and can evolve over a period of time, but crisis situations do not permit the luxury of time and the opportunity for debate and reflection that go with time. Crisis situations also typically involve national security or military challenges and situations. As a result the necessity for secrecy is also often present. Because of the suddenness with which crisis situations arise, the speed with which they must be responded to, and the secrecy which is often required, policy making in crisis situations differs markedly from policy making in noncrisis situations.

Basic Patterns

The single characteristic that dominates crisis policy making is the tremendous increase in the President's power and control in such a situation. This basic fact is a consequence of the three key marks of crisis decision making: the need for speed, the need for secrecy, and the great import of the situation.

Interest Representation The interest representation aspect of policy making is marked by the President's determining who is to be consulted and who is not. Interests typically do not have time to mobilize themselves and work their way into a position to influence policy development in a crisis situation. Factions within the Departments of State and Defense do not have time to crystallize and exert pressure as they do in noncrisis situations. Thus the President is left relatively free to pick and choose those whom he will call on for advice and information. Normally he relies on knowledgeable officials in the Departments of State and Defense and in the CIA, close personal advisers from his own inner circle, and his national security adviser from his White House staff. In the process Congress, the bureaucracies of the State and Defense Departments, and outside interest groups—all of whom normally play an important role in noncrisis situations—are excluded. Typically crises are the result of a foreign government making certain threats or taking certain hostile actions. That particular government is in effect making demands on the United States government that the President cannot ignore. Otherwise he is free, by and large, to determine what other foreign governments to consult.

Rule Initiation   Crises do not necessarily result in the initiation of a new rule—of a new direction in foreign policy. When they do, they tend to be specific, tailored to the immediate crisis. But crises do raise questions of whether or not a new direction is needed; if so, what that direction is to be; and if not, how is the old direction to be implemented. The making of such decisions rest almost totally with the President. From Truman's 1950 decision to intervene militarily in South Korea to Ford's decision 25 years later to intervene militarily to secure the release of the Mayaquez and its crew from Cambodian hands, basic policy initiatives come from the President. And "consultation" with Congress usually takes the form of informing key congressional leaders of the actions the President has decided to take, rather than actual consultation in which the congressional leaders have a veto or even influence over presidential actions. In the 1962 Cuban missile crisis, Kennedy kept congressional leaders ignorant of the Russian placement of missiles in Cuba for days while he and his advisers determined what the American response would be. He informed them of the threat and his planned response only hours before he went on television to inform the general public.[8]

The President has this sort of independence because he is usually able to act legally in his capacity as commander-in-chief of the armed forces or on the basis of other inherent powers. Even the 1973 War Powers Act, which requires the President to obtain congressional approval within 60 days of committing American troops to action, gives him considerable freedom in a short-run, crisis situation. In addition, the President has no need to depend on congressional appropriations to support his crisis actions as he needs to do in the longer-run, noncrisis situations. Opposition blocs in Congress (or elsewhere in government) have no time to form. The "rally round the flag" tendency—the tendency of the public to support

8. See Robert F. Kennedy, *Thirteen Days* (New York: Norton, 1969), pp. 52–55.

their President and their country when facing foreign challenge—is at its greatest in short-run, crisis situations. As a result the President is left pre-eminent in initiating responses to crisis situations.

Rule Application and Rule Interpretation   Crisis policy making at the rule application and the rule interpretation stages is marked by the President's continued oversight of the carrying out of presidential initiatives. Often the minutest details of policy implementation are observed and controlled by the President. Often, in fact, crisis decision making is largely a matter of the careful re-examination and implementation of long-standing foreign policy principles or rules. In his account of the 1962 Cuban missile crisis, Robert Kennedy describes how President Kennedy was informed minute by minute of the movement of Russian and American ships and personally gave orders concerning which Russian ships were to be intercepted and how it was to be done.[9] Modern communications make possible this type of presidential control over events unfolding thousands of miles away, and the importance and sensitivity of the crisis situations make Presidents desirous of exercising it. In addition, many noncrisis policies are constantly evolving and being implemented at once, and thus presidential attention must very often be elsewhere. But crises usually are of short duration and receive almost total presidential attention.

Because of the close presidential involvement in crisis situations, disputes between agencies over the application of directives that might require rule interpretation tend not to arise. When they do, they are quickly resolved by the President or a close adviser of his.

The Mayaquez: A Case of Crisis Policy Making

On the morning of Monday, May 12, 1975, the United States merchant ship Mayaquez was sailing on the high seas near Cambodian waters on a route from Hong Kong to Thailand.[10] A Cambodian torpedo boat challenged the Mayaquez and fired on it, forcing it to stop dead in the water. Seven youthful, heavily armed Cambodian soldiers boarded the ship and forced it to a small island off the coast of Cambodia. The ship's radioman was able to get off a distress message before being shut down, a message that was quickly relayed to Washington and President Ford. A foreign-policy crisis was thereby precipitated which was to last for four days and lead to a massive diplomatic and military effort that culminated in the release of the ship and its crew, strained diplomatic relations with Thailand, the death of 41 servicemen, and, some would claim, the re-establish-

9. Kennedy, *Thirteen Days,* pp. 67–74.

10. The following description was put together from contemporary newspaper accounts. With more time, the writing of memoirs by the participants, and the analyses of historians, additional information may modify some of the following observations.

ment of American prestige as a world power following the collapse of its Vietnam policy.

The key persons with whom Ford consulted during these intense four days of crisis were Secretary of State Henry Kissinger, Secretary of Defense James Schlesinger, CIA Director William Colby, the Joint Chiefs of Staff, and several other persons on the National Security Council. "Consultation" with Congress consisted of informing congressional leaders of Ford's decision to use military force after the decision had already been made. Because the entire crisis lasted only four days—96 hours—there was no time for interests among the public or in the Defense and State Department bureaucracies to emerge and exert influence. Time was of the essence because it was feared that the longer the United States waited the greater the chance that the crew members would be moved inland, into Cambodia, where it would be impossible to rescue them by a military assault.

Ford's initial decision was to seek the ship's and crew's release through diplomacy, approaching the Cambodian government directly through its representatives in Peking and indirectly through the Chinese government. After two days—on Wednesday—no response had been received from Cambodia. Thus a course of military action was decided on by Ford, in consultation with the close circle of advisers mentioned earlier. White House aides then informed congressional leaders of the decision.

Marines landed by helicopter on Koh Tang island, where the Mayaquez had been brought and where it was thought the crew was being held, and two air strikes on military and support facilities on the Cambodian mainland were carried out. The Mayaquez was found deserted and was towed away by an American destroyer, the Cambodians released the Mayaquez's crew, who had been moved to the mainland, and the marines were taken off Koh Tang under heavy fire. By Thursday, four days after the seizure of the Mayaquez, it was all over—except for the families of the 41 servicemen who died in the effort.

The underlying, undeniable feature of this incident is the extent to which Ford dominated the decision-making process. It was Ford—helped by his own select, small group of advisers—who decided first on a diplomatic approach and, when that failed, on a military approach. But Ford's control went beyond the outlines of the general response to be followed. It also covered the details of the execution of his decisions. The decision to use for the assault marines flown directly from the Utapao base in Thailand— an act that angered the Thais, who had not been consulted or even informed—was Ford's decision, as were the timing of the assault and the targets of the mainland air strikes. "Consulting" with Congress consisted of informing them of decisions already made. Public opinion and opposition groups within outside interest groups, the press, and governmental bureaucracies never had a chance to crystallize and exert their influence. The entire crisis broke open, reached a climax, and was resolved in the space of 96 hours. In such circumstances, it is not surprising that Ford was dominant from beginning to end.

Foreign-policy making differs from domestic-policy making—and foreign-policy making itself differs in crisis and noncrisis situations. The compressed time frame, the import, and the normal need for secrecy of crisis situations work to centralize decision-making power in the President's hands; whereas the longer time frame, the often more routine nature, and the possibility of free discussion of noncrisis situations work to open up and decentralize the decision-making process. This chapter has traced the different processes of foreign-policy making in crisis and noncrisis situations, processes that have an effect—direct or indirect—on all persons on our planet.

Some Exploratory Questions

1. Would noncrisis policy making be improved if there were less dissension in Congress, in the bureaucracies, and among the public, and more of everyone working together to promote the nation's welfare?

2. Is the crisis or noncrisis policy-making process more likely to lead to wise, effective policies?

3. In several respects the noncrisis policy-making process more closely approximates democratic norms than does crisis policy making. What, if anything, could be done to make crisis policy making more open and democratic?

Bibliographical Essay

Two brief books that give excellent overviews of the processes by which foreign policies are made and implemented are Roger Hilsman, *The Politics of Policy Making in Defense and Foreign Affairs* (New York: Harper & Row, 1971), and John Spanier and Eric M. Uslaner, *How American Foreign Policy Is Made* (New York: Praeger, 1974). For insight into the role of the bureaucracy in foreign-policy formation, see Francis E. Rouke, *Bureaucracy and Foreign Policy* (Baltimore: Johns Hopkins University Press, 1972). An excellent analysis of crisis decision making and the pitfalls small groups of policy makers can fall into is found in Irving L. Janis, *Victims of Groupthink* (Boston: Houghton, Mifflin, 1972).

Especially helpful in understanding the role that sources outside the political system have in the formation of foreign policy are James N. Rosenau, ed., *Domestic Sources of Foreign Policy* (New York: Free Press, 1967), and James N. Rosenau, *Public Opinion and Foreign Policy* (New York: Random House, 1961). Also still helpful is the somewhat dated book by Gabriel A. Almond, *The American People and Foreign Policy* (New York: Praeger, 1960).

Much can also be learned from the numerous books that analyze the content of existing and past foreign policies and how they were arrived at. Among the better ones are two that deal with American involvement in Vietnam: Chester L. Cooper, *The Lost Crusade* (New York: Dodd, Mead, 1970), and David Halberstam, *The Best and the Brightest* (New York: Random House, 1972). Also see John C. Donovan, *The Cold Warriors: A Policy-Making Elite* (Lexington, Mass.: Heath, 1974). The memoirs of George Kennan, an American diplomat and scholar who was at the center of the development of American foreign policies from 1930 to 1950, give many insights into foreign-policy-making processes: George F. Kennan, *Memoirs* (Boston: Little, Brown, 1967).

There are many books that advocate certain foreign policies or approaches to foreign-policy making. For three contrasting views, see Ernest W. Lefever, ed., *Ethics and World Politics* (Baltimore: Johns Hopkins University Press, 1972). Also see the strongly argued book by former Senator J. William Fulbright, *The Crippled Giant* (New York: Random House, 1972). Also see the collection of essays by Henry Kissinger written in the context of the United States' Vietnam involvement: Henry A. Kissinger, *American Foreign Policy* (New York: Norton, 1969). Taking a more theoretical approach is the able book by John C. Bennett, *Foreign Policy in Christian Perspective* (New York: Scribner's, 1966).

The Constitution of the United States

We the People of the United States, in Order to form a more perfect Union, establish Justice, insure domestic Tranquility, provide for the common defence, promote the general Welfare, and secure the Blessings of Liberty to ourselves and our Posterity, do ordain and establish this Constitution for the United States of America.

Article I

SECTION 1 All legislative Powers herein granted shall be vested in a Congress of the United States, which shall consist of a Senate and House of Representatives.
SECTION 2 The House of Representatives shall be composed of Members chosen every second Year by the People of the several States, and the Electors in each State shall have the Qualifications requisite for Electors of the most numerous Branch of the State Legislature.

No Person shall be a Representative who shall not have attained to the Age of twenty five Years, and been seven Years a Citizen of the United States, and who shall not, when elected, be an Inhabitant of that State in which he shall be chosen.

Representatives and direct Taxes shall be apportioned among the several States which may be included within this Union, according to their respective Numbers, *which shall be determined by adding to the whole Number of free Persons, including those bound to Service for a Term of Years,* and excluding Indians not taxed, *three fifths of all other Persons.*[1] The actual Enumeration shall be made within three Years after the first Meeting of the Congress of the United States, and within every subsequent Term of ten Years, in such Manner as they shall by Law direct. The Number of Representatives shall not exceed one for every thirty Thousand, but each State shall have at Least one Representative; and until such enumeration shall be made, the State of New Hampshire shall be entitled to chuse three, Massachusetts eight, Rhode-Island and Providence Plantations one, Connecticut five, New-York six, New Jersey four, Pennsylvania eight, Delaware one, Maryland six, Virginia ten, North Carolina five, South Carolina five, and Georgia three.

1. Portions of the Constitution that have been repealed or altered by subsequent amendments are italicized. In this case, see Amendment 14.

When vacancies happen in the Representation from any State, the Executive Authority thereof shall issue Writs of Election to fill such Vacancies.

The House of Representatives shall chuse their speaker and other Officers; and shall have the sole Power of Impeachment.

SECTION 3 The Senate of the United States shall be composed of two Senators from each State, *chosen by the Legislature thereof,* [2] for six Years; and each Senator shall have one Vote.

Immediately after they shall be assembled in Consequence of the first Election, they shall be divided as equally as may be into three Classes. The Seats of the Senators of the first Class shall be vacated at the Expiration of the second Year, of the second Class at the Expiration of the four Year, and of the third Class at the Expiration of the sixth Year, so that one third may be chosen every second Year; *and if Vacancies happen by Resignation, or otherwise, during the Recess of the Legislature of any State, the Executive thereof may make temporary Appointments until the next Meeting of the Legislature, which shall then fill such Vacancies.* [3]

No Person shall be a Senator who shall not have attained to the Age of thirty Years, and been nine Years a Citizen of the United States, and who shall not, when elected, be an Inhabitant of that State for which he shall be chosen.

The Vice President of the United States shall be President of the Senate, but shall have no Vote, unless they be equally divided.

The Senate shall chuse their other Officers, and also a President pro tempore, in the Absence of the Vice President, or when he shall exercise the Office of President of the United States.

The Senate shall have the sole Power to try all Impeachments. When sitting for that Purpose, they shall be on Oath or Affirmation. When the President of the United States is tried, the Chief Justice shall preside: And no Person shall be convicted without the Concurrence of two thirds of the Members present.

Judgment in Cases of Impeachment shall not extend further than to removal from Office, and disqualification to hold and enjoy any Office of honor, Trust or Profit under the United States: but the Party convicted shall nevertheless be liable and subject to Indictment, Trial, Judgment and Punishment, according to law.

SECTION 4 The Times, Places and Manner of holding Elections for Senators and Representatives, shall be prescribed in each State by the Legislature thereof; but the Congress may at any time by Law make or alter such Regulations, except as to the Places of chusing Senators.

The Congress shall assemble at least once in every Year, *and such Meeting shall be on the first Monday in December, unless they shall by Law appoint a different Day.* [4]

SECTION 5 Each House shall be the Judge of the Elections, Returns and Qualifications of its own Members, and a Majority of each shall constitute a quorum to do Business; but a smaller Number may adjourn from day to day, and may be authorized to compel the Attendance of absent Members, in such Manner, and under such Penalties as each House may provide.

2. See Amendment 17.
3. See Amendment 17.
4. See Amendment 20.

Each House may determine the Rules of its Proceedings, punish its Members for disorderly Behaviour, and, with the Concurrence of two thirds, expel a Member.

Each House shall keep a Journal of its Proceedings, and from time to time publish the same, excepting such Parts as may in their Judgment require Secrecy; and the Yeas and Nays of the Members of either House on any question shall, at the Desire of one fifth of those Present, be entered on the Journal.

Neither House, during the Session of Congress, shall, without the Consent of the other, adjourn for more than three days, nor to any other Place than that in which the two Houses shall be sitting.

SECTION 6 The Senators and Representatives shall receive a Compensation for their Services, to be ascertained by Law, and paid out of the Treasury of the United States. They shall in all Cases, except Treason, Felony and Breach of the Peace, be privileged from Arrest during their Attendance at the Session of their respective Houses, and in going to and returning from the same; and for any Speech or Debate in either House, they shall not be questioned in any other Place.

No Senator or Representative shall, during the Time for which he was elected, be appointed to any civil Office under the Authority of the United States, which shall have been created, or the Emoluments whereof shall have been encreased during such time; and no Person holding any Office under the United States, shall be a Member of either House during his Continuance in Office.

SECTION 7 All Bills for raising Revenue shall originate in the House of Representatives; but the Senate may propose or concur with Amendments as on other Bills.

Every Bill which shall have passed the House of Representatives and the Senate, shall, before it become a Law, be presented to the President of the United States; If he approve he shall sign it, but if not he shall return it, with his Objections to that House in which it shall have originated, who shall enter the Objections at large on their Journal, and proceed to reconsider it. If after such Reconsideration two thirds of that House shall agree to pass the Bill, it shall be sent, together with the Objections, to the other House, by which it shall likewise be reconsidered, and if approved by two thirds of that House, it shall become a Law. But in all such Cases the Votes of both Houses shall be determined by yeas and Nays, and the Names of the Persons voting for and against the Bill shall be entered on the Journal of each House respectively. If any Bill shall not be returned by the President within ten Days (Sundays excepted) after it shall have been presented to him, the Same shall be a Law, in like Manner as if he had signed it, unless the Congress by their Adjournment prevent its Return, in which Case it shall not be a Law.

Every Order, Resolution, or Vote to which the Concurrence of the Senate and House of Representatives may be necessary (except on a question of Adjournment) shall be presented to the President of the United States; and before the Same shall take Effect, shall be approved by him, or being disapproved by him, shall be repassed by two thirds of the Senate and House of Representatives, according to the Rules and Limitations prescribed in the Case of a Bill.

SECTION 8 The Congress shall have Power To lay and collect Taxes, Duties, Imposts and Excises, to pay the Debts and provide for the common Defence and general Welfare of the United States; but all Duties, Imposts and Excises shall be uniform throughout the United States;

To borrow Money on the Credit of the United States;

To regulate Commerce with foreign Nations, and among the several States, and with the Indian Tribes;

To establish an uniform Rule of Naturalization, and uniform Laws on the subject of Bankruptcies throughout the United States;

To coin Money, regulate the Value thereof, and of foreign Coin, and fix the Standard of Weights and Measures;

To provide for the Punishment of counterfeiting the Securities and current Coin of the United States;

To establish Post Offices and post Roads;

To promote the Progress of Science and useful Arts, by securing for limited Times to Authors and Inventors the exclusive Right to their respective Writings and Discoveries;

To constitute Tribunals inferior to the supreme Court;

To define and punish Piracies and Felonies committed on the high Seas, and Offences against the Law of Nations;

To declare War, grant Letters of Marque and Reprisal, and make Rules concerning Captures on Land and Water;

To raise and support Armies, but no Appropriation of Money to that Use shall be for a longer Term than two Years;

To provide and maintain a Navy;

To make Rules for the Government and Regulation of the land and naval Forces;

To provide for calling forth the Militia to execute the Laws of the Union, suppress Insurrections and repel Invasions;

To provide for organizing, arming, and disciplining, the Militia, and for governing such Part of them as may be employed in the Service of the United States, reserving to the States respectively, the Appointment of the Officers, and the Authority of training the Militia according to the discipline prescribed by Congress;

To exercise exclusive Legislation in all Cases whatsoever, over such District (not exceeding ten Miles square) as may by Cession of particular States, and the Acceptance of Congress, become the Seat of the Government of the United States, and to exercise like Authority over all Places purchased by the Consent of the Legislature of the State in which the Same shall be for the Erection of Forts, Magazines, Arsenals, dock-Yards, and other needful Buildings;—And

To make all Laws which shall be necessary and proper for carrying into Execution the foregoing Powers, and all other Powers vested by this Constitution in the Government of the United States, or in any Department or Officer thereof.

SECTION 9 The Migration or Importation of such Persons as any of the States now existing shall think proper to admit, shall not be prohibited by the Congress prior to the Year one thousand eight hundred and eight, but a Tax or duty may be imposed on such Importation, not exceeding ten dollars for each Person.

The Privilege of the Writ of Habeas Corpus shall not be suspended, unless when in Cases of Rebellion or Invasion the public Safety may require it.

No Bill of Attainder or ex post facto Law shall be passed.

No Capitation, or other direct, Tax shall be laid, unless in Proportion to the Census or Enumeration herein before directed to be taken. [5]

No Tax or Duty shall be laid on Articles exported from any State.

5. See Amendment 16.

No Preference shall be given by any Regulation of Commerce or Revenue to the Ports of one State over those of another: nor shall Vessels bound to, or from, one State, be obliged to enter, clear, or pay Duties in another.

No Money shall be drawn from the Treasury, but in Consequence of Appropriations made by Law; and a regular Statement and Account of the Receipts and Expenditures of all public Money shall be published from time to time.

No Title of Nobility shall be granted by the United States: And no Person holding any Office of Profit or Trust under them, shall, without the Consent of the Congress, accept of any present, Emolument, Office, or Title, of any kind whatever, from any King, Prince, or foreign State.

SECTION10 No State shall enter into any Treaty, Alliance, or Confederation; grant Letters of Marque and Reprisal; coin Money; emit Bills of Credit; make any Thing but gold and silver Coin a Tender in Payment of Debts; pass any Bill of Attainder, ex post facto Law, or Law impairing the Obligation of Contracts, or grant any Title of Nobility.

No State shall, without the Consent of the Congress, lay any Imposts or Duties on Imports or Exports, except what may be absolutely necessary for executing its inspection Laws: and the net Produce of all Duties and Imposts, laid by any State on Imports or Exports, shall be for the Use of the Treasury of the United States; and all such Laws shall be subject to the Revision and Controul of the Congress.

No State shall, without the Consent of Congress, lay any Duty of Tonnage, keep Troops, or Ships of War in time of Peace, enter into any Agreement or Compact with another State, or with a foreign Power, or engage in War, unless actually invaded, or in such imminent Danger as will not admit of delay.

Article II

SECTION 1 The executive Power shall be vested in a President of the United States of America. He shall hold his Office during the Term of four years, and, together with the Vice President, chosen for the same term, be elected, as follows

Each State shall appoint, in such Manner as the Legislature thereof may direct, a Number of Electors, equal to the whole Number of Senators and Representatives to which the State may be entitled in the Congress: but no Senator or Representative, or Person holding an Office of Trust or Profit under the United States, shall be appointed an Elector.

The Electors shall meet in their respective States, and vote by Ballot for two Persons, of whom one at least shall not be an Inhabitant of the same State with themselves. And they shall make a List of all the Persons voted for, and of the Number of Votes for each; which List they shall sign and certify, and transmit sealed to the Seat of the Government of the United States, directed to the President of the Senate. The President of the Senate shall, in the Presence of the Senate and House of Representatives, open all the Certificates, and the Votes shall then be counted. The Person having the greatest Number of Votes shall be the President, if such Number be a Majority of the whole Number of Electors appointed; and if there be more than one who have such Majority, and have an equal Number of Votes, then the House of Representatives shall immediately chuse by Ballot one of them for President: and if no Person have a Majority, then from the five highest on the List the said House shall in like Manner chuse the President. But in chusing the President, the Votes shall be taken by States, the Representation from each State having one Vote; A quorum for this Purpose shall consist of a Member or Members from two thirds of the States, and a Majority of all the States shall be necessary to a Choice. In every Case, after the Choice of the President, the Person having the greatest Number of Votes of the Electors shall be the Vice President. But if there should remain two or more who have equal Votes, the Senate shall chuse from them by Ballot the Vice President. [6]

The Congress may determine the Time of chusing the Electors, and the Day on which they shall give their Votes; which Day shall be the same throughout the United States.

No Person except a natural born Citizen, or a Citizen of the United States, at the time of the Adoption of this Constitution, shall be eligible to the Office of President; neither shall any Person be eligible to that Office who shall not have attained to the Age of thirty five Years, and been fourteen Years a Resident within the United States.

In Case of the Removal of the President from Office, or his Death, Resignation, or Inability to discharge the Powers and Duties of the said Office, the Same shall devolve on the Vice President, and the Congress may by Law provide for the Case of Removal, Death, Resignation or Inability, both of the President and Vice President, declaring what Officer shall then act as President, and such Officer shall act accordingly, until Disability be removed, or a President shall be elected. [7]

The President shall, at stated Times, receive for his Services, a Compensation, which shall neither be encreased nor diminished during the Period for which he shall have been elected, and he shall not receive within that Period any other Emolument from the United States, or any of them.

Before he enter on the Execution of his Office, he shall take the following Oath or Affirmation:—"I do solemnly swear (or affirm) that I will faithfully execute the Office of President of the United States, and will to the best of my Ability, preserve, protect and defend the Constitution of the United States."

SECTION 2 The President shall be Commander in Chief of the Army and Navy of the United States, and of the Militia of the several States, when called into the actual Service of the United States; he may require the Opinion, in writing, of the principal Officer in each of the executive Departments, upon any Subject relating to the Duties of their respective Offices, and he shall have Power to grant Reprieves and Pardons for Offences against the United States, except in Cases of Impeachment.

He shall have Power, by and with the Advice and Consent of the Senate, to make Treaties, provided two thirds of the Senators present concur; and he shall nominate, and by and with the Advice and Consent of the Senate, shall appoint Ambassadors, other public Ministers and Consuls, Judges of the supreme Court, and all other Officers of the United States, whose Appointments are not herein otherwise

6. See Amendment 12.
7. See Amendment 25.

provided for, and which shall be established by Law: but the Congress may by Law vest the Appointment of such inferior Officers, as they think proper, in the President alone, in the Courts of Law, or in the Heads of Departments.

The President shall have Power to fill up all Vacancies that may happen during the Recess of the Senate, by granting Commissions which shall expire at the End of their next Session.

SECTION 3 He shall from time to time give to the Congress Information of the State of the Union, and recommend to their Consideration such Measures as he shall judge necessary and expedient; he may, on extraordinary Occasions, convene both Houses, or either of them, and in Case of Disagreement between them, with Respect to the Time of Adjournment, he may adjourn them to such Time as he shall think proper; he shall receive Ambassadors and other public Ministers; he shall take Care that the Laws be faithfully executed, and shall Commission all the Officers of the United States.

SECTION 4 The President, Vice President and all civil Officers of the United States, shall be removed from Office on Impeachment for, and Conviction of, Treason, Bribery, or other High Crimes and Misdemeanors.

– Article III

SECTION 1 The judicial Power of the United States, shall be vested in one supreme Court, and in such inferior Courts as the Congress may from time to time ordain and establish. The Judges, both of the supreme and inferior Courts, shall hold their Offices during good Behaviour, and shall, at stated Times, receive for their Services, a Compensation, which shall not be diminished during their Continuance in Office.

SECTION 2 The judicial Power shall extend to all Cases, in Law and Equity, arising under this Constitution, the Laws of the United States, and Treaties made, or which shall be made, under their Authority;—to all Cases affecting Ambassadors, other public Ministers and Consuls;—to all Cases of admiralty and maritime Jurisdiction; —to Controversies to which the United States shall be a Party;—to Controversies between two or more States; *between a State and Citizens of another State,* [8]— between Citizens of different States;—between Citizens of the same State claiming Lands under Grants of different States, *and between a State, or the Citizens thereof, and foreign States, Citizens or Subjects.* [9]

In all Cases affecting Ambassadors, other public Ministers and Consuls, and those in which a State shall be Party, the supreme Court shall have original Jurisdiction. In all the other Cases before mentioned, the supreme Court shall have appellate Jurisdiction, both as to Law and Fact, with such Exceptions, and under such Regulations as the Congress shall make.

The Trial of all Crimes, except in Cases of Impeachment, shall be by Jury; and such Trial shall be held in the State where the said Crimes shall have been committed; but when not committed within any State, the Trial shall be at such Place or Places as the Congress may by Law have directed.

8. See Amendment 11.
9. See Amendment 11.

SECTION 3 Treason against the United States, shall consist only in levying War against them, or in adhering to their Enemies, giving them Aid and Comfort. No Person shall be convicted of Treason unless on the Testimony of two Witnesses to the same overt Act, or on Confession in open Court.

The Congress shall have Power to declare the Punishment of Treason, but no Attainder of Treason shall work Corruption of Blood, or Forfeiture except during the Life of the Person atainted.

Article IV

SECTION 1 Full Faith and Credit shall be given in each State to the public Arts, Records, and judicial Proceedings of every other State. And the Congress may by general Laws prescribe the Manner in which such Acts, Records and Proceedings shall be proved, and the Effect thereof.

SECTION 2 The Citizens of each State shall be entitled to all Privileges and Immunities of Citizens in the several States.

A Person charged in any State with Treason, Felony, or other Crime, who shall flee from Justice, and be found in another State, shall on Demand of the executive Authority of the State from which he fled, be delivered up, to be removed to the State having Jurisdiction of the Crime.

No Person held to Service or Labour in one State, under the Laws thereof, escaping into another, shall, in Consequence of any Law or Regulation therein, be discharged from such Service or Labour, but shall be delivered up on Claim of the Party to whom such Service or Labour may be due. [10]

SECTION 3 New States may be admitted by the Congress into this Union; but no new State shall be formed or erected within the Jurisdiction of any other State; nor any State be formed by the Junction of two or more States, or Parts of States, without the Consent of the Legislatures of the States concerned as well as of the Congress.

The Congress shall have Power to dispose of and make all needful Rules and Regulations respecting the Territory or other Property belonging to the United States; and nothing in this Constitution shall be so construed as to Prejudice any Claims of the United States, or of any particular State.

SECTION 4 The United States shall guarantee to every State in this Union a Republican Form of Government, and shall protect each of them against Invasion; and on Application of the Legislature, or of the Executive (when the Legislature cannot be convened) against domestic Violence.

Article V

The Congress, whenever two thirds of both Houses shall deem it necessary, shall propose Amendments to this Constitution, or, on the Application of the Legislatures of two thirds of the several States, shall call a Convention for proposing Amendments, which, in either Case, shall be valid to all Intents and Purposes, as Part of this Constitution, when ratified by the Legislatures of three fourths of the several

10. See Amendment 13.

States, or by Conventions in three fourths thereof, as the one or the other Mode of Ratification may be proposed by the Congress; Provided that no Amendment which may be made prior to the Year One thousand eight hundred and eight shall in any Manner affect the first and fourth Clauses in the Ninth Section of the first Article; and that no State, without its Consent, shall be deprived of its equal Suffrage in the Senate.

Article VI

All Debts contracted and Engagements entered into, before the Adoption of this Constitution, shall be as valid against the United States under this Constitution, as under the Confederation.

This Constitution, and the Laws of the United States which shall be made in Pursuance thereof; and all Treaties made, or which shall be made, under the Authority of the United States, shall be the supreme Law of the Land; and the Judges in Every State shall be bound thereby, any Thing in the Constitution or Laws of any State to the Contrary notwithstanding.

The Senators and Representatives before mentioned, and the Members of the several State Legislatures, and all executive and judicial Officers, both of the United States and of the several States, shall be bound by Oath or Affirmation, to support this Constitution; but no religious Test shall ever be required as a Qualification to any Office or public Trust under the United States.

Article VII

The Ratification of the Conventions of nine States, shall be sufficient for the Establishment of this Constitution between the States so ratifying the Same.

Amendment 1[11]

Congress shall make no law respecting an establishment of religion, or prohibiting the free exercise thereof; or abridging the freedom of speech, or of the press; or the right of the people peaceably to assemble, and to petition the Government for a redress of grievances.

Amendment 2

A well regulated Militia, being necessary to the security of a free State, the right of the people to keep and bear Arms, shall not be infringed.

Amendment 3

No Soldier shall, in time of peace be quartered in any house, without the consent of the Owner, nor in time of war, but in a manner to be prescribed by law.

11. The first 10 Amendments were ratified December 15, 1791, and form what is known as the "Bill of Rights."

Amendment 4

The right of the people to be secure in their persons, houses, papers, and effects, against unreasonable searches and seizures, shall not be violated, and no Warrants shall issue, but upon probable cause, supported by Oath or affirmation, and particularly describing the place to be searched, and the persons or things to be seized.

Amendment 5

No person shall be held to answer for a capital, or otherwise infamous crime, unless on a presentment or indictment of a Grand Jury, except in cases arising in the land or naval forces, or in the Militia, when in actual service in time of War or public danger; nor shall any person be subject for the same offence to be twice put in jeopardy of life or limb; nor shall be compelled in any criminal case to be a witness against himself, nor be deprived of life, liberty, or property, without due process of law; nor shall private property be taken for public use, without just compensation.

Amendment 6

In all criminal prosecutions, the accused shall enjoy the right to a speedy and public trial, by an impartial jury of the State and district wherein the crime shall have been committed, which district shall have been previously ascertained by law, and to be informed of the nature and cause of the accusation; to be confronted with the witnesses against him; to have compulsory process for obtaining witnesses in his favor, and to have the Assistance of Counsel for his defence.

Amendment 7

In Suits at common law, where the value in controversy shall exceed twenty dollars, the right of trial by jury shall be preserved, and no fact tried by a jury, shall be otherwise re-examined in any Court of the United States, than according to the rules of the common law.

Amendment 8

Excessive bail shall not be required, nor excessive fines imposed, nor cruel and unusual punishments inflicted.

Amendment 9

The enumeration in the Constitution, of certain rights, shall not be construed to deny or disparage others retained by the people.

Amendment 10

The powers not delegated to the United States by the Constitution, nor prohibited by it to the States, are reserved to the States respectively, or to the people.

Amendment 11[12]

The Judicial power of the United States shall not be construed to extend to any suit in law or equity, commenced or prosecuted against one of the United States by Citizens of another State, or by Citizens or Subjects of any Foreign State.

Amendment 12[13]

The Electors shall meet in their respective states and vote by ballot for President and Vice-President, one of whom, at least, shall not be an inhabitant of the same state with themselves; they shall name in their ballots the person voted for as President, and in distinct ballots the person voted for as Vice-President, and they shall make distinct lists of all persons voted for as President, and of all persons voted for as Vice-President, and of the number of votes for each, which lists they shall sign and certify, and transmit sealed to the seat of the government of the United States, directed to the President of the Senate;—The President of the Senate shall, in the presence of the Senate and House of Representatives, open all the certificates and the votes shall then be counted;—The person having the greatest number of votes for President, shall be the President, if such number be a majority of the whole number of Electors appointed; and if no person have such majority, then from the persons having the highest numbers not exceeding three on the list of those voted for as President, the House of Representatives shall choose immediately, by ballot, the President. But in choosing the President, the votes shall be taken by states, the representation from each state having one vote; a quorum for this purpose shall consist of a member or members from two-thirds of the states, and a majority of all the states shall be necessary to a choice. And if the House of Representatives shall not choose a President whenever the right of choice shall devolve upon them, *before the fourth day of March next following,* [14] then the Vice-President shall act as President, as in the case of the death or other constitutional disability of the President.—The person having the greatest number of votes as Vice-President, shall be the Vice-President, if such number be a majority of the whole number of Electors appointed, and if no person have a majority, then from the two highest numbers on the list, the Senate shall choose the Vice-President; a quorum for the purpose shall consist of two-thirds of the whole number of Senators, and a majority of the whole number shall be necessary to a choice. But no person constitutionally ineligible to the office of President shall be eligible to that of Vice-President of the United States.

Amendment 13[15]

SECTION 1 Neither slavery nor involunatary servitude, except as a punishment for crime whereof the party shall have been duly convicted, shall exist within the the United States, or any place subject to their jurisdiction.

12. Ratified February 7, 1795.
13. Ratified July 27, 1804.
14. See Amendment 20.
15. Ratified December 6, 1865.

SECTION 2 Congress shall have power to enforce this article by appropriate legislation.

Amendment 14[16]

SECTION 1 All persons born or naturalized in the United States, and subject to the jurisdiction thereof, are citizens of the United States and of the State wherein they reside. No State shall make or enforce any law which shall abridge the privileges or immunities of citizens of the United States; nor shall any State deprive any person of life, liberty, or property, without due process of law; nor deny to any person within its jurisdiction the equal protection of the laws.

SECTION 2 Representatives shall be apportioned among the several States according to their respective numbers, counting the whole number of persons in each State, excluding Indians not taxed. But when the right to vote at any election for the choice of electors for President and Vice President of the United States, Representatives in Congress, the Executive and Judicial officers of a State, or the members of the Legislature thereof, is denied to any of the male inhabitants of such State, being twenty-one years of age, and citizens of the United States, or in any way abridged, except for participation in rebellion, or other crime, the basis of representation therein shall be reduced in the proportion which the number of such male citizens shall bear to the whole number of male citizens twenty-one years of age in such State.

SECTION 3 No person shall be a Senator or Representative in Congress, or elector of the President and Vice President, or hold any office, civil or military, under the United States, or under any State, who, having previously taken an oath, as a member of Congress, or as an officer of the United States, or as a member of any State legislature, or as an executive or judicial officer of any State, to support the Constitution of the United States, shall have engaged in insurrection or rebellion against the same, or given aid or comfort to the enemies thereof. But Congress may by a vote of two-thirds of each House, remove such disability.

SECTION 4 The validity of the public debt of the United States, authorized by law, including debts incurred for payment of pensions and bounties for services in suppressing insurrection or rebellion, shall not be questioned. But neither the United States nor any State shall assume or pay any debt or obligation incurred in aid of insurrection or rebellion against the United States, or any claim for the loss or emancipation of any slave; but all such debts, obligations and claims shall be held illegal and void.

SECTION 5 The Congress shall have power to enforce, by appropriate legislation, the provisions of this article.

Amendment 15[17]

SECTION 1 The right of citizens of the United States to vote shall not be denied or abridged by the United States or by any State on account of race, color, or previous condition of servitude.

16. Ratified July 9, 1868.
17. Ratified February 3, 1870.

SECTION 2 The Congress shall have power to enforce this article by appropriate legislation.

Amendment 16[18]

The Congress shall have power to lay and collect taxes on incomes, from whatever source derived, without apportionment among the several States, and without regard to any census or enumeration.

Amendment 17[19]

The Senate of the United States shall be composed of two Senators from each State, elected by the people thereof for six years; and each Senator shall have one vote. The electors in each State shall have the qualifications requisite for electors of the most numerous branch of the State legislatures.

When vacancies happen in the representation of any State in the Senate, the executive authority of such State shall issue writs of election to fill such vacancies: *Provided,* That the legislature of any State may empower the executive thereof to make temporary appointments until the people fill the vacancies by election as the legislature may direct.

This amendment shall not be so construed as to affect the election or term of any Senator chosen before it becomes valid as part of the Constitution.

Amendment 18[20]

SECTION 1 *After one year from the ratification of this article the manufacture, sale, or transportation of intoxicating liquors within, the importation thereof into, or the exportation thereof from the United States and all territory subject to the jurisdiction thereof for beverage purposes is hereby prohibited.*
SECTION 2 *The Congress and the several States shall have concurrent power to enforce this article by appropriate legislation.*
SECTION 3 *This article shall be inoperative unless it shall have been ratified as an amendment to the Constitution by the legislatures of the several States, as provided in the Constitution, within seven years from the date of the submission hereof to the States by the Congress.*[21]

Amendment 19[22]

The right of citizens of the United States to vote shall not be denied or abridged by the United States or by any State on account of sex.

Congress shall have power to enforce this article by appropriate legislation.

18. Ratified February 3, 1913.
19. Ratified April 8, 1913.
20. Ratified January 16, 1919.
21. See Amendment 21.
22. Ratified August 18, 1920.

Amendment 20[23]

SECTION 1 The terms of the President and Vice President shall end at noon on the 20th day of January, and the terms of Senators and Representatives at noon on the 3rd day of January, of the years in which such terms would have ended if this article had not been ratified; and the terms of their successors shall then begin.

SECTION 2 The Congress shall assemble at least once in every year, and such meeting shall begin at noon on the 3rd day of January, unless they shall by law appoint a different day.

SECTION 3 If, at the time fixed for the beginning of the term of the President, the President elect shall have died, the Vice President elect shall become President. If a President shall not have been chosen before the time fixed for the beginning of his term, or if the President elect shall have failed to qualify, then the Vice President elect shall act as President until a President shall have qualified; and the Congress may by law provide for the case wherein neither a President elect nor a Vice President elect shall have qualified, declaring who shall then act as President, or the manner in which one who is to act shall be selected, and such person shall act accordingly until a President or Vice President shall have qualified.

SECTION 4 The Congress may by law provide for the case of the death of any of the persons from whom the House of Representatives may choose a President whenever the right of choice shall have devolved upon them, and for the case of the death of any of the persons from whom the Senate may choose a Vice President whenever the right of choice shall have devolved upon them.

SECTION 5 Sections 1 and 2 shall take effect on the 15th day of October following the ratification of this article.

SECTION 6 This article shall be inoperative unless it shall have been ratified as an amendment to the Constitution by the legislatures of three-fourths of the several States within seven years from the date of its submission.

Amendment 21[24]

SECTION 1 The eighteenth article of amendment to the Constitution of the United States is hereby repealed.

SECTION 2 The transportation or importation into any State, Territory, or possession of the United States for delivery or use therein of intoxicating liquors, in violation of the laws thereof, is hereby prohibited.

SECTION 3 This article shall be inoperative unless it shall have been ratified as an amendment to the Constitution by conventions in the several States, as provided in the Constitution, within seven years from the date of the submission hereof to the States by the Congress.

23. Ratified January 23, 1933.
24. Ratified December 5, 1933.

Amendment 22[25]

SECTION 1 No person shall be elected to the office of the President more than twice, and no person who has held the office of President, or acted as President, for more than two years of a term to which some other person was elected President shall be elected to the office of the President more than once. But this Article shall not apply to any person holding the office of President when this Article was proposed by the Congress, and shall not prevent any person who may be holding the office of President, or acting as President, during the term within which this Article becomes operative from holding the office of President or acting as President during the remainder of such term.

SECTION 2 This article shall be inoperative unless it shall have been ratified as an amendment to the Constitution by the legislatures of three-fourths of the several States within seven years from the date of its submissions to the States by the Congress.

Amendment 23[26]

SECTION 1 The District constituting the seat of Government of the United States shall appoint in such manner as the Congress may direct:

A number of electors of President and Vice President equal to the whole number of Senators and Representatives in Congress to which the District would be entitled if it were a State, but in no event more than the least populous State; they shall be in addition to those appointed by the States, but they shall be considered, for the purposes of the election of the President and Vice President, to be electors appointed by a State; and they shall meet in the District and perform such duties as provided by the Twelfth article of amendment.

SECTION 2 The Congress shall have power to enforce the article by appropriate legislation.

Amendment 24[27]

SECTION 1 The right of citizens of the United States to vote in any primary or other election for President or Vice President, for electors for President or Vice President, or for Senator or Representative in Congress, shall not be denied or abridged by the United States or any State by reason of failure to pay any poll tax or other tax.

SECTION 2 The Congress shall have power to enforce this article by appropriate legislation.

Amendment 25[28]

SECTION 1 In case of the removal of the President from office or of his death or resignation, the Vice President shall become President.

25. Ratified February 27, 1951.
26. Ratified March 29, 1961.
27. Ratified January 23, 1964.
28. Ratified February 10, 1967.

SECTION 2 Whenever there is a vacancy in the office of the Vice President, the President shall nominate a Vice President who shall take office upon confirmation by a majority vote of both houses of Congress.

SECTION 3 Whenever the President transmits to the President pro tempore of the Senate and the Speaker of the House of Representatives his written declaration that he is unable to discharge the powers and duties of his office, and until he transmits to them a written declaration to the contrary, such powers and duties shall be discharged by the Vice President as Acting President.

SECTION 3 Whenever the Vice President and a majority of either the principal officers of the executive departments or of such other body as Congress may by law provide, transmit to the President pro tempore of the Senate and the Speaker of the House of Representatives their written declaration that the President is unable to discharge the powers and duties of his office, the Vice President shall immediately assume the powers and duties of the office as Acting President.

Thereafter, when the President transmits to the President pro tempore of the Senate and the Speaker of the House of Representatives his written declaration that no inability exists, he shall resume the powers and duties of his office unless the Vice President and a majority of either the principal officers of the executive departments or of such other body as Congress may by law provide, transmit within four days to the President pro tempore of the Senate and the Speaker of the House of Representatives their written declaration that the President is unable to discharge the powers and duties of his office. Thereupon Congress shall decide the issue, assembling within forty-eight hours for that purpose if not in session. If the Congress, within twenty-one days after receipt of the latter written declaration, or, if Congress is not in session, within twenty-one days after Congress is required to assemble, determines by two-thirds vote of both Houses that the President is unable to discharge the powers and duties of his office, the Vice President shall continue to discharge the same as Acting President; otherwise, the President shall resume the powers and duties of his office.

Amendment 26[29]

SECTION 1 The right of citizens of the United States, who are eighteen years of age or older, to vote shall not be denied or abridged by the United States or by any State on account of age.

SECTION 2 The Congress shall have power to enforce this article by appropriate legislation.

29. Ratified June 30, 1971.

Index